THE ROAD TO
BOTANY BAY

An Exploration of Landscape and History

PAUL CARTER

Alfred A. Knopf • New York • 1988

THIS IS A BORZOI BOOK
PUBLISHED BY ALFRED A. KNOPF, INC.

Originally published in Great Britain by Faber and Faber Limited,
London.

Library of Congress Cataloguing-in-Publication Data

Carter, Paul.
The road to Botany Bay.

Bibliography: p.
Includes index.
1. Australia—History—To 1788.   2. Australia—
History—1788–1851.   I. Title.
DU98. 1. c37   1988   994   87-46076
ISBN 0-394-57035-9

Manufactured in the United States of America
FIRST AMERICAN EDITION

To Lucille

Contents

List of Illustrations

Sources

I am indebted to the University of Melbourne Library for plates 2, 3, 10, 11, 12, 15, 16 and 22.

My thanks to Mrs Marie Lever of Hall's Gap for allowing me to reproduce plate 13. For plate 20 I am indebted to Mr J. Tilgner of Drouin.

Plates 1, 14 and 21 are reproduced by permission of the National Gallery of Victoria.

Acknowledgements

In 1983–4 the Literature Board of the Australia Council awarded me a three month living and travelling grant: at a time when the book's development was both financially and conceptually uncertain, this meant a great deal. I am also grateful to the former editor of *'The Age' Monthly Review*, Robert Haupt, who in the book's early stages found room for some of its ideas even in their unlicked state.

Patrick Morgan was generous in sharing with me his knowledge of Gippsland history and literature. Terry Birtles of the Canberra College of Advanced Education forwarded me information about settlement on the Atherton Tableland. Geoff Tracey of CSIRO kindly provided the results of his vegetation survey in north-east Queensland. Brian Finlayson of the University of Melbourne shared with me his work on Major Mitchell and Lake Salvator. I am also grateful to Mrs Ida Stanton of Hall's Gap and to Mr Tom Horton of Coronet Bay for helping me to locate illustrations 13 and 14 respectively.

The kind and timely advocacy of David Malouf, Peter Carey and Professor Bernard Smith was instrumental in bringing my typescript to the attention of publishers: my thanks to them all.

For constructive criticism of the text I am grateful to historian Richard White. An extract of the book (chapter 4), which was published in *Scripsi*, gained in stylistic grace from the attention of the magazine's editors, Michael Heyward and Peter Craven.

My chief debt is to Martin Harrison. From the beginning he debated, encouraged and promoted this book with a rare combination of critical generosity and creative engagement. If *The Road to Botany Bay* traverses new historical ground in any way, it owes much to his adventurous guidance.

Needless to say, for whatever remains treacherous and ill-marked along the way, I alone am responsible.

Introduction:

A Cake of Portable Soup

It may, I think, be justly observed that few books disappoint their readers more than the narrations of travelers.

Dr Johnson, *The Idler*, No. 97, 23 February 1760

No sign of life on the shore this morning. From the bridge the glass picks out nothing. No wordless mime of figures crouched on their haunches; no Indians, more unaccountably still, pursue their way

> . . . in all appearance intirely unmov'd by the neighbourhood of so remarkable an object as a ship must necessarily be to people who have never seen one.[1]

But otherwise the physical conditions have scarcely altered. The shape of bay Cook surveyed, the tides, depths and weathers persist. To be sure: where cockatoos exploded out of the tree-tops, glittering across the bay, reflections of white hulls bob sedately at anchor. A cloud of historical consciousness must affect our vision, attributing to doubtful contours a permanent significance. A more sensuous trace of aircraft and oil refineries stains the prospect but, with a selective eye, the outlines of what Cook saw, the rim of shore on which Banks's natives remained absorbed in their own preoccupations, these material facts remain discernible. Botany Bay: if we believe the name, the place is still recognizable. Or is it?

Before the name: what was the place like before it was named? How did Cook see it? Barring catatonic seizure, his landing there was assured: but where to land, where to look, how to proceed? Where was the place as yet? Ahead, it was dense, cloudy; the report of small waves behind. The sound of voices calling to each other out of sight, displaying the invisible space, making it answer. Birds with human voices. The legend of giants. What we see is what the firstcomers did not see: a place, not a historical space. A place, a historical fact, detached from its travellers; static, at anchor, as if it was always there, bland, visible. Standing at this well-known point, the spatial event is replaced by a historical stage. Only the actors are absent. Even as we look towards the horizon or turn away down fixed routes, our gaze sees through the space of history, as if it was never there. In its place, nostalgia for the past, cloudy time, the repetition of facts. The fact that where we stand and how we go is history: this we do not see.

According to our historians, it was always so. Australia was always simply a stage where history occurred, history a theatrical performance. It is not the historian who stages events, weaving them together to form a plot, but History itself. History is the playwright, coordinating facts into a coherent sequence: the historian narrating what happened is merely a copyist or amanuensis. He is a spectator like anybody else and, whatever he may think of the performance, he does not question the stage conventions. The First Fleet reached Botany Bay early in 1788. Shortly after, Governor Phillip founded the first settlement (the future Sydney) at Port Jackson, a 'capacious' harbour immediately to the north of Botany Bay. This is how Australia's leading historian describes the scene.

> On 27 and 28 January the male convicts and the rest of the marines landed. Some cleared ground for the different encampments; some pitched tents; some landed the stores; a party of convicts erected the portable house brought from England for the Governor on the east side of the cove. So, as Collins puts it, the spot which had so lately been the abode of silence and tranquillity was now changed to that of noise, clamour and confusion, though after a time order gradually prevailed everywhere.[2]

Clark's description does not simply reproduce the events: it narrates them, clarifies and orders them. As history's secretary, Clark colludes in history's own wish to see chaos yield to order. Firstly, his syntax creates the sense of diverse activities converging towards the single goal of settlement. Indeed, the choice of events itself contributes to the illusion of growing purpose: for what is narrated are precisely those activities indispensable to foundation. It is their susceptibility to a cause-and-effect explanation which renders the landing, the clearing and the pitching of tents *historical* events, events that lead to other events.

In a theatre of its own design, history's drama unfolds; the historian is an impartial onlooker, simply *repeating* what happened. In Clark's account this illusion of the historian as *répétiteur* is reinforced by other, literary means. His second sentence, for instance, recalls the passage in Virgil's *Aeneid*, where Aeneas witnesses the founding of Carthage: 'Eagerly the Tyrians press on, some to build walls, to rear the citadel, and roll up stones by hand; some to choose the site for a dwelling and enclose it with a furrow . . .' In this sense the founding of a settlement at Sydney Cove is itself a historical repetition, a further enactment of a universal theme. Finally, of course, Clark draws attention to his own secondary role by letting the contemporary comment of Collins stand as a gloss on his own description: the historian does not order the facts, he conforms to them.

Such history is a fabric woven of self-reinforcing illusions. But, above all, one illusion sustains it. This is the illusion of the theatre and, more exactly, the unquestioned convention of the all-seeing spectator. The primary logic which holds together Clark's description is its visibility. Nature's painted curtains are drawn aside to reveal heroic man at his epic labour on the stage of history. The processes of clearing, pitching tents, erecting dwellings, are wholly ancillary to the main action. Their chief value is to set the scene. They are visible pointers to the swelling theme of foundation. What Clark gives us, in fact, is a series of stage directions, conventional and unexamined. For this is the irony: described in this way, from the imaginary spectator's point of view, these processes fundamental to the act of settlement are stripped of their historical meaning. Referring to the same events which Clark describes, another First Fleet chronicler, Tench, writing at the time, says: '. . . the scene to an indifferent spectator, at leisure to contemplate it, would have been highly picturesque and amusing'.[3] But this is the point:

there was no spectator, no gallery, no surveyor-like comprehension; it was precisely this that soldiers and convicts were about – and to picture their activities theatrically, according to the conventions of a unified viewpoint is, by a curious rhetorical trick, to efface the historical nature of the events described at the very moment their importance is apparently, and piously, asserted.

This kind of history, which reduces space to a stage, that pays attention to events unfolding in time alone, might be called imperial history. The governor erects a tent here rather than there; the soldier blazes a trail in that direction rather than this: but, rather than focus on the *intentional* world of historical individuals, the world of active, spatial choices, empirical history of this kind has as its focus facts which, in a sense, come after the event. The primary object is not to understand or to interpret: it is to legitimate. This is why this history is associated with imperialism – for who are more liable to charges of unlawful usurpation and constitutional illegitimacy than the founders of colonies? Hence, imperial history's *defensive* appeal to the logic of cause and effect: by its nature, such a logic demonstrates the emergence of order from chaos.

Hence, too, its preference for fixed and detachable facts, for actual houses, visible clearings and boats at anchor. For these, unlike the intentions which brought them there, unlike the material uncertainties of lived time and space, are durable objects which can be treated as typical, as further evidence of a universal historical process. Orphaned from their unique spatial and temporal context, such objects, such historical facts, can be fitted-out with new paternities. Legitimized by an imperial discourse, they can even form future alliances of their own. (It is precisely this family-tree myth of history which assures the historian his privileged status.)

Clark has been criticized for his tendency to moralize Australian history. His sense of a national destiny tragically unfulfilled has been found unfashionably biblical. But such criticisms make the error of lashing the person rather than the vice. For Clark's preoccupations are not personal foibles: they do not represent a peculiarly Australian preoccupation with questions of purpose and identity, but are inherent in the kind of history he practises so well. The fact is that, as an account of foundation and settlement, not to mention the related processes of discovery and exploration, empirical history, with its emphasis on the factual and static, is wholly inadequate. This is one reason why Australia's beginnings are felt to be so fragile, why it is felt that something more than Cook and the First Fleet is needed if Australians are to acquire a proper sense of their true and special destiny. For the result of cause-and-effect narrative history is to give the impression that events unfold according to a logic of their own. They refer neither to the place, nor to the people. Imperial history's mythic lineage of heroes is the consequence of its theatrical assumption that, in reality, historical individuals are actors, fulfilling a higher destiny.

Nor is the nostalgia for beginnings that this kind of history generates satisfied by pushing back the date of first discovery. It is well known from Dutch charts that by the mid-seventeenth century Dutch navigators had mapped the western half of Australia's coast, from Nuyts Archipelago in the south to Cape York in the north. Recently, considerable media interest has been aroused by the convincing-enough claim that, a century earlier, a Portuguese sailor, Mendonça, had mapped Australia's eastern coastline, from Cape York to Warrnambool on Victoria's southern coast. Five keys found (and since lost) near Geelong, a mahogany ship (found and since lost) near Port Fairy are thought to be relics of that voyage. And somehow the fate of these fragments emblemizes the strange lack of importance which attaches to their history. For, treated only as a question of priority, what does Mendonça's voyage tell us about our history? It serves simply to fill in a gap in Australia's imaginary chronology. Australia itself, the geographical object he and the Dutch helped to bring into being, is taken for granted. And so, by a characteristic paradox, Mendonça is relegated to the rank of a hero coasting a continent which was already there; as if the coast chose him, and not he the coast.

'In Sagres, in Coimbra, and elsewhere', writes McIntyre,

there are mosaic wall-maps, showing the outline of all the continents of the world, with proud ribbons radiating from

xvii

Lisbon along the track of the Great Discoverers. The discoverers who reached the shores of Australia are justly entitled to be joined in that distinguished company . . .[4]

There is something almost pathetic about this conclusion: as if, in the end, the only significance of Mendonça's voyage is as a heroic episode in an imperial pageant. Similarly, one is curious to know what our Sunday-historians will have learnt when they eventually find the lost caravel or the missing keys. But the pathos of these relics is a product of the historical method which constitutes them as facts, as evidence of a lost chronology. It is a method which does not, for instance, ask itself what 'discovery' means, which does not see the paradox inherent in writing a book about the 'secret discovery' of Australia. As if acts of discovery only differed accidentally from other voyages, and were not expressions of an imperial design; as if, for instance, a country which has not been named and brought into cultural circulation can, in any sense, be said to have been discovered.

There is no end to this filling in of the chronology, this cult of firstcomers: shards on the shores of the Gulf of Carpentaria bear witness to the regular visits of trepang fishermen from the north. And what of the Aborigines themselves, whose infiltration into the sub-continent is annually, as it were, pushed back a further thousand years? This dispersion of a too singularly British genealogy should not be mistaken for a desire to 're-think' Australia's beginnings. It represents nothing more than a transfer of power, a new nationalism as insular as the British connection it seeks to replace. The new chronology remains a form of legitimation. It continues to confuse routes with roots. When archaeologists 'push back' the date of first aboriginal settlement, who gains? To be sure, our legal preoccupation with issues of priority ensures each new date some political leverage. More profoundly, though, the increase of knowledge increases our control. For it is we Europeans who associate antiquity with 'a rich cultural heritage'. In discovering the Aboriginal past, we demonstrate our piety towards the household gods of our own history: the very variousness of Australia's cultural origins suggests an epic potential. The very elusiveness of any convincing cause-and-effect pattern becomes, paradoxically, evidence of a special destiny.

Viewed theatrically, there is nothing in Australia's prehistory which does not set the scene for Clark's description. There is no fact or artefact, however confusing, which does not, once located in the framework of European chronology, contribute to the emergence of historical order and narrative clarity. The historical eye may be seeking out more exotic objects, but its viewpoint remains fixed. History continues to unfold upon a stage: indeed, this is exactly what chronology is, a stage which nullifies time's cultural peculiarities. Chronology is the temporal counterpart of a Euclidean space: both are operationally efficient because they deny the historical nature of the realms they manipulate.

One of Australia's more popular, and avowedly nationalist, historians opens his account of the European settlement of what later became the state of Victoria in this way:

> As the sun rose on a winter's day in 1834, and the pale light successively shone on that wild coast stretching all the way from Bateman's Bay to the outskirts of Albany, only the sparsest signs of activity could be seen. Here and there the smoke drifted from a fire. On a few stretches of sand a rowing boat might be seen, resting well above the reach of the high tides. An alert eye might have discerned, in a few places, the green of a vegetable patch and the fresh unpainted wood of a hut and a new grave or two with a name and a date carved on a spar or the lid of a wooden cask. Along that three thousand miles of coast, Aboriginals were probably stirring in the early morning from their sleeping places beside their tiny fires. Maybe a hundred Europeans could be counted . . .[5]

And so on. Leaving aside the ancestor worship of smoke and spars and the paradigmatic yielding of pallor to verdure, the real mythologizing which occurs here is in the invention of a point of view, a panoramic eye before whose gaze the historical facts unfold again exactly as before. Only now – as never before – they are visible. If Clark's point of view is theatrical, Blainey's is sublime. Only it is the sublimity of a working model, a model which renders time clockwork and miniaturizes space. It is a world where events occur 'quietly', where change is always gradual and where, most significantly of all, nothing could have happened except in the way it did. It is, in short, diorama history – history where the past has been settled even more effectively than the country.

The satellite eye, and the commentary with it explaining how the model works, reveal a further distortion of this kind of history. The eye which sees is not the organic counterpart of Locke's blank mind: its gaze is not random, open-minded, equally attentive to all directions, all phenomena. On the contrary, it looks down a telescope. This is how epitaphs loom up – they were, after all, carved to be read. They were, from the beginning, historical sources. Smoke also was a signal. But this is why, too, the Aborigines fail to show up. The modesty of Blainey's remark that the 'Aboriginals were probably stirring . . .' is false modesty. For we do not need his stratospheric seer to establish their presence: some of those 'hundred Europeans' have left us 'eye-witness' reports. Still, by an unintended irony, Blainey's 'probably' reminds us that it was not only Banks's natives who went about their business apparently without seeing who was there: the gaze of most historians has been comparably partial.

Blainey's panoramic figure of speech, like Clark's theatrical description, does not refer to a physical invisibility. Rather, it outlines the selective blindnesses of a cultural discourse: imperial history. The Aborigines, for instance, were not physically invisible, but they were culturally so, for they eluded the cause-and-effect logic that made the workings of history plain to see. They did not share history's celestial viewpoint. Unlike ships at sea, their movements were unpredictable. Yet the former inhabitants of Australia were not unique in this respect: the diorama model of historical progress has equally obscured a fundamental dimension of the colonizers' history.

In the seventy years or so after the First Fleet's arrival, the Australian coastline was mapped – even discovered, since it was not until Flinders circumnavigated Australia in 1801–2 that it was established as a discrete and single land mass; the Australian interior was explored, its map-made emptiness written over, criss-crossed with explorer's tracks, gradually inhabited with a network of names; the Australian coastal strip, especially between the Great Divide and the sea, was progressively furrowed and blazed with boundaries, its estuaries and riverine flats pegged out for towns. The discoverers, explorers and settlers – and they were often one and the same person – were making spatial history. They were choosing directions, applying names, imagining goals, inhabiting the country.

And yet no history of these processes exists. We are well supplied with historical geographies, but these share the diorama mentality: they take it for granted that the newcomers travelled and settled a land *which was already there*. Geomorphologically, this was perhaps so – although even the science of landforms evolved as a result of crossing the country – but historically that country remained to be described. The diorama model shows us the river on the hill's far side; it shows us hills. But it was precisely such features which spatial history had to constitute. At the centre of the colonists' minds were not picturesque places, but what preceded them, horizons, possible tracks, bounding spaces.

The ironic result of not recognizing this is that those activities of exploring and settling, which nationalism elevates to an iconic status, become strictly superfluous. If the country was already there, laid out waiting to be found, why, anyone might have done it – and at any time. Landing might have occurred anywhere; any place might have been cleared; any site might have been chosen for the governor's house: and, from the point of view of history, the effect would have been the same. By the same token, when we reverently trace the explorers' tracks, we can claim to be explorers no less than they, and writing up our own experiences pretend it is history. A new genre is born, the explorer biography, where our own thoughts and feelings take an epic turn. Treating the historical space as 'natural', passive, objectively 'there', has the effect of draining what is most characteristic of Australian history of its historical content. The uniquely spatial experience is replaced by a ritual of repetitions. Putative journeys are effaced by a cult of places. And another genre emerges: the local history.

The Road to Botany Bay, then, is written against these mythic imaginings. It is a prehistory of places, a history of roads, footprints, trails of dust and foaming wakes. Within its domain fall the flight of birds, the direction of smoke, the lie of the land. Against the historians, it recognizes that our life as it discloses itself spatially is dynamic, material but invisible. It constantly transcends actual objects to imagine others beyond the horizon. It cannot be delimited by reference to immediate actions, let alone treated as an autonomous fact independent of intention. It recognizes that the spatiality of historical experience evaporates before the imperial gaze, like the lump of charcoal falling away from the undamaged diamond in the original ending of *His Natural Life*. The result may be legitimacy, but at the expense of a world of experience.

The Road to Botany Bay is concerned with the haze which preceded clear outlines, but this is no reason why it should imitate its subject. So, lest there be any misunderstanding (particularly perhaps amongst readers who have not thought of space as anything but an empty interval, a natural given), let it be stressed again: this book's subject is not a physical object, but a cultural one. It is not the geographer's space, although that comes into it. What is evoked here are the spatial forms and fantasies through which a culture declares its presence. It is spatiality as a form of non-linear writing; as a form of history. That cultural space *has* such a history is evident from the historical documents themselves. For the literature of spatial history – the letters home, the explorers' journals, the unfinished maps – are written traces which, but for their spatial occasion, would not have come into being. They are not like novels: their narratives do not conform to the rules of cause-and-effect empirical history. Rather, they are analogous to unfinished maps and should be read accordingly as records of travelling.

Indeed, to read them as self-evident sources for theatrical or nationalist plots – in the way that Clark treats Collins, say – or to regard their contents as little more than the raw material of heroic biography is to exclude precisely what distinguishes them: their active engagement with the road and the horizon. For the historical significance of the explorers' journals and the settlers' diaries does not reside in any stylistic illusion of picturesque completeness – a fact which Dr Johnson noted and lamented. Quite the contrary, it is their open-endedness, their lack of finish, even their search for words, which is characteristic: for it is here, where forms and conventions break down, that we can discern the process of transforming space into place, the *intentional* world of the texts, wherein lies their unrepeatability and their enduring, if hitherto ignored, historical significance.

Such spatial history – history that discovers and explores the lacuna left by imperial history – begins and ends in language. It is this which makes it history rather than, say, geography. If it does *imitate* the world of the traveller it is in a different sense. For, like the traveller whose gaze is oriented and limited, it makes no claim to authoritative completeness. It is, must be, like a journey, exploratory. It suggests certain directions in historical texts, leaves others for others to explore. Certain figures of speech draw it on; to others, no doubt, it is deaf. Certain historical characters loom large; others remain beyond its horizon. But like a journey it opens up the possibility of going back, of turning a private passage into a road, a road reaching more places than the first traveller imagined. 'A page of my *Journal*', Boswell once remarked, 'is like a cake of portable soup. A little may be diffused into a considerable portion'.[6] And his modern editor draws attention to an advertisement in the *London Chronicle* recommending such soup or 'solid broth', to gentlemen 'on journeys and at sea'. What follows is, I hope, useful to those modern travellers who emulate eighteenth-century gentlemen by writing and reading. And, as such, it suggests, perhaps, a ground-plan for exploring (even discovering) historical frontiers elsewhere – in the Old Country quite as much as the New World.

But where to begin? Late in 1616, Dirck Hartog of Amsterdam and his ship, the *Eendracht*, were blown on to the north-west coast of Australia. The skipper commemorated his involuntary landing on a pewter plate, which he affixed to a post. The island where Hartog landed was named after him; the adjoining mainland was called the Land of Eendracht. In 1697, another Dutchman, Vlamingh, also blown off-course, found Hartog's memorial. He had Hartog's inscription copied on to a new pewter plate and appended a record of his own visit. In 1699, the English seaman William Dampier also visited this coast. He let the island retain its Dutch connection, but renamed the country to the east Shark Bay. Then, in 1801, one Captain Emmanuel Hamelin discovered a pewter plate 'of about six inches in diameter on which was roughly engraven two Dutch inscriptions . . .', and named the place Cape Inscription.

The Road to Botany Bay is not about chronological priority: it is about *historical* beginnings. In this sense, the name Cape Inscription is emblematic of its approach. For such a name, as the earlier additions testify, belongs firmly to the history of travelling. Rewritten and repeated, it serves as a point of departure. But Cape Inscription, the name, is also the result of erasure: it also symbolizes the imperial project of permanent possession through dispossession. In short, the name oscillates between two extreme interpretations. It suggests a kind of history which is neither static nor mindlessly mobile, but which incorporates both possibilities. It points to a kind of history where travelling is a process of *continually* beginning, continually ending, where discovery and settlement belong to the same exploratory process. The 'facts' of this spatial history are not houses and clearings, but phenomena as they appear to the traveller, as his intentional gaze conjures them up. They are the directions and distances in which houses and clearings *may* be found or founded.

But Cape Inscription is also a striking figure of speech, an oxymoron yoking writing and landscape in a surprising, even grotesque, way. A geographical feature is made no bigger than a page of writing. A calligraphic flourish is able, it seems, to plume out like an ocean current one hundred miles long. This metaphorical way of speaking is a pointer to the way spatial history must interpret its sources. It also indicates, concisely and poetically, the *cultural* place where spatial history begins: not in a particular year, nor in a particular place, but *in the act of naming*. For by the act of place-naming, space is transformed symbolically into a place, that is, a space with a history. And, by the same token, the namer inscribes his passage permanently on the world, making a metaphorical word-place which others may one day inhabit and by which, in the meantime, he asserts his own place in history.

It is not, then, at Botany Bay, or anywhere else, that this

history begins, but in the name. Dr Johnson was right when he remarked, 'There is something in names one cannot help feeling.' But he meant much more than he intended.

THE ROAD TO
BOTANY BAY

1

An Outline of Names

. . . hanging Clowds and a thick horizon are certainly no known Signs
of a Continent . . .

James Cook to John Walker, Letter, 1771

Casting a jaundiced eye over burgeoning preparations for
Australia's bi-centenary, a weekend columnist of the Melbourne
newspaper *The Age* reported not so long ago a plan to replace all
Cook's Australian place names with others more congenial to
ordinary Australians. It is a measure of Cook's ambiguous role
in Australian history that one was not at all sure whether or not
the writer was serious. In the nearly two hundred years since
Arthur Phillip, commander of the First Fleet and first governor
of the colony of New South Wales, found Cook's description of
Botany Bay so inaccurate he had to transfer the settlement to
Sydney Cove, historical writers have eulogized and vilified
Cook with almost equal enthusiasm. He has been called the
founder of Australia; at the same time, he has been accused of
culpable indifference – his descriptions of the Australian coast
are said to be less than fulsome and, much worse, he never came
back. On top of this, whether rejecting or embracing his
memory, all writers on Cook have had to deal with the
awkward eighteen-year interval between the passage of the
Endeavour and the arrival of the First Fleet: why, if Cook's
excellent chart of the east coast of New Holland (as Australia
was then called) laid the foundations for a new colony, was the
British government so slow to take up the challenge? After all,
Cook had been dead ten years when Phillip sailed.

In the context of some Australian historians' largely imperial
assumptions, Cook's mixed historical fortunes are understandable. For what has been at stake in such debates is not Cook's
credentials as a navigator, but his status as a founder. Indeed,

one recently published book goes so far as to see in Cook a hostile father-figure, which, for the good of the nation, must be rejected once and for all.[1] Absurd as this Oedipal projection may sound, and though it confuses Cook the man with Cook the myth, in its own way it perpetuates the assumption that the chief task, so far as Australia's beginnings are concerned, is to establish Cook as a historical character, a personality separate from his travels. In flat contradiction to Cook's own propensity for coasting, Australian historians have in the past sought to haul him on land, and to anchor him statuesquely as an authority they can look up to.

The plausibility of that bi-centennial report did not only take advantage of Cook's enigmatic role in Australian history. More specifically, of course, it was a reminder of how little value our culture attaches to names, whoever may have given them. During the four months Cook spent in Australian waters, he named well over one hundred 'bays', 'capes', 'isles', and the like (see plate 2). In giving these names, Cook expended a good deal of ingenuity. There were names that were straightforwardly descriptive, like 'Point Upright' or 'Cape Manyfold'; but there were also names that were more fancifully evocative, like 'Pigeon House' and 'Glass House', applied to mountains. Other names, like 'Magnetical Island' and 'Eagle Island', referred to distinctive qualities or incidents associated with a place; yet others, like 'Thirsty Sound', 'Point Danger' and 'Cape Tribulation', alluded to the history of the voyage itself. Then there were the personal names: Cook commemorated some of his crew members, but perhaps a third of the hundred and fifty names he scattered along Australia's east coast celebrate nautical, political or aristocratic figures of the day.

Having studied Cook's manuscript journal, the great Cook scholar and biographer John Cawte Beaglehole had no doubt that Cook took the greatest care in bestowing names:

> There are numerous blanks left for geographical names, later filled in with a different ink and written very large and carefully. Some of these names are juggled and reassigned a good deal, particularly on the N. E. Australia coast, where the Lords of the Admiralty flitted from cape to cape, and in and

out of bays, according to decisions which it is impossible to account for now – though one sees that Cook was the reverse of casual in placing these names on the map: he was not a mere sprinkler of royal dukes.[2]

Despite this, it is fair to say that little attention has been paid to Cook's names, the general assumption being that, in contrast with Cook's journal itself and his excellent maps, the names have no particular relevance to the places, at any rate no or little objective relevance. At best they are anecdotal; at worst, adulatory. Any significance the names do have is biographical or circumstantial, hardly historical, even less scientific.

Thomas De Quincey probably articulates the insecurity associated with Cook's names where he writes in his essay 'On Style',

> Why are the local names, whenever they have resulted from the general good sense of a country, faithful to the local truth, grave, and unaffected? Simply because they are not inventions of any active faculty, but mere passive depositions from a real impression on the mind.

By contrast, De Quincey claims,

> Where there is an ambitious principle set in motion for name-inventing, there it is sure to terminate in something monstrous and fanciful.

As instances of the 'monstrous and fanciful', De Quincey cites sailors' names like 'Big Wig Island', 'The Bishop and his Clerks', 'Point Farewell', 'Cape Turn-again'. Pioneers' names are similarly culpable: names like 'Big Bone Lick' and 'Dismal Swamp' may be descriptive:

> Primary aspects of nature compose the scenery of their thoughts, and these are reflected by their names . . . There is a truth expressed, but again too casual and special.[3]

Certainly, Cook's names do not avoid De Quincey's criticism. By turns, his inventions are monstrous, fanciful, casual and special. If the criteria for good names are long residence and a local truth in which the mind is passively saturated, it is clear that Cook's names – and indeed almost all

3

Australian names – are doomed to the charge of wilful affectation. And yet Cook's choice of names was not casual: simply because it was active, it was not arbitrary. The fact that the names did not well up spontaneously from some sort of folk consciousness is undeniable, but it does not mean they have no historical import. Cook's knowledge of the Australian coast was a product of his mobility and his active engagement with its waters, reefs and horizons; at the very least, his casual and special names represent the conditions under which he aimed to make history. They underline the active nature of the explorer's space and time.

If we find names like 'Repulse Bay' or 'Cape Flattery' fanciful, it may reflect nothing more than a habit of minimizing the historical conditions that determine historical knowledge. It may be that, instead of seeing the process of exploration itself as history, we are too preoccupied with what Samuel Johnson called 'the fruits of travel'. Certainly, in most histories of exploration, Cook's voyages are treated as historical facts to be located chronologically in the history of Pacific exploration. Beyond placing Cook's achievement in the context of the state of navigational technology, there is little attempt to interpret what Cook's names themselves refer to – the specificity of his historical experience. And this is quite understandable, for it is the specificity of historical experience that is the enemy of positivist history: it is the active charge of historical time and space that undermines the cause-and-effect patterning of lives, events and facts into something significant. What would a history of Cook's names be? Their resistance to any kind of cause-and-effect classification becomes, then, proof of their historical insignificance.

Any attempt to classify Cook's names according to a static cultural taxonomy, whether etymological, semantic or bio-graphical, certainly reinforces this impression of insignificance. An etymological account has some value in ascertaining eighteenth-century meanings of words like 'hillock', but is evidently absurd in relation to proper names. Any attempt at a semantic classification soon runs into difficulties of reference: when Cook names a feature 'Ram Head', because it is 'very much like the Ram head going into Plymouth Sound', is the name descriptive or not? And, if it is descriptive, does it refer to a feature, a point of view, Cook's personal experience or what? Similarly, a biographical classification offers no singular, unequivocal key to the meanings of the names. You could almost think of the features Cook named after famous people in Ptolemaic terms, with Cook as the earth and successive spheres circling as far as the *primum mobile* of the royal house. Inside names like Northumberland Islands and Cumberland Isles, which both commemorate younger brothers of George III (in whose reign the *Endeavour* sailed), move places like Cape Grafton, Rockingham Bay and Shelburne Bay, all alluding to politicians influential at the time of the *Endeavour*'s sailing.

Closer to the biographical centre may be found commemorated Lords of the Admiralty, responsible for all marine endeavour, but responsible in particular for the *Endeavour*. These find their place in Cape Palmerston, Cape Sandwich, Edgcumbe Bay and elsewhere. Closer still are those luminaries with whom Cook himself was professionally acquainted, the naval commanders who served in the Seven Years War and, in particular, the officers who were his superiors on the Newfoundland Station. Here we find Cape Hawke, Cape Howe and so on. And a yet more intimate ring of names alludes directly to Cook's own career. Whether it is coincidence or not, Three Brothers, Eagle Island, Cape Grenville and Northumberland Isles punningly recall the vessels in which Cook had made his way as a seaman. With the *Three Brothers* Cook completed his apprenticeship and signed on for the first time as a seaman, in April 1750, 'perhaps with a little pride in his heart', remarks Cook's biographer, Beaglehole. He gained his Master's Certificate while serving in the *Eagle*, and had already applied that ship's name to an island in the Bay of Islands, Newfoundland. It was as master of the *Northumberland*, between 1759 and 1762, that Cook carried out his Draughts and Observations of part of the St Lawrence, Nova Scotia and Newfoundland, thus laying the basis of his reputation as a surveyor. 'Mr Cook the Surveyor' completed that survey while aboard the *Grenville* in 1765. His next command had been the *Endeavour*.[4]

Finally, there is an innermost circle of names arising, apparently, out of the immediate experiences of the voyage itself. These include descriptive names ranging from the blandly literal to the highly metaphorical, but having in common their focus on the permanent qualities of a geographical object – names like 'Red Point', 'Cape Dromedary', 'Pigeon House' and 'Sandy Cape'. These are complemented by names that, rather than evoke the physical appearance of objects, commemorate circumstantial events associated with them – names like 'Smoaky Cape', 'Magnetical Island', 'Islands of Direction'. And we can add to these occasional names those drawn from crew members – 'Point Hicks', 'because Lieutenant Hicks was the first who discovered this land'.[5]

Analysed like this, in terms of a static historical hierarchy, the relevance of these names to the coastline where they appear seems minimal. It is no wonder they appear to represent an 'ambitious principle' – and one rooted firmly in self-interest. The coastline appears as an occasion for self-glorification or, at any rate, as an opportunity to memorialize all the historical and personal facts that converged and found their historic climax in the *Endeavour* voyage. Cook may have been assuring his own career prospects in his flattering choice of names, but they hardly betray a founding vision of Australia's future. Why not, then, change the names?

But, even as one imposes this biographical interpretation on Cook's names, one sees that its coherence is illusory. For one thing, it is to forget that Cook's Australian names were but the final episode in a progress of naming that began off the South American coast eighteen months earlier. It is to suppose *a priori* a special relationship with the future Australia. For another, to attribute to Cook a summational impulse in his choice of names is evidently illogical. It is to unify them within a backward-looking, possibly imperial perspective. It is to ignore the historical circumstances in which the names were given – the fact that, like the places commemorated, they unfolded in time, and in space. Above all, perhaps, this impulse to classify Cook's names as if they amount to an enigmatic memorandum advocating colonization seems to assume that words apply uniquely to objects. It denies the possibility of equivocation, forgetfulness, even a sense of humour. It assumes Cook named his coast like a botanist naming plants.

In fact, despite Cook's historical reputation for unemotional coldness, his names are anything but dispassionately logical: they are not components of a cultural jigsaw or a sort of eighteenth-century dream to be deciphered according to an imperial codebook. Cook may have served in a ship called *Three Brothers*, but the fact is that, on 12 May 1770, he saw three hills which he named 'Three Brothers' as they 'bore some resemblance to each other'. Likewise, there was, after all, an eagle seen at Eagle Island.[6] The simple truth is that punning names like 'Eagle Island' are an instance of what, in a different context, Freud called overdetermination. They were names that bore more than one hidden allusion. In the context of the immediately preceding names, we might suppose that 'Green Island', for example, honoured the *Endeavour*'s astronomer, Charles Green. After all, geographical features just to the south were both named after contemporaries of Cook – the Frankland Isles commemorating a naval commander who had distinguished himself in the West Indies during the Seven Years War and Cape Grafton recalling the Prime Minister at the time of the *Endeavour*'s sailing. However, Cook's description of the island in question as 'low green woody'[7] seems to settle the matter: the name is obviously descriptive. Or is it? It might as easily be an allusion to Green Island, Newfoundland, dear to Cook as the site of his first important survey, work that led indirectly to the *Endeavour* commission.

The significance of this overdetermination of meaning does not lie in the direction of Cook's psychology, but in the revelation of the fact that Cook moved in a world of language. He proceeded within a cultural network of names, allusions, puns and coincidences, which, far from constraining him, gave him, like his Pacific Ocean, conceptual space in which to move. His was not the definitive univocal language of the dictionary. Unlike dictionary definitions, Cook's place names remained to be defined: they certainly claimed no finality or universal validity. On the contrary, they were deployed contextually, strategically. What they referred to was not a life elsewhere. It was not the imaginary leisure of an honoured retirement that they aimed to secure. They alluded to the journey itself, as it unfolded horizontally, revealing itself as a succession of events.

The idea of Cook spontaneously generating an imperial mythology is a biographical myth. It ignores the fact that exploration, no less than, say, botany was an intellectual discipline with its own distinctive scientific method, its own rules of description and classification. And, unlike the various branches of eighteenth-century natural history, whose classificatory system derived from Linnaeus and wholly ignored the circumstance of discovery, exploration was a *spatial* discourse. It was attentive to the where and how of objects, and its strategic deployment of names was integral to its transformation of the natural world into an object of knowledge.

Cook's names were neither meaningless nor arbitrary: they did have a genealogy, but it was a genealogy of particulars, a horizontal disposition to mark things where they occurred locally, rather than to organize them hierarchically or thematically. Cook's names were not proto-scientific or proto-imperial. Cook no more yearned for the exotically unique – always, potentially, the basis for a new taxonomy – than he disdained the continuously ordinary. The names Cook used in Australia he or others had used elsewhere; and he used some of them again. Names flattering the mighty (like Sandwich) he used on numerous occasions; others more sparingly. He took the Islands of Direction not only from observation, but also from Narborough, whose group he had passed as he neared Tierra del Fuego. In applying the name again, Cook implied no theory, no geomorphological speculation. Quite the opposite: he took advantage of the fact that proper names did not generalize or classify, but denoted particulars alone: however many places he named after Sandwich, the places themselves remained individual, uncompromised, unrelated. Their uniqueness lay not only in their spatial differentiation, guaranteed them by the map: it resided also in their textuality, in their belonging, each of them, uniquely to a journal, in which each had its own place.

Cook's attitude towards names is summed up in his first addition to Pacific knowledge, an island, which he called 'New Island', 'because it is not laid down in any chart'.[8] The unassuming circumspection of this is almost droll, but it embodies Cook's purpose precisely. For Cook, knowing and naming were identical, but there was no question of a direct relation between signifier and signified, any more than an imitative relationship existed between the uncompleted map and the world. To know the world in detail meant preserving its particulars. In this sense, the term 'New' *is* a name. It precisely delimits the conditions under which it came to be known; it resolutely refuses to say anything *about* the island. The name is, in fact, a pun on the fallacy of description. It is a subtle critique of those who might think a name with a history ('Old Island', perhaps) is somehow more appropriate. It is a name that refuses to admit the place was there before it was named, a name that celebrates the travelling mode of knowledge.

Consider in this context *the* foundational case in point: the name 'Botany Bay', which Cook gave to his first landfall on the coast of New Holland and in which he recorded the delight of his two botanists, Joseph Banks and Daniel Charles Solander, in finding a country so rich in floral novelties. If we are to replace empirical history's cause-and-effect preoccupation with founding fathers, and show Australia's true historical beginnings, in the traditions of exploration and discovery, our first task is to refloat Cook's static names and locate them once more in the light offing of travel. It is to dismantle names as definitive statements of arrival and let them function again as points of departure, as rhetorical lighthouses for getting on. We need, once again, to think of them, like the weather, the winds and clouds, which form so important a part of the ship's log, as metaphors of the journey. In this light, Botany Bay is, in more than one sense, a good place to begin.

The name has attracted speculation ever since John Hawkesworth published his edition of the *Endeavour Journal*, three years after the voyage in 1773. The fact that an anonymous version of the voyage, hurried into print before the official account, preserved an earlier name for the place, 'Stingray Harbour',[9] soon led critics, well disposed and otherwise, to ask why the name was changed. And the question has been raised again at intervals since. Was Cook generously paying tribute to his scientists? Or was he merely kowtowing to Banks, one of the richest and most influential men in England? Was he

9

perhaps translating the older name for that coast, 'Coste des Herbaiges', thereby conspiring in Britain's imperial ambitions?

Three historical writers in particular have addressed themselves to these questions: the nineteenth-century self-made historian, archivist and student of Aborigines James Bonwick; Frederick Watson, responsible among other things for carrying on Bonwick's pioneering work in compiling the *Historical Records of Australia*; and, of course, the magisterial Beaglehole. And, for all their differences, what is interesting is that all three writers assume that the explanation for Botany Bay's involved history lies in either the psychological or the political spheres. None of them seems to think the occurrence of the name in a journal of exploration in the least pertinent to its interpretation. Essentially, Bonwick and Watson both subscribe to a conspiracy theory. Beaglehole describes Watson's 1933 pamphlet 'Lieutenant James Cook and his Voyages in H.M. Bark Endeavour', as 'a rather silly, though fortunately small, book' – and much the same may be said of Bonwick's earlier effort, 'Captain Cook in New South Wales', published in 1901. Both writers assume an anonymous scribe in London was responsible for the change from 'Stingray Harbour' to 'Botany Bay'. Bonwick, for instance, guesses that the most likely interpolator was Hawkesworth, for

> Dr Hawkesworth meant to prepare as interesting a narrative as he could, and tried to please home parties as flatteringly as circumstances permitted. Thus, men of science would be gratified by the selection of the place as Botany Bay . . .[10]

Watson took a darker view of proceedings. He suspected 'Botany Bay' and 'New South Wales' 'were given after the return to England' and furthermore that the copies of Cook's autograph journal were for the major part 'compiled and written in England under official instructions and censorship'.[11] Watson agrees with Bonwick that the motive for altering Cook's 'Stingray Harbour' (or 'Bay', depending on the copy of Cook's journal consulted) to 'Botany Bay' was crudely imperialist. By appropriating the name 'Coste des Herbaiges' in the 1542 Rotz chart Whitehall wanted to leave the world in no doubt as to which coast it now claimed.

Beaglehole's more recent explanation of the name change is quite different and, in empirical terms, probably definitive. He is sure Cook alone was responsible for the changes, and the confusion was a product of his being in transit, nothing more. Beaglehole explains that Cook was writing up his *Endeavour Journal* before and after he reached Batavia. As he wrote it up, so his clerk, Richard Orton, successively transcribed corrected passages to furnish copies to be forwarded to London. This meant that not only might inconsistencies occur as a result of Cook correcting earlier passages as he went along; they might very well be compounded by the copyist. Firstly, Cook himself might be guilty of carelessness, failing, for instance, to change *every* reference to 'Stingray Bay' to 'Botany Bay'. Secondly, whether or not Orton picked up an afterthought of Cook's depended on whether he had already transcribed that part of the journal. The variant forms of Botany Bay that occur in the journal (and these include 'Botanists Harbour' and 'Botanists Bay' as well as 'Stingray Harbour' and 'Bay') are, says Beaglehole, not evidence of tampering. In fact, they reveal a process of conscious revision in which we can discern 'Cook's mind'. 'We have some indication', writes Beaglehole,

> that the change of name was no early decision; for 'Sting-ray Harbour', left in the entry for 7 May, occurs altered to 'Botanist' and then 'Botany' in the entries for 14, 23 and 30 May, and as late as 6 June unaltered, as 'Sting-ray Harbour', in a passage of three lines which were all deleted. In the general description of New South Wales, given under 23 August 1770, the variant 'Botanist' has disappeared; on f. 122a 'Sting Ray Harbour', and on f. 123c 'Sting Ray Bay', become 'Botany Bay'.[12]

Beaglehole's empirical rigour may make the conspiracy theories of Bonwick and Watson look foolish. But the fact remains that, for all three, the real question at issue is not the name itself, but the supposed biographical and political motives its changes represent. Underlying their wish to set the facts straight, all three authors suppose that the real subject under discussion is Cook's personality, his personal responsibility for the name, his personal integrity. If the text is problematic, it is only because the motives of the author (whoever he or they may be) are complex. In this sense, all three betray their common purpose, which is not to investigate the meaning of the name, but to establish an authentic genealogy for it. Their approach ignores entirely the fact that the name occurs in a journal of travelling and, just as the geographical feature it brings into scientific circulation has its own unique place on the map, so the name occupies a unique place in the text.

For all three writers, a place name like Botany Bay does not exist as a particularity, with a particular meaning in the context of the journal. Its significance is assumed to be hidden, perhaps deliberately suppressed. The corollary of this assumption is obvious: the historian must set himself up as an interpreter, revealing what is superficially arbitrary as a fragment of a repressed imperial discourse. Bonwick published his ideas in the year of Federation and his *An Octogenarian's Reminiscences*, published in the same year, reveals him as an ardent nationalist, a historian for whom the object of historical research was to promote a national consciousness and a sense of historical destiny. Looking down on Sydney Harbour 'as a historian', Bonwick wrote in his *Reminiscences*, 'I missed the dark-skinned fisher, but I beheld the arts of Civilization in full triumph. The white man had triumphed because he was progressive, and caught the note of advancing thought.'[13] In this vision of emergent nationhood – one admirably captured by E. Phillips Fox (plate 1) – a Cook unsullied by colonial taint was clearly much to be desired. Watson, too, was an out-and-out nationalist. 'The materials of this volume', Watson wrote in the preface to *The Beginnings of Government in Australia* (1913), 'collect for the use of the present and countless unborn generations the primordial documentary factors in the development and growth of the nation to which they belong.'[14] And an article published as recently as 1982 notes 'Watson's pride as an Australian and his sense of the uniqueness of the Australian experience'.[15]

Beaglehole's understanding of Cook and his writings is, of course, considerably more sophisticated and sensitive. His biography seeks to replace Cook in his appropriate historical context – not the context of imperial politics but of eighteenth-century scientific empiricism. Summing up Cook's character, Beaglehole writes:

He was not semi-mystical, striving as some rarefied explorers have done after the meaning of existence or some absolute human affirmation; he was not searching for or fleeing from himself. He had, so far as one can see, no religion. His was not the poetic mind, or the profoundly scientific mind. He was the genius of the matter of fact.[16]

Having persevered through nearly seven hundred pages of meticulous historical narrative, the reader may feel this represents a somewhat slender discovery. But, far from being an admission of biographical defeat, this litany of negatives vindicates Beaglehole's exhaustive detail. It underlines how the historian's task is to master the facts, to map in as much detail as possible the salient features, rather than to speculate about what lies beyond. In this sense, Beaglehole's approach imitates the empirical scepticism he finds so admirably characteristic of Cook. But Beaglehole's admiration is also a form of self-legitimation: for, of course, under the guise of writing Cook's life, Beaglehole is also furnishing a justification for his own historical method. His dispassionate empiricism finds its authority in Cook's own practice. Seen like this, Beaglehole's project also represents a form of historical imperialism. In treating Cook's biography as a network of dates, places and facts, Beaglehole assumes a natural consonance between the man and his age: he effaces the man's individuality at the very point that he asserts it. In this way, Cook becomes but another heroic variation on history's universal theme.

How, then, should we understand Cook's most famous name? The extraordinary effect of attempting to interpret a place name according to some kind of preconceived historical etymology is to empty the name itself of all meaning. The result of attempting to translate the name into psychological, biographical or empirically historical terms is to neutralize the name, to suggest that, so far as the 'place' goes, it is replaceable. The corollary of interpreting place names as disguised historical facts is that, more than ever, the name itself becomes an arbitrary imposition on the place, a linguistic gesture without a local topographical or traditional justification. And we may notice here another assumption implicit in this approach: the place itself, the 'bay', is taken for granted. Its existence as an already definite place is assumed, with the result that the name appears simply as an addition, a historical event that comes after the physical fact – and which is, accordingly, of relatively minor significance. The effect is to suppress the occasion of discovery, to treat the act of naming as if it represented nothing more than a postcard home, a personal memento of a journey completed. In the same spirit, a commission to commemorate Cook's landing at Botany Bay (plate 1) can stipulate that the painting be executed *in England*.

Suppose, though, we do not take a name like 'Botany Bay' out of context, but read it in the context of the journal where it occurs. Rather than attempt to explain it away, suppose we pay attention to its place in the text – a text, after all, with a definite narrative direction. Then, instead of appearing arbitrary, the name emerges as an accurate expression of the experience of travelling. It becomes a characteristic figure of speech to evoke the nature of exploration, with its zigzag course of erasures, revisions, provisional harbours and invisible reefs.

Cook's *Endeavour Journal* was the product of revision – on this at least Bonwick, Watson and Beaglehole all agree. In Batavia, for the first time, Cook could see the outline of his voyage. His voyage of discovery was over: but the memoranda of it remained to be 'written up', possibly for publication. Part of this process was, as Beaglehole has shown, a matter of elevating the general tone of the narrative by borrowing some passages of philosophical speculation from Banks's journal; partly it was a question of clarifying details. But what was the function of this revision? It was not to anticipate Hawkesworth: the object was not to give his narrative a discernible beginning and end, but rather to articulate it as a journey – this was what it meant to tell the 'undisguised truth and without gloss', as Cook put it.[17]

In this light, the meaning of Botany Bay emerges – and it begins, like the approach to New Holland, in New Zealand. Reading through the New Zealand section of the journal, it must have been clear to Cook that Endeavour Bay, the name he had originally given to his first landfall in New Zealand, hardly captured the place's significance in the voyage. In retrospect, the bay had not proved a haven to the little ship. 'It is a wild riding for a ship,' Robert Molyneux had written.[18] It had seen a bloody

14

encounter with the natives. In Cook's own words, the place 'afforded us no one thing that we wanted'.[19] In Batavia, therefore, Cook renamed it, more appropriately, 'Poverty Bay'. This change of name had not changed the place, but it had changed its place in the voyage. For, despite the unpropitious beginning, Cook's survey of New Zealand's two major islands had turned out to be, at least in retrospect, the major success of his *Endeavour* voyage. What had begun in poverty had ended in plenty: and it was no accident that Cook eventually named the bay corresponding to Poverty Bay on the north side of Cape East the Bay of Plenty (see plate 2).

After the Pacific's long, smooth horizons, the crew, if not Cook himself, had looked forward to surveying the substantial land mass of New Zealand from the time it first loomed on the horizon. Was it, as Banks conjectured, 'certainly the Continent we are in search of' – the great southern land Cook had been instructed to look for?[20] No doubt it was the surfacing of this question that led Cook to identify himself so firmly with his first landfall. In retrospect, though, his expectations had been surpassed. The successful circumnavigation of both islands – and indeed the discovery that there *were* two islands – had a significance that extended beyond the survival of the little community on board: the survey of New Zealand was a vindication of the whole *Endeavour* enterprise. In this context, it was appropriate to celebrate the authorities who had backed the voyage and made it possible. Thus Cook marked the culmination of the New Zealand survey by naming his point of final departure Admiralty Bay and, to underline its place in his career, its two capes were named after the signatories of his Instructions, the Secretaries of the Admiralty, Sir Philip Stephens and George Jackson. A survey that had begun at Poverty Bay now ended at Admiralty Bay: the grammatical similarity between the names marked them as belonging to the same journey; their semantic distance, on the other hand, told the story of changed fortunes crowned by success.

In the wake of these changes, the eventual appearance of the name 'Botany Bay' is understandable. Editing the text, reading back, turning the discontinuous repetitions into a continuity of experience, in the interests of investing the often puzzling

overlaps, backtracks and zigzags of the voyage with a narrative
direction, which would also preserve the sense of sailing on, the
feel of things appearing successively to the trained eye, the fact
that New Holland succeeded New Zealand became a connection
worth emphasizing. It lent, for instance, Cook's decision to
return via Batavia an air of reason. It transformed a region of
uncertainty into a bridge passage. It made sense to link his first
New Holland landing with his last New Zealand landfall. And,
having been impressed by Banks's enthusiasm for the place,
having decided to commemorate his botanists there, it was
logical to copy the arrangement he had just used in New Zealand
– or, at least, to have the two configurations conform. Out of
respect for their differing ranks in society (according to Beaglehole) or, perhaps more importantly, because of their close collab-
oration during the voyage, Cook accorded Solander a point,
Banks a cape. Cook first thought of 'Botanists Bay', but afterwards changed 'Botanists' to 'Botany': not, presumably, because
he was suddenly struck by the platonic grandeur of flower
hunting, but by analogy with 'Admiralty'. The analogy was not
justified empirically, but it did work rhetorically. It faithfully
preserved the traveller's sense of facts, not as discrete objects, but
as horizons increasingly inscribed with spatial meanings, defined
not in terms of objective qualities, but as directional pointers
articulating and punctuating the explorer's destiny.

   This account of how the name 'Botany Bay' emerged has, it
seems to me, a number of advantages. Even in conventional
biographical terms, it accords better with the image of Cook as
the 'genius of the matter of fact'. Beaglehole's rationalization of
the process of revision implies an introspective individual finely
sensitive to nuances of sound and sense. To speak in terms of
'variants' is to imply that Cook had the ambition and talent of a
poet, that he revised teleologically, towards the perfect expression he had in mind from the beginning. It suggests a middle-
class sensibility and leisure quite at odds with the portrait
Beaglehole elsewhere paints in his biography. In addition, of
course, the recognition that Cook actively engaged in his own
biography, and was not by any means a dispassionate observer
of events, puts paid to the notion that the character of the man
has to be sought elsewhere. In the open-ended form of the

journal, the making of history and the writing of history went together.

Seeing 'Botany Bay' the name as a characteristic device of travelling texts enables us to free the name of its posthumous mythology, to see it as a link forging the discontinuous entries of the ship's log into a continuous narrative. The world it refers to is the world of the text, not the mind of the author, nor even the collective ambition of the British government. Freed of these superstitious encumbrances, the name becomes one of a series of nominal strategies for articulating the dynamic of journeying; it discovers its logic in the twin processes of reading and travelling. In this strategic context, the fact that, on a later voyage, Cook named an island near New Caledonia 'Botany Isle' ceases to be surprising. In this instance, as before at Botany Bay, there was an anecdotal botanical circumstance justifying the choice of name; but the object was not to fix the place uniquely, to distinguish it uniquely – that was the task of the map – only to preserve, with Boswellian immediacy, the particularities of the journey.

To suppose that a name like 'Botany Bay' is, in some sense, arbitrary, that it lacks local authority, is to indulge in a form of linguistic animism – as if the soul of the object was, or could be, contained in a word. Its implication of a deep-rooted empathy between language and land represents a mythical nostalgia for a tradition, a tradition that, by supplying history with, as it were, a prehistory, serves only to eclipse the historical significance of the very event that might furnish the beginnings of a tradition. 'Botany Bay', the name, is no doubt replaceable – in the sense that 'Stingray Harbour' would serve equally well; but, and this applies to Cook's naming practice generally, no other name could improve on it. No other name could speak with greater authority about the place. For it was the shadowy outline of a place that Cook's name brought into being. The only argument for altering the name would have to be horizontal, in terms of the dynamic of the journey, not posthumously associative. And, even if renaming were to occur (as it has done in innumerable Australian instances), the replacement would still refer only to the particularity of a new journey, a new spatial horizon or orientation.

This kind of reading, which interprets, rather than explains, which relocates the text in the context of its writing, can be applied more generally: taken as a whole, Cook's place names express the navigator's active engagement with the space of his journey. They are figures of speech characteristic of the explorer's discourse. This much is clear, but what exactly is the explorer's discourse? How, for instance, does exploration differ from that other great eighteenth-century naming discipline, botany? In answering this question, the conjunction of Cook and Banks on the *Endeavour* voyage is a particularly fortuitous one. Historically speaking, the distinction between botany's concern to reduce the variety of the world to a uniform and universally valid taxonomy and exploration's pursuit of a mode of knowing that was dynamic, concerned with the world as it appeared, went back, on the one hand, to the Enlightenment project of universal knowledge and, on the other, to the trenchant criticism of its empirical assumptions mounted by David Hume. But nowhere is this methodological distinction brought out more clearly than in the contrast between the scientific practices of Banks and Cook.

Beaglehole shows that the more elaborate passages in the *Endeavour Journal*, where Cook attempts some form of reflective generalization regarding, say, the state of the Aborigines as noble savages or where he attempts a heightened descriptive prose (as in the account of the *Endeavour*'s holing) were, for better or worse, borrowed from Banks's journal, which Cook had an opportunity of consulting in Batavia – the same opportunity that gave him the idea of naming Botany Bay. But, significant as the borrowings may be in biographical terms, even more instructive is their dissonance within Cook's own text; and this dissonance did not mark a merely temperamental or social distinction, but also a difference in the kinds of knowledge the two men pursued. For where Banks was preoccupied with the typical, Cook was concerned with the singular; where Banks tended to generalize, Cook tended to specify. And this, indeed, was the difference between botany and geography as they were practised in the eighteenth century.

On the *Endeavour* voyage, Solander and Banks made use of the system of classification developed and popularized by the

Swedish botanist Carl Linnaeus. The Linnaean system was artificial in the sense that it derived from no detailed examination of plant morphology, which might reveal 'natural' affinities between distinct species. It was based instead on a superficial comparison of a limited number of characteristics. Once these characteristics had been defined for a type specimen, it simply became a question of seeing to what extent any new plant corresponded to it. If the new plant differed considerably, then it might itself become the type specimen of a new family. Whether these type specimens were actually typical of certain groupings in nature was not the issue. As the Linnaeus scholar William Stearn points out, the natural character of a genus had a single species as its basis, and he notes that

> Having once drafted a generic description, maybe at a time when only one species of the genus was known to him, he [Linnaeus] often left it unchanged from edition to edition of the *Genera Plantarum*, despite the addition to the genus of other species diverging in flower or fruit from the original species.[21]

Stearn quotes a letter, written by Linnaeus's son in 1778, in which Carl describes Linnaeus's 'secret of determining genera' as 'nothing more than his practice of recognizing plants by *externa facie* [general aspect]'.[22]

By 'Method' alone, as Oliver Goldsmith explained in his widely read *History of the Earth*,

> can we hope to dissipate the glare, if I may so express it, which arises from a multiplicity of objects at once presenting themselves to the view.[23]

And the great advantage of the Linnaean system over the other methods of classification was its simplicity: it made the getting of botanical knowledge beguilingly simple. The sole aim of it, as one of Linnaeus's disciples explained,

> is to help any one to learn the name and history of an unknown plant in the most easy and certain manner, by first determining its Class and Order in this system; after which its Genus is to be made out . . . and finally its Species . . .[24]

The great drawback of the system was that as a result

botany, as the nineteenth-century German botanist Julius von Sachs pointed out,

> ceased to be a science . . . in place of the morphological examination of the parts of plants there was an endless accumulating of technical terms devoid of depth of scientific meaning.[25]

Sachs was admittedly an evolutionist, who had therefore no time for the doctrine of the constancy of species on which Linnaean taxonomy rested. Even so, his outspoken dismissal of 'the dull occupation of plant collectors, who called themselves systematists', is just:

> It is true indeed that these adherents of Linnaeus did some service to botany by searching the floras of Europe and of other quarters of the globe, but they left it to others to turn to scientific account the material which they had collected.[26]

The pleasure of the plant collector, then, was a pleasure in naming uniquely and systematically. It was the pleasure of arrangement within a universal taxonomy, a taxonomy characterized by tree-like ramifications – in short, a pleasure analogous to that felt by the imperial historian, who assimilates occasions and anomalies to the logic of universal reason. Equipped with the artificial system of Linnaeus, novelty ceased to present a problem. Utterly strange forms became type specimens. Less curious plants might be assigned to existing genera. The taxonomy depended on no close examination. Accordingly, the botanist could concentrate on superficial differences between plants, rather than subtler likenesses: 'My business was to kill variety and not too many individuals of any one species,'[27] as Banks put it, referring to a bird-shooting expedition at Botany Bay. By the same token, once specimens of all that came immediately to hand had been collected, the botany of the place held no further interest. As Banks wrote, 'The Plants were now intirely compleated and nothing new to be found, so that sailing is all we wish for if the wind would but allow us.'[28] (And not long before, Banks had been sulking because Cook sailed too much and stopped too little!)

A significant corollary of Banks's Linnaean bias for the

history of early perceptions of Australian landscape is that, although he had an eye for superficial differences, Banks was likely to be insensitive to the appeal of likeness, of relatively undifferentiated continuity. Thus, at a distance from the New Holland mainland, he found, 'For the whole length of coast which we saild along there was a sameness to be observd in the face of the countrey very uncommon.'[29] Only at close quarters on land could Banks embark on that process of differentiation which, for him, constituted the pleasure of travel. The hint of contradiction in his remark that 'Of Plants in general the countrey afforded a far larger variety than its barren appearance seemd to promise,'[30] faithfully reflects the bias, even the impatience, implicit in his Linnaean strategy of possession.

Equally significant is the poverty of Banks's epistemology once he attempts to speculate beyond the immediate object. One of the temptations of the Linnaean system is to pass from species to classes, from particular differences to abstract uniformities. Banks's view, for instance, that, from the poor appearance of parts of the New Holland coast, the interior of the country must be equally barren – and hence entirely devoid of inhabitants[31] – is an exemplary instance of the indifference of the botanizing mind to the claims of locality and the limits of observation. Banks justifies his remarks, not by his own observation, but by quoting an authority on primitive people – to the effect that they are universally dependent on the sea for their subsistence. But such an authority serves merely to appropriate the Aborigines to a universal condition, to make them a further species in an already established family. Rather than encourage closer examination, it circumvents it. It denies the possible otherness that would render the unknown worth knowing. It renders the potentially interesting fact null and void.

Perhaps the most far-reaching implication of Banks's general outlook and the Enlightenment philosophy of knowledge that it represented was that the *spatiality* of experience could be ignored. Banks's interest in taxonomy quite excludes as part of his knowledge the circumstances of discovery. Knowledge, for Banks, is precisely what survives unimpaired the translation from soil to plate and Latin description. There is, in Banks's philosophy, no sense of limitation, no sense of what might have been missed, no sense of the particular as special. By a curious irony, even though he sets out to botanize on the supposition his botanical knowledge is incomplete, his knowledge is always complete: each object, found, translated into a scientific fact and detached from its historical and geographical surroundings, becomes a complete world in itself. It loses all power to signify beyond itself, to suggest lines of development or the subtler influences of climate, ground and aspect. In short, its ecology, its existence in a given, living space is lost in the moment of scientific discovery. And, we may add, what applies to Banks's botanizing is also true of empirical history – a discipline that, after all, is grounded in the same Enlightenment assumptions as botany: it is precisely the particularity of historical experience, the material hereness and nowness which cannot be repeated, that such history crowds out in favour of a transcendent classification in terms of multiplying causes and effects.

In all these respects, Cook differed from his botanists. Where Banks sought to build up, Cook aimed to pare away. His attitude is perfectly summed up, when he reports:

> In this Chart I have laide down no land nor figur'd out any shore but what I saw my self, and thus far the Chart may be depended upon.[32]

Cook prizes his lightness of touch; he finds blank spaces, gaps in his outline, as informative as the line itself. It may yield little of value to the traveller at home, eager for useful facts, but, as a document of travelling, to be used by those who follow Cook, the gaps are as significant as the discoveries. This anti-empirical focus on particularities, so characteristic of Cook's practice in mapping, is also evident in his attitude towards the 'natives'. Unlike Banks, he shows no interest in filling in the unavoidable blank spaces in his knowledge. Of the Australian Aborigines, he is content to say,

> Being wholly unacquainted not only with the superfluous but the necessary Conveniences so much sought after in Europe, they are happy in not knowing the use of them . . . they have very little need of Clothing and this they seem fully sencible of, for many to whome we gave Cloth &c to, left it carlessly

upon the Sea beach and in the woods as a thing they had no manner of use for. In short they seem'd to set no Value upon anything we gave them.[33]

Beaglehole dismisses this passage, with, as he sees it, Cook's uncharacteristic lapse into the mythology of the noble savage, as so much 'nonsense', although he admits that, since Cook repeated the description in a letter after returning to England, 'one must presume he was rather taken with it'.[34] But must Cook's sentiments be allied with those of Banks or even Jean-Jacques Rousseau? What fascinates Cook about the Australian Aborigines is, in contrast with the Tahitians, say, who swarmed over the ship after nails, their complete detachment, their lightness of touch in dealing with the world around them. In this sense, a parallel existed between their unassuming behaviour and Cook's own refusal to trade in hypotheses, to dress up (and thereby conceal) the naked truth.

The chief discovery of the *Endeavour* was its discovery of nothing or, rather, of the non-existence of a great southern continent: from an empirical point of view, this can only be construed as a failure. But, from the traveller's point of view, Cook's journal gains or loses nothing by its discoveries: what matters is the *quality* of the travelling it reveals. In contrast with the botanist, Cook's geo-graphy, his writing of lands, was inseparable from the conditions of the inquiry itself. The same calculations that enabled him to steer a course also enabled him to leave the coastlines he sighted where they were. This was the essence of the maps he made, that they did not mirror the appearance of natural objects, but preserved the trace of encountering them. Despite its *tabula rasa* appearance, the map was, from the beginning, designed to record particular information. As the spaces of its grid were written over, there was revealed a palimpsest of the explorer's experience, a criss-cross of routes gradually thickening and congealing into fixed seas and lands. In this context, the rubric 'New South Wales', disc. 1770' (see plate 3) named not so much a country as, by the direction of its writing, the course of a journey. By contrast, the illustrated plant and its Latin description belonged to a metaphysical system of classification from the moment of discovery. The nature of the discovering process was concealed. But, whereas the blank surround of the botanical plate was dead, the blank spaces of the map were active, locating future histories. For Cook, though, his knowledge was indistinguishable from the conditions of knowing. The fruits of his travel were directions to the traveller.

What could be further from Banks's eagerness to haul off and leave New Holland behind him than Cook's elaborate explanation of his zigzag route inside the Great Barrier Reef? As Cook wrote,

> I have engaged more among the Islands and Shoals upon this Coast than perhaps in prudence I ought to have done with a single Ship and every other thing considered, but if I had not I should not have been able to give any better account of the one half of it than if I had never seen it, at best I should not have been able to say whether it was Main land or Islands and as to its produce, that we should have been totally ignorant of as being inseparable with the other; and in this case it would have been far more satisfaction to me never to have discover'd it.[35]

No such scruples inhibited Banks: whether the flora of Botany Bay was typical or special, whether it was insular or coastal, was unimportant to him. For Banks, it was the aggregate of objects that counted, not their true relations. And, unlike Cook, Banks had no time for undiscoverable countries. The very syntax of Cook's explanation is symptomatic of his geographical practice: if Banks advances from superficial acquaintance to grand generalization, then Cook, from the certainty of a continuous coastline, entertains the possibility of having remained, after all, at sea.

Evidently, then, there was more to the dispute that led Banks to give up plans for sailing with Cook a second time than a personal difference. The disagreement was also methodological. True, the additional upper deck and extra cabin on the poop, which Banks demanded for himself and his scientific entourage, rendered the *Endeavour* unseaworthy, but, in ordering their removal, Cook was also asserting the secondary nature of the kind of knowledge they represented. Primary knowledge lay in the course of the exploration itself, not in the elaboration of possible discoveries. To ensure his ship handled well was not to exhibit the boorishness of a professional sailor, but to protect the integrity of exploring as a mode of knowing. It was to suggest travelling itself was knowledge and not merely the fruits of travel.

This difference between Banks's interest in botanical novelties and Cook's devotion to navigation can also be expressed in terms of the difference between exploration and discovery. For, while discovery rests on the assumption of a world of facts waiting to be found, collected and classified, a world in which the neutral observer is not implicated, exploration lays stress on the observer's active engagement with his environment: it recognizes phenomena as offspring of his intention to explore. Despite the tendency of most historians to regard the terms as virtually interchangeable, the pleasures of discovery and exploration rest on utterly opposed theoretical assumptions. The delight Banks took in discovery was summational, a matter of adding up discrete experiences. For Cook, it was quite different. To be an explorer was to inhabit a world of potential objects with which one carried on an imaginary dialogue. And, in so far as they had already been imagined, there was a sense in which the explorer's most valuable service lay in progressively clearing them away, in allowing the uncluttered space of the journey to emerge in its own right and speak. In this context, Banks's pleasure in finding Botany Bay surprisingly rich in flowers is as predictable as Cook's relative indifference to the fact.

In his letter to the Admiralty, dated 23 October 1770, summarizing the *Endeavour*'s progress, Cook wrote:

> Altho' the discoveries made in this Voyage are not great, yet I flatter my self they are such as may merit the attention of their Lordships, and altho' I have fail'd in discovering the so much talk'd of Southern Continent (which perhaps do not exist) and which I my self had much at heart, yet I am confident that no part of the failure of such discovery Can be laid to my Charge.[36]

Clearly, Cook is conscious here of the Admiralty's desire of tangible fruits of travel: he had, after all, been sent out, among other things, specifically to test the hypothesis of a great 'southern continent' (not, of course, to be confused with the already partially known land mass of New Holland later Australia). But equally impressive is Cook's assertion of the *quality* of his travelling, his confidence that the value of his journey is not in direct proportion to the discoveries made. And the belief that attentive exploring was a form of knowledge quite as valuable as actual discoveries is made explicit in Cook's post-*Endeavour* letter to John Walker:

> I . . . have made no very great Discoveries yet I have exploar'd more of the Great South Sea than all that have gone before me so much that little remains now to be done to have a thorough knowledge of that part of the Globe.[37]

It is perfectly possible to explore without discovering anything. In fact, it is precisely an exploring state of mind that renders discoveries significant, not accidental, not spuriously factual but authentically intellectual. It is this sense of intellectual discovery which explains Cook's 'possession' of the east coast of Australia. In his journal Cook reports:

> I . . . steer'd to the westward untill I fell in with the East Coast of New Holland . . . I coasted the Shore of this Country to the North . . .[38]

And, at the end of that coasting, he explained:

> Having satisfied my self of the great Probabillity of a Passage, thro' which I intend going with the Ship, and therefore may land no more upon this Eastern Coast of *New Holland*, and on the Western side I can make no new discovery the honour of which belongs to the Dutch Navigators, but the Eastern Coast, from the Latitude of 38° South down to this place I am confident was never seen or visited by any European before us, and Notwithstanding I had taken possession of several places upon this coast, I now once more hoisted English Coulers and in the Name of His Majesty King George the Third, took possession of the whole Eastern Coast, from the above Latitude down to this place, by the name of *New South Wales*, together with all the Bays, Harbours, Rivers, and Islands situate upon the said coast . . .[39]

What justified Cook in taking possession of the east coast was not his discovery of it: as his description of falling in with the coast indicates, he knew in advance (even if the sources of his knowledge are disputed) that such a coast existed. Cook's justification lay in the quality of his exploring, in the particular discoveries his meticulous navigation had yielded. As he said, regarding his discovery of the Great Barrier Reef, he may have 'engaged more among the Islands and Shoals upon this Coast than perhaps in prudence I ought to have done', but, had he not done so, 'I should not have been able to say whether it was Mainland or Islands . . . and in this case it would have been far more satisfaction to me never to have discover'd it.'

Cook's possession of the coast – and nothing more or less – reflects his confidence that the quality of his journey (evident in his charts and journals) has been the means of adding substantially to geographical knowledge. But it is not so much that New Holland has been possessed; rather it has appeared in the direction of Cook's sailing, it has fallen under his intentional gaze. It is this outlook which explains Cook's decision to claim the east coast for the crown by finally planting the British flag *on an island*. Imperial historians have always been puzzled by this: what could Cook possibly mean by not formally taking possession of the mainland, by laying claim only to an insignificant island? From the point of view of the imperialists, anxious to establish a direct link between Cook and 'Australia', this spatial dislocation between the place of possession and the place possessed appears like an act of wilful perversity or neglect. True, by 1787 Possession Island had aggregated to itself a group (see plate 3), but it remained resolutely moored off the mainland's northern tip. In fact, though, Cook's diffidence simply bears witness to the symbolic nature of his knowledge. For what Cook, his charts and journal knew was quite precisely a direction travelled. As Cook was an explorer of horizons, and not a discoverer of countries, his realm of competence was confined to a coastal swath bounded by the visible horizon: in the zigzag map created by his passage, Possession Island, far from appearing peripheral, stood as a symbolic centre, a jewel crowning his outline of names.

In this light Cook's place names suddenly grow eloquent. In adopting them, Cook's object was, as far as possible, to leave the 'places' as he found them, just as his maps did. To name them was to invent them, to bring them into cultural circulation. But the metaphorical function of his names – and this was embodied in their resistance to empirical paraphrase – was to leave the place uncharacterized. It was as if Cook's aim was not to fill the world up with objects but, rather, to erase its surface as far as possible of mythic excrescences. It was as if he wanted to bare the surface of the Pacific of imaginary objects in order to reveal the intentional space of his own experience, the sense in which it had produced his travelling. We see that Cook's name, Botany Bay, was given not without a sense of its irony. In yoking a scientific discourse that claimed universal validity to a place so particular, Cook registered a very proper sense of scepticism. As we shall see, the name's grandeur subsequently attracted a good deal of sarcastic wit, but there is no reason to suppose that Cook himself was wholly unaware of the name's pretentiousness. Rather, his name neatly recognized, and perhaps satirized, the difference between Banks's science, founded on changeless, universal axioms, and his own nomadic discourse, which, by contrast, engaged phenomena as they presented themselves to his problem-solving consciousness.

We can now make fuller sense of an interesting little correction that Cook made to Orton's fair copy of his journal. Referring to a New Zealand place name, Orton had inadvertently written, 'Banks names Sandy Bay.' Reading through Orton's copy, Cook came to this statement and wrote over Banks's name 'me'.[40] The temptation is to read this as evidence of personal animosity. After all, the name is hardly a distinguished one. But the truth lies elsewhere, in Banks's and Cook's differing attitude towards names. If Cook reserved to himself alone the privilege of naming places, it was not merely because he stood on his dignity as lieutenant-captain: it was because he knew where places were. And, in this sense, no name of his was casual, the mere product of circumstance. But the names that Banks gave, precisely because they were casually descriptive, superficially characteristic, tended to trail the place behind the namer's own destiny, attaching it to a point of view.

Returning to Beaglehole's conviction that 'Cook was the reverse of casual in placing these names on the map', we can now see that quite as significant as Cook's juggling of names are the 'blanks' themselves. These nameless gaps in the text symbolized Cook's concern to preserve, as he went along, his discoveries; to retain them provisionally within the open-ended domain of exploration, rather than commit himself to a premature, and artificially authoritative, definition. Unlike Banks, pressing his plants before hurrying on to the next discovery, Cook preserved *his* discoveries by not characterizing them on first acquaintance, by leaving them as they were where they first appeared in the text.

A profounder distinction between botany and exploration now emerges. For the difference between the two was not simply a matter of methodology: it embodied, more fundamentally, a disagreement about the nature of language and its relationship to the world. For Banks, names enjoyed a simple, Linnaean relationship with the object they denoted. They gave the illusion of knowing under the guise of naming. Cook's names obey a different, more oblique logic, the logic of metaphor. His names do not intend to preserve the delusion of objectivity, for his standpoint is neither neutral nor static. Instead, they draw geographical objects into the space of his passage. The paradox is that Cook's more wilful practice, his greater subjectivity, succeeds where Banks's unreflective objectivity does not in preserving what is named. A case in point is Banks's first attempt at Australian nomenclature. Banks writes, from on board ship, 'We could discern many cabbage trees but nothing else which we could call by any name.'[41] This seems straightforward enough, until we realize that, when Banks names certain trees on the shore 'cabbage trees', he is not identifying the trees, he is not naming *them*: he is only asserting their resemblance to a tree with which he is familiar. Under the guise of a scientific label Banks employs a simile based on what Erasmus Darwin later called 'intuitive analogy'; and, since he employs it in the absence of a proper name, we could say he employs the commonplace rhetorical trope of catachresis.

Banks's notion of a genuinely descriptive language spontaneously available to the empirical mind goes back to John Locke, who envisages scientific language as a language free of metaphorical distortion:

If we would speak of things as they are, we must allow that all the art of rhetoric, besides order and clearness, all the artificial and figurative applications of words eloquence hath invented, are for nothing else but to insinuate wrong ideas, move the passions, and thereby mislead the judgement, and so indeed are perfect cheats.[42]

Banks's 'descriptive' language, his lexicon-like invention and application of terms which are to be regarded as unequivocal and definitive, exemplifies Locke's position. But the language of things as they are is an illusion: as Banks's 'cabbage trees' illustrates, even the most factual name embraces the new figuratively. The illusion is compounded by the fact that, as Locke's own prose demonstrates, even the most dispassionate argument cannot dispense with figures of speech. Even to adopt the stance of a neutral observer is to adopt a point of view. The fact is that, however 'scientific' it may purport to be, the language of empiricism remains metaphorical. Even as Banks applied a name he resorted to figurative language; even as he denounced figurative language, Locke took advantage of it.

Indeed, Locke's imagery of sinuous paths is peculiarly interesting for, whether intentionally or not, it draws attention to a fact of the greatest significance for spatial history; which is that rhetoric, the whole range of figurative terms by which we denominate the world, attempting to translate it into plausible conceptions, is itself fundamentally spatial in nature. Metaphor, for instance, is quite literally a spatial figure of speech: in a static sense, it stands in for or in place of something else – in this way, it makes what was invisible or only dimly perceptible emerge clearly before our eyes; in a mobile sense, metaphor carries meaning over, brings distant things near or even runs alongside normal usage on a parallel track.[43] Figures of speech, place names among them, correspond symbolically to the scope of exploration itself: they are a means of making sinuous paths comprehensible, a means of recording the journey as it impresses itself on the consciousness. There may be nothing · objective about this, but then, as the philosopher Paul Ricoeur has observed, 'There is no non-metaphorical standpoint from which we could look upon metaphor, and all the other figures for that matter, as if they were a game played before one's eyes.'[44] Similarly, there is no non-directional, unimplicated point of view from which the traveller can describe the facts of the journey.

Cook's metaphorical mode of naming is not a peculiar whim of the namer: it represents an authentic mode of knowing, a travelling epistemology that recognizes that the translation of experience into texts is necessarily a process of symbolizing, a process of bringing invisible things into focus in the horizontal lines of the written page. So, where the metaphorical nature of Banks's discourse is suppressed, Cook feels under no such constraint. Names like 'Pigeon House Mountain' or 'Mount Dromedary' spectacularly depend on the namer's point of view. They assert no literal likeness but are offspring of the paradoxical miniaturization of the magnified image in the telescope; framed and isolated, such features are brought close, made homely, domestic. They are grand enough to hang on a wall; small enough to fit into a pocket. But Cook's seaworthy metaphors do not in any way diminish the otherness they make so readily accessible. For implicit in his metaphors is the figure of irony, a mode of description that passionately distances the observer from what he sees. If Banks's generalizations tend to belittle the coast, then the particularity of Cook's inventions suggests nothing so much as humility, a willingness to be dwarfed as well as to command.

To accuse Cook of insensitively reducing a foreign coast to certain local, biographical preoccupations of his own is wholly to miss the point that his names preserve and even enhance the otherness of the outline. The very violence of their metaphorical displacements preserves the irony of the explorer's position and the contingent nature of his knowledge. The *unnaturalness* of attaching ministers to mountains, secretaries to capes, the playful tautology of calling islands 'Islands of Direction', the unlikelihood of Botany *Bay*, as if the flora in question were marine: by all these figurative means Cook preserves the difference between the order of nature and the order of culture. If, as the Marxist historian Theodor Adorno argues, it is the loss of irony that characterizes the discourse of totalitarian regimes – 'Irony's medium, the difference between ideology and reality, has disappeared'[45] – then we can after all see in what sense Cook *was* a foundational figure. We do not have to invent an imperialist conspiracy, as Bonwick and Watson sought to do; nor, as Beaglehole has done, do we have to imagine a 'genius of the matter of fact'. It is enough to detach Cook from the company of the sedentary, speculative map-users and to replace him in the realm of the travelling map-makers.

Cook's place names were tools of travelling rather than fruits of travel. Rather than represent premature attempts to constitute Australia as a number of distinct physical parts, adding up to a metaphysical whole, their proliferation imitated the exploring process. Their concentration in north Queensland waters, for example, was not an objective mirror to the quantity of geographical objects found in that particular area, but a testimony to the extent of the exploring that went on there. Rather than iron out the coast, reducing its otherness to a placeless classification, Cook's names served to preserve the space of exploring, to spread the coast out. What they named were the individual moments that went together to form what James Boswell, referring to the contents of his own journal, called a series of uniformity. Their function was to preserve the means by which they came to be known, the occasion of places, the sense in which places are means, not of settling, but of travelling on.

Cook offered future travellers an accurate chart, an outline of names, but the essence of these texts was that they did not sum up a journey, but preserved the trace of passage. They were open-ended; their very accuracy invited further exploration, pre-empted premature possession. They – and this is what distinguishes Cook's achievement from that of his putative predecessors in the area – created a cultural space in which places might eventually be found. In this sense the superficial purchase of Cook's names is not a weakness but a strength. Where Banks's brief forays into the interior irremediably centred the future comprehension of the Australian flora on the narrowest of bases, Cook's un-cumulative, un-centred maps and travelling journal retained the possibility of multiple futures, endless journeys, arrivals and departures. It was hardly Cook's fault if, even before 1788, the gaps in his outline had been closed up (see plate 3) and map-makers serving the imperial cause were already representing New Holland as a bounded object, closed to future journeys. He was hardly to blame if the calligraphers were already capitalizing on Botany Bay, both literally and figuratively.

If Cook's voyage threatened to steady that line of foam, to have it coagulate into a possessable, a translatable territory, the integrity of his travelling nevertheless kept open (indeed, opened up) the possibility of other ways of possession. The world view embodied in his naming practice stood at odds with the aims of imperialism. Oriented towards the solution of problems, attentive to the changing hues of water and horizon, Cook's travelling embodied an attitude essential to the colonization of Australia. It was not Banks's imperial gaze, passive and static, that later explorers and settlers borrowed when they made their way in Australia, but the open-ended, imaginative vision of Cook. It was Cook's example they followed in writing up their journals and in drawing their maps. It is in this respect that Cook was a foundational figure: although he found a country, Cook did not aim to found a colony. Among contemporary historians he may not have the central place he once occupied. But what is needed is replacement, not displacement, a recognition that, by establishing a tradition of travelling, Cook inaugurated Australia's spatial history.

2

An Airy Barrier

We go by Analogy & judge from what we have seen & read before.

J. R. Forster, *The Resolution Journal*

Almost the greatest barrier to Australia's spatial history is the date 1788. On the one side, anterior to and beyond the limits of Australian 'history', lies a hazy geo-historical tradition of surmise, a blank sea scored at intervals down the centuries by the prows of dug-outs, out-riggers and, latterly, three-masters; it is a 'thick horizon', a rewarding site of myth and speculation. But it lacks substance; cause and effect do not converge in its events, but spread out behind like the wake. After 1788, all is solid. Even the weather seems arrested. In alighting at Botany Bay, Phillip steps out of Myth into History. His first concern is not, like Cook, to water his ships but to protect them permanently from offshore gales. He removes almost immediately to Sydney Cove: his means of passage become marks of place. Cook is cast off. A substantial history is inaugurated, an imperial tradition of names, years, floggings, heads of cattle, salaries. The sea, formerly an asylum, itself becomes a prison, a turbulent, unavoidable barrier to progress.

Botany Bay, the name, no sooner makes history than it is eclipsed, left astern. It ends up as it began: a rhetorical place, nothing more. It hosts the abuse that official histories suppress, the resistance to the logic of progress. 'Come with us, if we should go to "Bottomless Bay",' Eliza Darling writes to her brother in 1823.[1] Botany Bay's platonic grandeur is turned against it; it becomes an ironic figure of speech for all that is deceptive about the Enlightenment myth of order prevailing over chaos.

34

Therefore, old George, by George we pray
Of thee forthwith to extend thy sway
Over the great Botanic Bay.[2]

Thus Robert Southey in 1807, extemporizing his anti-monarchist sentiments one evening with William Wordsworth. And, thirty-two years after the event, De Quincey can still remember the lines. His memory may be imperfect but

> About the last I cannot be wrong; for I remember laughing with a sense of something peculiarly droll in the substitution of the stilted phrase – 'the great Botanic Bay', for our ordinary week-day name Botany Bay, so redolent of thieves and pickpockets.[3]

The fate of Botany Bay is of more than anecdotal interest. It illustrates a characteristic strategy of empirical history which a history of space is bound to resist. Botany Bay is a 'cause' so long as the First Fleet trends towards it; according to the First Fleet officer and chronicler, Watkin Tench, 'Ithaca itself was scarcely more longed for by Ulysses, than Botany Bay by the adventurers who had traversed so many thousands of miles to take possession of it.'[4] But, as this passage indicates, Botany Bay is a cause that surfaces only as an effect. In the event it inspires – possession – the place itself disappears, ceases to be an object of historical desire. This phenomenon can be generalized. It is the characteristic of such history that it is linear, that its causes are wholly spent in their immediate effects. No causes are, as it were, left over to remain a presence in future activity. There is no sense of cumulative effect. Although early maps (see for instance plate 4) write dates along sight-lines, suggesting how historical time was predicated on historical space, this historical relationship is soon effaced. Maps grow timeless; historical time becomes placeless. Events exhaust their origins. Thus Botany Bay is emptied of a future as the First Fleet renders it past. Similarly, like the Deist's First Mover, Cook is rendered invisible by his own motive power.

The year 1788, in this account, becomes an impassable barrier; it swallows up what went before; it starts the future on a new footing; sea yields to land; the sedentary replaces the dynamic; even the clouds become fixed historical objects. To quote Tench again, referring to the day of arrival in Botany Bay, ' "Heavily in clouds came on the day" which ushered in our arrival. To us it was "a great, an important day," though I hope the foundation, not the fall, of an empire will be dated from it.'[5] So, before we can, as it were, set foot in post-1788 history we have to dissolve this sudden, exclusive barrier. We have to divest the beginnings of their clear outline, their apparent solidity, recovering the lightness of Cook's glance. We have to show land and sea, observer and observed, future and past, in a dialectical relationship, rather than obeying the laws of organic growth and extinction. We have, in fact, to make cloudy again the line between language and space, to turn a barrier into a road, to recover the sense in which language did not simply delimit, but made a difference. We have to disperse the myth of spontaneous, theatrical settlement and linear progress, and to demonstrate the dialectical nature of founda- tion, the sense in which the new country was a rhetorical construction, a product of language and the intentional gaze, not of the detached, dictionary-clasping spectator.

Perhaps the most obvious example of this foundational process occurs in the way the First Fleet chroniclers read the journal of their distinguished predecessor, Cook. Historians anxious to defend Cook's reputation would have it that the settlers' rejection of his account of Botany Bay was total, immediate, dispassionate and, being empirically founded, authoritative. They would have it that Phillip's and Tench's revised estimates of the potential of the place as a site of settlement mark a decisive discontinuity between Botany Bay's discoverer and its settlers – a discontinuity that they have, in the interests of preserving the logic of cause and effect, to extenuate and, as far as possible, gloss over. But, in fact, the early readings of Cook – at least as his journal appeared in Hawkesworth's edition – were strategic, dynamic, dialectical. They expressed the intention of settlement and its progress, not the amused detachment of an imaginary onlooker.

The far from disinterested nature of Tench's attitude towards Cook's generally favourable description of Botany Bay is revealed, not only in the fact that it changes, growing increasingly critical, but also in the style, in the rhetorical devices, that Tench adopts to express his hardening disillusionment. Thus, in June 1788, a mere six months after the First Fleet's arrival, Tench was prepared to write only,

> Of the natural meadows which Mr Cook mentions near Botany Bay, we can give no account.[6]

By September 1789, however, when Tench accompanied the First Fleet surgeon, John Hunter, on his surveying expedition to Botany Bay, his uncertainty had become full-blown scepticism:

> Variety of opinion here disappeared. I shall, therefore, transcribe literally what I wrote in my journal, on my return from the expedition. – 'We were unanimously of opinion, that had not the nautical part of Mr Cook's description . . . been so accurately laid down, there would exist the utmost reason to believe, that those who described the contiguous country, had never seen it.[7]

And Tench's journal entry concluded, '. . . we did not find 200 acres which could be cultivated'. But the nadir of the bay's reputation was reached, for Tench, in December 1790. An abortive expedition against the Aborigines, to avenge the murder of a convict, led him into bogs from which he barely succeeded in escaping. Tench cites the phrase 'some of the finest meadows in the world', and appends this footnote:

> The words which are quoted may be found in Mr Cook's first voyage, and form part of his description of Botany Bay. It has often fallen to my lot to traverse these fabled plains; and many a bitter execration have I heard poured on those travellers, who could so faithlessly relate what they saw.[8]

In these successive judgements, Tench hardly proceeds empirically: it is scarcely calm judgement that replaces surmise with hard facts. Rather, he defines and redefines his position dialectically – in terms of and against Cook's earlier description. Nor is it as if Tench replaces Cook's account with a better, more objective one of his own. His outbursts are increasingly theatrical. Indeed, Cook's meadows seem to have little other function than to provide Tench with a convenient whipping-horse. They are little more than a pretext for Tench to indulge in self-dramatization. For all this, though, Tench's aim is clear: it is to dethrone Cook and substitute his own experience as authoritative. Yet he does not achieve this aim empirically, but rhetorically. Thus, he quotes Cook only to mock him; thus, too, he quotes himself. The dictionary-maker, like Johnson, or the Enlightenment-trained writer, like Tench, were quite familiar with the convention of quotation: to quote an independent authority in support of one's own statement was to lend one's own writing an air of disinterested authority. But what Tench's manipulation of this familiar device reveals is its rhetorical nature. If Tench refers to Cook's 'finest meadows', it is only to deny his authority. And what is disinterested about quoting *oneself* in support of a statement?

Seen like this, the date 1788 becomes something the newcomers had to construct: the difference was not there to begin with. The disagreement between Tench and Cook is not something to be explained inductively or deductively. It is a paradox which Tench went out of his way to emphasize. Similarly, there is no question of our trying to compare or to adjudicate: this would involve us in a form of historical reductionism that borders on the absurd. Should we, for instance, attribute Tench's bad humour on the last occasion to nothing more than frustration at finding himself 'in a rotten spungy bog . . . plunged knee-deep at every step'? Are we bound to gloss over any discrepancy by speculating it represented nothing more than the different circumstances (length of time, viewpoints, seasons and the like) in which Cook and his successors went over and described what was nominally the same place? But Phillip himself entertained this likelihood – and there is no reason to suppose Tench was less alive to this possibility.

The truth is that the invocation of Cook only to disparage him had little empirical merit. Its function was largely rhetorical. It bore witness to the fact that the newcomers set about making a place for themselves dialectically. Settlement did not occur on a pre-established stage. It resembled a road, where choices had to be made. As Dawes's map illustrates (plate 4), certain viewpoints had to be invented and upheld; others had to be rejected and placed behind. And this was not only a physical process but also a textual one. Cook's earlier account was the necessary departure point in terms of which the settlers could find their own way. Complete conformity between the two views – the continuity the imperial historian pines for – would, in fact, have rendered the process of settlement itself gratuitous and invisible.

In this interpretation, early readings of Cook demonstrate not his irrelevance post-1788 but his continuing presence. He continues to provide the frame of reference for the colonists' growing sense of self-definition. For the proper context in which to locate Tench's changing opinion is not psychological or empirical: it is spatial. His changing views refer, not so much to Cook, as to his and his colonists' changing sense of Botany Bay and their own spatial relationship to it as settlers. It is significant that Tench's initial suspension of judgement in June 1788 occurs in the course of a chapter entitled 'The Face of the Country; its Productions, Climate, &c.', which amounts to little more than a cautious, uncritical commentary on Cook's description of the country. In fact, for his account of the emu Tench is obliged to quote from Goldsmith's *History of the Earth* – apparently the First Fleeter's only 'authority' on antipodean nature.[9] There is, after six months in the new country, still very little sense that Tench is writing from a new centre, with a distinct point of view. Rather, his chapter resembles one of the compilations of an eighteenth-century editor like Hawkesworth, where more attention has been paid to reconciling the sources than to their critical assessment.

By September 1789, things had changed, and it was not merely that Sydney Cove was better established: it was also under greater threat. Convict desertions and depredations, conflict with the Aborigines and a keen awareness that the home country's supply ships were anything but reliable: these had combined to create a new sense of isolation, a new awareness of the social and political menace represented by those dreams of escape which, particularly in convict ranks, took the form of fantasies about other places. There was, correspondingly, a new explicitness about the ruling class's adherence to the only weapon it could claim wholly as its own, the logic of facts. It was in this situation that, 'for the preservation of public and private property', in the same month of September, Phillip drew up 'the first system of police'. In this context, John Hunter's survey of Botany Bay (in which Tench took part) had an obvious political value. It would, if it confirmed Phillip's first impression of the place, reinforce the governor's authority. It does not come wholly as a surprise to find, then, that Hunter concludes his remarks on the survey by fully confirming Phillip's original opinion: 'It is not possible to lie landlocked with a ship in any part of it; you will always be exposed to the large sea which tumbles in here with an easterly wind.'[10] In this context, Tench's own assertion, backed up with a quotation from his own field notes, that 'Variety of opinion here disappeared', is hardly to be taken as a disinterested geographical preamble.

Much the same may be said of Tench's final condemnation of Cook's report, in the wake of his official mission of retaliation against the Botany Bay Aborigines. As the editor of Tench's journal, L. F. Fitzhardinge, points out, this expedition 'is the only departure from Phillip's normal humanitarian approach to the aborigines'.[11] And Tench's account of the unsuccessful excursion is appropriately detailed. What is more, it is one of Tench's more self-consciously humorous passages: the *sang-froid* with which Tench greets every fresh disaster reveals him in a most attractive light. Despite the growing number of aboriginal attacks, culminating in the murder of the convict John McIntyre – the immediate cause of Phillip's attempted reprisal – Tench retains his respect for the temporary enemy. It is in this mock-heroic context, I suggest, that we have to read his remarks about Cook, for they occur at the climax or, more accurately, anti-climax of his narrative. In castigating the inventors of 'those fabled plains', he is, at least in part, satirizing his and his fellow officers' naive attachment to Reason. For only a fantastic belief in Reason could have launched so fruitless an expedition, putting into practice a military strategy that had no regard for the local, spatial obstacles.

Tench's changing views do not reflect a Lockean increase in empirical knowledge, but the dialectical process through which the new settlement constituted itself. And underlying this process of dynamic, historical self-definition, with all its legal, social, economic and political ramifications, was the dialectical nature of historical space. Space itself was a text that had to be written before it could be interpreted. This was the significance of Cook – that he provided such a text, something that could be interpreted, something with which a dialogue could be carried on, something against which places could come into being. And this argument can be extended to many aspects of the Sydney Cove experience. In a later chapter, in fact, I suggest that a full understanding of the textual character of the first European settlement requires us to take into account not only the texts of the official chroniclers but also the oral testimony of the convicts buried within them – testimony that teems with imaginary 'other places' in terms of which the real place of New South Wales was variously defined and denigrated.

First, though, we need to explore further those notorious meadows. The passage in Cook's journal Tench took such exception to was not after all penned by Cook himself. It was, in fact, an editorial paraphrase of Cook's journal whereby Hawkesworth hoped to make the notes of an unlettered sailor fit entertainment for a cultivated public. Where Hawkesworth has

> We found also interspersed some of the finest meadows in the world: some places however were rocky, but these were comparatively few . . .[12]

Cook's journal reads

> I found in many places a deep black Soil which we thought was capable of producing any kind of grain, at present it produceth besides timber as fine meadow as ever was seen. However we found it not all like this, some few places were very rocky but this I beleive to be uncommon.[13]

The difference between these two descriptions recalls the difference between discovery and exploration. For Hawkesworth has cut out what he sees as either circumstantial or subjective in order to concentrate attention on the factual core. He has summarized the increase in knowledge rather than the limiting conditions. But this empirical reduction to reason has not simply clarified the facts: it has altered them. Hawkesworth has not only excluded the circumstantial modifiers ('we thought . . .', 'at present . . .', 'I believe . . .'), which suggest the provisional nature of the report, he has also substantially altered the meaning of Cook's meadow. For while Cook's own words seem to mean only that the Botany Bay meadows were in no way inferior, no less *meadow-like*, than meadows seen elsewhere – their fineness referring to the degree to which they partook of the quality of meadows in general – Hawkesworth's phrase implies not that they *resemble* meadows elsewhere but that they *surpass* them, both in appearance and fertility.

This editorial sleight of hand may go a long way towards clearing Cook of the charge of wilful inaccuracy, but its true historical significance lies elsewhere, in the light it throws on the relationship between language and spatial history. Where Cook proceeds by analogy, describing the 'meadow' as being 'as fine . . . as ever was seen', Hawkesworth treats 'the finest meadows in the world' comparatively. Where Cook organizes his impression according to the logic of association, not going beyond his own experience elsewhere, Hawkesworth classifies the meadows hierarchically, as new facts conforming to a well-established and universally valid geographical taxonomy. It is not surprising that Tench took Hawkesworth's words at face value, for he was a man after Hawkesworth's own heart, an Enlightenment empiricist interested in objective data, not hazy surmise. But the truth was, of course, as Tench soon discovered, that the language of facts was a literary convention, a rhetorical trick: in describing novelties, one could not treat language as an objective mirror to reality. Language was not like algebra: it derived its meaning in new contexts from its meaning in old contexts. Even the most objective name was applied by way of analogy; even the least pretentious observation of a 'meadow' employed a figure of speech.

The significance of this discovery emerges when we consider the attempts of the early Australian travellers and explorers to *name* the country they passed through. Whether taken as a figure of speech or as a factual statement, Cook's description of 'meadow' had turned out to be incorrect. And the disillusionment of Tench was by no means unusual. Indeed, it was almost a commonplace among British residents that, in Australia, the laws of association seemed to be suspended. There seemed to be nothing that could be accurately named. There was, consequently, very little purchase for the imagination – that mental faculty which, according to associationist psychologists like David Hartley, was primarily a mechanism for making analogies. This was why Barron Field lamented in his *Geographical Memoirs* that Australia was quite unsuitable as a subject for poetry. Referring in particular to 'the eternal eucalyptus', the former dramatic critic of *The Times*, the friend of Coleridge and Wordsworth, wrote:

> No tree, to my taste can be beautiful that is not deciduous . . .
> Dryden says of the laurel
>
> > From winter winds it suffers no decay;
> > For ever fresh and fair, and every month is May.
>
> Now it may be the fault of the cold climate in which I was bred, but this is just what I complain of in an evergreen. 'Forever fresh', is a contradiction in terms; what is 'forever fair' is never fair; and without January, in my mind, there can be no May. All the dearest allegories of human life are bound up with the infant and slender green of spring, the dark redundance of summer, and the sere and yellow leaf of autumn. These are as essential to the poet as emblems, as they are to the painter as picturesque objects; and the common consent and immemorial custom of European poetry has made the change of the seasons, and its effect upon vegetation, a part, as it were, of our very nature. I can therefore hold no fellowship with Australian foliage . . .[14]

In an illuminating discussion of this passage, which he classifies among 'early reactions to Australian nature', the art historian and critic Bernard Smith has suggested that Field's opinions should not be seen 'merely as the prejudices of an homesick English exile': they should be read in the context of Baron von Humboldt's well-known praise of tropical vegetation, and interpreted as a criticism of Humboldt's views.[15] This may be true of Charles Darwin's view of Australian vegetation, which Smith cites in a footnote, but how far does it apply to Field? How far do rival theories of the picturesque account for Field's assertion that poetry thrives on the contrasts and comparisons offered by nature, that, in nature, are found 'All the dearest allegories of human life . . . essential to the poet as emblems'?

Field's real subject in this passage is not nature at all. It is language, and the impossibility of distinguishing the language of feeling from the language of description. The proper context in which to understand Field's uncompromising stance is not the history of taste but the history of mind. In particular, the point of departure for Field's animadversions is clearly the prevalent doctrine of associationism, which I have mentioned. The association of simple ideas to form complex ones depended on the ideas (or objects they derived from) being comparable. And first among the qualities of objects that made their comparison possible was, as Hume wrote, 'resemblance': 'This is a relation without which no philosophical relation can exist, since no objects will admit of comparison, but what have some degree of resemblance.'[16] European nature is an 'emblem' of human life because its cycle of seasons resembles the seasons of human life. Poetry, then, in so far as it evokes human life metaphorically, involves not the description of nature but its association with human themes.

But, as Barron Field's remarks bring out, the association of ideas depended on a profounder assumption. It depended on the assumption that distinct ideas existed to be related. But how is a distinct idea defined, except in relation to other ideas? Since, as Hume put it, 'all kinds of reasoning consist in nothing but a comparison, and a discovery of those relations, either constant or inconstant, which two or more objects bear to each other',[17] an absolute idea is a contradiction in terms. Hence Field's irritation with Dryden's laurel. Our ideas of freshness and fairness are relative. They derive their distinctness from our ideas of sereness and dullness. Their efficacy as metaphors of human life depends on our ideas of stale and withered age. But a tree eternally green offers the poet nothing. It defies the logic of association. It is not a distinct idea.

The far-reaching and astonishing implication of Field's remarks is, then, that Australia is, strictly speaking, indescribable. In so far as its nature is undifferentiated, it does not have a distinct character. Lacking this, it cannot be compared and so known. Its uniformity also means that it cannot be named, because no nameable parts distinguish themselves. Not amenable to the logic of association, Australia appears to be unknowable. A state of uniformity offers no starting point, whether for literary or physical travel.

The implications of this conclusion are not only literary. Bearing in mind that the prime responsibility of the early explorers was to *describe* what they saw, the dissonance between language and land presented a considerable challenge. There was no question of falling back on the logic of facts. There was no possibility even of allowing oneself the lazy luxury of comparison. Facts proved fancies; analogies proved false. Indeed, the spatial ramifications of Field's argument are well brought out by Field himself – in the context, significantly enough, of place names. Not surprisingly, Field is highly critical of Australian place names, which, he presumes, attempt to apply the principles of association. Given the 'prosaic, unpicturesque, unmusical' qualities of Australian nature, they are doomed, in his view, to failure. Here is Field's description of the country in the region of Mount York, between Windsor and Bathurst in the Blue Mountains, west of Sydney:

> The King's Tableland is as anarchical and untabular as any His Majesty possesses. The Prince Regent's Glen below it (if it be the glen that I saw) is not very romantic. Jamison's Valley we found by no means a happy one. Blackheath is a wretched misnomer. Not to mention its awful contrast to the beautiful place of that name in England, heath it is none. Black it may be when the shrubs are burnt, as they often are. Pitt's Amphitheatre disappointed me. The hills are thrown together in a monotonous manner, and their clothing is very unpicturesque – a mere sea of harsh trees; but Mr Pitt was no particular connoisseur in mountain scenery or in amphitheatres.[18]

This splenetic outburst against misnomers and misnamers is based on the assumption that the Australian names in question violate the logic of association. It is not so much a 'description' of nature as a critique of the absurdity of associative naming in Australia: the 'Tableland' in question does not really resemble a tableland; the 'Glen' does not really suggest a glen; the 'Valley' does not really recall a valley, because the Australian places fail to conjure up the proper associations. In Australia, therefore, class names of this kind fail.

The interesting thing about Field's view is that it underlines the perhaps surprising point that *both* elements in place names were figurative and non-factual: it is not only the particularizing element 'Botany' that is metaphorical; the apparently more objective term 'Bay' may be equally fanciful. What Field's remarks do not bring out, though, is the even more important point that follows from this – which is that the proper way in which to interpret geographical class names like 'valley' and 'tableland' is not in terms of imperial history, but within the perspective of the history of travelling. The imperial pretensions of particularizing epithets like 'King's', 'Prince Regent's' and even 'Pitt's' may seem all too obvious, but their concentration suggests that even they reflect the namer's intention to characterize a space. And, certainly, when we turn to the other element in such names, the spatial intention they express becomes inescapable. For the fact is that such names were given. In some sense they 'stuck'. And, even if we accepted Field's genealogical judgement and considered such classificatory names failures, we would still be left wondering why they were given in the first place. Why, if the newcomers were bound by the laws of analogy, by what they had formerly seen and read, did they not leave these nameless extensions, these culturally invisible intervals, unnamed and silent?

The truth is that the naming process may have been metaphorical and, to that extent, a kind of gnomic poetry *manqué*, but it was not associational in intent. It was not a retrospective gloss, after the event, a sort of gilding in bad taste round the physical mirror of history. It was the names themselves that brought history into being, that invented the spatial and conceptual co-ordinates within which history could occur. For how, without place names, without agreed points of reference, could directions be given, information exchanged, 'here' and 'there' defined? Consider those most beautiful of Australian names, names like Cape Catastrophe, Mount Misery, Retreat Well and Lake Disappointment. These names do not merely confirm Field's argument, that the logic of association breaks down in Australia, but also defy it, asserting the possibility of naming in the absence of resemblance. If a well is associated with water and is therefore regarded as an aid to the traveller, to describe it as Retreat Well is to say the conventional associations of the class name fail here. A mountain, associated with long views and perhaps with water, would, it might be thought, be welcomed by the explorer. To call it 'Mount Misery' is again to suggest that, in Australia, the normal logic of association breaks down. But, if these 'wells' are not wells, these 'mountains' unmountainlike, what do the names mean? What is their function? The paradox they express is not descriptive. Rather, it refers to the traveller's state of expectation.

More than this, such class names (as their riddling qualifiers often make explicit) do not reflect what is already there: on the contrary, they embody the existential necessity the traveller feels to invent a place he can inhabit. Without them, punctuating the monotony, distinguishing this horizon from that, there would be no evidence he had travelled. To be sure, the traveller might retain his private impressions, but, without names, and the discourse of the journal they epitomize, his experience could never become public, a historical fact leading to other facts, other journeys. Thus, the fundamental impulse in applying class names like 'mount' or 'river' was a desire to differentiate the uniformity.

Partly, of course, the uniformity defied easy differentiation because, in a quite simple way, the English language lacked words to characterize it. Alexander Hamilton Hume and William Hovell, for example, who led the first overland expedition from Sydney to Port Phillip in 1824, 'cross swamp which had been mistaken for a meadow'. As it turns out, it is neither one nor the other:

> This, like all other spaces of any extent, lying intermediately between the ranges, consists of a kind of meadow, divided along its centre by a small but rapid stream, is somewhat swampy, and in places near the water produces reeds.[19]

This was a case where a kind of country, far from rare, raised a problem of nomenclature. There was no English term for it, and yet in more arid regions the traveller sought it out. Indeed another explorer, Edward John Eyre, depended on it when making his attempt on the centre in 1841. Advancing northward parallel to the Flinders Range in South Australia,

> we just kept far enough into the plains to intercept the water-
> courses from the hills where they spread out into level country,
> and by this means we got excellent feed for our horses.[20]

As this fertile zone of passage was neither meadow nor swamp,
the explorer had no name for it. Passages like these come close
to vindicating the reductionist view of the American philosopher of language Benjamin Whorf. On the map at least, these
places do not exist simply because they cannot be named; reality
is a naive reflection of the language available to describe it. But,
even though Eyre and Hume and Hovell cannot name this
intermediate space directly, they can, after all, refer to it. What
limits their powers of description is not vocabulary but the
desire to differentiate, the necessity of naming in order to travel.
And, in so far as such nameless zones *can* be located syntactically
and spatially between 'plains' and 'hills', they have been
appropriated to the traveller's route.

In any case, the difficulty of vocabulary aside, the criteria of
differentiation were not simply empirical, naively describing the
nature of 'things' already there – it was precisely such objects
that names served to constitute. They were determined not
empirically but rhetorically. They embodied the traveller's
directional and territorial ambitions: his desire to possess where
he had been as a preliminary to going on. And this desire was
not placeless, it did not resemble the equal stare of the map grid.
It depended on positing a 'here' (the traveller's viewpoint and
orientation) and a 'there' (the landscape, the horizon). And
where such viewpoints did not exist, they had to be hypothesized, rhetorically asserted by way of names. Otherwise, the
landscape itself could never enter history.

This is the significance of the urgency, the premature
willingness, of Australian travellers to name 'mountains' and
'rivers'. Mountains and rivers were culturally desirable, they
conjured up pleasing associations. But, more fundamentally,
they signified differences that made a difference. They implied
the possibility of viewpoints, directions: to call a hill 'Prospect
Hill' (see plate 4) is to describe hills' historical function.
'Supposed course of the River Nepean': to write these words on

48

the map one after the other is to set out graphically the spatial intention implicit in invoking the word 'river'. Hills and rivers were, in fact, the kind of object that made travelling as a historical activity possible. They were the necessary counterpart of the traveller's desire to travel, to see to the horizon and to find a route there.

The sense in which such class names conjured up the country was particularly obvious in Australia. For, as numerous travellers reported, it was precisely rivers and mountains that Australia so conspicuously lacked. 'Nature', wrote the colonist and adventurer Lieutenant Breton,

> has distinguished New Holland and Van Diemen's Land by a character so entirely their own, that their appearance . . . is totally different from that of every other country; in both, the mountains are almost invariably rounded, nor did I ever observe, save once (near Mount Boorooran), an elevation which terminated abruptly, in craggy, perhaps inaccessible rocks.[21]

The South Australian explorer Charles Sturt amplified the point when he explained that Australian mountains were not mountains at all in the accepted sense:

> Many of my readers, judging from their knowledge of an English climate, and living perhaps under hills of less elevation than those I have mentioned, from which a rippling stream may pass their very door, will hardly understand this; but the mountains of south east Australia bear no resemblance to the moss-covered mountains of Europe.[22]

Elsewhere Sturt explained this contrast by saying that 'the peat formation' that characterizes the hills and mountains of the northern hemisphere was quite lacking here:

> In New South Wales . . . the rains that fall upon the mountains drain rapidly through a coarse and superficial soil, and pour down their sides without a moment's interruption.[23]

Associated with the term 'hill' or 'mountain' was the flow of water. But, in Australia, the logic of association did not apply. And the explorers reflected this failure in their names. When Eyre named 'Mount Deception', he did so because 'I had fully calculated upon finding permanent water at this very high range and was proportionally disappointed at not succeeding'.[24] The necessity to name in contradiction of associative logic is also the context of another of Eyre's names: 'Spring Hill', a name inspired by the fact that he discovered 'under a peak . . . a fine spring of water . . . about half way up it'.[25] In England the name would have been a tautology. Here it preserved the logic of association in the form of a paradox.

Other associations clung to the distinction of altitude, pre-eminent among them, visibility. In a flat world visibility was a property of even the smallest rise. Thus the marine surveyor John Lort Stokes names 'Mount Inspection, a hill 105 feet high, and the most remarkable feature hereabouts'.[26] Here the qualifying clauses make explicit that this is not a 'real' mountain. As is already implicit in the epithet 'Inspection', this is a mountain only by courtesy of the view it offers, not its height. Hills that *failed* to take one inside the country were proportionately disappointing. To quote Stokes again, Arthur's Seat 'had one of those unsatisfactory woody summits, of which it is difficult to ascertain the highest part'.[27] Faced with the forested summit of Mount Napier in Victoria's Western District, a more energetic surveyor, Major Mitchell, set about clearing it.[28]

In applying the class term 'mount' or 'hill', the observer was not describing a geographical object, he was attempting to differentiate the landscape in such a way that he could write about it and get on. Mountains or hills were essential in bringing space into the realm of communication. They transformed spatial extension into a spatial text, a succession of conceivable places that could be read. Whether they existed or not was by the way: they were necessary differences without which a distinct idea of the landscape could not be formed. It was as much for this reason as any other that, as a result of his coastal trek round the Great Australian Bight, Eyre lamented the fact he had 'no important rivers to enumerate, no fertile regions to point out . . . no noble ranges to describe . . .'.[29] And, as we see in a later chapter, the absence of geographical objects became, for both Eyre and Sturt, a decisive factor in determining the elaborateness of their exploration journals: the less there was to see, the greater the necessity to write about it.

The early travellers, then, invented places, rather than found them. This was what naming meant. To designate a place as 'mount' might express, in fact, the absence of that desirable feature. Paraphrasing one of his names, Sturt wrote,

> The peak itself was nothing more than a sandy eminence on which neither tree or shrub was growing, *and the whole locality was so much in unison with it, that we called it 'Mount Misery'.*[30] [My emphasis.]

In this instance, Mount Misery serves to create a rhetorical distinction that makes description of the 'unison' possible. Others went even further: Surveyor White in the sand dunes of the Victorian Mallee, for example, actually constructed hills. Geographical class names created a difference that made a difference. They rendered the world visible, bringing it within the horizon of discourse. If they were descriptive, they were descriptive not of a geographical object but of a place where travelling might settle down and become history.

This, incidentally, explains Major Mitchell's at first rather surprising approval of the name 'River Lett', a name that came into being in the following way:

> On 24 November 1813 Evans had reached the valley, commenting merely that 'the descent is rugged'. A day of rest was spent beside the Riverlett (i.e. rivulet and the name has remained as River Lett) . . .[31]

Mitchell evidently knew this history, but it did not prevent him from approving the name: 'A name derived from *rivulet*, and a very good one, being short.'[32] But why was the name good? After all, it did not describe a geographical object. Rather, it invented one. Had not the Major expressed the view in one of his own monumental journals of exploration that 'descriptive names' are 'best, such being in general the character of those used by the natives of this and other countries'?[33] So he had, but what he meant by 'descriptive' was a name that truly distinguished, truly differentiated, this place from that. What mattered was that the name described a conceptual place: whether it described a physical object was unimportant. Indeed, when an explorer did attempt to coin a name that was physically descriptive, more often than not he produced a name that was useless for all practical purposes. As a modern surveyor has pointed out, in connection with Victoria,

> An Index of streams shows that this small state has, at least, 63 watercourses called Stony, 45 Back, 35 Deep, 32 Spring and 32 Sandy creeks.

And the same writer comments,

> It is obvious that, in most cases, the surveyor had no intention of naming the stream in his note but of describing its characteristic at the time and place of survey.[34]

It is in this sense that a name like River Lett is 'descriptive', because by a happy chance it uniquely differentiates.

Mountains, like rivers, were cultural objects that made a difference. But, unlike rivers, they did not make a difference by themselves. From the traveller's point of view an isolated hill or, for that matter, a random or symmetrical arrangement of such hills was no more informative than an undifferentiated plain. This point had been made by none other than Immanuel Kant, who formulated it using the image of separate tables. 'An underlying assumption in orienting oneself in the space of the earth's surface', Kant pointed out, 'is that that space is asymetrical with respect to its objects.'[35] For instance, blindfold a man and place him in a room filled with symmetrically placed round tables: he might be able to feel his way 'forward', but he would have no idea where he was, nor what direction he walked in. The glare of an uninterruptedly symmetrical horizon blindfolded the explorer quite as effectively. He invented hills in order to see his way ahead, to map where he had been. Hills were essential to the description of the landscape only in so far as they inscribed the landscape with direction, and it was only in so far as they lent space direction that they were valued.

Characteristically, then, the early traveller denied to hills the name of 'hill' when they failed to distinguish his route. Where the Western Australian explorer John McKinlay, for example, came across 'a fearful jumble of broken sandhills', he expressed the opinion that the landscape was 'quite unfit to be described'.[36] The reason it was indescribable was that it displayed no clear differentiation, no sense of direction. Hills that failed to characterize their surroundings were useless. As another Western Australian explorer, Peter Warburton, complained, 'We had great expectations of this place, but distance had deceived us – the hill is rubbish, and we obtained no hopeful view from it.'[37] Nor did the view become hopeful simply because it presented objects. When John McDouall Stuart, the first European to make a return north–south crossing of Australia, commented (shortly after building a cairn at what he confidently declared the 'centre' of Australia), 'The view to the north is dismal; there are a few isolated hills,'[38] he revealed the fact that in any view the arrangement of objects was crucial. Only the clear directional arrangement of features, whether to form ranges or valleys, enabled the explorer to connect. As yet another surveyor and explorer, A. C. Gregory, put it, 'The country is, however, nearly level and it is difficult to ascertain the limits of the valley, as many portions of the original tableland exist as detached hills and ridges.'[39] And, just as the explorer deplored isolated hills, so he welcomed ranges of hills, hills that arranged themselves like a journey. One of the clearest expressions of this, as it turned out, misplaced confidence occurs in Eyre's journal of his inland expedition to the north of the Flinders Range. Having described the depressing appearance of Lake Torrens, Eyre continues,

> There was one feature of the landscape, which still gave me hope that something might be done in that direction and had in fact been my principal inducement to select a line nearly north from Spencer's Gulf. This feature was the continuation, and the undiminished elevation of the chain of hills forming Flinders Range, running nearly parallel with the course of Lake Torrens, and when last seen by me stretching far to the northward and eastward in a broken and picturesque outline. It was to this chain of hills I now looked forward as the stepping stone to the interior . . .[40]

Hills were of interest in so far as they gave access to an asymmetrical world. They might burst the bubble of the horizon. This, of course, was also the spatial value of rivers. More reliably than hills, flowing rivers lent the landscape direction. And, more than this, by the mere course they took, the very country they divided in two, they also related. They presented to the traveller who followed them a series of comparable objects. They initiated a series of resemblances that might be used to characterize the country. One of the pleasing ironies, at least for the traveller, was that rivers, in name at least, removed from him the burden of his responsibility. Rivers promised a self-evident mobility. He could relinquish the need to choose his direction, his horizon; he could let day and night and the chance conjunction of other streams determine the pattern of his journal. The events of his journey were given. And, in this profound sense, the mobility he felt, occurring as it did within the supposedly closed system of the river basin, was static. The dynamism implicit in the prospect of other routes was excluded. Rivers, more than any other feature, brought with them the prospect of arrival and ending. They were a kind of travelling that repeated itself: they anticipated the commerce of settled nations.

In this sense, they were the exact spatial corollary of the mechanism of mental 'attraction' on which, according to Hume, the process of association depended. In fact, Hume defined that principle of 'union and cohesion' with Isaac Newton's demonstration of the laws of gravity consciously in mind, asserting, 'Here is a kind of attraction, which in the mental world will be found to have as extraordinary effect as in the natural.'[41] The fall of rivers from their sources in the mountains to their final issue in the sea had its counterpart in the mental impetus to associate. In consequence, rivers were desired, not merely to assuage physical need, but as geographical objects satisfying intellectual thirst. They gave the explorer, weighed down physically and intellectually, a new lightness and direction. They relieved him in a double sense. As Warburton wrote, on at last coming across a river, 'We enjoyed floating in it, for we are so weak on land, we feel a peculiar delight in the support the water affords us.'[42] The water offered not only the sensation of weightlessness but also, for Sturt at least, a sense of direction, a sensation of mental and geographical expectations fusing. When the water-borne Sturt shot out of the Murrumbidgee into the broad stream of the Murray on his 1829–30 expedition (see plate 6), he reported, 'The boats were allowed to drift along at pleasure.' This was a metaphor of his own state of mind. As Sturt explained, the discovery of this river 'assured me of ultimate success in the duty I had to perform. We had got on the high road, as it were, either to the south coast, or to some other important outlet.'[43]

However unsatisfactory its mountains, Australia's rivers at least permitted the mind to wander from one thing to the next. They were poetic, in Barron Field's sense of the word. Or they would have been, had they behaved like rivers elsewhere. For in fact, of course, what the early travellers found was that, with the partial exception of the Murray, the country was *not* characterized by purposeful rivers. To quote Sturt again,

> Falling rapidly from the mountains in which they originate into a level and depressed country; having weak and inconsiderable sources, and being almost wholly unaided by tributaries of any kind; they naturally fail before they reach the coast, and exhaust themselves in marshes or lakes; or reach it so weakened as to be unable to preserve clear or navigable mouths, or to remove the sandbanks that the tides throw up before them.[44]

And notwithstanding his sanguine expectations of the Murray (expressing almost certainly the confidence of hindsight), as a rule Sturt recognized that Australian 'rivers' could not be relied on, either downstream or upstream. 'In any other country,' Sturt writes of the Macquarie River, 'I should have followed such a watercourse, in hopes of its ultimately leading to some reservoir; but here I could encourage no such favourable anticipation.'[45]

Throughout much of the Australian interior rain, when it fell, did not drain by way of tributaries into permanently flowing streams. Quite the contrary, rather than myriad trickles combining and contributing to form major rivers, the tendency was for flood water to spread out, to disperse through a lacework of temporary channels, which, far from concentrating the water, fanned it out to cover huge areas of normally waterless desert. Instead of contributing to rivers, watercourses acted as dis-tributaries. There was nothing intrinsically irrational about this system. Over a hundred years before Australia was colonized, Thomas Burnet, for example, had imagined just such an arrangement. Describing the hydrography of Paradise, which, incidentally, he located in the Antipodes, Burnet wrote,

> If you could turn our Rivers backwards, to run from the Sea towards their Fountain-heads, they would more resemble the course of those Ante-Diluvian Rivers; for they were greatest at their first setting out . . . like the Arteries in our Body, that carry the Bloud . . . and divide into a multitude of little branches, which lose themselves insensibly in the habit of the flesh, as these little Flouds did in the Sands of the Earth.[46]

This is an uncannily accurate description of Australian rivers, but it also underlines the point that the unwillingness of the nineteenth-century explorers and settlers to entertain it was due, not to a cognitive deficiency, but to a cultural context. Such 'rivers' were not inconceivable but, in the context of the explorer's historical responsibility to invest the space of his journey with meaning, they *were*, politically and economically, unthinkable. The pressure on the explorer to make 'interesting' discoveries, by which was meant, among other things, geographical objects likely to yield a profit, is clearly illustrated by a family letter that the prosperous Victorian squatter John Cotton wrote in 1845:

> Major Mitchell is still engaged in exploring the same quarter of the island (towards the Gulf of Carpentaria), but more to the westward, *so that we expect to hear of a vast extent of valuable country being opened for settlers before next year.*[47] [My emphasis.]

Explorers were not despatched to traverse deserts, but to locate objects of cultural significance: rivers, mountains, meadows, plains of promise. They had a social responsibility to make the most of what they saw, to dignify even hints of the habitable with significant class names. They were expected to arrest the country, to concentrate it into reversible roads which would summarize its content; they were expected to translate its extension into objects of commerce. They were, by a curious irony, meant to inaugurate a form of possession that would render the dynamic of their own journeys invisible.

The complacent expectations of John Cotton found their fantastic counterpart in a map prepared by T. J. Maslen, the putative author of a book called *Friend of Australia*. Maslen, an officer in the Indian survey corps, had never visited Australia but, on the basis of explorers' reports, he drew a speculative map (see plate 5) whose chief feature was the Great River or the Desired Blessing, a mighty current whose headwaters were in the south and east of Australia, and whose mouth lay in the region of King Sound, north of Broome. The map was drawn up in 1827 but, by the time the book went to press, Maslen had heard of Sturt's discovery of the Murray. It did not persuade him to redraw his map, though, so persuasive was the idea of an interior river that flowed to the north-west. And looking at the *design* of the map, one can understand why: for how strikingly the names of conquest and occupation, 'Eastern Australia', 'Anglicania' and 'Australindia', resemble mountain ranges, how much 'Western Australia' is like a tributary river. Rivers and ranges were explorers' aids but, in the context of Maslen's map, one is tempted to attribute their invention to the engravers of maps, even to the linear conventions of phonetic writing itself. What, one wonders, would a map look like written in a non-phonetic language? What for that matter would the country look like?

Understanding the strategic way in which class names like 'river' and 'mountain' were used, as means of getting on, and seeing how, implicit in their usage, was also the possibility of arrest, the reduction of the living space to a physically delimited, culturally valuable container of other events, we begin to perceive the ambiguity inherent in the explorers' condition. We can understand the apparent self-contradictions in their accounts. When, in 1846, Mitchell dignified a succession of ponds in south-west Queensland by the name 'river', it was as a potential highway to the Gulf of Carpentaria that he valued them, and, equally importantly, as a gateway to what would invariably be associated with rivers in Europe – fine pastures. And, indeed, before long the Major did come upon 'splendid plains'. His object was to fulfil the settling expectations of squatters like Cotton; it was to substantiate empirically the kind of economic blessing that Maslen had already mapped in desire.

But this imperial responsibility to organize the scattered appearance of phenomena into a series of logically related cause-and-effect facts was completely at odds with the explorer's habitual experience. Following 'rivers', whether wet or dry, had been for Mitchell, as for Sturt, almost invariably a frustrating process. Channels tended to fan out and lose themselves: they rebuffed, rather than encouraged, linear progress. They rebutted the whole logic of cause and effect, lacking either source or outlet. As it turned out, Mitchell's great river (which he left his second-in-command, Edmund Kennedy, to explore) formed part of the Cooper's Creek system (see plate 7), and its discovery was anything but consequential. In fact, it conformed to the other rivers Mitchell had seen on that expedition – and on earlier expeditions, too. As early as 1836 he had correctly described the relationship between the River Lachlan and Lake Regent:

> The fluviatile process seemed to be reversed here, the tendency of this river being, not to carry surface waters off, but rather to spread, over land where none could otherwise be found, those brought from a great distance.[48]

Encountering the same kind of system in 1846, during his fourth expedition, into south-west Queensland, he even went so far as to describe the tendency of the Macquarie River to 'spread out into a network of reservoirs that serve to irrigate vast plains' as an 'admirable distribution of water where water is so scarce'.[49] But none of this prevented Mitchell from discovering the longed-for 'river', any more than it dissuaded Sturt from pursuing an inland sea. The mountains, the rivers and lakes, the very words themselves, differentiated the space in the newcomer's mind. They supplied desirable directions, without which advance and settlement would have been impossible.

We may think, then, of the class element in place names as the agent of a linguistic fifth column, infiltrating and dividing the space stealthily, as an outpost supplying a ramifying network of grammatical and syntactical connections. Possession of the country depended on demonstrating the efficacy of the English language there. It depended, to some extent, on civilizing the landscape, bringing it into orderly being. More fundamentally still, the landscape had to be taught to speak. This was the source of the explorers' frustration with Australian rivers. Implicit in Sturt's disappointing Australian stream, which weakens and exhausts itself, is a comparison with an ideal, European river, supplied by copious and permanent springs. As it descends progressively from the mountains to the sea, it grows in volume and grandeur. Its strength increases. At length it issues from one mouth to the sea. It is, deliberately to borrow a cliché, like an orator's speech. By contrast, the Australian river, unlettered, undramatic, drops with an inarticulate exclamation into sullen silence. In this context, the syntax of Sturt's description, with its succession of unsubordinated clauses, linked only by 'and' or 'or', is not accidental: it is the equivalent of the Australian stream, which, far from culminating in a commanding statement, dissipates itself between alternatives. The truth was that the strategy of divide and conquer was, in the context of Australian settlement, first and foremost, a rhetorical exercise.

The investment of the landscape with rhetorical interest reflected the explorers' linguistic practice, for the language of exploration was not the language of dictionaries, but the active, dialectical utterance characteristic of travelling. If the landscape was realized associatively, then the mode of association was grammatical rather than conceptual. Australian features might not resemble features elsewhere, and this might mean that naming became difficult. But the difficulty itself was not beyond expression: even a sense of helplessness in the face of phenomena that defied description could be described. Nouns might let the travelling writer down: but there was still the logic of language itself, the resources of grammar and syntax that made even the inexpressible expressible. Often, in fact, the landscape was connected, not by invoking picturesque English scenes, but by following the direction of language itself, the way in which words became sentences, sentences conversations. When in the course of his journey from Sydney to the Australian Alps, John Lhotsky came across 'a chain of oval ponds', implicit in his comment is a linguistic analogy. Like Burnet borrowing an organic metaphor, he remarked,

They are strikingly analogous to the systema gangliosum of

59

animal bodies, the cosmic operations of the globe not having in our continent proceeded so far as to the formation of a vascular system, which in the organism of the globe is represented by rivers.[50]

The Australian creek Lhotsky describes not only resembles a primitive worm, each part being self-contained and a mere repetition of other parts, it also resembles the primitive language that Rousseau hypothesized in his *Essai sur l'origine des langues*. In its primitive state, according to Rousseau, language was characterized by a proliferation of synonyms, expressing the same thing from its different relations. What geographical object could resemble this primitive state of language more closely than the 'creek' with its succession of identical pools? Small wonder travellers, seeking direction and differentiation, sought to civilize these isolated pools and form them into chains. Even the term 'creek' stemmed originally from an attempt to impose on an unpredictable object at least a semblance of periodicity, the word being derived from the English term for tidal reaches.

The ambiguity inherent in names like 'hill' and 'river' was the ambiguity inherent in the discourse of travelling. If naming brought into being a dynamic world of passage, inaugurating a spatial history of particular routes, edges and centres, then such names also facilitated a process of association likely to subvert that momentum. The logic of association enabled the landscape the traveller had invented to be possessed. He opened it up only to find it, once again, closed off to further exploration. While the explorer attempted to trace (in journal form) his Boswellian experience, he was conscious of a Johnsonian public, a readership that wanted definitive results. And we should be clear: this was not a conflict about attitudes towards the country. It was not an incipient form of the current conservation/development debate – a debate in which neither side transcends the assumption of the landscape as an aggregate of objects. It was, if anything, a conflict rooted in rival theories of language. What did names name? Did they name facts or did they name intentions? Were they mechanically associative or spatially inventive?

In the context of Australian spatial history, these questions were anything but academic. It is arguable, for instance, that the fate of the Aborigines hung precisely on the outcome of this debate. For, if names preserved the spatiality of experience, there was no reason to prefer English names to aboriginal ones; indeed, aboriginal names, with their local genealogy and resistance to possession (even pronunciation and transliteration), were, in these senses, more appropriate. They could be said to express the 'otherness' of the traveller's experience, the sense in which it could not have been predicted and, for this reason, was valuable; the sense in which, too, any 'possession' was purely symbolic. But, if the essence of possession was to arrest, to enclose the mirage in a net of association, to neutralize the otherness, then the euphonious, but untranslatable, names with which Aborigines inhabited the landscape could have no epistemological place: they were not typical, obeyed no known rules, conveyed no useful facts.

This is the context in which to understand the widely disseminated view among early colonists that the Aborigines possessed no language, no grammar, no syntax and no generalizing vocabulary. For the implication of this deficiency was that the Aborigines not only could not defend their rights (could not argue their land claims) but did not even, in any recognizable sense, possess the land they occupied. Lhotsky expressed the view that the Aborigines 'referred to creeks and rivers by the name of the place through which they flowed'.[51] 'It is obvious to me', he wrote in the context of discussing the aboriginal name 'Meneru', 'that they have no general name for comprehending any aggregation of names whatever.'[52] It was a view largely shared by the far better informed, and well-disposed, E. M. Curr, writing fifty years later, who had this to say of 'Moneroo' or 'Manera':

> In connection with this name, Manera Plains, one suspects it at once, because, though the tribes have names for every remarkable spot in their territories, they have seldom collective names for large areas. What seems probable is, that the Englishman who first saw the plains had a Sydney Black in his party, who on being asked their name replied *manyer*, or *I don't know*.[53]

The Victorian writer Brough Smyth, in his comments on aboriginal languages, observed there were 'no articles; and, it is supposed, no distinctions in gender'.[54] Another Victorian writer referring to the inhabitants of the Goulburn and Loddon valleys, stressed the lack of an orderly grammar in the local tongues. He gave examples of how the 'few moods and tenses employed by inflexions' were 'exceedingly irregular in their construction'. And he also commented on 'the number and variety of their combinations' in the Jajowrong dialect, and how 'slight variations in the affixes' expressed 'important differences of meaning'.[55] Despite his alleged intimacy with the Murray natives, Peter Beveridge asserted, 'These dialects are quite innocent of everything in the shape of grammar, grammatical relations being denoted by prolongations, accentuations or position; each, or either of which, changes the meaning of different words entirely.'[56] And in view of Hume's definition of reason as the faculty of comparison, it is particularly significant that Beveridge asserted 'The entire absence of the organ of comparison in the native character'.[57] The implication of this lack of grammatical differentiation and syntactical direction was obvious to Beveridge: 'It would be infinitely better', he concluded, alluding to the aboriginal taboo on using the names of the recently dead, 'to have the aboriginal principle carried out in all its entirety [i.e. their persistent endeavour to forget] as regards their own tongues, and have the English language taught instead.'[58]

The true significance of these observations was neither anthropological nor philological. After all, the Whites, too, named rivers from the place where they were crossed. Eyre, for example, had bestowed the name 'Rocky River', explaining that the name was derived 'from the ragged character of its bed where we struck it'. But, of course, exactly the same limitations of time and place governed his assertion that what he crossed was a 'river'. The geographical term was, in fact, even more subjective than the particular term. The naming phrase taken as a whole named a spatial moment and a cultural expectation. Facts did not come into it. The various names that Peter Cunningham reports in 1802 for one New South Wales river make the point even more clearly: 'In Argyle, it is named the

Wolondilly; in Camden, the Warragamba; in Cumberland, the Nepean; and eventually it takes the appellation of Hawkesbury.'[59]

The Whites' assessment of aboriginal languages was hardly disinterested: rather, it mirrored certain preoccupations about the efficacy of their own language in possessing the country. Could English offer a more coherent rhetorical equivalent, a more logical arrangement, of what was to be seen? This, in effect, was the question. And the very positing of this question depended on a notion of possession as foreign to the Aborigines as it was to the traveller. How could the explorer share his culture's notion of space as passive, uniform and theatrical? How could he pretend there were no horizons to his knowledge, or that all directions were ultimately the same? To be sure, in an ideal state, where all Australia was mapped – and hence subject to the purely temporal logic of imperial history – space might be neutralized. But, until then, the explorer's dialect, his particular use of words and expressions, was essential to the progress of knowledge – essential, even if it led eventually to its own redundancy.

Exploration civilized the country by translating it into English, but it was hardly the English of Hawkesworth. The explorers' language was replete with misconceptions, repetitions: it was language in a primitive state of development. Its justification, though, was that it might lead to better things. Much the same argument lay behind the view expressed by Stokes, that 'no surer method of raising the Australian in the scale of civilization could have been devised than to put him in possession of the English language'.[60] Where the Aborigine's confinement within his own dialect 'absolutely tends to perpetuate the isolation in which the natives now live', English would 'give him an instrument which he could employ to enlarge his mind and extend his experience'. Where Beveridge proposes a merely pragmatic solution to the problem of controlling the Aborigines, Stokes, writing half a century earlier, retains a genuinely humanitarian interest in improving the Aborigine's lot. The Aborigine may, in his view, be primitive, but at least he belongs to the same order of being as the European and can consequently be improved. Still, what-

ever the motive, cultural eclipse is the intended result. It is the
nomadic attachment to locality that is being overruled. In this
context, Stokes's recourse to the image of *expansion* is not just
ornamental: it accurately embodies the nature of the imperial
project. For one thing, it implies a centre of power round
which the boundaries of the unknown are progressively
pushed back – a process quite alien to the explorer's experience. For another, it characterizes language as an instrument of
physical, rather than symbolic, colonization: more effectively
than stump-jump plough or roller, it translates the landscape
into a familiar arrangement of mental objects, tied together by
rules of grammar and syntax. By the same token, it irons out
the experience of travelling itself, the sense in which the
journey itself was history and territory a frame of reference.
Whatever its motive, to place the Aborigine in possession of
English was simply to possess him, to help him forget he was
ever at home.

Consequently, the same logic that sought to teach him
English also sought to deny the Aborigine possession of the
land he inhabited. Seeing that he did not classify it, did not
distinguish it from other places, seeing that he did not seem to
know 'it' as a 'place', could he be said to understand the notion
of possession at all? And, if his grasp of it were so tenuous, so
local, so incapable of generalization, then it was hardly a crime
to take possession of it. The Whites did not, in this sense,
possess the Aborigine's country, any more than they spoke his
language. They possessed a country of which the Aborigine
was unaware. To talk of contracts and boundaries to an
Aborigine was to talk a foreign language. Logically then,
possession could go ahead without consultation. As the
Hentys, a pioneering family in western Victoria, put it when
applying for legal recognition of their squatting rights,

> Due to their [the Portland Aborigines] having 'no conception
> of a right of property in the surrounding lands or of having
> anything in them to convey', it had not been thought sensible
> to conclude any treaty with them.[61]

Particularity, the very property of aboriginal place names
that made them so ineffectual in resisting the logic of coloniza-

tion, made them especially useful to explorers. As Mitchell explained,

> The great convenience of using native names is obvious . . . so long as any of the Aborigines can be found in the neighbourhood . . . future travellers may verify my map. Whereas new names are of no use in this respect.[62]

At the same time, though, Mitchell recognized that *mere* particularity was not enough. He could not ignore the fact that naming was an act of civilizing, that it did not refer naively to the locality, but was an assertion about possession, about the future world where exploration would no longer be necessary. It was not enough just to travel:

> He, alone, should be entitled to give a name to a river, who explored its course, or, at least, as much of it as may be a useful addition to geography; and when a traveller takes the trouble to determine the true place of hills or other features, he might perhaps be at liberty to name them also. The covering a map with names of rivers or hills, crossed or passed, merely in traversing an unknown country amounts to little more than saying, that so many hills and rivers were seen there.[63]

The irony of this lofty empiricism is that, in reality, even Mitchell's names amounted to little more than a statement that 'so many hills and rivers were seen there'. Mitchell, like other travellers, colonized the country rhetorically, with figures of speech rather than facts.

In this connection, Mitchell's attitude towards aboriginal names is particularly significant. His appropriation of native names was not inspired by any archaeological zeal: its object was purely rhetorical. When, for instance, Mitchell wrote that a prominent hill north of Melbourne, which he had named Mount Macedon, should be renamed 'geboor', this being the aboriginal name as ascertained by Phillip King,[64] it sounds at first like an admirable concern for etymological accuracy. In fact, though, the gesture is quite superficial – as Charles La Trobe found, when he discovered his aboriginal guide applied the same word to *all* mountains. Had Mitchell's suggestion been adopted, it would still have commemorated Mitchell, the explorer, not the local inhabitants. Much the same comment applies to the remarks of the author of *The Australian Race*, E. M. Curr, who wrote in the 1880s,

> Many of the names of places which Major Mitchell obtained from the Blacks, and gives in his works, turned out subsequently to be incorrect. As an instance, the Blacks who dwelt on the Goulburn near Seymour called that river *Waaring*, but Mitchell relates, from inquiries made on the spot, that its name is *Bayungan*. No doubt the Black from whom he made his inquiry replied *indunga*, that is, *I don't understand*, and that the Major took down the phrase, as nearly as he could, as the name of the river. Between *Bayungan* and *indunga* there is a good deal of similarity.[65]

No doubt, too, there is a certain piquancy in the idea of the white man displaying his own ignorance as he litters his maps with expressions of incomprehension. But it is a mistake to suppose that the issue is the truthfulness or otherwise of these borrowed names. In using what looked like aboriginal names, the newcomer's object was nothing more or less than to authenticate his own passage. If anything, he used aboriginal names in order to assert his own claim to priority within the history of travelling. If there is a joke, it rebounds on the Aborigines. On his 1846 expedition, for instance, Mitchell named a river 'Parachute' by analogy with the native name 'Baloon'.[66] Elsewhere he transcribed the native word for a slight elevation as 'too lowly' and commented that it was a 'fortunate pun'.[67]

These linguistic ploys might be interpreted as cruel attempts to efface the Aborigines from the cultural map – cruel in that they make the Aborigines collude in their own destruction. But is the true butt of Mitchell's irony the Aborigines? Irony only has any meaning in relation to a well-known semantic convention, a linguistic custom. But, in these cases, Mitchell knows nothing – either about the Aborigines or indeed about the country. If anything is being treated ironically it is the pretensions of a literary genre (that of travel writing) to provide what, according to Dr Johnson, was the only value of travel: 'useful information'.[68] Mitchell's playfulness in regard to names comes close to being a pastiche of the explorer literature. Pastiche is a kind of 'blank irony'; it is like parody but, as the critic Fredric Jameson has pointed out (in discussing the phenomenon of Post-modernism): 'it is a neutral practice of such mimicry, without parody's ulterior motive, without the satirical impulse, without laughter, without the still latent feeling that there exists something *normal* compared to which what is being imitated is rather comic'.[69]

At any rate, it is significant that Mitchell's preference for aboriginal names is highly local and largely confined to regions previously traversed by other explorers. In those regions, by seeking out the proper names he is not, in any sense, restoring the country, but rather overlaying it with his own history – to the exclusion of other names, earlier travellers. And, in this respect as in so much else, Cook had already set a precedent: when, on the *Endeavour* voyage, Cook restored St George's Island to its native name of Tahiti, he was not so much exhibiting his interest in Tahitian sovereignty as his self-interest in establishing his precedence there over the island's earlier English visitor, Samuel Wallis.

The historical space of the white settlers emerged through the medium of language. But the language that brought it into cultural circulation was not the language of the dictionary: on the contrary it was the language of naming, the language of travelling. What was named was not something out there; rather it represented a mental orientation, an intention to travel. Naming words were forms of spatial punctuation, transforming space into an object of knowledge, something that could be explored and read. Barron Field was mistaken in supposing Australian place names unpoetic. For, in fact, they were the first authentic Australian poems, the first non-associational metaphors which were at once unique and generally expressive, indicative of the nomadic condition before it stiffened into dams, roads and telegraph posts.

In short, before they were places, place names were friends of travellers – a truth Charles Darwin recognized when he wrote of his visit to Australia,

These Antipodes call to mind old recollections of childish doubt and wonder. Even but the other day, I looked forward to this airy barrier as a definite point in our voyage homewards; now I find it and all such resting places for the imagination, are like shadows, which a man moving onwards cannot catch.[70]

What were those definite points? They were nothing more than names and outlines on maps. They bore no relation to reality, but without them travelling was impossible. Whether or not they deceived with their promises of water and anchorage, they did not deceive in harbouring 'resting places for the imagination'. Without those airy barriers, how could the traveller measure his progress? Indeed, without *their* shadowy advance, as they slipped away from him like horizons, how could he know he was travelling at all?

The Charm of Novelty

I gaze on the eddying wreath
That gathers and floats away
With the surf beneath, and between my teeth
The stem of the 'ancient clay'.

A. Lindsay Gordon

The ambition to relate unrelated things, to bring distant things close, is, quite literally, the scope of Cook's or Mitchell's names; and it defines equally well the purpose of their journals as a whole. Explorers who wrote up their journeys aimed to bring the country before their readers' eyes. The logic they used to discover the country did not derive primarily from the realm of contemporary geographical hypothesis or even from the economic incentives offered by governments or squatters: it originated in the logic of travelling itself, in the continuity of the journal, which, kept day after day, left no spaces unrelated and brought even the most distant objects into the uniform, continuous world of the text. If there was a principle of association at work, it was to be found in the orderly succession of diary entries, not in any logic of the landscape.

The spacing of names, their disposition across maps and in the blank gaps of journals, was not an ornamental afterthought: it embodied the primary function of the journal as a whole, which was to name the world of the journey. This was the justification of the explorer's record that, whether he found anything or not (whether or not he found, as it were, objects that already had names), his account of his route would serve to bring the country into historical being; it was a metaphorical equivalent, figuratively bringing distant things into relation with each other. In this sense, travelling was not primarily a physical activity: it was an epistemological strategy, a mode of knowing.

None of this, of course, was lost on the journal writers

themselves or their contemporary readers. Explaining the journal form of his *Australasiatic Reminiscences*, the erstwhile companion (and critic) of the explorer Ludwig Leichhardt, Daniel Bunce, wrote,

> We shall abandon the old and hackneyed style universally adopted by all previous writers on the colony, who usually commence with 'Tasmania is an island'; or 'This interesting island lies between the parallels of . . .'[1]

Instead, Bunce writes,

> We confine ourselves to the incidents of travel which have fallen under our especial observation, during a period of twenty-three years.[2]

Bunce adopts this approach not for anecdotal convenience, but because he believes an account of his travelling gives the most truthful picture of the country's progress. As he explains,

> During the whole of this time, we have been actively employed in developing the resources of a country.[3]

In other words, Bunce's peripatetic narrative is a strategy for writing history in a country where space is as yet incompletely mapped and remains itself a matter of historical inquiry and manufacture. His routes are themselves part of the history and indeed the idea of a history that is *not* in some sense a form of spatial biography is premature. Geography, too, must wait on the traveller, although its later reduction of space to the universal uniformity of longitude and latitude effaces the process of map-making on which its own authority depends.

This last point was also recognized by the author of *Experiences of a Colonist Forty Years Ago*, George Hamilton, who, while content to turn his gun on real Aborigines, could also rhapsodize,

> Here was a country without a geography, and a race of men without a history.[4]

False with regard to the Aborigines, it was nevertheless a faithful reflection on his own condition. Whether officially or unofficially employed, in that partially or wholly un-mapped, un-described country, the journal was the newcomer's only recourse. And again, as Hamilton recognized, the choice of genre was, as much as anything else, a stylistic matter:

> The world did not require that Dr. Johnson should have written the tale of Rasselas, to teach it how often our hopes will be blighted and our aspirations smothered. At all events, experience does not give us long prosy introductions, drawn out in elaborate sentences, before it makes us learn its lessons.[5]

The open form of the journal, unlike the carefully balanced moral fable or the hierarchic structure of the essay, travelled light: it was responsive to every turn in the road (of fortune). It travelled without a map; it did not imagine itself at the end of the journey looking back. Unlike Johnson, it spoke in short sentences – it might be nothing more than a bare word or two ('Weather: Fair Again'); and, like Boswell's writing, it followed the line of the journey for its own sake, dotting the world with islands rather than weighty, putative interiors.

Both officially and by the reading public at large, the epistemological claims of the journal were well recognized. As Melbourne's first surveyor was informed, 'Every plan must be accompanied by a written report, the most convenient form of which in the survey of a new country is that of a Journal . . .'[6] Apart from anything else, these instructions remind us that, before it became the instrument of geographical knowledge, the map, too, belonged to the discourse of travelling. The map only gradually became flat and smooth, equally authoritative in every part: to begin with, it did not exist apart from the routes that scored it. It was not a collection of geographical objects imprisoned beneath the grid of latitude and longitude. It was closer to a picture or to the journal itself: its surface was littered with isolated trees, graphic outcrops of rocks with nothing behind them, and with descriptive comments (see, for instance, plates 4, 9, 12 and 15) – 'heavily timbered', 'flat, barren country' – which, far from being authoritative, recorded nothing more than the traveller's distant, one-sided impression as he reined in his horse and focused his glasses on the haze.

Only rarely did even the competent surveyor succeed in locating his position on the earth's surface accurately. The most he could usually hope for was to preserve the spatial relationship between whatever geographical objects crossed his path. The internal logic of his chart might be impeccable, but its relationship to other maps remained approximate. In the same way, the explorer's journal described an internally harmonious world, but there was no guarantee that, simply because travellers met, they necessarily met in the same place. And, indeed, had successive travellers agreed about the appearance of things, their real nature and character, the idea of writing their spatial history would be superfluous: it would be enough to assume, as most historians do, that any discrepancies between journal and maps represent nothing more than personal incompetence or idiosyncrasy – anomalies that the imperial discourse of geography has, thankfully, long since ironed out.

Inhibitions of this kind did not, however, affect the explorers' reading public – or the reviewers, for that matter. Saddled with neo-classical notions of literary genre, reviewers might not be able to *name* the literature of travelling, but they had no difficulty in distinguishing it. There was, for example, no danger of interpreting the explorer's report as a form of disguised autobiography. Nor was the journal to be read merely as random notes furnishing the building blocks of more scholarly works. As the *Atlas* said of Sir George Grey's *Expeditions*, which recorded the explorer's somewhat accident-prone journeys in north-western Australia, 'It unites the interest of a romance with the permanent qualities of an historical and scientific treatise.'[7] And one reviewer of Eyre's published journals declared, 'We rise from the perusal of them with a feeling similar to that which follows the enjoyment of a pleasant work of fiction.'[8]

Readers readily understood that, although journals might resemble poems or novels, they also fulfilled the factual demands of history and even science. What allowed the journal to meet these apparently antithetical conditions was, of course, its spatiality, its non-Euclidean metaphor of the world as a track. The journal narrative might resemble the plot of a novel, but it was not fiction. The journal was not simply rooted *in* a historical space: the explorer's unique experience, both histori-cal and spatial, formed its subject matter. In place of the fictional logic of the plot, the journal substituted the logic of the journey: it turned the world of the journey into a narrative. In place of the fictional characters of the novelist, the explorer–writer introduced the character of the country.

At the same time, though, his journal, like the world of his journey, was open. Views flowed in and through it, potential narratives waited in the wings. Nothing was unpredictable because nothing was predicted. It was a truthful account of the world's appearance, as it appeared in time and space. And it was in this sense that the journal resembled an empirical science: for, however elaborately the explorer might hypothesize (or simply dream) about what lay beyond the horizon, in the foreground, as it were, he gave himself up to the appearance of phenomena. A change of soil, a rise in temperature, an accident with a gun, were hardly facts of interest to science: but the explorer's attitude towards them was itself scientific, laconic. Illness, thirst and human error were treated as natural facts, events that, once classified, required no further interpretation.

Explorer–writers, from Matthew Flinders to Sturt and Eyre, were fully conscious of the hybrid nature of their journals. As narrators of their own histories, they adopted a distinct persona, whose reactions were quite as predictable as those of the hero in romance. The explorer–narrators of their journals exhibit, for instance, a gullibility with regard to the evidence of the senses that often borders on the comic. Geographical phenomena constantly confront them like giants. Thus Sturt writes,

> I fear I have already wearied the reader by a description of such scenes, but he may form some idea of the one now placed before him, when I state, that, familiar as we had been to such, my companion involuntarily uttered an exclamation of amazement when he first glanced his eye over it. 'Good Heavens,' said he, 'did ever man see such country!'[9]

At the same time, a passage like this serves to convey the explorers' fundamentally scientific outlook. The outburst of Sturt's companion indicates that they are not creatures of associative habit, but remain alert, free of prejudice, still ready to be surprised. And, indeed, it is this capacity to be surprised, this combination of lofty single-mindedness and naivety about the world's likely resistance to him, that characterizes both the knight of romance and the empirical scientist.

The explorer–writer did not simply transcribe the notes made in the field. He wrote them up, overlaying the bare data of star altitudes and barometer readings with descriptive detail, with rhetorical asides and philosophical interludes. He transformed his disconnected notes into a connected narrative of the road. And this process of overlaying the bare succession of events with a sense of unity and purpose depended, not on the explorer's ability to detach himself from his experiences, and put them in perspective: rather it followed from his ability as a stylist to articulate what lay hidden or partially hidden in his notebooks. Far from seeking to efface his own involvement in the interests of empirical accuracy, his object was to demonstrate the inevitability of his journey, the sense in which his travelling was itself the indispensable form of knowledge. This is achieved, not by a Hawkesworth-like reduction of incoherence to order, but by bringing events before the reader's eyes as never before. For, in order to preserve their original spatial occasion, the explorer's experiences must be amplified. They must, in short, be expressed metaphorically, rather than literally.

When Sturt wants to record the uniformity of the country, he does not imitate its evasiveness. On the contrary, he interrupts it with a rhetorical outburst. Whether or not the words Sturt quotes were literally uttered by his companion is by the way. What matters is their rhetorical effect: they are a metaphorical means of bringing Sturt's experience home to the reader – even if the quoted words were never uttered. Paradoxically, Sturt preserves the reality of his experience by constructing a fictional episode rather than sticking to the facts. (And, even if, in this instance, Sturt's companion *did* exclaim exactly as Sturt says, this would not affect my argument: for the important point here is not Sturt's factual accuracy but his editorial practice. Whether the incident occurred or not, in this form or another, the fact is that Sturt decided to make much of it.)

The journal is a 'telling' of the journey: a narrative. What is being told is the biography of the journey. The journal is not an objective slice through geographical reality, but a critical equivalent of the explorer's spatial experience. What the explorer–writer writes about is not the country or his own state of mind, but the process of exploring. This is what his journal is 'about'. The aboriginal Protector George Augustus Robinson tells a delightful story of the squatter Charles Hutton:

> Asked Mr Hutton if he ever kept a meteorological journal. Said he did once but it was for near 9 months all fine weather, and he got disgusted with putting down ditto, ditto, it was nothing but ditto.[10]

But the explorer's journal was not like this: it was, to borrow Boswell's phrase, a *series* of uniformity, and not merely a succession of sameness. Even to write 'Weather: Fair Again' is to introduce a note of surprise and expectation absent from the mere repetition of 'Ditto'. Whether the motion of mind described was physical or mental or, as usual, both, the journal aimed to capture the process of travelling. And, with this in mind, the journal was revised and polished, like any other work of literature. Boswell himself kept notes from which he wrote up his journals; and the explorer–writers were the same, working up their field books after their return, a process that, as we have already seen, involved, among other things, altering and replacing names.

The idea of revision as a process of articulating the *biography* of the journey was by no means unfamiliar to nineteenth-century Australian explorers. Just as the biographer treats his subject biographically, that is, according to certain conventions, so, too, the explorer–writer approached his expedition narrative with certain ideas of what was appropriate to the telling of a journey. And it should be stressed that these conventions were not a straitjacket, preventing the writer from expressing himself. On the contrary, they were what assigned his text to the genre of travel writing, and but for their rhetorical assistance his project of bringing distant things close would have been fruitless.

Perhaps the most obvious and, from the point of view of spatial history, fundamental convention that the explorer accepted in writing up his exploits, was the notion of the journey as a linear progression. This, of course, has its exact counterpart in the chronologically linear schema (birth–child-hood–youth–adulthood–death) of biography. Characters in history walk on and off the stage. In psychoanalysis, the model of the personality is sedimentary, layer forming on layer. But in biography the individual life remains at the centre and, shaking off imponderable origins, reveals itself in successive events. Similarly, in travel writing, the object is neither geographical nor geological. It is, rather, to constitute space as a track. The life of this space resides in succession, in the demonstration that its parts link up, looking forward and backwards along the orientation of the journey.

One need only plot the routes of the explorers and navigators to realize that their courses were anything but uniformly progressive. Quite aside from those whose journeys ended where they began (like Stuart and Sturt), other explorers followed routes that zigzagged, doubled back, even remained static for long periods. To stretch out these loops, retreats, side journeys, to suppress the (in the field) equally important journeys of other members of the expedition, was evidently to perpetrate a fiction. More exactly, it was to adopt a point of view within the journey and to refuse the overview of the retrospective historian or geographer. The writers were conscious of this, of course. 'I have made many twistings and turnings,' reported Stuart at Sturt's Plains, early on his final (and successful) attempt to cross Australia from south to north:[11] and, rather than resembling the narrowing flight of an arrow, his earlier forays to the north had been a series of divergences to left and right – like an arrow's flight feathers – from which he had had to retreat. Another transcontinental explorer, Leichhardt, considered that, 'Much, indeed the greater portion, of my journey had been occupied in long reconnoitring rides.'[12] But, in the published accounts, the meanderings and circlings, the backtrackings and side-steppings, have been ironed out. The actual progress of the expedition, which often closely resembled the character of an Australian river, an ever-widening fan of forays ending in disappointment (see, for instance, Sturt's numerous excursions to left and right on his last expedition, plate 9), is replaced by an impression of gathering momentum, of phenomena contributing to the explorer's advance, of nature funnelling to the horizon.

In fact, phenomena enter the traveller's narrative only in so far as they align themselves with the direction of his desire. His landscape is a landscape of portents, of possible arrows, purposeful skies and meaningful silences. When, for example, an explorer writes, 'I believe there will be rain tonight, which will be a great boon, and will enable us to travel on easily,'[13] it is by assuming the track-like character of the world that he succeeds in transforming the actual absence of journey-like phenomena into a prognostication of progress. It is a world where time and space have yet to be separated, where evening lies ahead and travelling is tomorrow. In the same spirit, that romancer of the centre, the explorer Ernest Giles, can assert, writing of his experience to the south-east of Ayers Rock in 1873,

> The country passed over between it [a range] and our encampment, was exceedingly beautiful; hills being thrown up in red ridges of bare rock, with the native fig-tree growing between the bare rocks, festooning them into infinite groups of beauty, while the ground upon which we rode was a perfect carpet of verdure. We were therefore in high anticipation of finding some water equivalent to the scene; but as night was advancing, our search had to be delayed until the morrow.[14]

The landscape emerges as an object of interest in so far as it exhibits a narrative interest. The day itself is track-like: somehow, whatever his direction, the traveller is always going towards the sunset. And, even where it fails to hold the promise of longed-for novelty, reflection on the fact serves to express the explorer's own sense of purpose, his distinctive identity and responsibility. This is true even of a matter-of-fact traveller like Augustus Gregory. When he reports, for 5 March 1858, in the course of his North Australian expedition, 'All was impenetrable desert, as the flat and sandy surface, which could absorb the waters of the creek, was not likely to originate watercourses,'[15] he is not reporting a bare hydrological fact – although it is a well-informed guess. He is alerting his reader to a shift in narrative direction – a shift already adumbrated the previous day when the explorer reported, 'As there was little prospect of water ahead and the day far advanced, we returned to one of the brackish pools and encamped.'[16] Absence becomes a metaphor expressive of his own presence. Lack of direction singles out the purposeful narrator, defining his intention. Paradoxically, it renders his journey progressive, even if it takes the form of retreat.

In the biography of the journey, even going back is progress. This emerges in the explorers' distinctive treatment of the birds. The explorers' interest in them was understandable. Stuart, the explorer most sensitive to birds in flight, and whose journals describe an extraordinary persistence in trying to break through the scrub north of the centre in an effort to reach Australia's north coast, remarks of the region where Sturt had anticipated an inland sea,

> From this place to the east, and as far as south-south-west, there is no rising ground within range of vision – nothing but an immense plain. The absence of birds proclaims it to be destitute of water.[17]

And, not without a sense of irony, Stuart named the region 'Sturt's Plains'. The presence of birds in the narrative did not reflect the interest of a naturalist. The birds were a figure of speech invoked to express the likelihood of water. But the birds were also invoked, less logically, as directional markers. In the explorer literature, birds in flight never fly *away*, but always *to* water. On first meeting the south-easterly flowing Finke, which he has approached from the east, Giles notes,

> Several hundred pelicans, those antediluvian birds, made their appearance upon the water early this morning, but seeing us they flew away before a shot could be fired. These birds came from the north-west.[18]

So far, so good, but it then occurs to Giles to comment,

> Indeed, all the aquatic birds that I have seen upon the wing, come and go in that direction.[19]

By the time Giles wrote up his journal for publication, subsequent explorations had shown the Finke flowed from the north-west, that there *was* water in that direction. At the time, though, the behaviour of those 'aquatic' birds was, if anything, presumptive evidence of the absence of water to the north-west. But, so strongly is the flight of birds associated with water in his and, he hopes, his reader's mind, that he perceives no illogicality in his remark. And, indeed, there was none. For such birds entered the journal only in order to articulate the direction of possible water and hence the logic of the track. It was a convention the explorer–writer bowed to even when experience showed it to be empirically false. As Warburton wrote,

> A flock of wild geese flew over in the evening from the west; we hail it as a good omen; but our speculations have not as yet turned out very happy ones.[20]

The explorer never entertained the possibility that birds flying his way sailed from absence to absence, that flight itself was a bad augury for what lay ahead. Sturt's avian argument is, of course, the notorious case in point. On the Darling at Fort Bourke, Sturt had observed that, 'The migration of the different kinds of birds . . . was invariably to the W.N.W.' He had also noticed that 'several of the same kinds of birds annually visited' the colony of South Australia, 'and that these came directly from the north'. Sturt argued from this that,

> If we were to draw a line from Fort Bourke to the W.N.W., and from Mount Arden to the north, we should find that they would meet a little to the northward of the Tropic . . . I was led to conclude that the country to which they went would in a great measure resemble that which they had left – that birds which delighted in rich valleys, or kept on lofty hills, surely would not go into deserts and into flat country.[21]

This geometrical proof of an inland Eden was, it must be said, greeted with some scepticism even by contemporaries. What evidence, for example, was there for Sturt's assumption of a single population originating from a single place? But, whatever else it was, Sturt's hypothesis eloquently expressed the explorer's responsibility, to constitute space as a narrow passage, a space funnelling the traveller towards the future.

In establishing a coincidence between the explorer's route and the course of events, the explorers also borrowed rhetorical devices more explicitly associated with the writing of fiction and poems. In particular, they gave a distinctive meaning to that semi-divine and definitely utilitarian figure, Providence. In eighteenth- and nineteenth-century historical writing of all kinds, Providence was regularly invoked as a convenient device to gloss events that cause-and-effect explanations seemed unable to plumb. It had, for instance, been very busy in the founding of Australia: Providence, in Mitchell's words, had provided a great southern land and left it vacant (*sic*) for His chosen race.[22] Providence had brought Cook to the Pacific.[23] Even the 'coercion of those Savages', who dwelt in New Holland, was the mechanism 'which it has pleased Providence to appoint for the extended cultivation of the human race'.[24] Providence enabled John, the sailor, in Southey's third *Botany Bay Eclogue*, to conclude 'all's for the best'.[25] And it was the same sentiment that informed Stokes's account of Cook's 'mishap' on Endeavour Reef, and his later escape to sea by way of Providential Channel: for, had not the former led to an important river, the latter to a passage through the reef, 'in a manner which can best be designated as providential'?[26]

But it was not only imperial apologists who found Providence a useful figure of speech. Land explorers, too, frequently employed this prosopopoeia to explain the happy outcome of 'situations that baffle their own exertions or foresight', as Sturt put it.[27] In this context, though, it also acquired a distinctive spatial meaning: it became the figure denoting a significant meeting place. It marked the spot where the explorer came across the footprints of a predecessor. There is even a passage in Warburton's journal where Providence emerges as the personification of direction. Charley, the aboriginal boy, sent to look for water, has failed to return. Warburton, who is travelling by night, decides to go on without him. Eight miles out, Charley miraculously intercepts Warburton, with the news he has located water:

> It may, I think, be admitted that the hand of Providence was distinctly visible in this instance. I had deferred starting until 9 pm, to give the absent boy a chance of regaining the camp. It turned out afterwards that had we expedited our departure by ten minutes, or postponed it for the same length of time,

Charley would have missed us; and had this happened there is little doubt that not only myself, but probably other members of the expedition would have perished from thirst. The route pursued by us was at right-angles with the course taken by the boy, and the chance of our stumbling up against each other in the dark was infinitesimally small. Providence mercifully directed otherwise . . .[28]

The Providence that permits Warburton to continue his narrative evidently shares the author's sense of direction: it brings the facts of the landscape to bear on his passage. At the same time, the providential *topos* also dramatizes the metaphorical nature of the text, the sense in which the explorer's space is, in fact, trackless. Its appearance and manner of intervening allegorize the explorer's way of thinking, his responsibility to connect the world up as a continuous path.

The landscape that emerges from the explorer's pen is not a physical object: it is an object of desire, a figure of speech outlining the writer's exploratory impulse. This is a point clearly illustrated by that highly self-conscious, and somewhat sentimental, explorer–surveyor, Stokes. Stepping ashore in the Gulf of Carpentaria, Stokes described himself as 'once more stepping out over a terra incognita; and though no alpine features greeted our eyes as they wandered over the vast level, all was clothed with the charm of novelty'.[29] Here 'the charm of novelty' is more than a conventional phrase borrowed from European travel literature: it names the theme that brings the explorer's route into being, that gives his track a narrative coherence and structure. As Stokes makes clear, the charm of exploring lies not in discovery, but in the act of exploring. It lies in a state of mind where potential mountains vastly outweigh the charm of any actually found. What invests the view with significance is the explorer's desire to make it signify: it is not that the explorer comes to the landscape with rigid preconceptions, European standards he is determined to impose. Rather, it is the mere fact of his 'advancing', the motive that moves him, that clothes all about him in a veil of mystery. The mystery is of his own making, a resistance dialectically constructed in order to give his own passage historical meaning. 'The charm of novelty' is the figure of speech by means of which the explorer translates the view into a text, by which he renders it of interest to the reader – a cultural object the reader will desire.

The basis of the explorer's interest in the landscape is neither objectively empirical nor is it merely literary or autobiographical: his stance is, rather, phenomenological in nature. It is grounded, that is, in his recognition that he, the observer, does not gaze on the world as through a window, but rather inhabits it. His perception of the world's appeal is inseparable from his own interest in it, from the 'intentionality' of his gaze. And the nature of that intentionality is not just personal, a matter of temperament or even professional calling: the explorer does not see the country differently merely because he is an explorer. His perception of space is grounded in his bodily nature, in the fact that his biological constitution is itself a spatial configuration. Thus we look forward; thus we expect symmetry to left and right, but not up and down; thus 'forwards' and 'backwards', though implying physically identical movement, bear very different cultural meanings.

In the context of these remarks we can interpret a passage that deserves to become a *locus classicus* for the emergence of an Australian spatial history. Viewing the plains near the future Burketown on the Albert River in west Queensland, on 25 July 1841, Stokes was led to reflect,

we stepped out over what we felt to be untrodden ground. It had often before been my lot to be placed in a similar position, and I have necessarily, therefore, given expression already to identical sentiments; but I cannot refrain from again reminding the reader how far inferior is the pleasure of perusing the descriptions of new lands, especially when attempted by an unskilled pen, to that which the explorer himself experiences. All are here on an equal footing; the most finished writer and the most imperfect scribbler are on the same level; they are equally capable of the exquisite enjoyment of discovery, they are equally susceptible of the feelings of delight that gush upon the heart as every forward step discloses fresh prospects, and brings a still more new horizon, if I may so speak, to view. And it may be added that, to the production of the emotions I allude to, beauty of landscape is scarcely necessary. We strain forward incited by curiosity, as eagerly over an untrodden heath, or untraversed desert, as through valleys of surpassing loveliness, and amid mountains of unexplored grandeur; or perhaps, I should say, more eagerly, for there is nothing on which the mind can repose, nothing to tempt it to linger, nothing to divert the current of its thoughts. Onward we move, with expectation at its highest, led by the irresistible charm of novelty, almost panting with excitement, even when every step seems to add certainty to the conviction that all that is beyond resembles all that has been seen.[30]

Here the journey is established in terms quite independent of a landscape. It is the charm of novelty that directs the explorer, that is the intentional mechanism focusing and unifying his actions. And, since novelties retain their novelty by never growing familiar, the explorer comes into being most completely in the *absence* of memorable geographical phenomena, not in their presence. It is the 'expectation' of objects that defines the explorer so that, in this context, it was wholly appropriate that Stokes should not only christen the field which so focused his feelings the 'Plains of Promise', but include in his narrative an illustration of them (plate 8). It emerges from a passage like this that the 'explorer', properly speaking, is not an interesting personality, whose adventures are ripe for biographical treatment: he emerges instead at the very moment his personality is submerged in a single-minded desire to realize space as an object of consciousness. He, the explorer, has no independent existence apart from his exploring. Nor should we expect the rest of his life to illuminate in some way this state of mind. Least of all should we suppose that his own character is in some way derived from the character of the landscape he discovers. It is precisely the lack of objects giving direction to the landscape, differentiating the horizon, giving focus to the journey, that brings home to the explorer the nature of his activity. What *he* brings home, despite himself, is a biography of the journey.

According to Stokes, his description cannot compare with the reality. But, in borrowing this well-worn rhetorical disclaimer, Stokes turns it on its head. For, after all, in the landscape Stokes describes, there is 'nothing on which the mind can repose'. There is nothing to describe except this sensation of nothing –

which is to say that, but for his ability as a writer, the reality of his experience would be lost. In this sense, in writing up his journal, Stokes surpasses the experience itself. But he does this, not by conjuring up imaginary landscapes, but by rejecting them – and at the same time rejecting the principles of association on which their appeal rests and which the picturesque poet exploits. It is in this way that, in his landscape, 'the most finished writer and the most imperfect scribbler are on the same level'. For, in the explorer's world, it is more important to clear the path than to clutter it up with distracting objects, whether physical, mental or rhetorical.

This desire to clear the way suggests an interesting parallel with psychoanalysis. The truthfulness of the explorer's testimony no more depended on the explorer's ability as a writer (his powers of invention and the like) than the interest of the analysand's dreams on his or her profession. If we can believe Stokes, the explorer–writer trusted in the inner logic of the track as completely as the analyst believed in the mechanism of wish fulfilment. There was implicit in the biography of the journey, as in the interpretation of dreams, a notion of naming and identifying neurotic distractions likely to block the emergence of the true path. In this context, the successful explorer narrative was one that regarded space as the place of 'distortion' or 'transposition', the place where all sequences of psychic activity (verbal, eidetic, associative) might occur and which, by its analysis, successfully revealed the true way. We might even want to claim the priority of exploring in this respect: after all, like the language of metaphor, psychoanalysis borrows its imagery from the realm of space. And who is to say that the spatiality of the discourse of the unconscious is merely a figure of speech?

The association between travelling and dreaming (both awake and asleep) was, in fact, a commonplace of the explorer literature. Giles, who gave to his published journals the subtitle 'The Romance of Exploration', describes just such an occasion of reverie:

Darkness began to creep over this solitary place and its more solitary occupant . . . I coiled myself up under a bush and fell into one of those extraordinary waking dreams which occasionally descend upon imaginative mortals when we know that we are alive, and yet we think we are dead; when a confused jumble of ideas sets the mind 'peering back into the vistas of the memories of yore', and yet also foreshadowing the images of future things upon the quivering curtain of the mental eye. At such a time the imagination can revel only in the marvellous, the mysterious, and the mythical. The forms of those we love are idealized and spiritualized into angelic shapes. The faces of those we have forgotten long, or else perchance have lost, once more return, seraphic from the realms of light . . .[31]

This reverie – and it continues at some length – should not be mistaken for a naive, and intrusive, autobiographical aside. For one thing, it serves a narrative function, dramatizing the explorer's feelings on temporarily losing contact with his party. For another, it conspicuously does not throw light on Giles's personal history. Rather, the writer seeks to persuade us of the universality of his experience. Such transcendent moments are part of the explorer's credentials. They are an indispensable element, if the biography of the journey is to be complete. They represent the secular, nineteenth-century equivalent of those mystical revelations in the wilderness, an obligatory episode in all early Lives of the Saints. More than this, Giles's revelling in 'the marvellous, the mysterious, and the mythical' is also a play within the play: it alludes to the appeal of his narrative as a whole, to the fact that, in the interior, all rules of association based on experience are suspended. There is nothing to impede the imagination on its own journey – in such states it is at liberty to wander backwards or forwards as it pleases. It is thus that, in the explorer's discourse, the cliché of 'the landscape of the imagination' is revitalized.

This analysis applies even to a passage that, on the face of it, appears explicitly autobiographical. At one point in the journal of his overland journey to Port Essington, Leichhardt recalls,

During the early part of our journey, I had been carried back in my dreams to scenes of recent date, and into the society of men with whom I had lived shortly before starting on my expedition. As I proceeded on my journey, events of earlier date returned into my mind, with all the fantastic associations of a dream; and scenes of England, France, and Italy passed successively. Then came the recollections of my University life, of my parents and the members of my family; and, at last, the days of boyhood and of school – at one time as a boy afraid of the look of the master, and now with the independent feelings of the man, communicating to, and discussing with him the progress of my journey, the courses of the rivers I had found, and the possible advantages of my discoveries. At the latter part of my journey, I had, as it were, retraced the whole course of my life.[32]

The Oedipal character of Leichhardt's dreams and the progress of the analysis backwards from the present to the earliest memories of childhood uncannily anticipate Freudian interpretations of the 'dream-work'. But Leichhardt's account is not to be taken as undisguised autobiography, as a spontaneous and prophetic description of the workings of the unconscious. To regard it or comparable passages as raw facts of personal experience – the tendency of most of our explorer–biographers – would be to detach it from the context of its appearance. And the context of its appearance was one of rereading and careful revision. It is not just, as Elsie Webster has pointed out in her book *Whirlwinds in the Plain*, that Leichhardt's journal was 'edited' for publication – P. P. King remedying its stylistic deficiencies with a liberal addition of classical allusions, interludes of elevated feeling (like the above), poetic description and moral reflection.[33] The conventional trope of life as a journey, on which Leichhardt bases his dream account, presupposes the journey has been completed. Leichhardt's elegant image of physical and psychic tracks converging in his success depends on the wisdom of hindsight. The notion of discussing with his former teacher 'the possible advantages of my discoveries', for instance, would clearly be senseless, had the expedition not succeeded. In other words, Leichhardt's account of his dream life is not to be taken as a truthful description of his experiences at the time: it is, rather, part and parcel of his rhetorical strategy for constituting his journey as biography. This is not to diminish its truth value. But it is to suggest that what we find illuminated in this passage is not Leichhardt's personal psychology but the life of the road. Journeying, as Boswell realized, transposed not only body but mind.

Recognizing the explorer's journal as an essentially metaphorical discourse, we can begin to understand the extraordinary appeal of two of the best-known exploration journals – Sturt's narrative of his expedition into central Australia in 1844–6 and Eyre's account of his overland journey from Streaky Bay to Albany in 1840–1 (see plate 7). Both these expeditions arose from a curiosity to discover the nature of the Australian interior. It was a curiosity with political and economic, as well as geographical, overtones: the South Australian government and powerful squatting interests were keen to find country that would extend the rather slender resource of grazing land available in the colony. And there was the possibility, mooted by Flinders and taken up by John Oxley in the 1820s, that, beyond the flat hinterland of the south coast, there might lie a considerable body of water: how else to account for the puzzling lack of major rivers flowing to the coast?

Quite why Eyre decided to make an overland journey along the edge of the Great Australian Bight, from Lincoln Peninsula in the east to King George's Sound at Australia's south-west extremity remains unclear. Partly, it may have been pique at his failure to fulfil his original instructions – which were to strike north from the head of the Bight in an effort to find a route inland. On previous expeditions, Eyre had followed the line of the Flinders Range only to have his progress arrested by a horseshoe of salt lakes. By striking north from farther west, it was hoped to avoid this impediment. Whatever the case, Eyre found the more westerly route equally difficult and elected instead to continue along the coast. Sturt was more successful: striking inland three years after Eyre, and approaching from the east via the Darling, he was able to penetrate as far as the edge of the Simpson Desert (see plate 7) – some 150 miles from the centre by his own calculations. In the course of his journey, which took well over a year to perform, on account of the need to time any advance with the extremely scarce rains, Sturt discovered the Stony Desert and Cooper's Creek – but not an inland sea.

The suffering and deprivation endured by both explorers is not in question: their journals are classics of the romantic genre of travel literature. And from the point of view of spatial history – illustrating the place where language and spatial experience intersect to make history – they are also uniquely interesting. When, for example, Eyre writes, 'As fast as we arrived at one point which had bounded our vision (and beyond which we hoped a change might occur), it was but to be met with the view of another [unbroken line of cliffs] beyond,'[34] we recognize at once the explorer–writer at his double task of differentiating the space in order to unify it as a track. The very statement itself is the rhetorical means of bringing space into the realm of discourse, of rendering it distinct and conceivable. Or, again, when Sturt reports that, 'We stood as it were in the centre of barrenness,'[35] we recognize, not an objective description, but a characteristic oxymoron expressive of the explorer's responsibility to link what has gone before with what is to come. So Sturt continues, in the next sentence, 'I feel it impossible, indeed, to describe the scene . . .', to say, that is, which way to go.

The common reader may have understood these conventions, but not, for the most part, critics, biographers or, for that matter, the makers of television serials. As titles like *Sturt: The Chipped Idol* and *The Hero as Murderer* (dealing with Eyre's life) indicate, explorers' biographers have tended to assume that the explorers' journals are transparently autobiographical; or, rather, since they are clearly 'worked up' versions of the events, more or less elaborate fictions to be dismantled in search of the truth. Far from being read as symbolic representations of journeys, they have been interpreted as offering little more than a stage on which the explorer hero worked out his personal destiny. So, writing of Eyre, the distinguished Australian biographer and historian Geoffrey Dutton speculates in reference to the explorer's decision to push on round the Great Australian Bight to King George's Sound in Western Australia, 'Pride, his sense of duty, and perhaps deepest of all some passion to create his own fate, drove him on.'[36] No doubt, but why this route rather than another? Suppressing the spatial occasion in this way has the result of inventing a historical character of surprising wilfulness, a wilfulness that, once invented, has to be explained.

To take two illustrative instances: Sturt's field journal for 9 September 1845 records that 'Mr Browne has also had severe pains in his Muscles and limbs, prognostics I hope of a change of weather.'[37] In the published journal, these symptoms of scurvy are brought forward to 29 August and, by 7 September, 'a gloom hung over' the surgeon: 'His hands were constantly behind him, pressing or supporting his back, and he appeared unfit to ride.'[38] Despite this, the following day John Browne was out on horseback, reconnoitring to the north-east with Sturt. Even more curiously, Browne himself reports that when he returned to camp on 1 October, 'The men in the Camp said they saw no difference in me.'[39] These editorial emendations, and the discrepancies between Sturt's account and that of Browne, have been taken by at least one biographer as evidence of Sturt's incompetence or lack of candour. But they are better understood as revisions intended to articulate the dynamic of the journey. For instance, it was on 7 September that Sturt, according to his *Narrative*, gazed out 'from the summit of a sandy undulation', and 'saw that the ridges extended north-wards in parallel lines beyond the range of vision, and appeared as if interminable. To the eastward and westward they succeeded each other like the waves of the sea.'[40] It was on 7 September that, 'within 150 miles of the centre of the continent', Sturt, 'with a bitter feeling of disappointment', turned back. In correlating Browne's illness with his decision to retreat, Sturt was not so much falsifying the medical evidence as making it subsidiary to the main story, drawing it into the line of the journey. As he explained, 'I could not make up my mind to persevere, and see my only remaining companion perish at my side, and that, too, under the most trying, I had almost said the most appalling circumstances.'[41] It is in this context that Browne's illness appears, not as a fact, but as the main theme in a minor key.

And another example – this time from Eyre: well on the way to Albany, John Baxter, Eyre's overseer, was murdered by two of the aboriginal guides (who themselves immediately absconded). This was, of course, a human tragedy – this time one that served to drive the explorer on, not back. But the horror of the incident does not explain the prominence it receives in Eyre's published account. Whatever its personal meaning, it serves there mainly as a structural device, a dramatic means of punctuating the narrative and marking the journey's watershed. Thus it is no accident that Baxter's death occurs at the end of chapter six, and at the end of volume one of Eyre's two-volume journal. Standing at the exact midpoint of Eyre's twelve-chapter narrative, the desert drama draws attention not only to human perfidy but to the hostility of the country itself, a land, as he puts it, 'inhospitable even to death':

> The frightful, the appalling truth now burst upon me, that I was alone in the desert . . . At the dead hour of night, in the wildest and most inhospitable wastes of Australia, with the fierce wind raging in unison with the scene of violence before me . . .[42]

A more dramatic ending to the first act could hardly have been devised.

Of course, the explorers themselves promoted the image of the explorer as hero. Warburton, for example, thought Eyre's trek had placed 'unexampled demands on human endurance'. Grey spoke of 'dauntless courage', Sturt of 'untiring perseverance' and, in another context, of Eyre's 'chivalrous spirit'. And, it is true, heroism is a significant ingredient of all their narratives. It is not, however, to be attributed naively to the explorer himself. The heroic explorer exists, rather, as a convention of the explorer discourse. He is a figure who emerges from the explorer–writer's abilities in transforming the country into a narrative. It is the explorer–writer's talent for forging a metaphor of himself as traveller that makes the narrative heroic, not the country and even less the personal qualities of the explorer.

This is the context in which we can understand the appeal of Eyre and Sturt. From an imperial point of view, anxious to install them in Australia's pantheon of founding fathers, the chief problem both their narratives present is the conspicuous uselessness of their journeys. As Eyre himself wrote, he had 'no important rivers to enumerate, no fertile regions to point out . . . no noble ranges to describe . . .'.[43] Sturt, even more dramatically, wholly failed to find the inland sea on which he (and others, it must be said, including John Oxley) had pinned his hopes. And, unlike Eyre, Sturt even had to admit defeat and turn back. Faced with this apparently embarrassing lack of geographical achievement, the biographical ploy of shifting attention away from the journey towards the personality of the explorer, the positing of a personal flaw, is no doubt under-standable – and it is supported circumstantially by the explorers themselves. Sturt openly admitted that his last expedition was a final attempt to advance himself and provide for his children. Eyre as readily acknowledged that his journey stemmed from his frustration with trying to reach the centre; and he made a point of informing his readers that he refused the South Australian government's offer of a ship to supply him for 'any examinations I might wish to make from the coast northwards' – a refusal that, combined with his decision to go it alone, seemed to most, as he says, 'little less than madness'.

Yet it was madness the readers could interpret, the sort of madness of which dreams were made. It was a visionary state of mind which cleared the way of obstacles. Eyre might lament his failure to make discoveries, but the mountains and lakes he longed for *were* there in his narrative – as potential objects. It was his ability to suggest this that made his journey readable. Similarly, even when Sturt had proved to the satisfaction of all (except himself) the non-existence of the inland sea, he did not let this cloud his narrative. Without its rhetorical presence, the nobility of his journey, the importance of his route and indeed the fertility of his imagination might have been lost. And contemporary readers, unlike our biographers, seem to have grasped this: it was not Stuart, who successively traversed the centre twice, but Sturt (who failed to reach it) who was remembered, and he was remembered not for his journey but for his narrative, his power of transforming the landscape into a symbolic journey.

Eyre may have travelled west along the coast; Sturt may have gone north towards the 'centre'. But what unites their narratives is their unusual ambitiousness in attempting to constitute their journeys under the aegis of a single, unifying metaphor: that of the sea. Figuring forth the spaces of their journeys as sea-like, as resembling the sea, as contiguous to the sea, even as contrasting with the sea, both Sturt and Eyre were able to orchestrate the variousness of their experiences into a single, swelling symphonic theme. Whether the sea was 'real' or imaginary was, from the point of view of the interest of the narrative, by the way. Its significance lay in its symbolic fertility as a hypothesis of exploration, as a device suggesting the journey's inner logic and, above all, as a means of bringing remote things close, vividly before the reader's inner eye. And it should be stressed that the importance of the sea in both narratives is *metaphorical*. It is not invoked simply as a simile, a decorative but essentially trivial trope. Rather, it represents an attitude towards reality, a model for constructing the truth.

Paul Ricoeur writes, 'the shared characteristic which supplies the basis of metaphor does not necessarily lie in a direct resemblance between tenor and vehicle: it can result from a common attitude taken to both.'[44] This is the case with Sturt's and Eyre's sea. And the common attitude of the explorers to both is one of ambiguity. It is the uncertainty whether what lies ahead is sea or land (and, more profoundly, the possibility that the properties appropriate to one may be transposed to the other) that makes the metaphor so attractive. At the same time, of course, this metaphorical suspension of definition is the best possible means of giving the narrative direction and interest. Explorer and reader alike travel along an imaginary boundary, where opposites meet and threaten to become each other. The interest of the narrative lies precisely in the infinite deferral of any resolution of this ambiguity. It is the continuing metaphorical ambiguity that constitutes the track. It is the perceived ambiguity that provides the incentive to travel on.

It should perhaps be stressed that the sea–land metaphor was not just a literary trick. The choice of image was neither straightforwardly empirical, nor was it arbitrarily wilful. Its power to figure forth the nature of the explorer's experience lay, in fact, in its very lack of originality. From Homer onwards, the metaphorical intercourse of land and sea has been conventional. But the likeness in difference felt in contemplating the sea as land-like, the land as sea-like, goes deeper than this. It is rooted phenomenologically in our most primitive sensations of earth and water and of their common heritage in the wind-filled sky.

If at times the sea promises an ease of passage impossible on land, at other times it seems disastrously flat, depressed, pointless. 'A spacious Horizon is an Image of Liberty,' wrote Addison, and thought the horizon in question might equally well contain 'a troubled Ocean' or 'a spacious Landskip'. To some of Australia's explorers, it was the antithesis between the two that was felt more strongly. To Stokes, 'Pent up for some time on board ship a very barren prospect may seem delightful.'[45] To Banks, escaping the shipwreck, on the other hand, 'That very Ocean which had formerly been look'd upon with terror by (maybe) all of us was now the Assylum we had long wishd for and at last found.'[46] In fact, we may hazard the guess that the true liberation that sea and land offered lay in the realm of metaphor – in their power to intimate each other, to suggest an imaginary meeting place, where one became the other and both were transcended.

At any rate, it is clear that Eyre's attitude towards the barren coast he was obliged to follow as he rounded the Bight was not wilfully subjective. He did not make the pathetic fallacy of treating nature as an extension of his own feelings. Rather the reverse, in fact: his personal feelings entered the biography of the journey in so far as they could be expressed in terms of the narrative's overriding metaphor. On the one hand is 'this wild and breaker-beaten shore', strewn at intervals with the wrecks of 'unfortunate' vessels. It offers no relief, only the illusion of it: 'It required our utmost vigilance to prevent the wretched horses from drinking the salt-water.' On the other hand is a country 'inhospitable even to death', a country that resembles the sea remarkably. This is how the explorer's destiny becomes bound up with the journey. On the one hand, 'The whole region around appeared one mass of dense impenetrable scrub running down to the very borders of the ocean.' On the other, periodically, 'The tide became too high for us to continue on the shore.'[47] The coast of Eyre's journey exists as a narrow passage. It is the track where opposite possibilities continue to meet, continue threatening to cancel each other out. The coast is the metaphor of exploring, not of the explorer.

In this context we can understand the significance of the *Mississippi* episode in Eyre's narrative. Just short of Esperance Bay, Eyre and his surviving aboriginal companion are rescued by a French whaling vessel, the *Mississippi*. They spend a fortnight aboard the ship recuperating, before continuing their overland journey. It is an incident that any biographer of heroes is likely to find embarrassing. It risks revealing the arbitrary nature of Eyre's journey, the artificial gravity of the dangers he has exposed himself to. But Eyre himself treats it rather differently, not as an indictment of his journey, but rather as a welcome occasion to reflect on it. To be taken on board was, he writes,

> a change in our circumstances so great, so sudden, and so unexpected, that it seemed more like a dream than a reality; from the solitary loneliness of the wilderness, and its attendant privations, we were at once removed to all the comforts of a civilised community.[48]

Described like this, the rescue is another expression of the sudden and unpredictable reversals of fortune that characterize the explorer's track. The *Mississippi* episode appears to provide a non-metaphorical point of view from which to contemplate reality. In fact, though, it is itself a further metaphor bringing home to the reader a metaphorical journey. After weeks of viewing the land as sea-like, it offers an opportunity of contemplating the sea as land-like; and in this way it merely articulates the effect of Eyre's journey as a whole.

What Eyre could take largely for granted as the groundswell of his metaphorical narrative, Sturt, of course, had to spell out. Not having the sea consistently on his left hand, the land on his right, Sturt constantly has to remind the reader of their possible meeting. But the metaphorical function of the sea–land image remains the same as in Eyre's narrative, to express the direction of desire, to characterize the ambiguity inherent in an activity where wanting to find always exceeds the sum of objects found. Still, Sturt's appropriation of the sea–land metaphor is remarkable for its persistence and unifying power.

Looking north-west from the Main Barrier Range on 8 November 1844, Sturt remarks, 'One might have imagined that an ocean washed their base, and I would that it really had been so.'[49] A few days later, looking back at the Barrier Range from the north-westerly plains, Sturt could not help feeling a conviction that 'they had once looked over the waters of the ocean as they then overlooked a sea of scrub'.[50] Further north (see plate 9), at Depot Glen, in May 1845, Sturt laments the lack of rain: 'The wide field of the interior lay like an open sea before me, and yet every sanguine hope I had ever indulged appeared as if to be extinguished.'[51] By 5 September, across the Stony Desert and following Eyre Creek, the view westward and eastward 'was, as it were, over a sandy sea; ridge after ridge succeeding each other as far as the eye could stretch the vision'.[52] And the same image is used a few days later, on 8 September, the culminating day of Sturt's expedition, when he finally turned back.

Elsewhere, the device of metonymy serves to evoke the likelihood of ocean. Where, for instance, 'coasts' occur, they are seen to stand for the sea itself. On 19 January 1845, Sturt thinks, 'We could not be very far from the outskirts of an inland sea, it so precisely resembled a low and barren sea coast.'[53] Eight months later, the appearance of the Stony Desert 'was like that of an immense sea beach'. Equally, isolated hills remind him of islands; he himself is a navigator. So, in the Stony Desert, 'we could no longer see the sand hill just noticed, but held on our course like a ship at sea . . . As we approached, it looked like an island in the midst of the ocean.'[54]

Sturt's expressions are not highly original. But nor are they conventional. Stuart, for instance, who travelled with Sturt on this expedition, and who later traversed similar country on his own trans-Australian expedition, makes no use whatsoever of the land—sea metaphor. This underlines the point that Sturt did not use it ornamentally. Whether or not latter-day travellers following Sturt's route are able to see exactly what he meant when he described a feature as coast-like, is quite beside the point. The verisimilitude of his descriptions is not in question. What matters is the *attitude* that informed them. For Sturt did not use such images descriptively, but as a mode of knowing, as a model of reality which might lead him to make a discovery. They were hypotheses making the prospect of the longed-for inland sea ever more plausible.

However, the distribution of these images throughout the text has the effect of altering the nature of the desired blessing. The inland sea ceases to be a geographical object waiting, in some sense, at the end of the narrative. It is the coherent metaphor running throughout the narrative, which gives the journey its identity. When, on 24 August 1845, for instance, well-grassed plains encourage Sturt 'to hope we were about to leave behind us the dreary region we had wandered over, and that happier and brighter prospects would soon open out, to reward us for past disappointment',[55] it is the ever-present sea–desert ambiguity that makes Sturt's allegorical landscape plausible. What keeps the explorer going is not so much a cycle of hope and disappointment as the continuous potential for both. The whole journey occurs in a potentially metaphorical realm, a realm of promising mirage. And it is worth adding that, if the sea–land prospect ceased to be a mirage, the interest of the narrative would also disappear.

As we might expect, Sturt's sense of the journey occurring in a metaphysical zone between opposite views emerges in other ways. There were occasions when the explorer physically straddled the difference:

> So closely was the Desert allied to fertility at this point, and I may say in these regions, that I stood more than once with one foot on salsolaceous plants growing in pure sand, with the other on luxuriant grass, springing up from rich alluvial soil.[56]

In such a world, where nothing was constant, it was logical to expect change. But the changes could not be foreseen; they were as unexpected as metaphorical shifts of meaning: 'As the changes . . . in this singular and anomalous region had been so sudden and instantaneous, I still held my course,'[57] Sturt wrote on 6 September 1845, and his remarks succinctly express the nature of his journey, a journey into the spaces of metaphor, a journey characterized by the spaces metaphors made.

A readiness for change characterizes the narratives of both Eyre and Sturt. As it happens, the two journeys were from a geographical point of view markedly different. If Eyre did indeed encounter a country that was dispiritingly uniform, then Sturt's experience was quite different. Indeed, there was a pattern about the mutability of his experience that was in itself finely dramatic: sandhills (14–18 August 1845), creek country and bare plains (18–22 August), well-grassed, park-like plains

(23–24 August) and sandhills (24 August), on the south side of the Stony Desert (see plate 9), are matched, on the desert's north side, by sandhills (28 August), waterholes, pools, plains or flats (29 August–3 September), open and grassy country (4–6 September) and sandhills (7 September). What would a structuralist critic make of this? Symmetrical about the Stony Desert, does not this structure reveal the book's true centre? In a sense it does, but the fact is that such 'sudden' changes are a feature of that region, at least to the traveller. In this context, what is more interesting is Sturt's attempt to turn these changes at right-angles, as it were, to their appearance, and translate them into characteristics of the journey itself – to refuse, that is, to see these geographical changes as anything more than a sign nothing was certain. In the narratives of both Eyre and Sturt, the process of change, and its perpetual possibility, replaces an interest in the changes themselves.

Read in this way, it becomes comprehensible that Sturt's readers regarded his false hypotheses lightly. Eyre might disagree with Sturt about the nature of the interior, but it did not prevent him paying handsome tribute to Sturt's qualities as an explorer. True, Sturt's geographical surmises were not wholly fanciful, particularly when he modified his hypothesis to suggest merely that the desert he crossed was *once* a sea. The geologist Hutton, for instance, had argued that 'the greater portion, if not the whole, of the solid land' had been 'originally composed at the bottom of the sea'.[58] Hutton's original 'spheroid of water, with granite rocks and islands scattered here and there', bears a striking resemblance to Sturt's view 'that the continent of Australia was formerly an archipelago of islands'.[59] But the appeal of Sturt's narrative did not arise from any vindication of Hutton. To the end, Sturt remained 'of the opinion that there is more than one sea in the interior of the Australian continent'.[60] To the end, he insisted on the uncertainty of the country.

In this sense, Sturt's journey was a success. For, in the metaphorical world he creates, even the Stony Desert is an intimation of its opposite. It is not a question of persuading the reader of his hypothesis, that the Stony Desert, that 'adamantine sea', was once a real sea: the context of its occurrence is enough, its emergence in the course of a metaphorical journey. And

Sturt was quite conscious of this. As he explains,

> Neither can I, without destroying the interest my narrative may possess, now bring forward the arguments that gradually developed themselves in support of the foregoing hypothesis.[61]

The sea was the current carrying his story forward. The success of Sturt's narrative as the biography of a journey lay in keeping the sea–desert metaphor in play. It lay in keeping alive the difference. It was along the boundary of that difference that Sturt was able to make his way. In deferring the discovery that might destroy the interest of his narrative, Sturt succeeded in producing a pure narrative of exploration. Like Eyre, he defined the explorer as the chief mover of events, as sole centre of interest. Recalling his discovery of Cooper's Creek, Sturt wrote,

> When I sat down beside the waters of the beautiful channel to which Providence in its goodness had been pleased to direct my steps, I felt more than I had ever done in my life, the responsibility of the task I had undertaken.[62]

The biblical allusion was quite in place: the object of Sturt's description was not the promised land, but its promise. And this he successfully conveyed.

At the end of chapter 1 I suggested seeing Cook's voyage, not as an event occurring peripherally along the margin of a static land mass, but as a passage central to the spatial constitution of Australia. In defining their routes as coasts in the making, this was exactly what Sturt and Eyre did.

4

Triangles of Life

Farewell to thy mountains, Australia,
To the high icy peaks and the snow,
The tempests that round me did play there,
To the heat and the hatred below.
Deep, deep in thy rocks, O Australia,
I carved out my sovereign's name;
By the side of the banished but faithful,
I climbed up the steep hill of fame.

Sir Thomas Livingston Mitchell, 'Farewell to Australia', 1852

Sturt and Leichhardt may have been good biographers of the journey, but when it came to *surveying* the country they passed through, their journals were less satisfactory. Equipment failures aside, comparison with journals kept by other expedition members suggests that their estimates of latitude and longitude (where they are given) sometimes seem based on quite inadequate observations. There are discrepancies between the published and unpublished data. Sometimes curious lacunae appear in the journals – days go missing. Another explorer, Giles, candidly admits to losing track of time. Estimates of distance are impressionistic and, in many instances, insufficient angles seem to have been taken to plot the route of the expedition accurately. The accounts of the country passed through may be tolerably reliable, but *where* that country is exactly on the map often remains hard to tell. Grey, exploring the headwaters of the Victoria River in north-western Australia, remarks, of an excursion made by Mr Lushington, that the only detail of his report he doubts is

> that of the distance they went, which I believe to be overrated; having always found the estimates of everyone of the party, as to the daily distance travelled, very erroneous, and sometimes more than doubled. This, indeed, is a mistake well known to be of common occurrence, and very difficult to guard against in a new and wild country.[1]

And Sturt himself concedes that his calculation of distances as he sailed down the Murray was of necessity largely guesswork.

The provisional nature of these explorers' reports has been one reason why their authors have attracted biographers. It is almost as if the personality of the explorer emerges in the difference between the country as it is and the country as the explorer reported it to be. When every allowance has been made for the notorious unreliability of the climate, the fact remains that places Sturt described as barren are now inhabited – and indeed were inhabited even before the discovery of artesian basins. The fact is that Stuart traversed country Sturt found impenetrable; and country Stuart found dismal Giles described in tones of rapture. It becomes easy to conclude that the explorer's reactions were subjective, even essentially imaginative. There is a temptation to make the landscape a reflex of the explorer's mind, even to speculate that in some way what the explorer found was himself rather than anything external. But, as I have already suggested, this kind of treatment rests on dubious assumptions – both about the nature of historical space and about the nature of exploration. The explorer was not on one side with nature on the other. Rather, the two emerged as historical objects through and in terms of each other.

From the perspective of spatial history, the personality of travellers is not something there from the beginning, a quotient of inheritance and environment: it is an identity consciously constructed through travelling. It is in this context we can begin to understand the historical significance of Major Mitchell, Surveyor-General of New South Wales between 1827 and his death in 1855, and during that time the leader of four expeditions (see plates 6 and 7). Very briefly, the historical reputation of Mitchell is somewhat ambiguous. While he is acknowledged as a highly competent surveyor and artist, his personal arrogance and the inflated claims he made for himself as an explorer indicate an all too human weakness hardly compatible with a hero's life. The tendency has been to divide Mitchell into two parts, to judge his professional achievements favourably, his personality unfavourably. As a result, historical geographers have paid his surveys of New South Wales handsome tribute, but the biographers have largely ignored him – for it must be said that, although invaluable as a source of information, the long-awaited biography of Mitchell by William Foster[2] is too much of an admirer's account to address itself critically to the paradox of Mitchell's character and career.

The paradox is there, though, and in my view it results from a historical and biographical tradition that ignores the historical claims of spatial experience. It is partly a consequence of imposing on him a biographical model that takes for granted the formation of personality in early life. Partly, it is based on a notion of geographical knowledge that is both narrow and, in the context of exploration, perhaps quite anachronistic. For Mitchell's personality cannot be dissociated from his spatial experience: he did not just become a surveyor, he made himself one. In the process, he came to recognize that the survey did not simply imitate physical space: it translated it into a symbolic object whose properties were as much historical as geographical. Similarly, to be a surveyor was inevitably to annex oneself to a future history. For Mitchell, biography and history emerged dialectically from the survey.

Mitchell himself had no doubts about the historical significance of the survey, and it was one reason why he had scant respect for the reports of fellow explorers like Sturt and Leichhardt. His criticism can be put succinctly: if sufficient angles and distances could be obtained to fix accurately the relative positions of prominent geographical objects, and if the survey itself could be connected with a base line whose latitude and longitude were accurately known, then, and only then, could the explorer claim to have surveyed, as well as explored, the country. It was on these theoretical grounds that Mitchell disparaged Sturt's voyage down the Murray in 1829. As he wrote in a draft introduction to his own *Three Expeditions*:

> Of the various methods of exploring an unknown region a less satisfactory can scarcely be adopted than that of embarking in a stream . . . the only compensation that can be hoped for is the barren discovery . . . of the actual course of the river itself . . . Without horses . . . no one of those excursions so necessary

for the examination of the country to either side can be made
. . . neither can any knowledge be obtained of hills, rocks,
soils or products . . .[3]

Mitchell, by contrast, was a man with a method. As he had
explained in his little book *Outlines of Surveying*, 'The most
essential operation, in taking a plan, consists in laying down
points representing the true relationship of the most prominent
objects on the face of the earth.'[4] In this definition of 'taking a
plan', 'prominent objects' were not simply *what* is mapped: they
were also the *means* of mapping. They not only provided the
surveyor with worthwhile objects to plot: they also supplied
him with indispensable points of view. The explorer might
proceed like a ship at sea, but the surveyor had to tack between
definite points of reference. Triangulation was essential to the
surveyor's progress. Indeed, progress by any other means was
not, scientifically speaking, possible. This, as Mitchell pointed
out in the same draft introduction (in another passage he later,
and perhaps prudently, deleted), was the argument for proceeding by way of hills rather than rivers. Mitchell's own original
proposal for exploring the junction of the Murray and the
Darling had been based on the supposition of a convenient
east–west range of hills marking the division of the northern
and southern watersheds of Australia. The great advantage of
following this range was that 'such ranges . . . afford the means
of accurate survey . . . commanding extensive views of . . . the
distant country around . . .'.[5] But, Mitchell complains, on
Sturt's advice the colonial administration rejected this plan in
favour of a more circuitous route following the line of rivers.
(The fact that an east–west range turned out not to exist did not,
in Mitchell's view, affect the principle at stake.)

This, in essence, was Major Mitchell's argument for distinguishing his own geographical endeavour from that of other
explorers. And he had good grounds for feeling superior. When
Mitchell arrived in the colony in 1827, and shortly thereafter
replaced Oxley as Surveyor-General, he came armed with
qualifications both as a draughtsman and as a surveyor. One of
Wellington's surveyors in the Peninsular War, he had been
selected in 1814 to stay on in Portugal and Spain to work on

drawings and plans of the principal battlefields. Five years in the field and, somewhat spasmodically, as many more at his drawing board, led in 1841 to his contributing nearly half the material in James Wyld's monumental *Maps and Plans showing the Principal Movements, Battles, and Sieges, in which the British Army was engaged during the War from 1808 to 1814, in the Spanish Peninsula and the South of France.* An earlier outcome of Mitchell's Peninsular experience had been his *Outline of a System of Surveying for Geographical and Military Purposes,* which, published in 1826, had no doubt been influential in his appointment to Sydney.

Between 1827 and 1855 (the year of his death), Mitchell took the opportunity to put his *Outline* into practice, leading no fewer than four expeditions of exploration. If it was the hypothesis of an inland sea that preoccupied Sturt and Eyre, Mitchell's primary ambition, it seems, was to discover a great inland river. His first expedition (plate 6) had been inspired by a bushranger's report of the Kindur, a river supposedly to be found to the north-west. His second and third expeditions (plate 6), in 1835 and 1836, both explored the possibility that the Darling did *not* join Sturt's Murray, but flowed instead westwards and possibly north-westwards into the interior. (It was after concluding that the Darling did enter the Murray that Mitchell, ignoring instructions, struck out from the Murray south-west across what was to become Victoria, traversing the fertile country he decided to christen Australia Felix.) But, if the tally of navigable rivers from the earlier expeditions had been disappointing, the fourth and last expedition made up for it (plate 7). In south-west Queensland in 1846. Mitchell discovered a river which, he claimed, enabled him 'to solve the question as to the interior rivers of Tropical Australia'.[6] Rather confusingly, Mitchell called his north-westerly trending stream the Victoria – the name that Grey had already used for another river on Australia's north-west coast.

Like Cook, Mitchell prided himself on the *quality* of his travelling. Sturt may have pre-empted him in discovering a great river (the Murray); Leichhardt may have pipped him at the post in travelling across northern Queensland to Port Essington in 1844–5 (incidentally casting doubt on Mitchell's claim that the Victoria would flow to the Gulf of Carpentaria). But what did their work amount to? Leichhardt might have been a competent naturalist; but he was no surveyor. Sturt, in Mitchell's view, was bereft of method either as a surveyor or as a scientist. Theirs had been more obviously heroic journeys, with adventures of considerable anecdotal interest, but, since they were unable to say exactly where they had been, their permanent contribution to geography – or, indeed, to the process of colonization – was, in Mitchell's view, minimal. Nor was this all. Mitchell had another quarrel with these self-proclaimed discoverers: whatever their powers of literary description, they were not artists. They could not draw. A draughtsman's skills were as essential to scientific exploring as a facility in trigonometry. How could one follow in the explorer's footsteps, if they had not been reliably measured or accurately depicted?

Perhaps more profoundly, in what sense could such explorers truly claim to be 'first' in the field, if they furnished insufficient data to equip subsequent travellers? In this context, what right had these wanderers to give place names? As Mitchell explained,

> when a traveller takes the trouble to determine the true place of hills or other features, he might perhaps be at liberty to name them also. The covering of a map with names of rivers or hills, crossed or passed, merely in traversing unknown country amounts to little more than saying, that so many hills and rivers were seen there.[7]

Quoting this passage before, I pointed out that Mitchell's own naming practice was hardly dispassionate: it told the story of a journey. But for Mitchell what was at stake was the *quality* of the journey – a quality which Mitchell's own names were designed to proclaim in no uncertain terms.

At the time of his death, Mitchell's Survey Department was under official investigation. Mitchell's inability to get on with successive governors (aggravated by his claim that he derived his instructions directly from the home government), his extended leaves of absence in England and the slowness of his department's progress in producing a trigonometrical survey of the colony, together with what his most recent biographer calls Mitchell's 'independent spirit': these were all factors in Governor Denison's decision to set up a Commission of Inquiry. But, despite (perhaps because of) Denison's transparently political motives, the report of the commissioners did not seriously impugn Mitchell's posthumous reputation. As a surveyor, if not as an administrator, Mitchell's *Map of the Colony of New South Wales* (1834), no less than the roads he had surveyed in the colony, continued to be praised.

Mitchell's skills as an explorer were not in question. Had they been, the testimony of Mitchell's second-in-command on the third expedition ought to have been decisive: Granville Chetwynd Stapylton did not return to Sydney in late 1837 with any great respect for Mitchell as a leader (he had found him overbearing and dictatorial), but his qualities as a surveyor were unquestionable. Stapylton, it appears, had been sceptical at first:

> Sur. Gl. makes capital way across the country, keeps his line wonderfully well and shews a complete knowledge of his subject. I have already got a few hints altho I must confess I at first thought that with my experience little or nothing to learn . . .[8]

On another occasion, Stapylton writes,

> of all men I believe the Sur. Gl. has the most correct idea of geographically laying down & ascertaining to a mathematical nicety all points of importance in a country however extensive provided you give him Mountains of elevation from whence to draw his conclusions.[9]

And one cause of Stapylton's later estrangement from Mitchell was undoubtedly the younger man's growing frustration with a journey that seemed to be endless, and endlessly slow, because of the Surveyor-General's dogged pursuit of trigonometrical accuracy.

This, then, is the surveyor. Now to the paradox of Mitchell's personality. Despite his respect for Mitchell's professional abilities, Stapylton describes him as a man who, when any error occurs, 'will not scruple at a falsehood to declare the officer the sole cause of any inconvenience that may arise therefrom'.[10] And even if this rebuke reflects as much on the egotism of Stapylton as on that of his leader the geographical claims that Mitchell made for his last expedition certainly seem to support Stapylton. For, in September 1846, in south-west Queensland, Mitchell, according to his published journal, made a great discovery:

> a river leading to India; the 'nacimiento de la especeria' or *region where spices grew*: the grand goal, in short, of explorers by sea and land from Columbus downwards.[11]

It was a river

> typical of God's providence, in conveying living waters into a dry parched land, and thus affording access to open and extensive pastoral regions, likely to be soon peopled by civilised inhabitants.[12]

A river whose naming required careful thought:

> It seemed to me, to deserve a great name, being of much importance, as leading from temperate into tropical regions, where water was the essential requisite.[13]

Mitchell named it the 'Victoria', and he described his feelings in epic terms:

> Ulloa's delight at the first view of the Pacific Ocean could not have surpassed mine . . . the river . . . thus and there revealed to me alone, seemed like a reward from Heaven for perseverance, and as a compensation for the many sacrifices I had made.[14]

Mitchell's biographer, Foster, assumes that Ulloa is a mistake for Balboa[15] and, if so, the mistake is a significant one: in confusing the discoverer of the Pacific with the discoverer of the Colorado River, Mitchell was subconsciously revealing his real motive, which was not so much to record the geographical facts as to establish himself at any cost as a great discoverer of rivers.

At any rate, Mitchell's purple prose was, to say the least of it, premature. And, what is even more curious, rather than embark on the exploration of a river he confidently expected to flow to the Gulf of Carpentaria, at this propitious but inconclusive moment, Mitchell turned back, leaving his second-in-command, Kennedy, to complete the exploration of the river. By the time Mitchell had published his glowing account in London, Kennedy had informed the Sydney public that, far from leading to a second Eden or an 'El Dorado', as the Major hoped, the

Victoria wound serpentine through a wilderness. Far from opening a way to India, it dissipated itself in the desert near Cooper's Creek (see plate 9), Sturt's discovery of two years earlier – in fact, Kennedy suspected the two 'creeks' were one and the same: 'I would gladly have laid this creek down as a river, but as it had no current I did not feel myself justified in doing so.'[16] It was a nice irony that Kennedy's report was published as an appendix in Sturt's account of his own unsuccessful attempt on the centre. Even in defeat Sturt had the last laugh, it seems.

Here, then, is the enigma of Mitchell. It is not even as if the river were an isolated blemish on an otherwise untarnished trigonometrical record. Earlier in the same expedition, over-optimism, to put it at its most charitable, had led him to describe, to mark on his map (see plate 12), and even to depict, a lake where no lake exists. According to a modern geologist, Brian Finlayson, an examination of the surface morphology and of the sediments underlying the bed of the 'lake' which, on 7 July 1846, Mitchell discovered and named 'Lake Salvator' 'clearly show that there never was a lake on this site'.[17]

The obvious explanation for these misrepresentations is the one retailed in an Australian school textbook published in the early 1960s: 'In the end,' Mitchell's 'great weakness, his desire for enduring glory as an explorer, ultimately defeated his scientific honesty.'[18] Two impulses were at work in Mitchell's nature and, finally, the worse overwhelmed the better. Here is a theme fit for the stage: an idealist with a tragic flaw, a visionary corrupted by his lust for fame. But, on reflection, does not this interpretation reveal itself as rather stereotyped? Indeed, is to describe Mitchell in this way anything more than a means of fitting him into that hackneyed paradigm of the man of good family dragged down by life in the colony? Stapylton wrote scornfully of Mitchell's 'overweening vanity of character' and his 'fondness of alluding to the intercourse he has had with persons of distinction'.[19] The man of honour thrust out to the further end of the world who, in his efforts to recover his lost self-esteem and social position, sacrifices the very standards he holds so dear: who could fit this colonial paradigm better than Mitchell, a man as unscrupulous in denigrating others as in praising himself, shamelessly ambitious and, where ambition was rewarded, shamelessly obsequious?

Rather than seek to fit Mitchell into this biographical framework, rather than try to extenuate his faults, I want to suggest that Mitchell's geographical fantasies were not embarrassing weaknesses, but were, in fact, essential to his notion of travelling. They were ways of rendering the country habitable – the grander project which distinguished the surveyor from the explorer and which justified Mitchell in taking his historical role so seriously. Indeed, rather than interpret Mitchell's geographical claims in psychological terms, it makes better sense to see them in terms of the distinction he himself insisted on – that between exploration and the survey. This not only has the advantage of accounting better for Mitchell's cantankerous independence of spirit: more importantly, it reveals his significance in Australia's spatial history.

One way of defining the difference between the explorer and the surveyor is to contrast the explorer's desire to constitute space as a track with the surveyor's interest in regionalizing it. If, for the explorer, mountains and rivers were both means of getting on, then, for the surveyor, they functioned primarily as natural boundaries. They were geographical givens which helped the surveyor bound a useful space, a space that was conceptually and trigonometrically consistent. As Mitchell wrote in his *Outlines*:

> A ridge or chain of heights affords also the most favourable line for the boundary of a plan, or for joining two plans together. Mountains divide the sources of rivers, govern the direction of roads, and bound the visible horizon.[20]

Where the explorer saw ranges as roads, the surveyor thought of them as bases. Where the explorer's space was two-dimensional, backwards and forwards, the space of the surveyor was triangular, extending in depth to either side. Clearly, as a matter of fact, Mitchell frequently behaved like an explorer, taking the easiest route: but this did not compromise his attitude towards the route itself – which remained for him invisible, little more than the necessary means of bringing him to fresh pastures, vistas new and regions full of promise. If the narratives of Sturt and Eyre have the melodramatic appeal of serialized stories, then the journals of Mitchell suggest operatic pageants, where scene after scene of exotic incident has the paradoxical effect of making the reader forget exactly where he is.

Certainly, one major drawback of the fatal flaw thesis, with its suggestion of innumerable causes welling up to produce one climactic infamy, is that it overlooks the fact that the discoveries of 1846 were by no means the first that Mitchell had 'invented'. Lake Salvator and the Victoria River were not the geographical dying fall of a disappointed explorer: they resembled the kind of desirable object that Mitchell had been keen to discover from the time of his first expedition in 1828 in search of the fabled river 'Kindur'. Nor was it by any means the first time his language had been found inflated, misleading, infuriatingly vague. Take the experience of the squatters Henry and David Monro, who made two excursions into central and northern Victoria on the basis of the descriptions of Australia Felix in Mitchell's *Third Expedition* and, on both occasions, returned disappointed. After the first trip down the Campaspe had failed to reveal the rich plains recorded by Mitchell, 'David Monro refused to concede Mitchell to be completely wrong.'[21] He persuaded Henry to make a second expedition – this was in 1842, six years after Mitchell's passage – 'to examine the country on the Loddon and Avoca Rivers (see plate 6) on Mitchell's track, of which he [Mitchell] had spoken most enthusiastically'.[22] Paraphrasing Monro's manuscript narrative, J. O. Randell writes,

> They arrived at Mitchell's 'Vale of Avoca' and found the water 'nearly as salt as the sea' . . . Monro felt that, although Mitchell had seen all this country in an extremely favourable season, he was a sufficiently experienced bushman to know this and to have indicated in his writings that it would not invariably present the same bountiful impression . . . Henry and David Monro returned to the station near the Campaspe, disillusioned and certain Major Mitchell had misrepresented the quality of the country.[23]

Or consider the uniformly dismissive remarks of George Augustus Robinson, who visited parts of south-western Victoria in 1840 and 1841 – five years after they had been described by Mitchell:

> This is the hill Mitchell focused his praise on, was given to the sky's [*sic*], and from which he saw and made his sketch of the Mammeloid hills. The hill does not answer his description: the grass which grows between the stones is thin as to afford no feed. The plains over which the Major's Line runs is quite bare . . .[24]

At the same time, Robinson acknowledges that 'the sketch in the Major's book was a faithful delineation'. Again, Robinson reports,

> Major Mitchell makes a sad mistake where he says he saw the sea from Mount Cole – the distance is too great. He must have seen the Lake Corangamite and which he says is an inlet of the sea.[25]

Mitchell was little more reliable in the matter of descriptive names. According to Robinson, most of what Mitchell called 'lakes' were never more than 'lagoons covered with thick reeds and grass'. And of two 'lakes' south of Mount Abrupt at the southern end of the Grampians (see plate 6), he writes,

> These places, called by Mitchell lakes, had no doubt water in them. But even then it must have been so shallow that had he examined them he would have seen the grass. They are now dry . . .[26]

The climax of these derogatory remarks occurs in Robinson's references to Mitchell's much vaunted description of south-western Victoria as Australia Felix, a country like Eden. Referring, in particular, to the plains between the Loddon and the Pyrenees neighbouring on the same 'Vale of Avoca' visited a little while later by the Monros, Robinson writes,

> The banks, or bergs of the river as Mitchell called them, are covered with grass it is true but so very thin as not to hide the ground. The Major's Line was through the sweep of this plain and he describes it in glowing terms, his usual practice – see book. He came to a level plain resembling a park, hence he called it Major Mitchell's park. The banks of the river Lodden,

which was on the E. side, are abrupt but covered with grass. And the river, he said, was north among some hills, probably to water a country of a fine and interesting character. Now this is all fudge. Better the Major had not published such nonsense as it has occasioned an expedition of time and money to numerous emancipists who have gone in search of this country of interesting character. The Major's Eden is another specimen of his puff: excellence not yet located. Eden though it be, the same fate extends to the greater part of his Australia Felix.[27]

So much for 'this Eden' of which Mitchell boasted:

I was the first European to explore its mountains and streams – to behold its scenery – to investigate its geological character, and, by my survey, to develope those natural advantages certain to become, at no distant date, of vast importance to a new people.[28]

What are we to make of this? If we were dealing with one of those unscientific explorers, castigated by Mitchell himself, whose map filled with place names 'amounts to little more than saying, that so many hills and rivers were seen there', then these imaginary features could be attributed to inaccuracies in the survey itself. Perhaps there was a lake, but not where the traveller plotted it on his map. Or perhaps Mitchell was simply deceived by the country. Mitchell traversed the Grampians region during a very wet season; during a very dry season, the same country wears a quite different appearance. Or, if it seems unlikely that Mitchell, the scourge of untrained travellers, was so gullible as to take appearances at face value, perhaps we should attribute these discrepancies not to him but to Robinson. Certainly, there does seem to be some personal animus behind Robinson's criticism. But in spite of this his criticism stands, and can be corroborated. And, even if extenuating arguments can be brought to bear on the third expedition, they hardly apply to the fourth expedition – in the Preface to which Mitchell made a point of asserting,

The new geographical matter is presented to the public with confidence in its accuracy, derived as it is from frequent and careful observations of latitude; trigonometrical surveying with the theodolite, wherever heights were available; and, by actual measurement of the line of route . . .[29]

Rather than dismiss this claim, we should value it for the light it throws on Mitchell's notion of geographical knowledge, the outcome, after all, of the survey. Although Mitchell aims at a geographical knowledge that would fix the country from every direction, he is fully aware that exploration is a necessary preliminary. 'That a country may be mapped, it must be traveled over,' observed Dr Johnson and, evidently approving of the remark, Mitchell copied it into his 1835 notebook. And it is worth noting that at least one cause of Mitchell's conflict with the colonial administration was his advocacy of 'trigonometrical surveying with the theodolite'. Under Governor Brisbane, and therefore up until 1825, the kind of survey favoured in the colony had been the American-style rectilinear grid system. This had the advantage of expediency and speed: provided that he could determine the delimiting longitudes and latitudes of a region, a surveyor could proceed to its rectilinear subdivision without ever setting foot there. In theory, it meant that orderly, taxable settlement could proceed without the delay and expense of government-funded explorations. In practice, it often meant, as later settlers found who purchased selections surveyed in this way, that country which looked uniformly attractive on the map turned out in the field to be anything but uniformly inhabitable.[30]

Mitchell's trigonometrical method, on the other hand, was a features survey: it was a way of getting to know the country, and not simply a geometrical accessory to taxation. The essential function of the travelling survey was not to explore what lay beyond the horizon; nor, of course, did it aim to equalize topographical differences. Its object, rather, was to characterize the country, to 'square' horizons and to group geographical features by way of significant viewpoints. Where the explorer aimed to differentiate geographical objects, the surveyor aimed to arrange them significantly. His aim was to centralize features, to compose them into regions. Where the explorer was always anxious to travel on, the surveyor always had it in mind to stop: against the explorer's high road, the surveyor was an advocate of fertile basins – conceptual places where the imagination might be enticed to settle.

There was actually a working relationship between these

imaginary centres and the scale of the map: for it made little practical sense to produce charts where rivers crawled in and out of the edges. The eye read inwards from the borders. Maps were understood as ways of getting in. More subtly, the map-maker himself was drawn to regions that the map could characterize. Exploring and surveying were, in this sense, two dimensions of a single strategy for possessing the country. The map was an instrument of interrogation, a form of spatial interview which made nature answer the invader's need for information. And it is in the context of this military metaphor that we should, I suggest, understand Mitchell's imaginary rivers and lakes; indeed it is the necessary context for understanding more generally Mitchell's historical significance. For Mitchell, the survey, with its triple artillery of map, sketches and journal, was a strategy for translating space into a conceivable object, an object that the mind could possess long before the lowing herds.

Strategy immediately suggests the idea of military manoeuvres, the picture of a general deploying his troops. As a metaphor of exploration, it was commonplace in Mitchell's day. One contemporary historian, commenting on the fourth expedition, compared Mitchell's achievements with those of Xenophon. Much as military campaigns must inspire admiration,

> amid difficulties and privations as great as ever beset an army engaged in warfare, to prepare the way for the establishment of numerous and important states, is an achievement which falls not below the standard of heroism.[31]

More specifically, in the same book where he had hypothesized a great inland river, the author of *Friend of Australia* had argued that exploring should be carried on exactly as if it *were* a military campaign.

He thought that the chief impediment to the development of Britain's newest and potentially greatest colony was ignorance of the interior. *Friend of Australia* was, among other things, a modest proposal for overcoming that ignorance. Maslen had studied the efforts of Oxley and Sturt and he was firmly of the opinion that, 'As the examination of the interior is impeded for want of navigable rivers, the plan of an expedition must be adapted entirely for marching.'[32] But such an expedition required a generous complement of men. Maslen thought that Sturt might have continued his advance beyond the mouth of the Murray, 'provided he had had enough men with him'. A larger number of men meant, though, that,

> All the members of the expedition should be subject to the articles of war, the same as if it were a detachment or company belonging to one of His Majesty's Regiments of foot, and the commanding officer should be vested with the power of ordering courts-martial, and of inflicting punishments, for the due preservation of discipline and good order among so many.[33]

In all these respects, Maslen closely anticipated Mitchell's own practice as an explorer. Maslen was also insistent that any assault on the interior required setting up a depot. The depot should be located near Mount Granard on the Lachlan (see plate 5) – a position remarkably close to Mitchell's later Fort Bourke – and Maslen recommended enclosing it 'with a slight breastwork and ditch'. Maslen even shared Mitchell's view that any survey be 'undertaken in the wet season'.[34]

The campaign as a metaphor of exploration was very much in the air. It helps explain why Mitchell's cumbersome bullock drays and flocks of sheep, apparently so ill-adapted to long-distance travelling, could find official approval and funding. The expedition was not a dash for the other shore, a sort of guerrilla assault on the Gulf, like Leichhardt's or Stuart's. It was a scientific and cultural invasion, a civilizing process, even an act of liberation, and no doubt one with a particular appeal to those officials in the colony who, like Mitchell or Sir George Gipps, were veterans of the Peninsular War. It is here, if anywhere, that Mitchell's personal history intersects with Australia's spatial history: for in the years leading up to his colonial appointment, it is clear that Mitchell studied to make himself an expert in strategic survey. As a stylist, as an artist, as a map-maker, he worked to translate the language of war into a metaphor of cultural invasion; and, in the process, he made himself a man fit to found and not merely find places.

During the three years (1811–14) he was stationed in Portugal with the 95th Regiment of Foot, Mitchell saw relatively little active service. While he surveyed, the battles based on his maps were fought by his colleagues. It was a matter of bitter regret to Mitchell as a soldier that he had not been at Waterloo – and not only 'as a soldier': Mitchell later claimed it had prejudiced his chances of promotion. The five years that Mitchell spent after the event in meticulously surveying, sketching, painting and finally engraving the battlefields of Wellington's campaign represented, in a sense, the active service Mitchell had not known during the campaign itself. But they also represented something more, of course: they were a strategy for possessing the country permanently – as Wellington himself had never done. It emerges very clearly from Mitchell's notebooks that he was under no illusion about the task before him. His commission was not simply to record, it was to make history. He had to show the campaign to its best advantage. He had to imagine viewpoints that would render the events of battle clear, comprehensible, inspiring.

His assiduousness in cultivating these skills is evident from his notebooks, as well as from the maps and engravings published much later by Wyld. Notebook C21, evidently compiled over a number of years, includes, for example, trigonometrical tables, extracts from a *Traité de perspective linéaire* by L. N. Lespinusse and from Emerson's *Mechanics*. Equally significant are the extensive notes on watercolour technique. In 1815 Mitchell was apparently studying 'Mr Burr's *Method of Drawing Landscapes.*' He also familiarized himself with the methods of Mr Payne, Mr Varley, Mr Nicholson and Mr Gilpin. Gilpin, Mitchell noted, thought that,

> Among all the beauties of nature nothing is so transient as a tree, which is liable to so many accidents. A scene therefore which depends merely on a few trees, is not worth recording.[35]

And, following Gilpin's advice, Mitchell paid particular attention to the picturesque possibilities of sunsets. C26 contains a description of an evening sky 'observed from Mafra over the Atlantic' in January 1819. Finally, eight years after this, when Mitchell was putting the finishing touches to some of his finest

Peninsular landscapes, we find him receiving 'hints from Mr Martin about my view of Ciudad Rodrigo'. Martin had advised Mitchell to put in 'a very faint cloud behind the mountain to relieve it'.[36]

Mitchell was not simply making up for some supposed shortcoming as a soldier. He was discovering how, in a narrative of travelling, history could not be distinguished from geography. How, to preserve the spatiality of events, the chronicler had to invent rhetorical viewpoints. More profoundly still, as he went over the ground his survey had opened up to Wellington, he was struck perhaps by the prehistorical role of the survey, the sense in which the rhetoric of its viewpoints made spatial history possible. In this context, Mitchell's reading during these years is quite as significant as his visual education. Notebook C21, again, which Mitchell described as a 'Book of Useful Notes', contains a transcription of a narrative of the Battle of Wagram, a description of the Siege of Olmitz, translated from Jomini's *Traité sur les grandes opérations militaires*, as well as extracts from French military reconnaissances and communications. An interest in ancient warfare and, more particularly, in the qualities of great leaders is equally obvious. At one time or another, Mitchell read Caesar's *Gallic Wars*, Pliny, Plutarch, Sallust and Seneca. He copied out Livy's account of Philopoemon, impressed by the Achaean's 'unusual astuteness . . . in choosing positions':

> When he was travelling anywhere and had reached a pass difficult to get through, viewing the character of the ground from every angle, when he was travelling alone, he would consider with himself, when he had companions, he would ask them, if the enemy had shown himself at this point, what plan should be adopted . . .[37]

In another notebook, we find Mitchell studying rhetorical tactics. The six parts of a speech, as defined by Cicero, are copied out and below them stylistic hints useful to the writer bent on persuasion. Such a writer (or orator) should, in the exordium or opening of his discourse, affect

> modesty without meanness – deference with a sense of dignity arising from a sense of the justice or the importance of the subject.

In the second part, where the subject and its divisions are laid out, the writer/orator should aim to be

> clear and distinct, probable, concise – names, dates, places. Exhibit character of persons and shew their actions proceed from natural emotions and likely to gain belief – all superfluous circumstances rejected.

Lastly, Mitchell notes that, with regard to arguments, 'invention' is 'the most material and basis of the rest'. And he notes it is the 'common rule to advance . . . to the most forcible, placing the most feeble, though proper to be used, in the middle'.[38]

Given Mitchell's later 'lakes' and 'rivers', which appear at the midpoint of his narratives, this last remark is highly suggestive. And there is one other suggestive literary project from the Peninsular years worth mentioning here. It was in the years he spent in Portugal that Mitchell began his translation of the national epic of Portugal, the account of Vasco da Gama's voyage to India, the *Lusiads*, by the sixteenth-century poet Camões. Just as Mitchell had served with Wellington, Camões had sailed with Vasco da Gama. Like Mitchell surveying the battlefields, Camões, in writing his poem, was, in part, telling his own story. In this respect, both men had fully anticipated the condition of the Australian explorer, who made history twice over, first by his journey and then by his journal.

In short, by the time Mitchell was offered a post as assistant Surveyor-General in New South Wales, he was equipped to survey the country, not only trigonometrically, but as an artist versed in the picturesque and as a writer familiar with figures of speech. He had interested himself in such things strategically and when, prior to sailing, Mitchell sought instructions 'as to the manner of going over a country geologically' from Murchison, had Herschel help him with his astronomy, McCullough give him surveying tips and Leadbetter explain how to skin and stuff birds, he was merely putting the finishing touches to a training that would enable him, not merely to traverse a country, but to know it, the true relation of its geographical objects, as well as its 'rocks, soils or products'.[39]

Mitchell saw the expedition as a rhetorical campaign. The

trigonometrical survey, the sketch and the words of description were instruments of cultural conquest, not scientific observation. Mitchell was a geographical Wellington, or so he liked to think. He reminded readers that the third expedition, for instance, commenced on the anniversary of the taking of Badajoz. Four months later, it was the fall of Salamanca in 1812 that came to mind – and Mitchell commemorated Wellington's success by christening an outcrop west of the Grampians 'Mount Arapiles', after the hill overlooking Salamanca and, as we learn from Mitchell's notebooks, an important 'landmark or reference point' in Mitchell's retrospective survey.[40] Ten years later, in the narrative of the fourth expedition, Mitchell again remembered 22 July as the anniversary of that victorious day thirty-four years earlier.[41] The parallels were intimated in such asides as 'I felt the ardour of my early youth, when I first sought distinction in the crowded camp and battlefield, revive . . .'[42] (at the beginning of volume 1 of *Three Expeditions*) or, again,

> Even war and victory, with all their glory, were far less alluring than the pursuit of researches such as these; the objects of which were to spread the light of civilization over a portion of the globe yet unknown.[43]

It was spelt out in Mitchell's choice of names. At what he would persuade his readers were the victorious culminations of his journeys of exploration, in the Australia Felix of south-west Victoria in 1836, and ten years later in south-west Queensland near the head waters of what Mitchell reported as a great inland river flowing to the Gulf of Carpentaria, the explorer lapsed into Peninsular names.

And these regions of Australia Felix and the Victoria River were constructed in other rhetorical ways. It is no accident, for instance, that the textual, if not geographical 'gateways' to these rich regions received the same name. South of Swan Hill in 1836 it was the view from what he called Mount Hope that persuaded Mitchell to depart from his instructions and, instead of following the Murray to its sources, to explore south-west. Ten years later, the promising country was prefaced by mountains which Mitchell called the Tableland of Hope or

Hope Tableland (see plate 12). These mountains marked the edge of regions, the edge of maps.

It was the explorer *as surveyor* who rivalled the feats of the military commander. On completing the survey of a road in 1830, possibly the Great Southern Road, Mitchell observed in his field book (C42), 'I certainly felt almost as well pleased with . . . the new line of road as a General could after gaining a victory.'[44] If Wellington had brought the restoration of order, Mitchell in a sense could claim to have achieved something more radical, the initiation of order. Introducing the account of his 1846 'Expedition into the interior of tropical Australia', Mitchell claimed,

> In Australia, the great family of civilized man seems still at that early period between history and fable, upon which, even in 'the world as known to the ancients', the Roman poet had to look very far back:

> > Communemque prius ceu lumina solis et auras
> > Cautus humum longo signavit limite mensor[45]

'And the ground which had hitherto been a common possession like the sunlight and the air, the careful surveyor now marked out with long-drawn boundary line' – the implication of this quotation from Ovid, which Mitchell had culled over twenty years earlier when preparing his *Outlines of a System of Surveying*, was clearly that the surveyor was far more than a humble measurer: with his boundaries, he was also a legislator and leader. He ushered men out of the age of myth into an age that, according to Ovid, was characterized by voyages of discovery, by mining and by war. For Mitchell, at least, the connection between the beginnings of enclosure and the beginnings of history appears to have been obvious.

Mitchell, then, did not simply assert a parallel between his own exploits and those of a military commander: he worked out the parallel in detail, 'possessing' a country with names and views quite as effectively as a general deploying his troops. Unlike the explorer who left hardly any trace of where he had been, and whose journey often seemed to leave the country emptier than before, the surveyor was a harbinger of civilization. He saw his task as preparing the path for orderly colonization. He was the means of transforming the dynamic space of travelling into the fixed and passive space of settlement. But he effected this transformation by positing a plausible place rather than by discovering it. He viewed the country he passed through as if with the eyes of the future.

Before there were central places, there were central names or constellations of names forming. Mitchell's naming practice faithfully embodied the strategic character of his invasion. I have mentioned elsewhere his habit of writing over earlier names with his own. This was not just selfishness: it was part of translating the world of the map into an imperial possession. We learn from Stapylton that Mitchell's first name for the Yarrayne (later River Loddon) had been Ilyssus (sic), 'in reference to Queen Dido's plan of forming her new colony as related by Virgil'.[46] Thus the imperial theme was announced before Mitchell 'discovered' Australia Felix. If the decision to retain the aboriginal word, Yarrayne, was a second thought (reflecting perhaps Mitchell's discovery of his true imperium further to the south-west), Mount Arapiles was, apparently, a third one: Stapylton reveals that Mitchell originally replaced 'Mount Broughton' with 'Mount Salamanca' – and, giving the Major's reasons, Stapylton makes it clear that the name change was dictated by imperial, rather than personal pretensions: 'It so happened that the Sur. Gl. ascended it on the anniversary of that Battle . . .'. But Stapylton added,

> Another good hit at the Frenchmen who have been very active with their designations of Capes on the Southern Coast of our Territory.[47]

Stapylton's journal dramatically suggests a more immediate political context for these changes too. At Portland, on the south-western Victorian coast, where, to his surprise, Mitchell found a fishing settlement, he also learnt that a new government had been formed in England. Something of this was intimated to Stapylton when Mitchell returned to camp, and Stapylton writes,

> Most anxious to know who forms the new ministry. Sur. Gl. does not inform me. Hear that Broughton is styled His Lordship the Bishop in Sydney. Quite enough for me to know

that Wellington and his party are the men and that Mr
Goulburn if his health permits it . . . must be one of the
Secretaries of State perhaps for the Colonies . . .[48]

The Stapylton and Goulburn families were connected by
marriage, and Stapylton was quick to see what the change of
government might mean for his own career. But Mitchell was
quicker: he elaborated a system of names that commemorated
Wellington's Peninsular campaign – Arapiles overlooked Salamanca, the scene of one of Wellington's greatest victories – and
he rapidly placed Stapylton's patron on his own map (see plate 6).

And, if this seems strategy of the most self-serving kind, we
should remember that these names were applied within a region
already delineated in imperial terms. Thus, Mitchell explains his
naming of Mount William on the same third expedition in this
way:

> The capes on the coast I was then approaching were chiefly
> distinguished with the names of naval heroes; and as such
> capes were but the subordinate points of the primitive range, I
> ventured to connect this summit with the name of the
> sovereign in whose reign the extensive, valuable and interest-
> ing region below was first explored . . .[49]

In this way, a network of names defined a geographical region
strategically, historically, as a place whose relations made travel
possible and settling imminent. In this way, too, Mitchell
subordinated his own claims on posterity to those of his
geography.

Mitchell's strategic view of surveying extended to the writing
of his journals as well. His journals were not simply dramatic
accounts of journeys; they were not confined, like those of Sturt
and Eyre, to a metaphorically constituted track. They were,
rather, tactical weapons, adding up to a strategy for invasion.
They represented designs on the country to left and right. They
suggested secure depot camps and sources of supplies. In
writing up his journeys, Mitchell's attitude was not one of calm
detachment. Mitchell was not compiling a lexicon of interesting
facts. His journals, like the survey, like his names, were planned
as instruments of persuasion. Their elaborate preparation, their
ornate style and picturesque illustration brought into being a

country that readers could imagine, and therefore inhabit. In this sense Mitchell's reports were blueprints for the movement of people; they provided, not simply the maps, but the rhetorical incentives to travel. They made places where people could settle, could imagine settling.

This is the context of Mitchell's lifelong interest in the *Lusiads*, Camões's epic poem of exploration. Mitchell recognized in Camões's poem a literary model well suited to the expression of his own ambition as a cultural strategist, as one responsible for discovering an uninhabitable country. In Camões's subject matter, his style and method of composition, Mitchell saw a rhetorical strategy that perfectly complemented the spatial strategy of the survey. Camões's poem was distinguished from other epic poems by its theme and by its picturesqueness – the fact that its best verse was descriptive. It suggested to Mitchell the possibility of marrying his skill as a topographical draughtsman and his ability as prose writer in the form of journals that would portray his surveying expeditions as epics of the picturesque.

When Mitchell finally published his translation of the *Lusiads* in 1853, he added a preface that made these connections very clear. Firstly, there was the subject itself. Camões's poem accorded the explorer a cultural significance rivalling, if not surpassing, the ideal of the heroic warrior celebrated by Homer and Virgil. For, in Camões's treatment, Vasco da Gama's voyage signified much more than the discovery of a new country: it represented the spread of civilization, the triumph of Christianity over paganism. For such reasons, Vasco da Gama's voyage formed a subject superior, in Mitchell's view, to 'either the destruction of a city; a navigation in the Mediterranean; a Garden of Eden; or a descent into Hell'.[50] Mitchell writes of the Portuguese epic in terms he might well have applied to his own journals of exploration,

> Here . . . we have celebrated . . . the first progress to trace out, and ascertain the full extent of 'man's only dwelling place', with brilliant descriptions of natural phenomena, gracefully combined with not only all that we believe, but with all that has been created by man's own imagination.[51]

Even the trappings of the epic genre itself, Camões's introduction of the classical pantheon ('all that has been created by man's own imagination') into a poem narrating the progress of Christianity ('all that we believe'), were not without significance to Mitchell. In his opinion,

> The historical comparisons and classical allusions, by which the poet elucidates events, and dignifies his reflections, seem not the least important features in the poem.[52]

And Mitchell was also drawn to Camões's poem by its style and its structure which, in his view, were closely linked. For what distinguished Camões's poetic style was its 'pictorial' quality; and the painterly genius of the poet emerged not only in individual descriptions but in his juxtaposition of pleasingly contrasted episodes. If this was the technique of a great story-teller, it was also the method the artist used to compose the elements of a painting. In short, Mitchell found in Camões an exemplary master of the literary picturesque. In discussing the sixth canto of the *Lusiads*, he writes:

> The effect of contrast is also brought out with the skill of a great painter. The tale of a tournament in England, for instance, is told to beguile the dull tedium of a night-watch on an unknown sea, – a violent storm, and the loud shouts of the boatswain suddenly interrupt the narrative, and the vessels are in the greatest danger – when Venus and Nymphs come to the assistance of the Lusians, and by their influence over Boreas, and the 'fierce south', allay the tempest. The bright planet rises in the east, on the dawning of a serene morning, when the Indian mountains are disclosed at length on the distant horizon.[53]

And Mitchell comments,

> The skill of this arrangement is as remarkable as its beauty – and is alluded to here chiefly because it has not been noticed hitherto by critics. The arrangement is as artistical as poetical – shewing the intimate connexion there is between composition in poetry and painting.[54]

In all these respects, Mitchell modelled his own journals on Camões's epic example. He alluded frequently, for instance, to his own role in ascertaining the full extent of 'man's only dwelling place'. In the journal of his first expedition, he fancies himself as the Moses of white civilization:

> He, who led Israel like a flock, would guide and direct our little party through the Australian wilderness. [55]

He congratulated himself, in his account of the third expedition, that

> We had at length discovered a country ready for the immediate reception of civilised man. [56]

At the climax of the fourth expedition, and on the eve of discovering the Victoria 'river', Mitchell assured his readers that

> Here was an almost boundless extent of the richest surface in a latitude corresponding to that of China, yet still uncultivated and unoccupied by man. A great reserve, provided by nature for the extension of his race where economy, art, and industry might suffice to people it with a peaceful, happy and contented population. [57]

If the parallel with Vasco da Gama's India is implicit here, it becomes explicit when Mitchell greets the Victoria River as

> leading to India; the 'nacimiento de la especeria' or *region where spices grew*: the grand goal, in short, of explorers by sea and land from Columbus downwards. [58]

Mitchell took equal advantage of Camões's poetic theology. Even if he did not import Camões's Olympian *dei ex machina* wholesale, he took over Camões's habit of describing the gods in painterly terms, particularly in his own descriptions of the Aborigines. And, in doing this, his object was not to amuse, but to elucidate events by rendering the parts of his narrative 'clear and distinct', 'to gain belief' for his story through the rhetorical skill of his 'Invention', which, as he had recorded in his notebook, involved the 'proper disposition and arrangement' of materials. [59] He wanted, like Camões, to introduce pleasing contrasts into his work. Perhaps the most dramatic and sustained use of historical and literary allusions to these strategic ends occurs in Mitchell's account of his second expedition (see plate 6).

This expedition to find the junction of the Darling and the Murray turned back partly because of the hostility of the Aborigines, who consequently form a prominent part of Mitchell's narrative. It was in his own interests as well as the interests of the narrative to bring the Aborigines into sharp relief, comparing and contrasting the various nations met with and, in general, amplifying in the reader's mind their unpredictable singularities, discontinuities and contrasts. In this sense, by dramatizing their irregular appearance and habits and then harmonizing them within his masterly narrative Mitchell possessed the Aborigines as he could not possess their country. His strategy is evident, first of all, in his choice of names. Between Fort Bourke, which Mitchell left on 10 June 1835 and returned to on 8 August, and Menindee or Laidley's Ponds, his lowest point on the Darling (see plate 6), the Major identified six distinct 'tribes' of Aborigines: the 'Fort Bourke' tribe (7–10 June and 8 August onwards) at and around Fort Bourke; the 'Puppy' tribe (12 June and 6 August) near the present Dunlop Homestead, north of Mount Glass (Mitchell's Dunlop Range); the 'Occa' tribe (15 June and 2 August), slightly north-east of the present Tilpa; the 'Red' tribe (22 June and 26 July), in the region of Marra; the 'Spitting' tribe (27–29 June and 22 July), downstream from the present Wilcannia; and, finally, 'King Peter and the Icthyophagi', which first joins a previously met 'friendly' tribe on 9 July, and is itself reinforced by a 'newly arrived' tribe on 11 July. It was the hostility of this larger aboriginal force that, Mitchell says, persuaded him to turn back on 12 July.[60]

Mitchell's names do not correspond to genuinely distinctive characteristics or habits. Taken together with his extended descriptions, they represent picturesquely strategic mnemonics, nothing more. Mitchell might refer to the Red tribe, but three weeks before, among the Fort Bourke people, he had already described 'a wild looking young one, covered with red ochre'.[61] It was not only the Puppy tribe but also the Red tribe that was 'quite delighted' with 'a greyhound pup and a tomahawk'.[62] The Spitting tribe[63] and the Icthyophagi shared the peculiar 'fire-throwing' habit.[64] The 'Occa' tribe may have been named for its cupidity,[65] but cupidity was a trait of all the Darling tribes[66] . . . and so on.

Mitchell's descriptions of the Aborigines along the Darling elaborate the picturesque strategy implicit in his names – and, as a result, Mitchell's decision to retreat seems transformed into a drama that culminates, on 11 July, in a struggle apparently with the Devil himself. In Mitchell's description, the Aborigines of the Darling become like characters in a Renaissance masque. Earlier in the piece we have met a member of the Red tribe who was 'such a figure as Neptune or Jupiter are usually represented';[67] a 'monotonous hymn' chanted by the 'priest' of the Spitting tribe has suggested to Mitchell 'the idea of the ancient druids';[68] a dance performed by the same tribe 'seemed a fitter spectacle for Pandemonium, than the light of the bounteous sun' – the 'savages' retired 'like the witches of Macbeth';[69] the branch-burning ritual of the Icthyophagi, Mitchell notes, recalls the Greek Pyrophoroi, who bore torches and laurel branches, and were ambassadors 'when armies were about to engage'.[70] Thus, when, on 11 July, the leader of the hostile Aborigines appears, Mitchell's description of him does not appear exaggerated but is wholly in keeping with the picturesque expectations these earlier episodes have aroused. The major aboriginal actor in the drama is described as a

> very remarkable personage, his features decidedly Jewish, having a thin aquiline nose, and a very piercing eye, as intent on mischief, as it had belonged to Satan himself.[71]

The picturesque style and construction of Mitchell's narrative had the useful effect of diverting attention from the geographical failure of the second expedition. In particular, it enabled Mitchell to leave unelaborated the remarkable claim, slipped in as it were among the other events of 11 July, that, at the very moment the Aborigines were making further progress impossible, he had in fact discovered what he was looking for:

> I became now apprehensive, that the party could not be safely separated under such circumstances, and when I ascertained, as I did just then, that a small stream joined the Darling from the west, and that a range was visible in the same direction beyond it, I discontinued the preparations I had been making for exploring the river further with pack animals, and determined to return. The identity of this river with that which had been

seen to enter the Murray, now admitted of little doubt, and the continuation of the survey to that point, was scarcely an object worthy the peril likely to attend it.[72]

Interestingly, that 'small stream', nowhere else mentioned in the text, is shown on Mitchell's map as flowing from slightly east of north. And what of the 'range'? Since Mitchell has not moved, the mountains must have come to him. The features of the landscape seem to be deployed with the same cavalier panache Mitchell brings to his depiction of the natives. As the instructions of the third expedition made plain, the government did not share Mitchell's view that the location of the Murray–Darling junction was an unimportant 'object', but Mitchell's picturesque veil of dancing savages at least served to disguise his somewhat threadbare geographical achievements.

However, we should not make the mistake of supposing Mitchell's strategic prose style and the method of pleasing contrast he admired in Camões were merely fictional devices designed to conceal his personal deficiencies as an explorer and surveyor. As far as one can tell, and given his short time in the area, Mitchell's anthropological observations were remarkably accurate. When he speaks of the Darling tribes' extensive use of fishing nets, he may well have been referring, in particular, to the Ngemba tribe, whose territory, according to Norman Tindale, extended from Brewarrina, upstream from Fort Bourke, down as far as Dunlop. Again, the first element in 'Calle-warra', which Mitchell thought meant the Darling River, and which he heard just downstream from Fort Bourke, bears a close resemblance to 'Kula', the name of the tribe that lived 'chiefly on the western banks of the Darling from near Bourke to Dunlop'.[73] Tindale himself identifies Mitchell's 'Occa' tribe with the Barkindji, who occupied the Darling downstream from Wilcannia, 'Ba:ka', Mitchell's 'Occa', being their name for their stretch of the river. But this appears to be a mistake, since Mitchell did not encounter this tribe at Wilcannia, but some hundred miles upstream. Perhaps Mitchell's Occa tribe corresponded to the Naualco people, whom Tindale describes as 'perhaps only a northern portion of the Barkindji'.[74] Certainly, though, it was the Barkindji that Mitchell described in King

Peter and the Icthyophagi. This aggressive tribe, further distinguished by having all their teeth intact, occupied the Darling River 'from Wilcannia downstream nearly to the Avoca and extended 20 to 30 miles [30 to 50 kms] on either side of the river'.[75]

Like Camões, Mitchell brings out contrasts 'with the skill of a great painter'. Indeed, for Mitchell, artistic and rhetorical composition were almost interchangeable. A nice illustration of this occurs again in Mitchell's *Second Expedition*. Repulsed by the Aborigines and retreating along the Darling towards his base camp, Mitchell had, as he put it in his rough journal, 'a little more time for the picturesque'. On Sunday 9 August 1835, he found himself camped before a river view where

> everything [had] . . . been combined in the most picturesque beauty under some of Australia's glowing skies.[76]

There follows in the rough journal more than a page of notes, carefully detailing the picturesque elements of the scene.

> the curiously gnarled and twisted branches of an enormous gum tree . . . the man conducting the cattle to water . . . Weatherworn clothes, originally blue, had become of a purple colour, finely contrasting with the warm green of the foliage and harmonising equally well with the purple distance . . .[77]

Such comments suggest nothing so much as instructions to a painter. Perhaps we should not be surprised, then, that not a trace of this poetic description survives in the published journal. There, instead, facing the entry for 9 August, we find an engraving of the scene (plate 10). The literary picturesque has been translated into the pictorial picturesque.

Mitchell did not adapt the picturesque devices of Camões's epic to disguise the facts, but rather to order and articulate them. It was not by discovering novelties but by ordering them, rendering them conceptually and culturally visible, that the great work of colonization went ahead. In a sense, it was the process of surveying itself that constituted the decisive discovery, rather than the fruits of exploration. It was the method of giving objects great and small a place in the world, the picturesque logic of connection and contrast, that ensured they could never be lost again or overlooked.

For, whatever else had been lost by it, the 11 July defeat had won a place for itself in history. It was the culmination of a succession of contrasting scenes that were like the overhanging cliffs, clumps of shadowy trees and diagonal hillsides, which, in a picturesque composition, focus attention on the river and the distant hills. They fed the current of the narrative, they concentrated it on that distant prospect, the decision to retreat. In a way, it became impertinent to ask what might have been beyond the horizon.

All of which brings us back to the Victoria River. Mitchell not only arranged individual scenes and episodes in the manner of Camões's picturesque epic: in his *Journal of an Expedition into the Interior of Tropical Australia in Search of a Route from Sydney to the Gulf of Carpentaria* he actually imitated the *structure* of the *Lusiads*. In disposing and articulating the events that led to the discovery of the Victoria River, Mitchell used the same structural strategy Camões had used in the *Lusiads* to set the scene for da Gama's discovery of India. The salient part of the *Lusiads* is the section that Mitchell himself praised so warmly in the Preface to his translation – canto VI, where the Portuguese, apparently nearing their destination at last, are diverted and almost destroyed by a storm. At the beginning of the canto, Vasco da Gama's ships are, after many trials, 'ploughing/ Straight through the seas of India', and 'their ardent designs seem almost over'. At this moment, though, Bacchus, who represents India and the forces of Islam, once more intervenes in an attempt to thwart the Portuguese forces. He descends to the submarine quarters of Neptune and persuades Neptune to raise a tempest. As a result, back on board ship, Vellosa's courtly tale, which Mitchell so admired, is suddenly and rudely interrupted. The ships are enveloped in a storm so fierce that da Gama is for a moment brought face to face with the 'termination to his hopes and wishes'.

All turns out happily, though. Like Aeneas, da Gama is protected by Venus. Seeing her protégé's plight, Venus quells the storm, harmony is restored and, by the end of canto VI, a new morning appears and with it 'the mountain tops of India'. By stanzas 17 to 22 of canto VII, the Portuguese have before them a land abounding in riches and, most importantly, fed by a mighty river, a land, in short, ripe for colonization:

Now they found themselves at length beside the land,
So much desired by so many and so long,
Enclosed between the great Indian currents, and
The Ganges dwelling terrestrial Heavens among.
Behold! brave people, work now to your hand,
To grasp the palm of victory, so strong.
Now ye are arrived, now before ye such is
The land of India which abounds in riches.[78]

In prose, but rather less prosaically and certainly, but no less deliberately, Mitchell prepared the ground for his own discovery in the same way. By the end of chapter 5 of his fourth expedition, all the auguries suggest that the explorer is within reach of his 'goal'. Mitchell has located a valley which, *merely on account of its surpassing picturesqueness*, seems to intimate geographical victory:

The hills overhanging it surpassed any I had ever seen in picturesque outline. Some resembled gothic cathedrals in ruins; others forts; other masses were perforated, and being mixed and contrasted with the flowing outlines of evergreen woods, and having a fine stream in the foreground, gave a charming appearance to the whole country. It was a discovery worthy of the toils of a pilgrimage. Those beautiful recesses of unpeopled earth could no longer remain unknown. The better to mark them out on my map I gave to the valley the name of Salvator Rosa. ('His soul naturally delighted in scenes of savage magnificence and ruined grandeur; his spirit loved to stray in lonely glens, and gaze on mouldering castles,' Allan Cunningham (the Poet) [Mitchell's footnote].) The rocks stood out sharply and sublimely from the thick woods just as John Martin's fertile imagination would dash them out in his beautiful sepia landscapes. I never saw anything in nature come so near these creations of genius and imagination.[79]

The effect of contrast Mitchell notes here recalls his earlier evocation of the picturesque Darling. And, had Mitchell worked up his impressions of the Darling and decided to publish them, they would probably have acquired the ornateness of this passage, complete with its thickets of footnotes and artistic allusions. As it is, this passage is not only picturesque in

1 E. Phillips Fox, *Landing of Captain Cook at Botany Bay, 1770*
oil on canvas, 1902

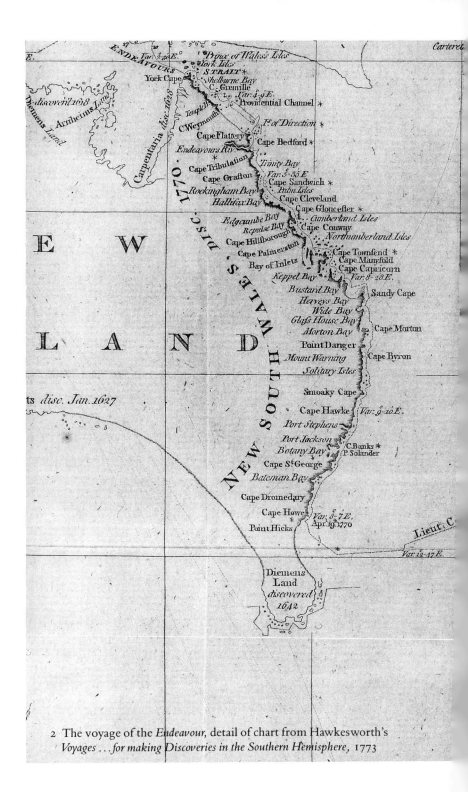

Var: 2 30 E.

ENDEAVOURS

Prince of Wales Isles

York Isles

STRAIT

York Cape

Shelburne Bay

C. Grenville

Var: 4 9 E.

Diemens Land

discover'd 1618

Arnheims Land

Temple B.

Carpentaria disc. 1628

Providential Channel

I.ˢ of Direction

C. Weymouth

Cape Flattery

Cape Bedford

Endeavours Riv.

Cape Tribulation

Trinity Bay

Var: 5 35 E.

Cape Grafton

Cape Sandwich

Rockingham Bay

Palm Isles

Hallifax Bay

Cape Cleveland

Cape Gloucester

Edgcumbe Bay

Cumberland Isles

Repulse Bay

Cape Conway

Cape Hillsborough

Northumberland Isles

Cape Palmerston

Cape Townsend

Cape Manyfold

Bay of Inlets

Cape Capricorn

Keppel Bay

Var: 8 28 E.

Bustard Bay

Sandy Cape

Herveys Bay

Wide Bay

Glass House Bay

Morton Bay

Cape Morton

Point Danger

Cape Byron

Mount Warning

Solitary Isles

ts disc. Jan. 1627

Smoaky Cape

Cape Hawke

Var: 9 10 E.

Port Stephens

Port Jackson

C. Banks

Botany Bay

P. Solander

Cape Sᵗ George

Bateman Bay

Cape Dromedary

Cape Howe

Var: 8 7 E.

Apr. 19 1770

Point Hicks

Lieut. C

Var: 12 17 E.

Diemens
Land
discovered
1642

DISC. 1770

NEW SOUTH WALES

N E W   L A N D

2 The voyage of the *Endeavour*, detail of chart from Hawkesworth's
Voyages ... for making Discoveries in the Southern Hemisphere, 1773

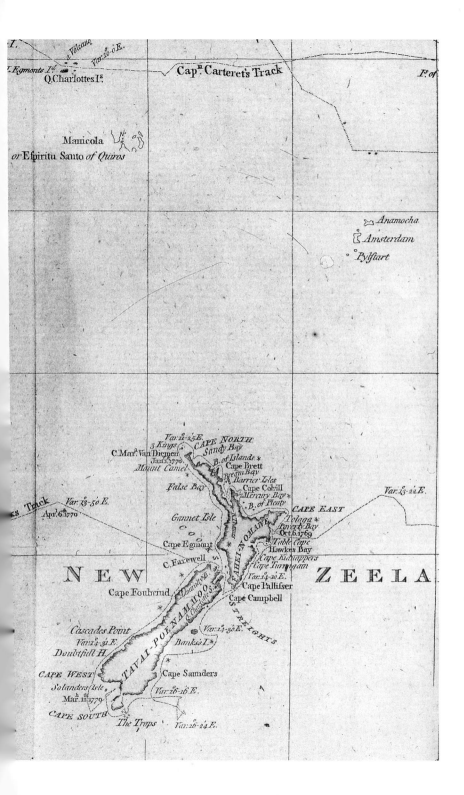

_L._

L. Egmonts I.ᵈ _a Volcano,_ _Var: 10. 0 E._
Q. Charlottes Iˢ.

Capⁿ Carteret's Track

F. of

Manicola
or Eʃpiritu Santo of Quiros

~◁ _Anamocha_
₹ _Amsterdam_
° _Pylʃtart_

Var: 14-25 E. CAPE NORTH
3 Kings _Sandy Bay_
C. Marⁱ Van Diemen _B. of Islands_ *
Jan: 3. 1770. _Cape Brett_
Mount Camel _B. of Islands_
Barrier Isles
False Bay _Cape Cohill_
Mercury Bay *
B. of Plenty

ss Track _Var: 13-50 E._ CAPE EAST
Apr: 6. 1770 _Tolaga_ *
Poverty Bay
Gannet Isle _Oct. 6. 1769_
Table Cape
Cape Egmont _Hawkes Bay_
C. Farewell _Cape Kidnappers_
Cape Turnagan
Var: 14-20 E.
Var: 13-22 E.

Cape Foulwind _Cape Pallisser_
Cape Campbell

Cascades Point
Var: 14-31 E. _Var: 14-30 E._
Doubtfull H. _Banks's I._ *

CAPE WEST
Solanders Isle _Cape Saunders_
Mar: 11. 1770 _Var: 16-16 E._

CAPE SOUTH
The Traps _Var: 16-24 E._

N E W Z E E L A

TAVAI-POENAMMOO
Charlotte's B.
S T R E I G H T S
EAHEI-N'OMAWE

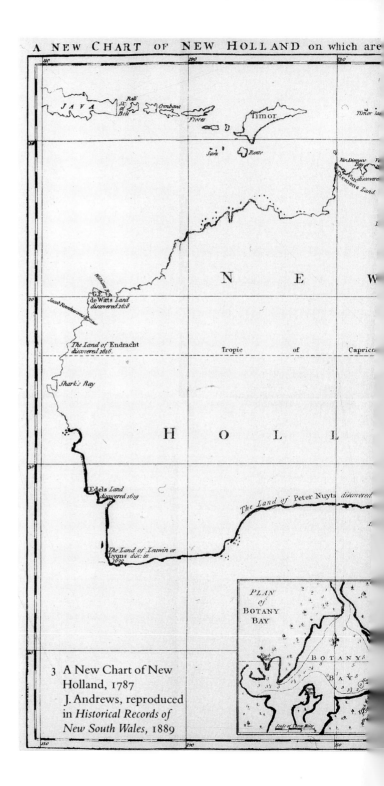

3 A New Chart of New
Holland, 1787
J. Andrews, reproduced
in *Historical Records of
New South Wales*, 1889

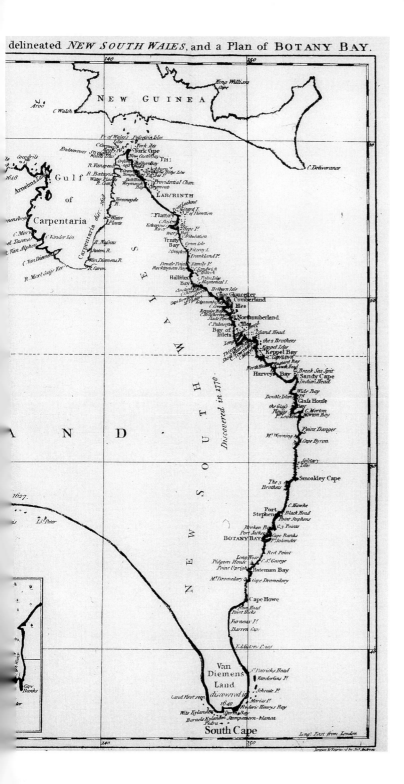

delineated *NEW SOUTH WALES*, and a Plan of BOTANY BAY.

King William Cape

NEW GUINEA

C. Walsh

Aroo

C. Deliverance

Prince of Wales's Islands

York Cape
York Isles

New Caledonia

Providential Chan.

Gulf

of

Carpentaria

LABYRINTH

Cocodrils

R. Batavia

R. Nassau

R. Coen

R. Maet Suijs Ker

Van Diemen R.

Endeavour Str.

Flattery

Trinity Bay

Double Point

Hallifax Bay

Cape Gloucester

Cumberland Isles

Northumberland

Bay of Inlets

Island Head

the 2 Brothers

Keppel Isles

Keppel Bay

Bustard Bay

Break Sea Spit

Harvey's Bay

Sandy Cape

Indian Head

Wide Bay

Glass House Bay

the Glass House

C. Morton

Morton Bay

Point Lookout

Point Danger

Mt Warning

Cape Byron

Discovered in 1770

Solitary Isles

Smoakley Cape

The 3 Brothers

C. Hawke

Port Stephens

Black Head

Point Stephens

Broken Bay

C. 3 Points

Port Jackson

BOTANY BAY

Cape Banks

Pt Solander

Red Point

Long Nose

Pidgeon House

C. St George

Point Upright

Bateman Bay

Mt Dromedary

Cape Dromedary

Cape Howe

Ram Head

Point Hicks

Furneaux Pt

Barren Cape

1627

Ls Peter

Van Diemens Land

discovered in 1642

St Patricks Head

Maria's Pt

Frederic Henry's Bay

Wit Eylanden

Boreels Eylanden

Pedra

South Cape

Longe East from London

Cape Banks

Drawn & Engraved by Jno. Andrews

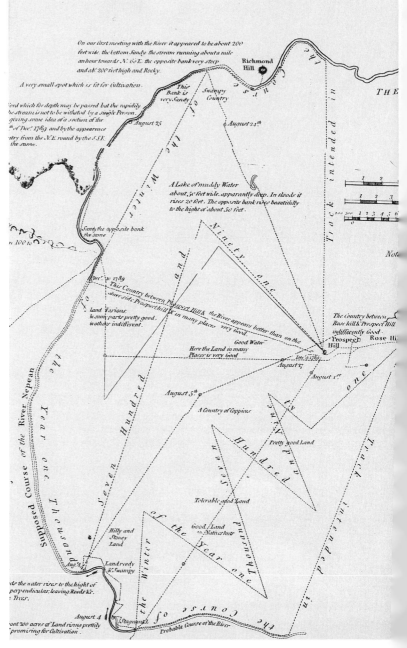

4 A Map of New South Wales (detail), 1792
W. Dawes in Hunter's *A Historical Journal*

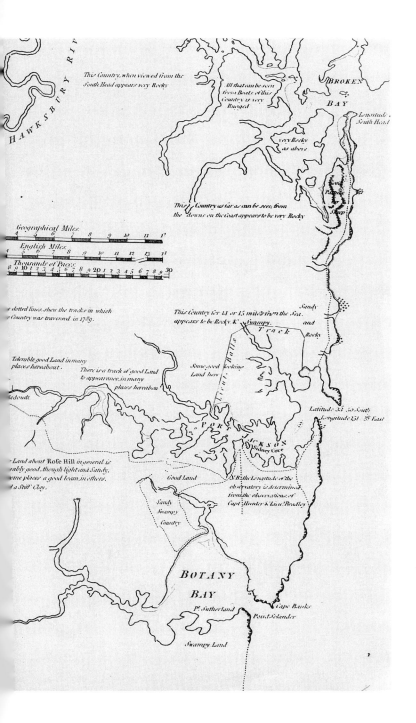

HAWKSBURY RIV

This Country, when viewed from the
South Head appears very Rocky

All that can be seen
from Boats of this
Country is very
Rugged

*BROKEN
BAY*

Longitude
South Head

very Rocky
as above

This Country as far as can be seen, from
the downs on the Coast appears to be very Rocky

Sandy

Geographical Miles.
4   5   6   7   8   9   10   11   12

English Miles.
4   5   6   7   8   9   10   11   12   13   14

Thousands of Paces.
8 9 10 1 2 3 4 5 6 7 8 9 20 1 2 3 4 5 6 7 8 9 30

e dotted lines shew the tracks in which
e Country was traversed in 1789.

This Country for 14 or 15 miles from the Sea
appears to be Rocky & Swampy.   and

Track

Rocky

Tolerable good Land in many
places hereabout.

There is a track of good Land
to appearance, in many
places hereabou

Some good looking
Land here

Latitude 33. 50 South.
Longitude 151. 28 East

Redoubt

PORT   JACKSON
Sidney Cove

e Land about Rose Hill in general is
rably good, though light and Sandy,
me places, a good loam, in others
a Stiff Clay.

Good Land

NB. the Longitude of the
observatory is determined
from the observations of
Capt Hunter & Lieut Bradley

Sandy
Swampy
Country

BOTANY

BAY

Pt. Sutherland
Point Solander

Cape Banks

Swampy Land

5 Map of Australia, 1827
from T. J. Maslen's *Friend of Australia*

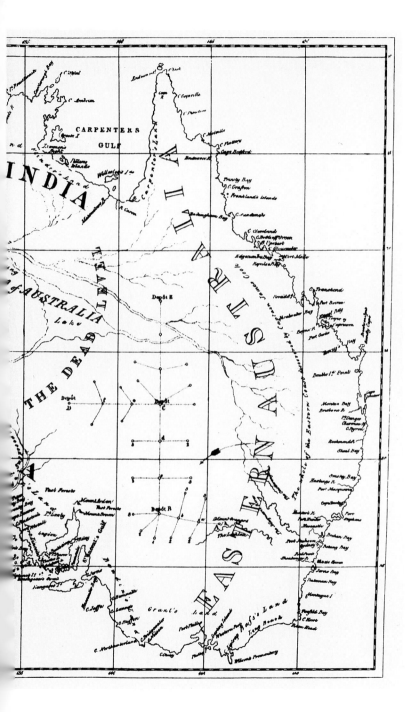

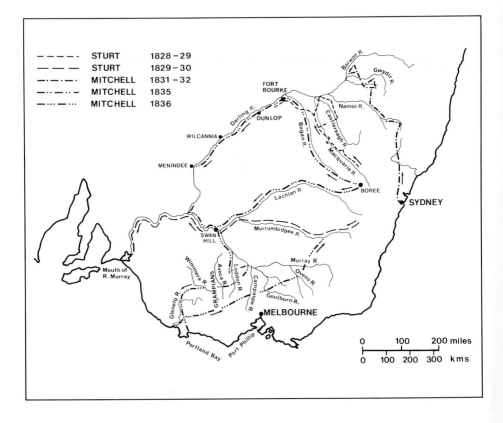

STURT   1828 – 29
STURT   1829 – 30
MITCHELL   1831 – 32
MITCHELL   1835
MITCHELL   1836

Barwon R.

Gwydir R.

FORT
BOURKE

Namoi R.

Darling R.

DUNLOP

Bogan R.

Castlereagh R.

WILCANNIA

Macquarie R.

MENINDEE

BOREE

Lachlan R.

SYDNEY

SWAN
HILL

Murrumbidgee R.

Murray R.

Mouth of
R. Murray

Winnmera R.

Avoca R.

Loddon R.

Ovens R.

GRAMPIANS

Campaspe R.

Goulburn R.

Glenelg R.

MELBOURNE

Portland Bay

Port Phillip

0   100   200 miles

0   100   200   300   km s

6 Inland Exploration I

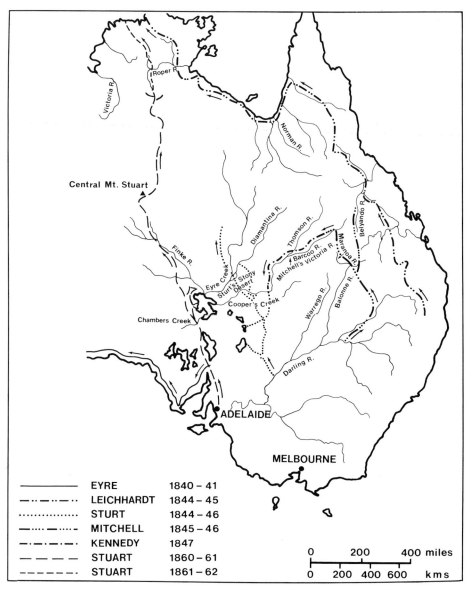

———————	EYRE	1840 – 41
—··—··—··	LEICHHARDT	1844 – 45
··············	STURT	1844 – 46
—·——·——·	MITCHELL	1845 – 46
—·—·—·—·	KENNEDY	1847
— — — —	STUART	1860 – 61
– – – – –	STUART	1861 – 62

7 Inland Exploration II

G. Gore, del.

Last View of the Plain

8 "Last View of the Plains of Promise," engraving from
Stokes's *Discoveries in Australia,* 1846

f Promise, Albert River.

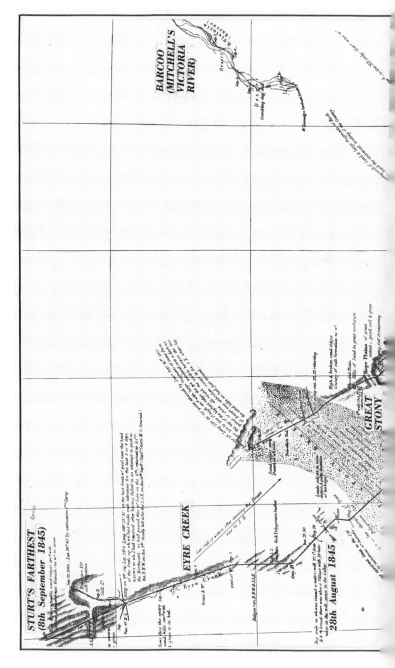

9 Sturt's Farthest, detail of map from Sturt's *Narrative of an Expedition into Central Australia*, 1849

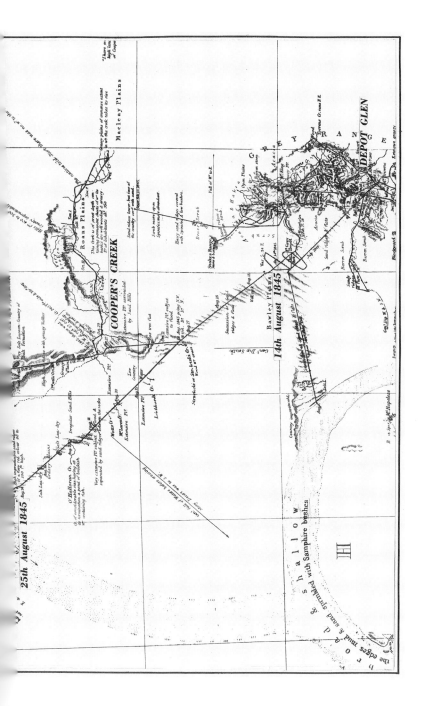

10 "A View on the Darling," engraving
from Mitchell's *Three Expeditions into the Interior of
Eastern Australia,* 1839

itself: like the Darling notes, it serves as instructions to a painter. Printed shortly after Mitchell's purple prose is a view of Martin's Range, complete with a recumbent shepherd – no doubt lost in the contemplation of nature's gothic castles. It is this engraving with its lake in the foreground (in fact Lake Salvator) which Finlayson presumably refers to in his article as evidence of Mitchell's perfidy.[80]

Mitchell named a neighbouring river after Claude and the plateau region associated with these artists

> after such individuals of our own race as had been most distinguished in the advancement of science and the pursuit of human knowledge.[81]

With a nice sense of mingling the visible with the invisible – a quality he admired in Camões – Mitchell commemorated two geologists, John Playfair and James Hutton, and the pagan god who came closest to being an appropriate patron of their discipline: Pluto. At this culturally auspicious juncture, though, Mitchell comes across another stream, the Belyando (see plate 7), and the larger part of chapter 6 is an account of Mitchell's journey down this misleading channel. Instead of trending north-west, as Mitchell hopes, the Belyando continues obstinately east of north until Mitchell is eventually forced to admit that the river he has been following is none other than the Suttor of Leichhardt. Mitchell does not exactly blame Leichhardt, but he does intimate that his detour has been unnecessarily extended by Leichhardt's self-interest and incompetence as a surveyor.

In consequence, Mitchell is forced to retrace his steps to the Claude and to underline the point that *this* is the picturesque focus of his expedition. It occurred to him, he writes,

> that the scenery of the Mantuan bard, which this painter has so finely illustrated with pastoral subjects, deserved a congenial name; and that this country might, therefore, be distinguished by that of the Mantuan Downs and Plains.[82]

By the close of chapter 6, his fruitless wanderings behind him, Mitchell is once more back on course. He has just witnessed a 'gorgeous sunset . . . to the westward of the beautifully broken rocky woody range beyond Lake Salvator'.[83] He is in sight of Mount Pluto, on whose other side, in the next chapter, the

Victoria River awaits him. It is hardly an accident, then, that just at this point Mitchell depicts the Salvator River and the picturesque backdrop of the Martin's Range for a second time (plate 11) and, again, the river looks ambiguously like a lake. By this structural ploy, Mitchell not only recalls the reader to his first discovery of this place of picturesque promise seventy pages and almost two months earlier, he also brackets off his recent excursion along the Belyando, characterizing it as a misleading anabranch, a distraction from the expedition's swelling theme. Accordingly, on 15 September 1846, early in chapter 7, Mitchell comes upon the view that makes him compare himself with Ulloa:

> From that rock, the scene was so extensive as to leave no room for doubt as to the course of the river, which, thus and there revealed to me alone, seemed like a reward direct from Heaven for perseverance, and as a compensation for the many sacrifices I had made, in order to solve the question as to the interior rivers of Tropical Australia.[84]

The following day he reports:

> The 'gorgeous curtains of the East' over grandly formed clouds harmonised well with my sentiments on awaking, again to trace, as if I had been the earliest man, the various features of these fine regions of earth.[85]

Mitchell, it appears, adopted the model of the *Lusiads* tactically, as part of his strategy as a surveyor for bringing into being a habitable country. It is interesting that, despite his comprehensive rhetorical attack on the country, Mitchell was also able to write in his journal that, from his short examination, the Victoria River

> consisted of firm clay, and contained deep hollows, and the beds of long reaches, then, however, all dry.[86]

In other words, Mitchell could vouch for the geographical accuracy of his narrative. But geographical accuracy was only part of his brief. Far more important was the discovery of a country fit to be settled. And, in this context, what mattered was that Mitchell's discovery *looked like* a river: it bore a picturesque resemblance to the reality and therefore it was surely reasonable to conclude, as Mitchell did, that the remains of mussel shells were

> testimony that water was seldom so scarce in this river, flowing as it did through the finest and most extensive pastoral region I had ever seen.[87]

The same applies in the case of Mitchell's disappearing lake, Lake Salvator. It was not a wilful fiction – Mitchell had little to gain by inventing so insignificant a feature: it belonged, rather, to a picturesque discourse designed to open up the country. It was one element in a picturesque strategy for persuading the Australian public there was a place there they could make their own. The difference between Mitchell's account of Lake Salvator and his picturesque engraving of it as a lake is therefore crucial for, much as he vaunted its picturesque promise, Mitchell also noted in his journal for 7 July that 'We . . . heard the current of water amongst the reeds.'[88] More spectacularly, on returning to this lake two months later, Mitchell observed 'The surrounding grass, and also the reed in the lake, had been very extensively burnt along our former tracks.'[89] As Finlayson notes

> An audible current of water and extensively burnt reeds suggest conditions that would not usually be expected in a lake.[90]

And, indeed, Mitchell's scattered remarks, fulfilling his promise to present the 'new geographical matter' accurately, do suggest the kind of 'braided stream' Finlayson found characteristic of this area. Finlayson's mistake, though, is to assume that Mitchell's illustration of Lake Salvator is simply a gloss on the verbal description – and this despite the fact that, as Finlayson himself admits,

> The picture is geometrically inaccurate. The vantage point from which he has apparently sketched Martin's Range does not exist and the high banks of the lake shown in the foreground are also fictitious.[91]

The fact is that neither Mitchell's view of Martin's Range nor Mitchell's engraving of the River Salvator (plate 11) is a naive representation of the geographical matter contained in the text:

both are advertisements, enticing the prospective settler to an imaginable country. Their position in the text is quite as important as their imaginary (and imaginative) point of view. They no more represent Mitchell's experience than Mitchell's elaborate set pieces of Peninsular battlefields describe Wellington's viewpoint. For the purpose of evoking the place, it was enough that the depression in question looked like a lake, could be named and possessed in that form.

Besides, by way of a coda to Mitchell's epic theme, it is worth remembering that he was not alone in using the term 'lake' to describe *likely* lakes. In 1839, with much the same strategic motive, Eyre had named a considerably less propitious stretch of saltbush 'Lake Torrens'.[92] Mitchell was not the only one to treat exploration picturesquely or to approach expeditions like military campaigns. When Mitchell named the Ilyssus on his third expedition, Stapylton did not find the classical allusion inflated or inappropriate. On the contrary, he observed:

> Very appropriate when taken in reference to Queen Dido's plan of forming her new colony as related by Virgil and prospectively as relative to the probability of this region being also shortly colonised.[93]

Again, it was not Mitchell, but Stapylton, who found in the Vale of Avoca (which the Monro brothers found barren beyond belief)

> everything available and at hand for the future inhabitants of this portion of New Holland.[94]

It was Stapylton, not Mitchell, who greeted the native report of a river larger than the Murray in the following glowing terms:

> Thus at last we have accomplished the glorious summit of all our hopes.[95]

In short, the character of exploration as a rhetorically consistent gesture, a strategic previsioning of occupation, is not to be construed as a personal idiosyncrasy of Mitchell's. He simply maintained a culturally coherent view of his spatial – and hence historical – responsibilities.

But what of the settlers who attempted to follow in Mitchell's footsteps? True or false, Mitchell's descriptions opened up the country. His surveys were sufficiently accurate for overlanders to follow – and, as I show in chapter 8, in persuading them to go that way, Mitchell's picturesque prose was at least as significant as his maps. And when the wanderers found the promised land? Well, they were at least 'there' and could hardly retreat. If occupation was the goal, Mitchell's strategy had worked. He had conquered. And he had conquered precisely because he had not kept to the 'barren facts', but instead had invented a country for others to live in. Of Lake Salvator Finlayson reports:

> So compelling has been the myth that Mitchell started that it has been accepted unquestioningly by all who have subsequently been associated with the area.[96]

But did Mitchell dupe them? Were they the unwitting victims of a cruel geographical joke? Could it not be that the settlers *wanted* to believe in Mitchell's country? Without his myth there would have been no pretext for setting out, nowhere to settle. Without his lake, there would have been nothing to explain why they had chosen so barren a stretch of country or why they had failed. From the point of view of colonization Mitchell's imaginary country was more real than any empirical one. It had, after all, provided a legend from which history could flow.

5

Debatable Land

Home, after all, is home the world over . . .

John Lort Stokes, *Discoveries in Australia*, 1846

I love to loaf along the fence . . .

Barcroft Boake, 'On the Boundary,' in
Where the Dead Men Lie and other poems, 1897

East of Melbourne and north of Westernport Bay, there is an area that early maps showing aboriginal tribal divisions describe as 'Debatable Land'. It was land that no one laid claim to, or it was land whose ownership was disputed. Either way, it was land that had not been settled. Whether the Aborigines saw it in this light is extremely doubtful: the phrase 'Debatable Land' refers not so much to aboriginal beliefs, as to certain assumptions of their white interrogators. Implicit in the question, to whom does this land belong, are territorial notions possibly incomprehensible to those questioned. To debate the ownership of land is to think of the land in question as a region, a geographical object that can be treated in isolation, as a legal or economic unit. Again, to suppose that aboriginal inability to give clear answers about the area raises questions for debate implies that what is at stake is a boundary of some kind. It is but one step from 'debatable land' to the border dispute. In fact, the real boundary implied by the phrase may be the one separating two quite distinct notions of cultural space.

But the descriptive phrase 'Debatable Land' has another significance. It reminds us that the process of settlement was not a laconic replacement of one culture by another, a mechanical imposition of superior technology, a simple, physical 'taming' of the land, but, on the contrary, a process of teaching the country to speak. One facet of this process involved asking the Aborigines their names for the country – and it may well be that the relative failure of Whites in Australia to incorporate aboriginal concepts into their language is one reason why

English here continues to float, as it were, off the ground and why, despite its ability to name isolated objects, its poetic power to evoke the living space remains patchy. Particularly in the absence of a bilingual nomenclature, the would-be settler was more than ever obliged to settle the country rhetorically, rather than etymologically: he had, more than ever, to conjure up the object of his desire and, through the act of articulating it, to bring it into being.

According to family tradition, when the first of the Austins took up his selection near Geelong, this exchange occurred between him and his wife:

> I am going to make a township of that paddock running down to the river. What name shall I give it? Mrs Austin at once said, 'Call it Chilwell, after my old home.'[1]

A gloss on this passage which points out that Chilwell is a village in Derbyshire, so named on account of its springs, may have etymological curiosity but wholly misses the anecdote's spatial significance. The Austins were bringing into being a place by announcing their intention to do so: from that time on, whether it mushroomed foundations and roofs or remained a paddock, Chilwell was a point of reference; it had become an intentional object; a place had been linguistically settled. And the result was not silence but, one imagines, a growing babble of speech, building plans, family jokes, legal disputes, over-drafts and endless disagreements about curtain material. By naming that paddock, the Austins settled their own history, mapping out a family future.

In naming Chilwell, the Austins behaved as Sturt did when he named Mount Misery: in both cases, names preceded places. The spatial effect was to render what lay 'yonder' central, to transform a former boundary into a communicable space; 'there' became 'here' and an exchange of opinions could occur. This process of 'settling' the country can be expressed in grammatical terms: to name a space, to turn it into a negotiable place, was like constructing a sentence. But the sentence was not of the form 'I cut down a tree' or 'I push back the frontier'. It was not, that is to say, a sentence consisting of a subject, a verb and an object. Rather it took the form of a subject and predicate:

'The tree is there', 'That house is where I live'. The predicate or describing phrase evokes a new state of mind; it refers to a new 'place' where meanings, associations can accrue. Where the transitive verb of the subject–object sentence implies the exclusion of one thing by another ('I' replaces the tree, the frontier), the predicate is inclusive: much more can be said about the 'house' or the 'tree', and the result will be to enrich, rather than to suppress, their meaning.

This distinction relates also to the difference between an imperial history and a spatial history. For the former tends to regard historical statements as transitive, as verbal glosses on physical actions; but the latter, by contrast, interprets statements as indicative of states of mind, as symbolic representations of intention. In the context of settlement, the assumption of a transitive relationship between subject and object (between the settler and the land he settles) results inevitably in the myth of the pioneer, a man who recklessly hacks down every vestige of the wilderness and then, amid his fertile plains, falls, historically speaking, silent. At the very least, spatial history's stress on intention dismantles the myth of the mindlessly destructive newcomer. And, by drawing attention to the linguistic character of the settling process, it also shows why, after all, there was a limit to his destructiveness.

To understand the settling process we need to bear in mind that, contrary to the imperial paradigm of colonization, in which settlement follows on smoothly from discovery and exploration, the settlers inhabited the new country strategically. They were themselves discoverers and explorers. Rather than think of the process as a one-way road coming to a full stop outside a cottage door wreathed with roses, we should think of settlement much more as a stop along the road. The relationship between travelling and settling was not causal, but dialectical: roads might lead to houses, but houses were human mountains, depot camps foddering departure. The process of settlement, like the process of travelling, depended on a continuing tension between mobility and stasis: neither made sense except in terms of the other. For how could one find Mitchell's habitable dreams except by travelling? And what were houses if not places for dreaming, for bringing one's journal up to date and describing one's adventures along the road?

The explorer did not yield in the second act of the great drama of colonization to the pioneer: they were, in reality, more often than not, one and the same person. Take the pioneer squatter Thomas Learmonth. As an explorer, he had set out from Port Phillip (Melbourne), making his way north-west of Ballarat as far as the Mount Beckwith Ranges in search of good grazing. His initial impressions had been unfavourable, as he indicated in his first place name:

> ... being in great distress from want of water, we passed a most uncomfortable night under the highest point of them, which we called Mount Misery – a foolish name, which it has unfortunately continued to bear ever since.[2]

In the event, Learmonth found this country highly suited to his pastoral purposes. Not unnaturally, he came to regret his too hasty reaction. As he later explained in his letter to the Victorian Governor, La Trobe, Mount Misery

> is one of the most conspicuous peaks in the country . . . it is seen as a landmark perhaps further than any other single elevation in the colony, being the culminating point from which rivers flowing into the basin of the Murray on the one side, and into the sea to the westward of Cape Otway on the other, take their rise. I cannot but regret therefore, that it should continue to bear a foolish name, that originated in a foolish moment.[3]

Were he in a position to rename it, Learmonth concludes, he would suggest calling it after Governor La Trobe himself. La Trobe, he explains,

> assumed the reins of government when Port Phillip was the weakest of the British possessions . . . [He] is now about to leave it the fairest colony annexed to the British crown.[4]

There is, Learmonth implies, a parallel between the geographical position of Mount Misery and the strategic position achieved by La Trobe.

Learmonth's criticism of his own first impressions strongly recalls Mitchell's criticism of explorers. And Learmonth shares with Mitchell a surveyor's sense of the country as a strategic challenge. His regionalization of the country around Mount Misery is reminiscent of Mitchell's unified viewing and naming of Victoria's Western District under the imperial aegis of Mount William. And his magnification of Mount Misery recalls Mitchell's own extravagant claims for the view from Mount Cole. Indeed, Mount Cole is easily visible from Learmonth's Mount Misery and it may be that Learmonth was influenced in his description by Mitchell's journal.

When such explorers settled down, they did not lose their taste for travelling. Learmonth had no doubt read Mitchell. Other prosperous squatters roved further afield. John Cotton, another settler in Victoria's south-west, looked forward, as I mentioned earlier, to reading about Mitchell's discoveries. And, while here his interest was strictly utilitarian, the same letter to his brother also asked him to procure, among other books, 'Smith's Journal in South Africa', 'Darwin's Journal', and 'Rambles by Rivers'. Cotton shared with another squatter, E. M. Curr, an admiration for perhaps the pre-eminent travel writer of the day, Chateaubriand. It is highly likely that, like Curr, Cotton possessed on his companionable shelves Mitchell's narrative of Australia Felix, and perhaps the journals of Sturt and Eyre.[5]

It was not so much that explorers wrote for settlers. Rather they provided symbolic blueprints for settlement, and would-be travellers, looking for habitable country, read them according-ly. They read them as they read the country, with a definite end in mind. And, just as Tench defined his own place against Cook, so the settlers, men like the Monro brothers, interpreted what they read contextually, looking at the words from where they stood themselves. But the close relationship between settler and explorer, the sense in which 'settling' and 'exploring' simply refer to two aspects of a single epistemological mode, to do with the getting of spatial knowledge, is brought out most clearly in the fact that both adopt the journal as their obvious literary medium. This was not merely a matter of convenience, but reflected the peculiar circumstances in which they wrote – and indeed the conditions in which writing itself was possible. To put it at its simplest, the traveller who kept a journal did not write as he rode: he took advantage of stopping places to bring his record up to date. As the overlander Thomas Walker explained:

> I could write a great deal more to you than I do, but I have little convenience or time for the purpose. I can only do so at night when the others are asleep. I shall just describe to you my present situation; I am sitting on my mattrass in our tent . . . my paper is on my knees, the candle on my hat, in my left hand I hold my ink-stand . . .[6]

This is a good example of a subject-and-predicate description. For, although Walker says he will 'just' describe his 'present situation', the predicate of spatial details is, in fact, what brings his present situation fully into being. But his journal entry is also about the conditions in which writing is possible. This entry describes the material conditions of its own production. It reminds us that even the journal of travelling depends on moments of stasis: successive entries may symbolize the progress of the road, but they do not imitate the horse's motion.

The fact that journals described the places of the journey, rather than any external 'natural' place, explains why they flourished on board ship – and why perhaps the greatest bulk of primary material relating to Australia's early spatial history is probably contained in relatively obscure and unpretentious journals kept during the 'voyage out'. Ships were houses on the move. They had something of the convenience of home with the advantage of enforced leisure. They enabled one to write the letters one would never have written otherwise. Despite the salt spray, the heaving deck, the stench and the poor rations, they offered marginally superior conditions in which to record one's experience than a campsite in the bush. It was not that life on board ship was more 'interesting', that there was more incident to record: quite the contrary, it was the very monotony of sea travel that made it a pre-eminent site of journal writing. For what the emigrants wrote about was the experience of travelling and nowhere was that experience brought home to them more clearly than in an environment devoid of external distractions.

It is this self-referential character of the journals that most historians overlook. Bernard Smith, for instance, in his invaluable book, *European Vision and the South Pacific*, quotes the following passage from Bacon's essay 'Of Travaile'. Bacon, the first of the modern empiricists, claims to find it

> a strange Thing, that in Sea voyages, where there is nothing to be seene, but Sky and Sea, Men should make Diaries; but in *Land-Travaile*, wherin so much is to be observed, for the most part, they omit it.[7]

Ignoring the paradox Bacon is drawing attention to, Smith comments,

> Such an observation . . . serves well to illustrate the connection already existing in Elizabethan times between sea voyaging and empirical observation.[8]

Smith's conclusion may be generally true, but it does not follow from Bacon's remark. The fact is that diaries and journals were not kept solely for empirical purposes. Even the most laconic of official journals was a record of travelling first and foremost, and not a catalogue of remarkable incidents. And, when a sea passenger undertook to keep a journal, it was the absence of incident as much as anything else that forced his hand.

Take, for example, this extract, selected almost at random, from an emigrant journal of the early 1840s:

> Our days now pass away in so monotonous a manner, not even a new bird or fish breaking the dull routine of time, & the difficulty of finding employment for such a party as mine is so great, that I can hardly make out a few notes, without repetition of same uninteresting trifles.[9]

This is but one step away from the squatter reported by Robinson, who gave up his diary because it was 'ditto, ditto, . . . ditto'.[10] But the difference is perhaps more striking than the similarity. For this passage with its amplification of absence, its syntactical progress making up for the lack of any perceptible change, is, among other things, a kind of commentary on the historical tradition that supposes only external events and novelties worthy of record. It shows us that, even in the absence of such stimuli, it is possible to speak and write; that, in fact, the true dialogue the writer conducts is not with external reality, but with language itself. What he explores is the resources of meaning implicit in the mere repetition of conventional phrases. And this is not a solipsistic exercise shutting out the world: on the contrary, it faithfully records the existential condition of its own appearance as a diary entry. It is only that what this emigrant's words refer to is not an event, but a spatial occasion, a moment on the journey when the journey became an object of consciousness.

The essential journeying recorded by both the traveller and the letter writer at home was *intentional* in character. The motive of the writer was always, in some sense, to project himself where his writing was addressed. It was not simply that by naming and describing a place the travel writer brought distant things near: he also put himself where his thoughts were. The place he described was one he intended to inhabit. It was where his mind was oriented. In this sense, when the traveller wrote up his journal, when, that is, he detailed where he had already been, his thoughts were always ahead as well as behind. His 'here' implied a 'there' towards which he trended. His 'here' was a place for writing; his 'there' a place to write about. This was as true of the settler who was settled as it was of the traveller. It is from the fastness of her home in the Gippsland forest that the poet Nellie Clerk writes,

> And then (could I fly from the forest,
> O'er its dark barriers rise . . .),
> Far out on the limitless ocean,
> I would feast my long-prisoned eyes . . .[11]

But the longing to be somewhere else is predicated on the fact of being where she is – and, as I suggest in a later chapter, the true subject of this poem is not nostalgia or escape but the rhetorical reinforcement of 'home', a place always made precious by thoughts of elsewhere.

If the journal of travelling was testimony to a series of temporary shelters where writing could occur, then the journal of settling down recorded the emergence of places from which new travelling, imaginative as well as physical, could begin. The essential function the journal served in both situations, whether of settling down or moving on, was that of naming. It was the act of language that brought a living space into being and rendered it habitable, a place that could be communicated, a place where communication could occur. In passing, it is interesting to note that James Mill, a utilitarian philosopher prepared to entertain a policy of rational colonization on the basis of an aggregate gain in human happiness, fully anticipated the argument advanced here. According to Mill, experiences impress upon the mind ideas, not only of themselves, but of their order. It is to record their order, whether in time or space, that the mind employs the 'artifice of Predication'. Mill offers this example of predication marking the order of place:

> The house is on the hill; a lawn is in front; a stable is on the left hand; a garden is on the right; a wood is behind.[12]

Thus, Mill says, is the house more comprehensively named, and the reader 'can trace the sensations, the order of them, and the mode of the marking'.[13]

Mill bases his argument that language names not only objects but the relations between them on the psychological principle of association. According to Mill, the very construction of sentences illustrates the process of association. Grammatical relationships express mental relationships, 'the order in which sensations and ideas follow one another in a train'.[14] And, as we have seen, this argument can be extended to the journal itself as a literary genre; the journal is a naming of space in the order of its appearance. At the same time, though, as pointed out in chapter 2, the principle of association presupposes a profounder (and active) principle, that of differentiation. While naming allows associations to congregate, in the first instance it serves to *dissociate* this from that. In spatial terms, the important thing is not that 'Chilwell' resembled Chilwell – for it clearly did not – but that it created a new region. In this sense, what was named was not so much an area, a spatial extension, but the boundary conditions differentiating such a place.

This is a point illustrated by the distinctively Australian nuance given to the word 'plain' or 'plains'. Connoting both flatness and openness, it was the latter characteristic that was emphasized in the Australian use of the term. As Michael Williams reports in his book *The Making of the South Australian Landscape*,

Many place names exist today with the element 'plains' in the name, at places which are not particularly level. Their origin lies in the openness of the locality compared with the surrounding dense scrub.[15]

Similar considerations determined names like Pine Plains in the Victorian Mallee (see plate 18). In fact, levelness was an almost incidental quality in defining the attractiveness of the Australian plain. A correspondent to the *Pastoral Times*, writing in 1866 of the country between Deniliquin and Hay, reported that the landscape was

> amazingly level, it is often beautifully diversified with graceful clumps of trees, terminating in wavy points.[16]

The appeal of such country lay in its openness. But it was not an unlimited, horizon-wide openness. Describing his reaction to 'plains' near the Liverpool Ranges, William Henry Breton wrote that,

> Although the effect of the first view, when upon the Plains, was striking . . . the eye becomes fatigued with so extensive a view, bounded only by the level horizon, and the fancy can but imagine a continuance of a similar series of flats.[17]

The attraction of extension lay in the contrast it made with their surroundings. As the late nineteenth-century author of *Bush Life in Tasmania*, John Fenton, wrote,

> It is easy to imagine how gratified a man must feel who has been out exploring for days through dense scrubs when he comes suddenly upon a beautiful undulating expanse of country quite clear of the everlasting forest that intercepts his progress in every direction. Dooley's Plains stand up prominently on rising ground, with a gently undulating surface . . .[18]

Such openings permitted physical activity; they could even perhaps be associated with certain forms of mobile pleasure:

> The plain upon which I had entered was covered all over with wombats, feeding vigorously like a flock of sheep. There were at least a hundred of those curious animals . . . I started off at a canter, thinking to give them a chase and have a little sport; but they only stared with innocent curiosity . . .[19]

But, first and foremost, these open regions marked a threshold of mental activity, a place where the act of association could occur. As Fenton implies, they enabled the traveller to get his bearings. Precisely because they were *not* an environment as clear as the scrub was dense, were not equally infinite, but rather a place of limited extent, they acted as a distinct point of reference. A distinct idea could be formed of them. And, consequently, by a process of association through contrast, they also enabled the traveller to grasp that apparently undifferentiated zone, the forest.

The essential appeal of plains lay in their visibility, and this was a corollary of their boundedness and even of the picturesque arrangement of objects within them. They were an aid to the inland navigator because they furnished him with an artificial horizon, a coastline and archipelagoes of islands to steer by. Breton, an earlier travel writer in New South Wales, illustrates these Australian connotations when he writes of the Bathurst Plains:

> The plains or downs (they undulate considerably) are twelve miles in length, about five in width, and contain 30,000 or 35,000 acres destitute of timber, and surrounded by open forest.[20]

Breton notes that the inland plains are variegated, rather than uniform:

> I had received quite a false impression of these regions, having been led to suppose from various accounts, they constituted one boundless flat, unbroken by hills, denuded of trees, and completely covered with such high grass, as to be almost impassable . . .[21]

In consequence, he was agreeably surprised: 'This is clearly a wrong description of them.' As he discovered:

> They may rather be likened to a lake, interspersed with islands, clothed with wood.[22]

Breton's remark, testifying to the travelling emphasis on boundedness, rather than flatness or openness, illustrates the existential necessity the newcomer felt to differentiate, to delimit and name in order to possess. The stress on openness was, in this context, premature. To find boundless extents attractive, the newcomer needed a bounded place of his own. The pleasure of open horizons was best appreciated from a veranda. In the first place, though, their enclosure was essential. Thus bounded plains permitted a greater mobility but, more fundamentally, their limited extent gave the newcomer a heightened sense of stability. Replacing the endlessly receding natural boundary of the horizon, a limit that was invisible and intangible and that could never bear more than one name, the extensive enclosure the name 'plain' implied was visible, finite, fixed and possessable. In consequence, the traveller could locate himself in a landscape. He could possess the view merely by looking. Curiosity could be assuaged without exploring. Enclosure extended his grasp.

The significance of these sensations for the spatial history of settlement is amply brought out by E. M. Curr. In his *Recollections of Squatting in Victoria,* he recalls how his decision to move from the relatively settled region of Wolf's Crag on the Campaspe River, in the Victorian Divide north of Melbourne, to a new run, 'Tongala', at the junction of the Murray and the Goulburn, was resisted by his shepherds. Only one day out from Wolf's Crag, they were all for turning back. The reason they gave was the 'wildness' of the bush:

> They not only objurgated it as 'wild', but I overheard one of them appealing to his neighbour as to whether the water in the creek, which they were drinking at the time, was not 'the wildest water that ever was'.[23]

Why did they find the country 'wild', Curr asked himself, and he answered:

> I was unable to guess what it was which was affecting my men disagreeably about the camp, and in what the uncongenial 'wildness' consisted – and, indeed, why wildness should be thought objectionable . . . On my men, all of them old hands, unoccupied country had a depressing effect, their ideas being that we should all be killed by the Blacks.[24]

But, as the sequel proves, the imaginary threat from the 'Blacks' was merely symptomatic of a profounder spatial nausea, a sense of being out of bounds, of being invisible to themselves, though visible (and a prey) to others: in short, a sense of placelessness. By contrast, when Curr's party at length clears that placeless zone: 'emerging from the scrubby country on to the beautiful plains of Colbinabbin and Coragorag', Curr recalls that it

> tended to raise the spirits of the party and allay their discontent, which arose entirely from fear; in fact, I heard some of them declare the plains to be less 'wild' than the scrub, and more homely . . .[25]

In short, according to Curr's account, the essential sensation evoked by the plains was a sense of homeliness. The plains Curr crosses could be visibly possessed. They were, writes Curr, 'undulating and sparsely timbered' and he reports that,

> On the eastern side of the plain, fifteen or twenty miles away, I could just make out a faint line of smoke, rising, no doubt, from a native encampment on the edge of the forest.[26]

The plains are perhaps even less free of 'Blacks' than the forest, but they nevertheless induce in the travellers a sense of security, a feeling that they can be inhabited. And, if we ask what quality of the plains communicates this sensation, the answer is their edge, that smoking boundary which informs Curr and his men exactly where they stand. The smoke is a hieroglyph emblemizing now, not the threat of annihilation but the nearness of settlement. It is, accordingly, where Curr decides to locate his new station, where, shortly after, is heard 'the crash of the trees falling on the edge of the little plain'.[27]

Such boundary zones transformed space into place, making roads rebound and turn into enclosures. When, forty years later, the first pioneer at Hall's Gap in the Grampians sited *his* hut on the edge of a plain, a photograph (plate 13) captured him standing proudly amid ring-barked gums: as if to give the lie to the myth of the pioneer's destructiveness, a gum tree appears to grow out of his chimney, a visual pun testifying to the metaphorical nature of boundaries and the places they create.

Curr's narrative throws light on the historical significance of the word 'plains'. It also illuminates another word with a characteristically Australian meaning: 'bush'. From early on in the post-1788 period, 'bush' came to replace 'bushes' as a description of the country which lay beyond the bounds of settlement. We may speculate that the contraction of bushes into one collective bush had much to do with the rhetorical establishment of the open place of settlement. As the boundary between one and the other grew clearer, as the distinction between settled and unsettled areas, lawful and lawless zones, hardened, so the beyond of nature was seen to close ranks. To call what lay out there 'the bush', was to urge colonists to a comparable sense of unity and common destiny. Out there was also 'outback', that is to say, amongst other things, culturally invisible. To invoke another Australian colloquialism, what was 'beyond the black stump' belonged to the realm of cultural darkness. Physically, the 'black stump' had been charred by fire; the country beyond was occupied by the 'Blacks': but, culturally, their darkness was the absence of enlightenment.

Curr's journey brings us then in sight of the settler's thoughts, his intention to mark out and build a home for himself. But here, on the threshold, as it were, of a sedentary history emerging, we encounter a difficulty. The very journals which have been so informative in describing the journey peter out. There is no end of settler diaries detailing the journey out. They have been equally informative about their ports of arrival, generations of settler writers recording their first impressions of the new country. Nor, even, do we run into any difficulties *once* the newcomers have settled down: letters, diaries and journals, both published and unpublished, abound detailing the established settler's business affairs, social life, even his passing reflections. But the intermediate period, when the settler is actually settling, this, it seems, is beyond description.

Relatively few contemporary records exist of that transitional moment where the home came into being. Where records of the first days of settling can be found, they are invariably written after the event. In general, even the most scrupulous diarist and letter writer who, before arrival, notes every incident of life aboard ship and, after settling, records every day's weather, every head of stock bought and sold, seems to neglect his diary during that period of transition from traveller to settler. His silence may only last a few weeks or months. Or it may be a matter of years, even decades, before those first days are written up. But the records become *contemporary* accounts again only at some time after the act of settling.

The act of settling itself is sometimes recollected, but it is not described as an immediately present event. Why should this be? Why should the letters and diaries evoking the first days always be written well after the primary act of settling down? Why at the time are the settler-writers silent about the environment they are making? The answer usually given is that the pioneer chroniclers were simply too busy. One Sarah Midgley, for instance, gave up her diary for three years after reaching Victoria because, according to her editor,

> With so much work to be done and living under such primitive conditions, Sarah must have found it impossible to continue writing her diary . . .[28]

Only some years after, when Sarah had again taken up her diary, did she describe the first days of settling. Yet it appears the passage of time had done nothing to dim her impression of the original aspect of the place:

> seven years have transpired since we came to what was then a desolate spot surrounded with dense scrub, stringy bark and gum trees with an occasional Blackwood interspersed and not a single house within a mile, where all was solitary and still except the singing or screeching of the different birds.[29]

At first sight, one could hardly ask for a clearer evocation of the sensation of home-making in a strange country. Certainly this is how historians have tended to read such passages: as empirical accounts no different from what would have been written at the time, had there been time. In the absence of contemporary accounts, surely they can substitute perfectly well. At any rate, nothing crucial has been lost. But the very clarity of a description like this is a product of *hindsight*. The associative principles on which the intelligibility of Midgley's recollection depends were precisely what the location and inhabitation of a house rendered possible. Only by differentiating the 'desolate spot' was it possible to name it predicatively, in relation to the scrub, the absence of houses, the birds. And, even then, in evoking that first impression, her prose is hardly descriptive. It is, rather, a rhetorical strategy for conjuring up what is strictly indescribable. What is defined is largely by what was *not* there, the absence of relations. In this context, the connotation of 'desolate', its idea of a once inhabited place abandoned, is peculiarly accurate. For, in order to inhabit that 'spot', to imagine it as it was, Midgley has to strip it of the human associations that have since accrued to it.

If the process of making a place for oneself was as much a process of bringing symbolic boundaries into being through language as it was a question of wielding the axe, then the absence of written accounts is explicable. It was not only a dwelling place which had to be built, but a language of place as well. This does not mean we cannot expect to find accounts of settling. But it does mean that the literary evidence for settling will not be naively descriptive or expository. Rather than search for 'scientific' accounts in the colonial literature, we need to acknowledge those documents which evoke the act of settling metaphorically, obliquely. For how, except by rhetorical means, can a place be described before there is a place to write?

The Land of the Lyrebird, published for the Committee of the South Gippsland Pioneers' Association in 1920, is one of the most remarkable compilations of settler records. Originally mooted in 1914, it represented an initiative to collect together in a permanent and coherent form the pioneers' recollections of the early days of settling in Gippsland's rain forests in south-eastern Victoria. The result was much more than anecdotal reminiscences: fully-fledged essays, often of great stylistic sophistication and confidence, suggest the guiding hand of a gifted editor, perhaps that of T. J. Coverdale, one of the Association's most active committee members. And it was perhaps the same editor who inspired the attempt which some of the contributing pioneers made to evoke the 'early days'.

Whatever the editorial influence, there was no question of Gippsland pioneer W. W. Johnstone describing the first day dispassionately. To recollect it was clearly a rhetorical skill, like telling a good story:

Through the dense forest we pushed our way – we walked

along logs, climbed over logs, crept under logs, crawled through logs, but seldom or never did our feet touch the ground. At last we came to an enormous log. Oh, what a monster! and father said that on the other side of that big log lay our selection. Anxious to view the promised land, we made a desperate effort and clambered on top and had a look, and what do you think we saw? – why, more logs. Were we downhearted? No! Eager for the fray, we slid down off the log and swung our axes, and in less than an hour our first tree came crashing down, and the battle had begun.[30]

Not the least interesting feature of Johnstone's account is that it concludes here. It ends at exactly the point where settling might be thought to begin. Yet the writer evidently feels he *has* described the sensation of settling – and so he has obliquely, metaphorically, by creating an imaginary place in advance of the physical one.

How Johnstone has created that place is by inventing a rhetorical boundary. This, of course, is the significance of Johnstone's 'big log'. On his own admission, it made no physical difference: there were as many logs on the other side of it as there were on this side. But it did make a rhetorical difference. Without it, the writer could not have communicated his sense of arrival. The significance of the log is not that it marks a division in the spatial uniformity, but that it creates a difference that can be talked about. It establishes a place of exclamation, of dialogue. It enables the writer to bring the 'other' into focus, if only as an enemy, as a perceivable space. It is a plain that is bounded, whose edge can be conceptualized, and hence expressed.

In order to communicate the act of settling Johnstone has to invent a boundary. He has as it were to delineate a potentially nameable zone. Only having denominated the space in this way, can he pass to other things: only once the site of his future history has been cleared in this way, can the physical progress of clearing be taken for granted. In other words, it is clear from Johnstone's description that enclosure is essential, not only to the act of settling, but also to the *description* of settling. Where there is no enclosure, no desolate spot, it must be invented: the settler's first axe cut could not be substituted for this prior rhetorical incision.

Johnstone's log is a symbolic boundary marking the difference between culture and nature. In that difference, in the space it creates for talking and doing, the settler's history begins. And, having begun in this way, the settler's fundamental intention to create a home, a place where he belongs, proceeds to articulate itself through the proliferation of symbolic boundaries. The account of settlement given by another Gippsland pioneer in *The Land of the Lyrebird,* Mrs W. J. Williams, eloquently illustrates this process. Mrs Williams recalls her first log house:

> As the logs did not touch each other in places, there was plenty of ventilation, and the wind blew our hair about in the night.[31]

She 'cut strips of tree ferns and put them in the crevices on the inside'; then, she and her husband started 'to line the rooms with hessian and paper'. Next they turned their attention to furniture:

> He made a sofa, cot, and two easy chairs, which, when covered with cretonne, looked very nice and comfortable.[32]

Comparable developments occurred outside: 'When we had a little enclosure, we thought we ought to have a pig.'[33] This reminds Mrs Williams of a story, about the time she prepared a feast for a fishing expedition, and the pig escaped, got into the kitchen and gobbled up all her precious cooking. And, now she thinks of it, the pig episode reminds her of another episode involving a goanna or iguana. The 'large iguana came close to the door' and, frightened as she was, she chased it off:

> Sure it would come back again . . . I got the gun which had been left loaded, and rested it on the fence.[34]

The iguana did come back and it was shot.

Mrs Williams's account of the early days of settling is articulated in terms of the multiplication of symbolic boundaries. Firstly the interior of the house is sharply differentiated from the exterior: crevices are filled in, walls lined, furniture covered to make it look 'nice and comfortable'. Comparable enclosure occurs outside: not only is the garden enclosed with a fence; a pig is enclosed as well. But, in expressing her spatial history, it is not so much the enclosed spaces themselves as the boundaries that enable her to speak, that give her something to say. It is around wall, doorstep, gate and fence that Mrs Williams's recollections cluster. Her anecdotes concern border disputes. In this sense the boundaries are spatial metaphors through which her own history can be told. So, she does not speak directly of the wildness, but of the wind blowing her hair about during the night. She evokes her feelings metaphorically, by way of an illegitimate transgression. Similarly, the furniture is a focus of memory because it symbolizes a boundary dispute satisfactorily resolved. It is 'nice and comfortable' *as furniture*, because the wildness of the wood has been tamed, covered in cretonne. Equally, the pig makes its mark in Mrs Williams's early pioneer history, not by being enclosed, but by breaking out. The same applies to the unfortunate goanna. And, while the goanna is despatched beyond the fence and the pig merely replaced in its pen, both incidents serve to articulate the real story Mrs Williams has to tell – about how a symbolic zone was established, sufficiently differentiated to bear a history; about how, in short, she made a home.

In this light we can explain the 'paradox' that, while the pioneers destroyed the bush, there is every evidence that they admired and drew sustenance from it. It is Mrs Williams who not only recalls the death of the goanna but rhapsodizes:

> Oh! how I used to love the early mornings, when everything awoke to new life; I would just stand and feast on the beauty and glory of it all. There was a spot down by the river which I never tired of looking at, the tall tree ferns, with their graceful spreading plumes, the bracken, swordgrass, clematis, maidenhair fern, and Xmas trees, etc., made a picture impossible for me to describe.[35]

As this passage indicates, before nature could be loved, it had to be conceptualized as a place, a visible object. A distance had to be created between the observer and what she saw. To embrace the inexhaustible wealth of nature, she needed to be able to stand back from it, pointing it out from a secure vantage point.

In other words, Mrs Williams's favourable view of that 'spot down by the river' depended on the fence that separated it from her garden. For it was the fence that established it as a spot clearly outside the clearing. By the same token, though, the *pleasure* she takes in the view depends on trespassing there: for home does not shut out the forest, but transforms it into a cultural object, a wildness into a kind of beauty.

Much of this argument is illustrated in an early photograph depicting a farm on Bass River, on the fringes of Gippsland (plate 14). In Kruger's photograph, it is not simply that the settler's cottage stands out from the surrounding scrub, separate and enclosed within its picket fence, but the fact that we glimpse home from the wildness of the bush, parting, as it were, the fronds of the tree ferns, that assures its appeal. The attraction of the settler's cottage is expressed in the form of a visual transgression. At the same time, though, the figure on the veranda looks back, we imagine, towards the photographer: the fern tree gully viewpoint itself becomes desirable, not least as a place where one can look back, reflecting on one's history. Inside the fence, it is the wildness beyond that becomes the place of writing, the site of reverie.

The settler's proliferating boundaries are not simply physical necessities: they serve the symbolic function of making a place that speaks, a place with a history. The straight lines of the roof edge, the palisade of the picket fence or a row of tree stumps carefully saved from the general wreckage communicate the settler's presence. Equally important, though, they enable the settler *to speak and write about himself.* His house and garden are where he can tell stories about travelling – even stories about animals that went where they were not allowed. For, even when he settles down, the stories he tells are stories of motion in one form or another. And one can say that the chief symbolic function of boundaries is, among other things, to incorporate the sensation of travelling into a static or near-static existence. Fences translate physical travel into literary travel, journeys into journals. Drama clusters about fences. Narratives begin and end there. They are places of exchange where the sensation of journeying is vicariously relived.

In this sense, the act of enclosure permeates the entire

structure of settler society: for without the invention of differences, communication would have been impossible. The social behaviour associated with such eloquent differences is well illustrated by that characteristic nineteenth-century institution, the picnic. The Australian picnic was an occasion which expressed its social function spatially. Its appeal rested on the recognition that to transgress spatial boundaries licensed the breakdown of social, and even personal, barriers. Men and women came back from picnics having enjoyed illegitimate intimacies which only society could legalize. In this sense, picnics resembled the old custom of beating the bounds for, by celebrating the distinction between settled and unsettled places, they served to reinforce social cohesiveness.

Picnics were pre-eminent 'places' for tales as well as trysting. Take, for instance, this account of a Christmas outing on the Murray, written by a young member of the Beveridge family. Brother Harry has gone on ahead in the small buggy:

> [Mother] said she would have so much tidying up to do after we had left, that she was staying at home to do it. So we just waved her goodbye as she stood at the porch watching us move off.
>
> We soon overtook Harry as we trotted off quickly, and we didn't stop until we reached the two big boundary posts. There, father pulled up and waited until we saw Harry coming up over the rise and round the bend. We waited for him so he could see which turn-off we were taking. As father said, 'It would never do for him to miss the right turning, because he has all the tucker boxes on board with all our lovely Christmas dinner!' We left the road soon after that, and went down the track which led right into the gums. Within seconds we were surrounded by great gum trees towering above us. It was all so cool and mysterious. Even the horses trod softly and carefully . . . The track wound in and out amongst the gums for quite a long way, till at last we came right to the edge of the creek. There, father pulled up under the shade of a big tree with wide-spreading branches. 'Now gals,' he said, 'how's that for a spot for boiling the billy?'[36]

What makes the outing possible? Or – perhaps it is the same question – what makes it an event worth writing about? (For

here history and the making of history are scarcely distinguish-
able.) Home and creek are not only spatially distinct; situated on
opposite sides of the boundary, they offer a symbolic contrast
which has within it the seeds of a story. It is this incipient plot
which the boundary posts, in a sense, bring out. For in the
Beveridge picnic, the boundary posts are turning points in a
double sense: they inspire speech, articulating the outing as a
symbolic journey, a journey about the pleasure of journeying,
but they also make the *narration* of the outing possible.

This kind of analysis explains perhaps the phenomenon I
alluded to before – the fact that the first days of settling are
recollected rather than recorded and, eluding the diarist, for the
most part, fail to find a place in colonial history. It is not simply
that the newcomer is too busy to write. He has yet to enclose a
place in which history can begin to occur, a clearing where he
can express himself. The dependence of writing on a place to
write is, then, anything but trivial. It turns out to be a boundary
condition for the production of history. So it may be no
coincidence that the phrase 'to set down' describes the essential
character of both settlement and writing. For, as the phrase
implies, both cultural activities have a double aspect, vertical
and horizontal. In its vertical aspect, the root meaning of 'set'
and its cognates (settle, seat, etc.) has to do with the notion of
coming to rest. The idea is of a burden transferred. The settler is
one who sits down, who gravitates, who establishes a balance.
He is distinguished from the traveller by the fact that he
externalizes his existence as a place. He transfers the burden of
himself to the world around him. He takes the weight off his
legs. In this sense, the place stands in for him even in his
absence.

Comparable constraints clearly delimit the writer's activity.
The setting down of thoughts on paper is (or was) a product of
the vertical stylus and the horizontal page. We clarify our ideas
by setting them out. By covering the previously clear page, we
give our unruly thoughts an order and perspicacity all their
own. The linearity of writing (in contrast with the multi-
dimensionality of experience) and the linearity of the logic it
expresses reflects neither the nature of experience nor, for that
matter, of history, but rather the limitations of the medium.

Because of these limitations Jacques Derrida has called for a different kind of writing, one that lets one 'reread past writing according to a different organization of space'.[37] Presumably, one effect of the kind of rereading Derrida advocates would be to render the hitherto marginalized act of settling a central object of historical study.

Reconstructing the spatial history of settlement has implications, not only for the myth of the pioneer, but also for the associated myth of 'the frontier' – a persistent figure of speech, not only in the United States, but also in Australia. Essentially, the frontier is usually conceived of as a line, a line continually pushed forward (or back) by heroic frontiersmen, the pioneers. Inside the line is culture; beyond it, nature. As the frontier moves, nature is bulldozed into submission. There is no negotiation, simply the imposition of a new regime by force. Culture does not evolve or adapt: it simply replicates itself over an ever-growing territory. The frontier signifies the decisive exclusion of all that is not culturally familiar: and it excludes it even when it incorporates it. For the act of incorporation involves the complete silencing and obliteration of whatever it was that made the frontier necessary in the first place. The rhetorical significance of the frontier is that it empties the beyond of any cultural significance even before it is subdued. Savages are, by definition, what are found beyond the pale of civilization: there is no question of letting them disperse the boundary or turn their backs on it, for this would undermine the imperial logic of opposition on which the frontier myth rests. As the 'Star Wars' project of the 1980s reminds us, one tragic irony of the frontier dream is that its proponents can never cease to feel surrounded. For, however far back the frontier is pushed, there is always something threatening on the other side.

From the point of view of spatial history, though, the notion of a one-sided, unified line of defence or attack has little value. For, as I have suggested, the essential function of the boundary is to facilitate communication. It enables places to appear and be named. It enables the settler to establish who and where he is. This is my clearing, that beyond is not. But this difference does not imply an exclusive opposition. You grasp the settler and the place that declares his presence by seeing them in relation to the surrounding bush. The settler himself takes advantage of this distinction to make his own position clear. The boundary is not a barrier to communication. Quite the opposite: it gives the settler something to talk about. Of course, this is not to say such communication is always friendly. A Castlemaine pioneer, for example, recalls getting lost on his way back from the Bendigo diggings in mid-Victoria. On the fifth evening he and his mates came across a squatter's hut, or homestead, and found the 'Gent of the Wool' in his garden.

> When I approached the fence I asked him if he would kindly sell us some flour, mutton or corned beef. He said he supposed I was one of those accursed diggers who were bringing ruin on the land, and had come to invade his run.[38]

At first sight, this anecdote might appear to reinforce the accepted imperial view of boundaries, that they symbolize exclusion and silence. But, even if we accepted this, we would have to admit that, friendly or not, the squatter's fence was the place where communication occurred.

However, underlying the apparent opposition between squatter and digger is a deeper significance. In effect, the brevity of their dialogue reflects the squatter's unwillingness to enter into any kind of symbolic exchange, whether verbal or monetary, with the visitor. And, if we ask why this animosity, the squatter himself explains: the digger and his mates are wanderers, they have no fixed abode, they lie out of bounds. No relationship based on reciprocal rights and responsibilities can be established with them. In this sense, the diggers resemble the untamed bush. They will reduce the land to a kind of ruin resembling, presumably, the desolateness of the wilderness in its original state. The true function of the fence, in this context, is to define the difference between squatter and digger. In refusing to hold intercourse with them, the squatter refuses to give the diggers a place from which to speak, he refuses to recognize them *even* as opponents.

Of course, some historians have questioned the value of the frontier as a historical term. A case in point is T. M. Perry, in his scholarly history of settlement in New South Wales, *Australia's First Frontier*. In the introduction to his book, Perry gives qualified support to the idea of the frontier initially put forward by the American historian F. J. Turner in *The Frontier in American History*. But, if anything, Perry's own study only demonstrates the elusiveness of Turner's concept. In fact, Perry is obliged to conclude that 'The frontier was not a homogeneous entity in New South Wales. In 1829 there were in fact three major frontiers in existence . . .'[39] In short, at least in New South Wales, the invention of a metaphysical entity, known as the frontier and revealed in such phenomena as the 'frontier mentality', does not serve to elucidate the historical facts. As Perry shows, 'The processes of transformation were clearly different in each region.'[40] One is left wondering why the author saddled himself with so useless a concept in the first place.

The answer may well have to do with the lack of a critical method, whether historical or geographical, capable of describing those boundary experiences which define the act of settlement. Certainly, this would appear to be true of another historian, Henry Reynolds, who has enshrined an oppositional notion of the boundary in the title of his book *The Other Side of the Frontier*. Reynolds's book has been praised as a valuable assemblage of information about aboriginal experience and perception of white settlement. And, certainly, bearing in mind the tendency of Australian historians to minimize the brutal facts associated with the progressive extermination of the Aborigines, Reynolds's book is deservedly influential.

But how far is the Aborigines' cause served by any account of their history that takes as its premiss the existence of a frontier? Within the limits of the information available to him, Reynolds's object is straightforward: 'to put down as clearly as I could my vision of how the Aborigines reacted to the invading Europeans'.[41] But in what sense does Reynolds's intention to 'bring the other side of the frontier within the compass of our scholarship'[42] actually describe the aboriginal experience? Bringing together a host of scattered oral and written data, in a manner wholly foreign to an oral culture, ordering them under the aegis of a culture-specific discourse known as history, does not Reynolds's book merely continue by other means two hundred years of white history, a history founded on the successful appropriation (and suppression) of neighbouring cultures? This is not Reynolds's intention, of course, but it is an unfortunate consequence of his assumption that what goes on on the other side of the fence is strictly comparable with what goes on here. Is this assumption justified? What, in fact, does it mean to speak of 'aboriginal history'? Mircea Eliade, for instance, has pointed out that Australian Aborigines and other primitive peoples

> do not have a historical awareness comparable, say, to that of Westerners . . . The Aborigines do not record historical events in an irreversible chronological order. The changes and innovations, which imperceptibly and continuously trans-formed their existence, were telescoped into the mythical era.[43]

But, as the perpetuation of concepts like 'the pioneer spirit' reveals, it is not only Aborigines who mythologize changes they cannot account for.

Reynolds's assumption that aboriginal history can be treated in the same way as white history is itself a form of frontier rhetoric. For, unintentionally no doubt, it has the effect of suppressing the difference of Aboriginal history – a difference not simply of content but of form. Reynolds maintains that,

> The barriers which for so long kept Aboriginal experience out of our history books were not principally those of source material or methodology but rather ones of perception and preference.[44]

He concludes, with unconscious irony,

> It is clear, now, that the boundaries of Australian historio-graphy can be pushed back to encompass the other side of the frontier.[45]

No doubt white historians have suppressed or disregarded much aboriginal evidence. But simply to bring such evidence to light does not of itself constitute an accurate account of the aboriginal experience. The evidence still stands in need of interpretation.

This emerges perhaps even more clearly when we turn to a group of white scholars who might be thought to have, if anything, a prejudice in favour of the Aborigines: the anthropologists. But certain perennial questions Australian anthropologists debate, in particular to do with the definition of such terms as 'tribe' and 'territory', illustrate that methodology is, in fact, at the heart of the matter. One might have thought that any attempt to define concepts like 'tribe' or 'territory' would have involved some prior reflection on the nature of boundaries. Clearly, if the idea of the boundary as a barrier is one peculiar to our culture, it is of little use in describing aboriginal concepts of social and spatial organization. But, although anthropologists have differed in their definitions, they have generally attempted to define the 'tribe' and its 'territory' in terms of each other. Radcliffe-Brown, for example, defined his tribal unit, the 'horde', as a 'small group of persons owning a certain area of territory, the boundaries of which are known, and possessing in common proprietary rights over the land and its products'.[46] More recently, Birdsell and Tindale have respectively used linguistic and ecological data to reinforce this notion.

True, formulated in these terms, it is a notion that other workers have criticized as simplistic. Territory, according to writers like R. M. Berndt, Robert Dixon and D. H. Turner, is not the static, spatial counterpart of the tribe. Rather, it is a product of diverse social relations, based on kinship ties, totemic affiliations, language, age and sex. As Biernoff notes, for the traditional Aborigines of Arnhem Land at least, 'In a general way access to land is determined by social identity.'[47] And this is a remark that applies reciprocally to the idea of the tribe. Referring to the use of the term 'tribe', again in eastern Arnhem Land, Turner has concluded, 'it is probably best to abandon the concept altogether.'[48] But, whether finding the concepts useful or not, it is significant that the terms of the debate have not themselves been greatly questioned. For, implicit in any discussion of tribe or territory are, of course, certain assumptions about boundaries. As Nicholas Peterson, the editor of *Tribes and Boundaries in Australia* (1976), remarks:

Boundedness has an aesthetic and analytic appeal, because by creating a finite universe it allows for the total exhaustion of a topic in the course of analysis and makes for ease of comparison. It is this intellectual appeal that transforms what are often really gradients, clines, areas of intergradation or zonation into discontinuous or bounded units.[49]

There is much truth in what Peterson says, but a boundary that is not a barrier is not necessarily imperceptible. It may be a place of communication. The anthropologist Berndt might have thought he was making a witty academic joke when he suggested his colleague Birdsell rechristen his notion of a 'dialectical tribe' 'dialectal' because ' "dialectical" . . . could be interpreted as having something to do with philosophy, perhaps defining a tribe on the basis of its members being dialecticians'.[50] But the joke rebounds on Berndt. For, leaving aside Birdsell's attempt to define the tribe according to linguistic criteria, there is little doubt that, if tribal identity means anything, it means the tribal member's sense of difference from non-tribal members. His self-definition may not depend on his dialect but, in so far as he defines his identity *against* Aborigines who for whatever reason are unlike him, his self-definition is very definitely dialectical. It preserves and respects symbolic boundaries, whatever form they take.

Redefining the boundary as the place of communicated difference, rather than as a 'veil' or 'barrier' to knowledge, has the decided advantage of corresponding to the behaviour of the Aborigines themselves. For it appears reasonably clear from the anthropological literature that, to speak very generally, the Aborigines recognize boundaries or, rather, decisive differences. But, it is equally true that they are rarely able to say precisely where the boundaries lie. Boundaries are, indeed, *debatable* places: not just zones of uncertainty, but places where intertribal communication can occur in a controlled way. Certainly this seems to be the assumption determining the 'Corroborras or Theatrical Merry Meetings', as William Gardner called them, writing in 1854, and which occurred when 'at certain seasons of the year the various tribes of the interior meet at appointed places'.[51] 'At these general rendez-vous', Gardner explained, 'their disputes were adjusted and settled.'

The function of such places as debating grounds seems to have been fully grasped by early missionaries. The Wesleyans responsible for establishing the Buntingdale Mission near Geelong in Victoria in 1839 selected a site, conscious that 'each tribe has a particular location and boundaries beyond the limits of which they seldom go except on special occasions when they formally visit each other'.[52] Rev. Joseph Orton and Rev. Francis Tuckfield therefore chose their ground where such formal visits could occur: about 40 miles to the westward of Geelong on the south side of the River Barwon, 'the junction of the Barrabool and the Lake tribes'. 'Being central to several tribes', it was, as the Colonial Secretary noted, 'well adapted for the objects of the Mission.'[53] Intentionally or not, the same practice was followed by the Moravian missionaries, who set up the Ebenezer Aboriginal Mission on a corroboree ground at Antwerp in the Wimmera. Nor does the significance of such places for white spatial history end there. To take two further Victorian examples, Nhill, again in the Wimmera, and even Melbourne, are founded on corroboree grounds.

The implications of these facts for our understanding of Aboriginal–European relations in the early period of colonization may be considerable. Consider, for instance, the question of aboriginal acquiescence in the occupation of their land. Tindale, who takes the view that aboriginal tribes occupied discrete territories, envisages the boundary as a kind of no-man's-land between tribes, a neutral, usually relatively infertile strip. If this is so, it throws light on the history of white exploration. Many explorer and pioneer tracks 'happen to be boundaries between tribal groups' and Tindale speculates,

> Where such men were accompanied by aborigines with local knowledge, it is probable that to avoid transgression of the territories of others, for which the aborigines could be held responsible, pioneer whites were always steered along tribal boundaries and through other neutral areas.[54]

Tindale's view hardly squares with the opinion expressed by Berndt, according to whom 'empty spaces unallocated in human terms are not "empty" in mythic terms, and they are always potentially owned'.[55] Nor do Tindale's observations explain the fact, frequently noted by Robinson and other early observers, that in many cases the most fertile localities had first been shown to the squatters by aboriginal guides. It is true that Tindale himself acknowledges that 'neutral ground' may be neutral precisely because of its social importance. As he says,

> The boundary may run from the named watering place *a* to the one *b*, or, where the waters are shared by both clans, the habitual camping spots, one on each side of the water, are regarded as limiting such territory with the water as constituting neutral ground.[56]

And Reynolds's observation is also pertinent:

> Unless forewarned Aborigines probably had no appreciation of the European's determination to stay indefinitely.[57]

Even so, these attempts to reconstruct the first moments of intercultural contact rest on a cultural assumption about the symbolic significance of the boundary. Rather than regard the track as a neutral boundary bordering territories, it might make more sense to see it as a corridor of legitimate communication, a place of dialogue, where differences could be negotiated. Boundaries may themselves have been significant narratives. The track itself, replete with mythic as well as human meaning, may have been a form of communication. In this context, there is a certain poignancy in the idea of the white pioneer ignoring the route itself and casting his eyes instead, left and right, towards the kind of space that spoke to *him*.

Against this background, white invasion was a form of spatial writing that erased the earlier meaning. Settlement then became a question of giving back to a desolated, because depopulated, land a lost significance. This is, for instance, true of all the pioneers represented in *The Land of the Lyrebird*: taking up selections made available only in the 1870s and 1880s, they entered a country from which over the preceding forty years the cattle-running squatters had almost completely banished the aboriginal population. The extent of that massacre is only now beginning to emerge, but the result was that the pioneer selectors entered on a literally unsettled country: and there was no one with whom to debate it. The myth of the frontier and the pioneer bushman, which the contributors to *The Land of the Lyrebird* were more than happy to promote, was a necessary myth to make the artificially silent land speak. Theirs had been a peaceful war with nature, a translation of trees into houses which had given back to the forest its human meaning.

Other pioneers inscribed themselves on the landscape in other ways. The overlander John Hepburn, for example, records how, after journeying from Sydney, he reached a place north of the Victorian Divide:

> Here we took a day's rest admiring the beauties of this interesting spot. I was so much delighted with it that I cut my initials on a large tree, and said this will be my abode at some future period.[58]

Hepburn's gesture, the carving of his initials, neatly illustrates the intimate connection between the making of spatial history and its writing. For the physical marks the newcomers made were primarily symbolic: the first axe blows, a gun shot fortuitously taking a cockatoo out of its path of flight, even the fording of a creek, these spatial gestures marked their intent to construct a new country, to write over what was there before, to revise it until it appeared like an Eden. And in this sense 'writing' was not history's amanuensis: it was the place where history announced itself. As Hepburn remarks, after cutting his initials, 'The next step towards settling was making a station, which was done.'[59]

A less destructive, less heroic image of the pioneer conforms to the historical facts but raises questions of its own. Whether the squatter and, later, the selector intended it or not, the fact is that the country they took over, mainly for farming purposes, was in many instances utterly transformed. Gippsland in Victoria must be the most dramatic Australian example, where an entire temperate rain forest was effaced to produce denuded downs, whose emerald glaze is at once glowingly fertile and strangely sterile. But, even in drier regions right across the southern states, the 'bush' was systematically removed and, as a result, the country rendered increasingly susceptible to the erosive power of wind and rain. How is this destructive neglect to be reconciled with the picture of the traveller settling down, even writing his story?

Perhaps the answer is to be found in our redefinition of the boundary. Despite the surveyors and more recently the historical geographers, the first settlers did not inhabit a discrete territory with definite boundaries. A map of the Victorian squatters' runs between 1837 and about 1870 prepared by the historians A. S. Kenyon and R. V. Billis shows a jigsaw of contiguous estates, with clearly defined boundaries.[60] The surveys prepared for selectors after the Land Acts of the 1860s use the same strategy. But, needless to say, the row upon row of rectangular blocks on the map bore very little relation to what the purchaser found when he attempted to take up his selection. And, similarly, the earlier squatters often had only the dimmest idea of where their land ended and their neighbour's began. In this context, the tentatively indicated outlines of the first squatting runs, as represented on early surveys (see, for instance, Pine Plains, plate 18), more nearly represented spatial experience. Indeed, the sense they give of directions petering out, of lookouts and surrounding blankness, may apply equally to the selector's early experience. The sharp contrast between the numbered, rectilinear plots of the selection acts (again see plate 18) and the sprawling indistinctness of the squatter's run, with its network of names, may be largely a cartographical artefact.

The truth is that definitive boundaries of any kind had very little to do with the settlers' experience of settling. Randell's monographs on pastoral settlement in northern Victoria contain numerous illustrations of the point that, in the early days, station boundaries were still undefined. In the early days, boundaries were rather zones of unoccupied, unspoken for, land.[61] They could be as vague as horizons. Another local historian, Susan Priestley, accurately evokes the character of the squatters' runs on the Wimmera in western Victoria, when she describes them as 'huge, their boundaries ill-defined and running away into the distance'.[62] Selectors had much the same experience: the map boundaries had very little to do with the boundaries that mattered to them in the field. The 1869 Land Act, for example, permitted selection before survey, requiring only that the boundaries of the selection be marked with 'conspicuous posts or cairns of stones'. But, as Ross Hartnell has remarked, in the context of Gippsland settlement:

Even this requirement illustrated that the Act had not been designed with such a region as the 'scrub country' in mind. In that dense, and at times almost impenetrable scrub, finding even the approximate boundaries of selections was a major problem.[63]

As for the further requirement that the selector should fence his land within two years,

No selector in his right mind would attempt to enclose his property with a 'good and substantial fence' until clearing was completed, both on his property and those of his neighbours. To do so would involve running the risk of the fences being promptly burnt to the ground when clearing by fire got underway.[64]

The act of settling was not a matter of marking out pre-existing boundaries, but one of establishing symbolic enclosures. It depended on establishing a point of view with a back and front, a place with a human symmetry, a human focus of interest. Boundaries were the means of expressing this ambition, of articulating presence. They represented acts of spatial translation, which did not exclude but set up a dialogue with the outside environment they created. Hence the widespread destruction and silencing of the bush was not necessarily intentional. In a passage that deserves to become another *locus classicus* for the history of Australian space, the Gippsland selector already quoted, Mrs W. J. Williams, illustrates how, for an individual settler clearing his block, the *general* clearance of the land could still come as a surprise:

As time went by we could hear what seemed to be thunder in the distance, but it was in reality the noise made by scrub falling as it was cut. One day when up the track, my husband saw what appeared to be a break in the tops of the trees to the North; so, the following Sunday we climbed to the top of the hill, and, behold! there was a gap in the scrub. Someone was clearing, and each week the gap grew larger. Then, in other directions, the same thing would occur, and the following February or March, we would see clouds of smoke. Each year the clearings grew larger, and the smoke more intense, and as the years passed, the great walls of scrub were cut down, and bands of men could be seen chopping the logs up after the fire had passed over them.[65]

This account strongly suggests that denudation was the result of the grid-system of surveying and selecting which took no account of the topography of the country. Perhaps, had a Mitchell surveyed south Gippsland, there might perhaps have been some incentive for the government to set aside public reserves, even to promote central settlements. As it was, the country was divided into selections which, while equal on paper, did nothing to preserve the necessary differences essential to homemaking. More than this, the selections were offered indiscriminately to individual owners – with the result that, instead of creating a network of public and private spaces, the Land Acts simply encouraged the proliferation of clearings. Each clearing in itself may have depended upon, and drawn sustenance from, the 'wall' of rain forest – at least when it had been pushed back a decent distance beyond the fence; but the cumulative effect of these uncoordinated local acts was the creation of a landscape from which difference had been excluded. A new uniformity of blandly smiling slopes came to replace the inscrutable impenetrability of the primeval bush.

Some idea of the significance of this bureaucratic failure of imagination can be gauged by comparing the Gippsland experience with that of settlers on the Atherton Tableland in northern Queensland. The subtropical rain forest which covered the Atherton Tableland began to be cleared in the period 1870 to 1900 in the wake of a succession of mineral rushes in the region. In contrast with events in Gippsland, the primary motive of the Queensland axemen was not settlement but profit – particularly from selling the valuable 'cedar' and they were evidently wantonly destructive. By the turn of the century, though, the first wave of invasion was being followed by a second, more pacific immigration of selectors, primarily interested in farming. Over the next decade or so, more and more land was thrown open for selection. Indeed, by 1914 nearly the whole of the 700-square-kilometre plateau had been selected. Even so, despite the rapacity which characterized this rapid settlement, the Atherton Tableland, in sharp contrast with south Gippsland, retains a considerable number of isolated pockets of original rain-forest vegetation. How did these come to survive?[66]

Short of examining each selection's individual history, it is not possible to give any comprehensive answer. But one factor at least seems to have been crucial. In contrast with the pattern of individual settlement in Gippsland, a significant part of the Atherton Tableland was taken up by *groups*. The membership of one might be dominated by farmers from northern New South Wales or from the Manawatu lowlands of New Zealand; another group selection was composed largely of German Jews or Irish selectors; and so on.[67] Group selection made it possible to formulate a coherent land management policy: instead of shaving the forest back hard against a neighbour's boundary, it became possible to cooperate with the same neighbour in preserving a screen of trees, valuable not only aesthetically but also in providing shelter for animals. Nor did this cooperative policy arise by chance: it was the direct offspring of a series of government measures designed 'to encourage bodies of selectors to come from other states'[68] and which gave preference to group applications.

There is a poem, entitled 'Retrospect', by the Gippsland pioneer W. Johnstone, which begins,

> When I first came to Gippsland, no seer could foretell,
> That the light-tapping axe rang the forest's deathknell.

Johnstone goes on to lament that 'Ever gone are the gumtrees that covered the hills' and 'the tree ferns that sheltered the rills' –

> And gone are the dells where I oft loved to roam
> And bring in wild flowers to garland my home.

Never more, he regrets, 'shall I list to the lyre bird's song' or 'wander, awe-struck and subdued . . .'

> And feel, when along those great aisles I have trod,
> I worshipped alone in the temple of God.

But, at this heartfelt point, Johnstone shakes himself out of his retrospective reverie: 'away with these fancies' –

'Tis better today
Where the forest encumbered, the children now play
In meadows bespangled with flowers whose hue
Is brighter than those that the pioneers knew.

Where the forest delighted, perchance, two or three,
The present rich meadows fill hundreds with glee.
Our wives and our children, our homes and our farms
Are dearer and better than Nature's wild charms.[69]

It is difficult not to sense in this poem a conflict. Far from
wholeheartedly approving the destruction of the natural environment, Johnstone finds some difficulty in rationalizing it: his
utilitarian argument that 'the present rich meadows fill hundreds
with glee' sounds hollow in comparison with the lyrebird's song.
The new community of farms and families seems less persuasive
than the lost congregation, of trees. It may be that the relative
absence of community, a consequence of the manner in which the
selection acts were framed and the country surveyed, also has
something to do with the relative lack of conviction in Johnstone's conclusion.

At the same time, the poem is an attempt to resolve the
pioneering paradox, that what is gained occurs at the price of
irremediable loss; and, in this respect, it aptly illustrates the
argument of this chapter. For, from the position of settlement,
the forest now appears as a place where the imagination was at
home. It is now conjured up as a place of mental and emotional
travelling. Stasis endows it with a sense of freedom. It becomes
the site of the imaginary travelling which only a house with
windows, table and chair makes possible. With its cover of gum
trees, its shelter of tree ferns, it becomes the image of home.
Thus, in retrospect, is the wilderness cultivated and preserved as
a cultural site, a place where the settler can reflect on his own
condition, understanding perhaps the intention to settle as a
question of spatial and psychic stability, as well as pride in having
an address. Plainly our contemporaries, the 'developer' and the
'environmentalist', spring from one and the same tradition. Why
then can they not talk to each other? Whatever the stated reasons,
one cannot help feeling that, underlying it, is their mutual appeal
to the false rhetoric of the frontier.

6

A Thorny Passage

Thus kindred objects kindred thoughts inspire,
As summer-clouds flash forth electric fire.

Samuel Rogers

Going and coming back are by no means the same thing. The mileage may be the same and, to judge from the map, the route identical. But, to the traveller on the road, the difference is obvious. Retracing his steps, he now faces the country which, on the outward journey, was always behind him. Instead of spreading out, it converges. In this sense, he once again enters a new country. But he does not experience the charm of its novelty as he would were he travelling on. His attitude towards it is different. Retreating, he is able to go forward without fear of being forced to retreat. No longer do promising views dictate the direction he takes: they belong to the already constituted road. Less functional than ornamental now, they are like pearls strung along the way. He has more time for the picturesque. He can afford to dream. But, if the country ahead has lost its exploratory charge, by the same token it can, as it were, be taken as it comes.

If the traveller on the outward journey is preoccupied with making a track, on the backward journey he can begin at last to look at the country. What he sees is not wholly unfamiliar, but nor is it wholly familiar either. Distances that previously seemed enormous now appear almost domestic. Hills that once looked impassable now melt away because one knows what is on the other side: in a sense, one is already there. On the other hand, places that had previously looked like natural campsites, approached from the opposite direction, and with the advantage of experience, now compare poorly with other 'places' further on. Other favoured stops have disappeared, while land that formerly looked barren beyond belief is now inhabited by companionable birds and flowers. At worst, one is accompanied by one's own footsteps; and, even if the expedition's supply of geographical magazines is exhausted, there is at least the pleasure of reading through one's own journal.

Coming back is not only essential to the traveller's personal survival: it is also essential to his historical future. For, in so far as the journey has to become a journal, a map or a drawing in order to enter spatial history, going back is the traveller's opportunity to check his facts. It is analogous to the process of revision. Indeed, these two processes are very closely related. If, for instance, we look at the journals of Sturt or Stuart or Mitchell, all of which recount double journeys, outwards and backwards, we find that a very small proportion of the text is given over to describing the return journey. The larger part of their journals is taken up with a narrative of the journey out. If, as I have suggested, the journal is not primarily a description of the country, but a symbolic representation of track-making, this is understandable. But it does not mean that the return journey has been left out: rather, it has been incorporated into the account of the outward journey as a series of marginal interpolations, erasures and name changes which, at a yet later stage of revision, can be woven into the narrative to increase its dramatic interest.

The seamlessness of the journals is a literary illusion. Unfortunately, though, it has too often been taken at face value, with the result that the *reflective* attitude the explorer and settler literature embodies has been overlooked. Instead, the historical experience it records has been subjected to an 'I came, I saw, I conquered' mythologizing, as if the explorers did not criss-cross their own tracks a hundred times, did not ride in elaborate circles, taking hours and sometimes days to get back where they had last begun; as if pioneers did not reconnoitre, did not go back to town, stake legal claims, take out loans, buy supplies and (perhaps only after half a dozen journeys, and even perhaps after rejecting half a dozen other places) eventually set about the business of making a home for themselves. And not only have the backtrackings implicit in such spatial experiences been ironed out, but the *order* of them has been linearized, subjected to a one-way imperial chronology.

But spatial history does not advance. Or, better, it only advances by reflection, by going back and looking again at already trodden ground. The ground is not virgin: it already has a history. It is not a question of correcting what is already there, of replacing it with a better route. It is a question of interpretation, of attempting to recapture and evoke more fully 'the world of the text' – not just the biographical and stylistic history of the journals, but the 'world' they refer to. If this process is not to become a tyranny, effacing what it attempts to describe, if it is to avoid falling into the positivist fallacy of supposing its own account of events decisively replaces the original one, then it is essential that it respect the *difference* of the historical texts it deals with.

We can illustrate this by the journey analogy: however many times an explorer's biographer takes the route first taken by the explorer, he can never take it for the first time. The route has already been constituted for him. In this sense, his journey is always a return journey; and, if he ignores this, imagining himself in the explorer's place, the result may be good fiction, but not good history. For, by a too zealous and unreflective imitation, the explorer's experience has been rendered infinitely repeatable. It has been translated into an experience anyone can have: it is but a matter of time before the television crews and the motorcyclists will be there.

But, except by going over the ground again, how can the explorer's experience be relived? Except by narrating his adventures once again, how can his memory be kept alive? A reflective history is less ambitious: it recognizes that things now are not as they were; that reading now is not the same as writing then, nor travelling either. This difference is what history is and what makes it an object of reflection. The historian himself is embedded in history, is himself a product of historical consciousness. He cannot take refuge in a timeless logic of cause and effect. His aim should be, rather, to articulate the difference. It is this which, if anything, can make what he writes 'relevant to today'.

But how is the past conjured up without destroying it? It seems to me that essential to this reflective process is a recognition that it must be metaphorical. Metaphors, after all, not only give us an insight into unexpected similarities: the pleasant feeling of deeper understanding they give us depends on actual differences between the things compared. In the context of writing spatial history, the essential metaphor whereby we 'bring to life' the explorers without pretending *we* are explorers is perhaps that of writing and reading. As I read and write, so, perhaps, they travelled. But what makes this a comparison that is historically illuminating – and not just flashily fashionable – is that language, like travelling, gives space its meaning. It does not report the world: it names it.

To interpret the spatial history embedded, say, in an explorer's life, we have to pay attention to the metaphorical nature of his own knowledge. There is also a need to be aware of the sense in which he himself was conscious, not just of travelling unknown regions, but of inventing his own history – the sense, too, in which he himself recognized the difference between his own voyaging and that of travellers before him. It is in this context that the career of Australia's first circumnavigator assumes perhaps its full historical significance. For Matthew Flinders not only made discoveries, helping to establish that Van Diemen's Land (later Tasmania) was an island, as well as exploring the coast where the future Adelaide was situated; he also had unusual (if unwanted) opportunities to reflect on the meaning of his own journey for, on returning to England after sailing round Australia, he was arrested by the French in Mauritius, and confined there for no less than six years (1803–10); and, finally, Flinders had a highly developed historical consciousness. In this last respect, his profound admiration for Captain Cook means that, in some way perhaps, to write about Flinders is also, albeit indirectly, to begin to retrace our own steps to Cook.

Although Matthew Flinders has received a fair amount of biographical attention, from novelists as well as historians, he has invariably been treated as the stuff of romance. His youth, his newly married wife left behind, the 1801–3 *Investigator* voyage, its circumnavigation of Australia and its tragic sequel – Flinders's arrest and imprisonment – all this, combined with his premature death in 1814 at the age of forty, has made it easy to see in Flinders yet another variation on the theme of the doomed romantic hero. In the sense that Flinders was fully conscious of his own bad fortune and, like a romantic poet, consciously set out to write his own life in terms of it, this image is not wholly mistaken. What it tends to overlook, though, is the terms in which Flinders constructed his life – the fact that, in order to memorialize himself, Flinders set out, during his enforced confinement, to write his life *as a journal*. It was in this way that Flinders found a route out of his physical isolation and a way back into history.

The story of how Flinders came to write up the journal of his *Investigator* voyage and produce what eventually became the monumental, and portentously entitled, *A Voyage to Terra Australis* is straightforward enough. When, in 1801, Flinders sailed for Australia, his attitude towards the possible publication of his journal was that of Cook thirty years earlier: he assumed the task of editing it into publishable form would be given to what he later called a 'literary man'. At the time, in fact, Flinders wrote to his cousin, John (later Sir John) Franklin, then studying at Oxford, to suggest he might like to consider taking on the job himself. If Franklin seeks a literary career, Flinders writes, he might make a good beginning in writing up the *Investigator* voyage.

> I am now engaged in writing a rough account, but authorship sits awkward upon me, I am diffident of appearing before the public, unburnished by an abler hand.[1]

Flinders invites Franklin to prepare himself for the task of authorship:

> A little mathematical knowledge will strengthen your style, and give it perspicuity. Study the writings of different authors, both for the subjects, and the manner in which they are treated. Arrangement is a material point in voyage writing as well as in history: I feel great diffidence here. Sufficient matter I can easily furnish, and fear not to prevent anything unseamanlike from entering into the composition; but to round a period well, and arrange sentences so as to place what is meant in the most perspicuous point of view, is too much for me. Seamanship and authorship make too great an angle

with each other: the farther a man advances upon one line the farther distant he becomes from any point on the other.[2]

It is clear from this that Flinders had in mind a considerably more sophisticated account than that which Cook furnished of the *Endeavour* voyage. Bearing in mind the interest that Cook's erstwhile companion, Sir Joseph Banks, was now taking in promoting the *Investigator* voyage, it is likely that Flinders anticipated a full-blown scientific report being published – the sort of comprehensive ethnographical, geographical and natural historical description, in fact, that J. R. Forster had hoped to publish of Cook's second, *Resolution*, voyage. Understandably, Flinders expressed misgivings about writing it. At the same time, though, the advice Flinders gave Franklin, together with his charming figure of the widening angle between the courses of authorship and seamanship, suggest a style and a personality themselves well fitted to the task.

By 1810, when at long last Flinders had been released from Mauritius and was once again back in England, his attitude towards authorship had changed. As he wrote to his friend J. Wiles,

> The original plan was that all my charts and accounts, and those of the men of science, should be put in the hands of some literary man, to be employed by the admiralty to write the account from our documents; and this plan I would suppose Sir J. would still wish to be pursued, but I find an opinion prevailing at the admiralty that it would be better done by me; so that I know not yet what plan will be adopted.[3]

By early 1811 the question had been resolved in Flinders's favour: 'It is agreed that Flinders will write the Narrative himself – as he now earnestly wishes.'[4] During the remaining three years of his life Flinders worked almost ceaselessly, writing his own account and collating the scientific reports of others, drawing and redrawing charts, having views engraved and, last but not least, bestowing names on his discoveries.

The major cause of Flinders's new confidence in his literary abilities was, ironically, his six-year sojourn in Mauritius. The enforced idleness there, together with the likelihood that the achievements of the *Investigator* might be appropriated by the

French and Flinders's own claims as a scientific navigator and discoverer denied, provoked him to the kind of literary and cartographical work that otherwise he might have neglected. It was, for instance, in 1806 that Flinders began in earnest his researches into magnetic variation. And, throughout this time, Flinders occupied himself redrawing his charts, enlarging their scale, filling in details. It is curious to imagine the passion with which Flinders battened on to the outline of certain Australian coasts, willing them into life, as if in the mere act of representation a meaning might be found.

At the same time Flinders was learning to speak and write French. As a prisoner, he had ample occasion to practise the art of petitioning. He learnt to match his turn of phrase to the subject and the recipient: he quotes, in writing to his wife, part of a letter he had addressed to Captain Bergeret in 1806, regarding the possibility of release. 'Adieu, worthy sir,' it concludes, 'may the winds be propitious, and may you never be reduced to the bitterness of sighing after justice in vain.'[5] Flinders learnt something of the art of 'arrangement' as well: he produced 'an analytical account' (or summary) of 'several manuscript travels and journals in the interior and along the coasts of Madagascar'.[6] Flinders was made conscious of the deceptiveness of language, the ease with which it conspired against 'perspicuity', for his servant was under the delusion the whole island was in conspiracy against them – even 'the political articles in the gazettes', he thought, 'related in a metaphorical manner the designs carrying on' against the English prisoners.[7] And then there was Flinders's own correspondence with his wife, bearing witness to the widening range of Flinders's reading, as well as the depth of his feelings.

As a result, when, after returning to England, Flinders came to write his account of the voyage, he was able to invest it with a scientific rigour and stylistic sophistication any account of his written seven years earlier would have lacked. By the time that *A Voyage to Terra Australis* was ready for publication, it was not merely the account of a voyage: it had become a model of how explorations should be written up. It had become the exploration of a literary genre as much as the record of a journey. A rather too lengthy bivouac, Mauritius was the necessary resting place the explorer needed in order to write up his journal. And, while the discoveries reported may have been modest, the literary influence of the *Voyage* was not.

For one thing it set a monumental precedent for the explorer to appear as his own historian and biographer. *A Voyage to Terra Australis* is prefaced by a historical introduction that runs to no fewer than 204 pages. This might seem excessive, except that Flinders devotes some 550 folio pages to the two years of the *Investigator*'s voyages. The introduction is matched in length by Book Three of the *Voyage* – which is not about the voyage of discovery at all, but is a detailed account of the circumstances surrounding Flinders's detention and imprisonment in Mauritius. A voyage that begins in history ends in biography.

In effect, *A Voyage to Terra Australis* is the first great Australian work of spatial history. Flinders emphasized this point by the arrangement of his material, notably of the historical data in the first volume. The chapter divisions not only correspond to the history of the voyage, they also articulate the place of the voyage of the *Investigator* in the tradition of Australian sea exploration. While chapter 4, for example, describes the zone of the south coast previously visited by Bruni d'Entrecasteaux, chapter 5 covers the coast further east, which the older navigator Pieter Nuyts had visited (see plate 3). Thus, by chapter 6, tracking back through history as he sails forward, Flinders literally and metaphorically opens a new chapter in exploration. Thus, too, where exploration begins history and biography intersect.

A Voyage was also a formal and stylistic model. Its two-volume division, for example, was adopted by King, Stokes, Sturt, Eyre and Mitchell, who used it in a variety of ways to lend their explorations an air of symmetry and, hence, dramatic interest. To a lesser or (mainly) greater extent, all these writers followed Flinders in dwelling on their own feelings and impressions as an authentic aspect of their expedition's history. Again, they imitated Flinders's voluminous appendices, in particular the floral descriptions contributed by *Investigator* botanist Brown. Characteristically, Mitchell, with a greater flair for the picturesque than the informative, made it a habit to footnote all novel flora with an elaborate and Latin morphology. Eyre thought it appropriate to append an essay on the state of the Aborigines, Sturt on the state of South Australia.

As we might expect, in revising his journal and writing it up, Flinders paid considerable attention to place names. He recognized they were not arbitrary impositions on the map, but rather referred to the progress of the voyage. They referred not to appearances, but to the experience of appearances appearing, in short, to the dynamic of the journey – and therefore to the traveller's recollection of travelling. And, just as Flinders's *Voyage* was the result of almost unprecedented literary and graphic revision, so, too, his place names revealed an unprecedented biographical coherence. This is particularly apparent in the group of names in Spencer Gulf that Flinders derived from his 'native province' of Lincolnshire (see plate 15).

The region of Spencer Gulf, east of Nuyt's easternmost point and west of Encounter Bay, where Flinders met the French navigator T. M. Baudin (also on a voyage of discovery), was the only portion of the Australian coast that Flinders could claim to have discovered in his 1802 circumnavigation – Australia's northern, western and eastern coasts had all been previously coasted, if not surveyed. As a result, perhaps, Flinders took the unusual step of naming nearly thirty islands, bays and headlands in Spencer Gulf after places in his home county. The motive for this comprehensive commemoration of his natal place might be thought to have been straightforwardly self-promoting, a matter of making the most of what were, after all, modest discoveries.

But more hung on the existence of Spencer Gulf than Flinders's rather slender reputation. As Flinders reports in his *Voyage*, on the afternoon of 20 February 1802, after more than a month following the unbroken coast of the Great Australian Bight, the shore was seen to veer away to the north and a passage became visible. Flinders recalls the reaction of the *Investigator* crew:

A tide from the north-eastward, apparently the ebb, ran more than one mile an hour; which was the more remarkable from no set of tide, worthy to be noticed, having hitherto been observed upon the coast. No land could be seen in the direction from whence it came; and these circumstances, with the trending of the coast to the north, did not fail to excite many conjectures. Large rivers, deep inlets, inland seas, and passages into the Gulph of Carpentaria, were terms frequently used in our conversations of this evening; and the prospect of making an interesting discovery, seemed to have infused new life and vigour into every man in the ship.[8]

In other words, in the discovery of Spencer Gulf lay the possible key to the enigma of the Australian interior. Why Flinders should have thought so is not explained in the published account. But, in the *Abridged Narrative*, which Flinders prepared in Mauritius – a much slighter document than the later *Voyage*, but anticipating its biographical focus – Flinders enlarges on his reasons. Referring, firstly, to his own earlier discovery of Bass Strait, dividing Tasmania from the Australian mainland, he writes:

The currents, which had been found to set out of the unknown space between Van Diemen's Land, at the southern extremity of the continent, and New South Wales, had induced a pretty general belief that a strait existed here; and this was partly confirmed in 1798 by my friend Mr George Bass . . . I fully demonstrated the existence of the strait, by sailing through it and making the circuit of Van Diemen's Land . . .[9]

It is in this context that the unusual behaviour of the tides at the entrance to Spencer Gulf excited so much interest:

One separation being thus clearly ascertained, the opinion of further intersections was strengthened by analogy; and it was further countenanced by a tradition or report amongst the native inhabitants of Port Jackson. They said, that on the west side of their mountains existed a people, who planted potatoes and maize; and when asked of what complexion were these people, they shewed the inner side of their hands, of an olive colour. Now supposing the country to be intersected by straits, or occupied by a Mediterranean sea, it was possible that some Malay vessel had been lost there; and that the crew, finding a fertile country, had established themselves in the part specified by the natives.[10]

In the event, Flinders's argument from analogy broke down. Within two days of departing north-eastwards from what Flinders later called 'Port Lincoln', hopes had been 'considerably damped by the want of boldness in the shores, and the shallowness of the water'; by 11 March, Flinders had located the gulf's 'termination'.[11] In adopting Lincolnshire names here, then, Flinders was not commemorating a discovery so much as a disappointment; he was not drawing attention to his claim to fame, but to the way in which fame had eluded him. The termination of Spencer Gulf could almost be said to have marked the end of Flinders's career as an explorer. Why, then, did Flinders go to such lengths to name this region of defeat? Why, in writing up his journal, did he retrace his steps so obsessively in this region?

Up until now I have drawn attention to the way in which explorers and settlers 'constructed' their biographies spatially – and, by the same token, made places where they lived. But there has been absent from this discussion any recognition of what might be called the personal factor. Now, though, having established how, as travellers and travelling writers, men and women as diverse as Mitchell, Cook and Mrs Williams belonged to the same spatial history, we are in a much better position to interpret the significance of individual differences. Mitchell did not travel as Sturt did; Banks did not sail as Cook. But, as I have already suggested, the significance of these differences is to be sought less in individual psychology than in differing attitudes towards the getting of knowledge. Where such travellers disagreed, it was not so much (or not simply) because of a personality clash, but because they differed over the proper objects of knowledge.

It is at this level, I think, that we need to turn to Flinders's Spencer Gulf place names – not as personal advertisements but as testimonies to a geographical intuition, to a sense that something *objective* linked the traveller to the place he had discovered, and not just the accident of his being first there. When we explore them in this way, something else emerges: we also begin to see how, after all, geographical knowledge was personal knowledge and, in the naming and description of places, it was possible to intimate the very ground of one's own identity. In this respect, to explore the meaning of Flinders's names is also to propose a reflective reading applicable to other travellers, a means of reinserting biography into history.

The first point to make is that, like Cook, Flinders did not give his names at the time. According to H. M. Cooper, an examination of Flinders's preliminary charts and the *Investigator* log books reveals that, of the 140 names Flinders bestowed on the Unknown Coast only 18 were bestowed at the time,[12] and these did not include the Lincolnshire names. Most of the names were added later, perhaps, Cooper speculates, in Mauritius, where, as Flinders notes in the *Voyage*, the fair log was worked up and the charts revised and enlarged. It is more probable, though, that Flinders decided on his names in or around 1812, after he had finally returned to England and was hard at work writing the *Voyage* and preparing his charts for publication. In a diary entry for 27 March 1811, Flinders reports dining with Lord Radstock and notes 'where were Ld Waldegrave and some others, all unknown to me'.[13] It was presumably only after this encounter that Flinders decided to name Cape Radstock 'in honour of admiral Lord Radstock'[14] and the first two islands to the east of it 'Waldegrave's Isles'. At any rate, the conjunction of these names on the southern coast which Flinders discovered is suggestive. Again, in a postscript to a letter, dating from December 1812, Flinders informs his friend, Wiles, 'Upon the before unknown south coast of Terra Australis, you will see Cape Wiles and Liguanea Island.'[15] (Liguanea was the name of Wiles's plantation in Jamaica.) Flinders had been in regular contact with Wiles ever since his return to England in 1810. Thus this postscript suggests the naming was quite recent. And these names like the others occur in the immediate vicinity of the Lincolnshire names.

In selecting Lincolnshire names some ten years after the event, there were obvious personal and political motives. In 1809, while still in captivity, Flinders learnt 'from a Moniteur of July 1808 . . . that French names were given to all my discoveries'.[16] However, by 1813, the authors of these names, François Peron and L. C. Desantes de Freycinet, had still not published charts to support their claim to priority in the area. Flinders's publication of his charts would establish Spencer Gulf as his discovery, and his choice of names connect it even more pointedly with him and him alone. Besides this, there was the vexed question of Flinders's promotion. Flinders saw in his *Voyage* his only chance of obtaining the advancement he thought he deserved. In this context, too, his names and especially his complimentary references to both his patrons, the Admiralty Lords (commemorated in the name Spencer Gulf) and Sir Joseph Banks (who had a group of islands named after him), in the region of his own discoveries, would be a strong hint about another reputation worth advancing, namely his own.

But this reduction of Flinders's naming strategy to purely personal motives will not do. For one thing, it ignores the context of their appearance – the exhaustively comprehensive and scientific *A Voyage to Terra Australis*; for another, it ignores the spatial arrangement of Flinders's place names. In his selection and arrangement of names, Flinders was not lapsing into naive autobiography; he was saying something about his life as an explorer, something about exploring as a mode of knowing. This emerges clearly when we compare the disposition of his Australian names with their Lincolnshire counterparts. Flinders's Lincolnshire names do not merely recall, in an anecdotal and sentimental fashion, familiar places of his childhood. No doubt Donington, 'the birthplace of Matthew Flinders, is a charming old-world market town, set amidst the fens'. True, 'Sibsey is a large but straggling village and parish.'[17]

But the essential point about Flinders's Lincolnshire names in Spencer Gulf is that they preserve the spatial and topographical relationship of the Lincolnshire villages (see plate 16). Take, first of all, the Lincolnshire villages whose names Flinders transposes. On the map, they fall into three constellations. In the south-west, proceeding south and westward, one finds successively Kirton, Sleaford, Bicker, Donington, Surfleet, Spalding, Grantham and Stamford. To the north-east, on the other hand, cluster the villages of Langton, Winceby, Dalby, Partney, Lusby, Hareby, Spilsby, Bolingbroke (Old and New), Reevesby, Kirkby, Stickney and Sibsey. These two zones are divided by the crescent of (reading from north to south) Louth,

Tumby and Boston, a sort of barrier between the two larger groups of names.

The same tripartite arrangement characterizes Flinders's names in Spencer Gulf (plate 15). To the south and south-west of Port Lincoln we find Cape Donington, Bicker Island, Point Kirton, Surfleet Point, Spalding Cove, Stamford Hill, Grantham Island and Sleaford Mere. To the north-east of Port Lincoln is located the Sir Joseph Banks Group of islands. From north to south, these are Winceby, Reevesby, Lusby, Kirkby, Dalby, Hareby, Langton, Sibsey, Spilsby and Stickney. Kirkby Island, Flinders notes, stands 'nearest to the point' on the mainland which he called Point Bolingbroke. The equivalent of the Lincolnshire crescent in Spencer Gulf is the coastal arc of Tumby, Louth and Boston islands and bays.

Of course, the antipodean Lincolnshire is not an exact spatial replica. As the flagship of these names, Port Lincoln occupies a central position, in contrast with the peripheral location of Lincolnshire's county town. It is hard to see why Flinders reverses the relative positions of Louth and Tumby. Again, on his map, the south-western group has been drawn together, while the north-eastern group is more decisively isolated. In short, Flinders's names do not reproduce the layout of English Lincolnshire exactly – they could almost be said to revise and clarify its spatial relationships. And much the same is true of the implied topographical resemblances. The three groups of English names are associated with three distinct types of country. Those to the south-west lie on limestone uplands which decline north-east from Lincoln edge. It is a country of orchards and small farms, in Flinders's day already largely enclosed. The villages to the north-east, on the other hand, lie huddled in the troughs of the upland Wolds. But between these two elevated areas lie the Fens, unenclosed and, in Flinders's day, still subject to inundation. In short, a wide coast. From Keal Hill near Spilsby one can look south-west 'where the greensand ends and the road drops into a plain which is without a hill for the next fifty or sixty miles'. The Fens extend, not only south and east to the Wash, but north and west among the Rivers Witham and Bain (on which Tumby stands).

These extended views and the regions associated with them also played their part in influencing Flinders's final choice of Australian names. In one of his manuscript charts, he wrote, instead of Stamford Hill, 'Keal Hill'. The panorama of land, sea and islands, which had unfolded before him as he stood on his Australian hill, enabling him to take 'numerous bearings', made Keal Hill an obvious choice of name. Why, then, did he replace it with 'Stamford' Hill?[18] No notable elevation distinguishes the English Stamford. It is plausible to speculate that Flinders recognized that, whatever its individual aptness, Keal Hill disrupted the wider spatial correspondence he wanted to establish. Similarly, perhaps, it may not be too far-fetched to wonder whether, when Flinders recalled how near the watering places at Port Lincoln 'small shells and bits of coral might be picked out' and reflected that 'this part, at least, of Terra Australis cannot have emerged very many centuries from the sea',[19] he was struck by the resemblance to fields near his home town of Donington, where shells littered the fields, a visible reminder that, before the sea dykes, it too had lain under water.

What is the significance of Flinders's elaborate and, one is tempted to say, laboured analogy between Lincolnshire and Spencer Gulf's coasts and islands? Perhaps in choosing homely names Flinders anticipated the views of De Quincey. Perhaps he wanted to avoid the 'ambitious principle' in name-inventing which results in 'something monstrous and fanciful'. But such an idea does not take us far. After all, Flinders was quite capable of coining the kind of name to which De Quincey objected, names like Haul-Off Rock and Cape Catastrophe, whose 'truth' would seem to be 'casual and special' in the extreme. Still it does seem that, while individually arbitrary, Flinders's names were, taken as a whole, a sustained effort to respect what De Quincey called the 'local truth'. In Spencer Gulf, Flinders had run into the difficulty later described by Barron Field: the principle of analogy had broken down. Tides did not foretoken, as they had done elsewhere, promising passage. And the gulf itself, with its hazy, hard-to-define low horizons, was difficult to characterize.

In this context, Flinders adopted a different strategy: he captured his experience of that sea and its islands by a process of *spatial* association; and, in this way, instead of reducing geographical objects to an ambitiously motivated personal mnemonic, he suggested an objective, geographical association between his own earliest experiences and his career as a navigator. There was a sense in which this naming strategy enabled him to transcend the merely accidental. And the accidental had been rudely brought home to Flinders at the entrance to Spencer Gulf by the shocking death of no fewer than six of his crew through drowning. But Cape Catastrophe, which resulted from this, was not an isolated geographical epitaph: for Flinders commemorated the dead sailors in the names of six islands that stand offshore there and, respecting the ranks of the lost men, he named the largest of the islands after John Thistle, their officer. In this way Flinders commemorated his men by a form of spatial association. In some way, by perpetuating their relations in the seascape, he raised geometry to the status of myth. He wrote out their memory geographically, as places related to one another on a map, in this way preserving the historical moment where death and geography met. And, to underline his spatial biography, with characteristic irony, Flinders called the sea between Cape Catastrophe and Thistle Island 'Thorny Passage'.[20]

What was true of Flinders's names was no less true of the *Voyage* as a whole. In writing his history of a journey Flinders aimed to give his personal experience a scientific value; he wanted to show his method of exploring as a mode of knowing, and the means of doing this was to reveal the true nature of associative logic and, in particular, the validity of the argument from analogy. The country Flinders discovered did not in any naive way reflect his own personality or personal history. Yet it was, in some sense, a product of his mind: what he saw, where he went, and how he ordered the results, all of this was an intellectual activity. And, if the organization of this complex experience of exploring, and the discoveries it brought, were not to be arbitrary, it had to be grounded in some coherent theory of knowledge. Without some grasp of how the mind worked, it was impossible to know anything about the world.

This, for Flinders, was the significance of the psychological doctrine of associationism; for the way in which philosophers like Hume and Hartley had described the mind joining together ideas to form associative chains of reasoning was also a way of explaining the logic of discovery. A good introduction to this doctrine, particularly as it pervaded Flinders's thinking, is a letter Flinders wrote from Mauritius in 1804 to his wife. He tells her that he has dedicated the first day of the year to ' "the pleasures of memory" '.[21] This phrase, which Flinders placed inside quotation marks, almost certainly alludes to Samuel Rogers's popular poem, 'The Pleasures of Memory', published in 1792. There was much in Rogers's poem, one imagines, that must have appealed to the proud, perhaps over-proud, Flinders in Mauritius – Rogers's picture of the slave, for instance, a prisoner transported to a foreign coast, 'Crushed till his high, heroic spirit bleeds':

> Yet here, even here, with pleasures long resigned,
> Lo! MEMORY bursts the twilight of his mind.[22]

But the real interest of Rogers's poem lay in its philosophical argument. 'The Pleasures of Memory' was, in fact, a poetic exposition of the philosopher Hartley's doctrine of association-ism. The basis of this theory, as Rogers himself explained in his preface, was the notion of attraction:

> When ideas have any relation whatever, they are attractive of each other in the mind; and the perception of any object naturally leads to the idea of another, which was connected with it either in time or place, or which can be compared or contrasted with it. Hence arises our attachment to inanimate objects; hence also, in some degree, the love of our country . . .[23]

This kind of connection, Rogers explains, follows a mechanical process, acting 'in subservience to the senses'. Had Flinders, for example, named Port Lincoln in Spencer Gulf because the place brought to mind (as a picture might) the town he knew well in England, then he would have been following this mechanical principle of connecting.

But Memory is by no means limited to this. The second canto of Rogers's poem evokes the active Memory, which is not 'excited by sensible objects', but is 'an internal operation of the mind'. This faculty does not merely associate ideas, but transforms them into complex ideas. The active Memory 'preserves . . . the treasures of art and science, history and philosophy'. It is responsible for 'every effusion of the Fancy who with the boldest effort can only compound or transpose, augment or diminish the materials she has collected and still retains'.[24] The most significant feature of this faculty of active transformation is that it can pass from what has been to what may be, from what is to what is not. It is the power of concluding and, as Rogers says, 'We can only anticipate the future, by concluding what is possible from what is past.' Rogers does not enlarge on how this process occurs, but it is evidently by way of what Hartley (and Hume before him) calls analogy.

The relevance of this to Flinders's speculation about the interior of Australia is obvious. Having found on an earlier occasion that strong tides were associated with a strait, when he again encounters unusual currents Flinders is able to argue by analogy that another strait must be found nearby. That is, by an internal operation of the mind, Flinders can argue from the past to the future, from what was before to what is possible again. In this way, he can advance logically beyond the horizon. It is worth pointing out here that the logic of this argument is in complete contrast to that which Banks earlier used to 'prove' the uninhabited nature of the interior. For Banks's logic was only capable of denying difference: interpreting a particular case (the observation of Aborigines along the New Holland coast) in terms of a universal truth (that all savages are said to depend on the sea), Banks reduces the possible future to conformity and uniformity with the present.

Flinders, by contrast, employs what might be called a logic of travelling. Certainly, this idea of a travelling logic is particularly relevant to Flinders's investigation (and solution) of the problem of compass variation, which occupies an expansive appendix to his published Voyage. It had long been recognized that the compass showed different variations from true north when it was moved about the ship. But Flinders was the first to observe that 'a change in the direction of the ship's head was also found to make a difference in the needle'.[25] Flinders's discovery was a triumph of argument by analogy. Since movement of the compass about the ship had an influence on the needle, it was reasonable to argue by analogy that the movement of the ship itself might have an effect. But this reasoning had another significance. It underlined the point that, for Flinders, motion and orientation, the twin conditions of travelling, were instrumental aspects of knowledge. Travelling, if it was properly understood, if it was subjected to the proper reasoning processes, could yield a truth that eluded merely static deduction.

Flinders himself made the point that, in reaching his conclusion, he had adopted an approach that differed from that of many of his predecessors. There was, Flinders writes, an 'injudicious practice' among earlier navigators of not entering a compass variation in the journal when it was thought to differ too much from 'what was thought to be the truth'. This suppression of the inexplicable difference was, of course, part and parcel of the same reductionism that characterized, for example, Banks's reasoning. Flinders noted, 'There are however many honourable exceptions; and at the head of these must be placed the immortal Cook.'[26] Cook, by suspending judgement, had allowed inexplicable novelties, departures from the normal, to appear. Flinders went one step further and *anticipated* them. He adopted an expectant attitude; he looked for signs of change in the belief that the contrast they made with what was already known was itself a source of comparison. It was associative reasoning itself that drew the explorer on. Like a ship at sea, the explorer advanced on the current of his own reasoning. By his mental attitude, he attracted the world to him; and, vice versa, he found himself oriented towards the magnetic north of discovery.

In this context, Flinders's solution of the problem of compass drift was a particularly appropriate triumph for associative reasoning. It had been Hume's ambition to provide a theory of mind analogous to Newton's theory of the physical world. Hume had sought to elucidate a principle of mental attraction comparable to Newton's theory of gravitation in the physical world. What, then, could be more apt than that Flinders should take advantage of Hume's theory to solve a problem in Newton's domain?

In place of a science of facts, Flinders pursued a course of investigation based on the interpretation of signs: nothing was too insignificant to count. Hence Flinders resisted classifying phenomena hierarchically, treating the ephemeral and the permanent as strictly comparable in significance. It is this attitude which throws light on the extraordinary detail of his *Voyage*. Take, for example, this passage:

> The wind was light at east, and the weather fine over head; but there was so dense a haze below, that the true horizon could not be distinguished from several false ones, and we had six or seven different latitudes from as many observers: those taken by me to the north and south differed 19 minutes. This dense haze, from its great refractive power, altered the appearance of objects in a surprising manner: a sandy beach seemed to be a chalky cliff, and the lowest islands to have steep shores.[27]

This is an entirely empirical or scientific description but, rather than record reproducible facts, it describes phenomena as they appear in all their elusiveness. It is a passage about the conditions of travelling, therefore a passage about the conditions of knowledge. In offering this account, Flinders suspends the question of discoveries in favour of a detailed description of the nature of exploration. And the detail into which Flinders enters is in inverse proportion to the general truth of the phenomena. It is exactly because the haze creates highly particular effects that it warrants close analysis; for it is in particularities that the associative mind glimpses passages to grander truths.

Flinders's belief that knowledge emerges by way of analogy (we might almost say, metaphorically) explains why equal space is given to all objects of scientific interest, whether small or great. A striking instance of this occurs in the first volume of the *Voyage* on facing pages 68 and 69. While the left-hand page is dominated by two columns of anatomical measurements of an Aborigine, 'one of the best proportioned of our visitors', met at King George's Sound, the right-hand page deals with the latitude and longitude of Bald Head at the entrance to King George's Sound, to ascertain which involves a discussion of the relative accuracies of the ship's 'time keepers'. The discussion is supplemented by a footnote recording the situation assigned to Bald Head by the two earlier explorers, George Vancouver and d'Entrecasteaux.[28] Flinders feels no embarrassment of perspective in presenting these data side by side. The extent of an Aborigine's nostrils is as significant as the position of a continent. And this is characteristic of *A Voyage to Terra Australis* as a whole. At one moment we gaze with Flinders towards the stars. At another, the telescope is replaced by the magnifying glass, and we are down on our hands and knees, searching the arenaceous hinterland for water.

But, as I suggested earlier, this way of describing the world, according to a distinct and coherent theory of mind, not only throws light on Flinders the explorer: it also has biographical implications. In exploring the affinity Flinders felt with the world of appearances and the richness of associations that congregated in certain parts of the text, we can begin to see where his own interests lay. We are able to penetrate aspects of his personality that conventional biography overlooks. And we can see how, after all, in a certain way Flinders did write himself over Spencer Gulf.

Flinders knew his poets and certainly, finding how he reflected on his own mind, it is hard not to be reminded of Coleridge and Wordsworth – so closely does his psychology of mind and his optimism that it is a tool for knowing the world resemble theirs. On top of this, they share his own view of what a man's biography is, and how it is made. When, for instance, Wordsworth expressed his disapproval of 'poetic diction' and called for a new empiricism of the heart, he did so in the spirit, not of an eighteenth-century classifier, but of an experimental scientist:

> I have at all times endeavoured to look steadily at my subject; consequently there is I hope in these poems little falsehood of description, and my ideas are expressed in language fitted to their respective importance.[29]

But this interest in the particular was not disinterested or unselective. Like 'The Man of Science', 'who feels that his knowledge is pleasure; and where he has no pleasure he has no knowledge',[30] the poet was drawn to certain subjects by the pleasure they gave him. And what was this pleasure but the pleasure of sympathy or imagination, the possibility of beholding through sympathy with the particular 'the great and universal passions of men, the most general and interesting of their occupations, and the entire world of nature before me'.[31] Working associatively, the active mind, the imagination, could combine particulars to reveal a moral and intellectual universe extending beyond the immediate horizon.

Coleridge is equally eloquent in expressing the biographical implications of Flinders's recognition of the imaginative principle in exploring. Flinders's biographer, Ernest Scott, says that Flinders had a particular love of Defoe's classic, *Robinson Crusoe*. What drew Flinders to Defoe? Not a somewhat puerile taste for the exotic, as Scott supposes.[32] Rather, he appealed to Flinders for much the same reason he appealed to Coleridge. 'De Foe's excellence it is', wrote Coleridge, 'to make me forget my specific class, character, and circumstances, and to raise me while I read him, into the universal man.'[33] The significance of this praise is that it recognizes that the notion of the 'universal man' has by 1800 become out of date. The passive empiricist has been overtaken by the active associationist. As Coleridge himself exemplified in his own life, the man who aims at universality does so now by way of cultivating singularity. 'There is in the heart of all men', wrote Coleridge,

> a working principle – call it ambition, or vanity, or desire of distinction, the inseparable adjunct of our individuality and personal nature, and flowing from the same source as language, – the instinct and necessity in each man of declaring his particular existence, and thus of singling or singularising himself.[34]

Judging from his journals, his letters and the *Voyage to Terra Australis*, what Flinders admired most of all in Defoe was his almost affected plainness of style and, what went with this rhetorical abstinence, his hero's almost obtuse refusal to take advantage of his cultural inheritance. Robinson Crusoe was not a man without a history but, if the castaway was to succeed in making a place for himself, every proposition had now to be tested empirically. A man without innate qualities, Crusoe acquired his character from the environment. Perhaps it was this fiction which appealed to Flinders but, if it did so, it was for the same reason that Defoe's book appealed to Coleridge – nostalgically. For, as we have seen, only by singularizing himself could Flinders find a way of possessing Australia, the island whose integrity he had ascertained.

For Flinders, unlike Cook, could not possess Australia by coasting alone: he aimed at possessing its interior imaginatively. Flinders's Spencer Gulf names were a strategy for possessing the country imaginatively. They shifted attention from objects to intervals, to the mode of knowing them. They showed how an explorer carried with him the memory of places, not in the form of a host of individual sensations, but as an associative network. In this sense, just as Coleridge in 'The Ancient Mariner' reinvested Cook's voyages with the very aura of superstition Cook himself was at pains to dispel, so Flinders, in a different way, once more made Australia's coast problematic, a site of unexpected places, a host to unforeseen fates – and it may be symptomatic that, in connection with the loss of men at Cape Catastrophe, Flinders reports that, according to the men, this disaster had been foretold by a fortune-teller in London.

By reflecting on it, Flinders turned his Australian experience into biography. But it was his own mind, its explorational intent, that had been the means of characterizing Australia as a discrete object – an island, a distinct geographical unit that could be named unequivocally. The two aspects of discovery could not be dissociated: and it is in recognizing this that we can glimpse the nature of Flinders's own spatial biography. It is, for instance, a mistake to imagine that the name of the tiny boat in which, in 1798, George Bass and Flinders began their Australian explorations has a merely anecdotal interest. The *Tom Thumb*, and the kind of exploration carried out in it, belonged to the same order of miniaturization that enabled Flinders to juxtapose an aboriginal cranium and a coastal cape.

This spatial metamorphosis was not an agoraphobic reaction: it had a demonstrable epistemological value. Crouched in the *Tom Thumb*, the navigators were not crushed by the immensity of the continent. They felt, as it were, its ground, read the palm of its currents. Emphasizing how little they had seen for themselves, they became, paradoxically, authorities. Stressing that they possessed no place, they found no horizon foreign to them. But, without the artificial horizon of their own singularity, the strategy of association possessing wider views would have been impossible. For miniaturizing himself, Flinders also magnified his control: his Lilliputian stature comparably reduced the Australian coast to human proportions, to the intimate aspect of a house, a body. Thus among the names that Flinders gave in the region of his later Spencer Gulf discoveries, we find Elbow Hill, Antechamber Bay and Backstairs Passage.

Flinders's sense that the microscopic hidden truths might be used to magnify was also characteristic of his own spatial biography. It was not only that, in attending to the details of Spencer Gulf, the whole of Australia might be unlocked. Nor, merely, that a quivering needle, a lull in the wind or a paler hue of water contained in them, properly entered into, hints of hidden causes. These particularities also expressed, metaphorically, Flinders's own spatial fantasies. They were transformations of a phenomenological tension that found its first site in the Lincolnshire of Flinders's childhood. Referring, in his *Voyage to Terra Australis,* to his eventual release from Mauritius, Flinders writes,

> Those who can receive gratification from opening the door to an imprisoned bird, and remarking the joy with which it hops from spray to spray, tastes of every seed and sips from every rill, will readily conceive the sensations of a man during the first days of liberation.[35]

Despite its conventional language, this is a passage that, in its almost unconscious adoption of a double perspective, unmistakably reveals Flinders's characteristic outlook. If, on the one hand, Flinders identifies with the human liberators who set free the bird, on the other, he seems to share the sensations of the bird itself. He is gratified, we might almost say magnified, by the thought of his own pleasure. But, to enter into the sensation of freedom itself, he identifies with the 'imprisoned bird'.

The interest of this passage goes further. For it suggests that the long solitude Flinders experienced in Mauritius, giving as it did ample scope for fanciful reflection and the pleasures of memory, may have refined his associational inclination. Rogers would have thought this perfectly natural. For, as regards Memory, Rogers writes,

> The world and its occupations give a mechanical impulse to

the passions, which is not very favourable to the indulgence of this feeling. It is in a calm and well-regulated mind that the Memory is most perfect; and solitude is her best sphere of action.[36]

In this sense, there was a certain fatefulness about Flinders's time in Mauritius, and his refusal to countenance illegal escape; for, in Mauritius, Flinders found the solitude in which he could cultivate his mind. There, in enlarging his maps, and in concealing, as best he could, his precious bearings, Flinders laid the groundwork of his spatial biography. In his cage, he compassed the world.

Certainly, there is a passage in Flinders's Mauritius journal that supports these conjectures. In August 1805 Flinders was given permission to quit the Garden Prison and was allowed to lodge with a French family in the interior of the island. On 21 October 1805, in the course of exploring the surrounding mountains, Flinders went with his friend Pitot to visit one of the island's more spectacular waterfalls. The experience set off a train of association:

It appears to me that originally there had been only one great cascade or declivity at the mouth of the valley, but that the water draining through the crevices of the rock above caused pieces to fall down, forming another cascade. The same thing, happening further and further back in the course of time, has brought them to what we now find them; and it is still going on . . . thus nature proceeds in reducing all things to a level as well in the moral as the physical world . . . From reflections of this sort which I pursued much farther, I passed to the vicissitudes of my own life. I was born in the fens of Lincolnshire, where a hill is not to be seen for many miles, at a distance from the sea, and my family unconnected with sea affairs, or any kind of enterprize or ambition. After many incidents of fortune and adventure, I found myself a commander in the Royal Navy, having been charged with an arduous expedition of discovery; have visited a great variety of countries, made three times the tour of the world; find my name known in more kingdoms than where I was born, with some degree of credit; and this moment a prisoner in a mountainous island in the Indian Ocean.[37]

It would be hard to imagine an autobiographical account that demonstrated more clearly how 'the centres of our fate', to borrow Gaston Bachelard's formulation, are located in 'the spaces of our intimacy'.[38] For the profound tension between the horizontal and the vertical, which Flinders describes here, is not only a spatial opposition that goes back to his earliest memories of the Fens: it also expresses the ambiguity of Flinders's fate – where the ambition 'to get on' has led, despite himself, not only to horizontal, but also to vertical, advancement. But we notice that it is in the opposite, the threateningly vertical, environment of Mauritius that this process of reflection occurs. For much as the contemplation of the waterfall depresses Flinders, it also elates him. And this dialectical tension informs his recollection of home. If, in one mood, the flatness of the Fens, their open horizons, induces a delicious sense of retirement and refuge, in another, their unadventurous equilibrium provokes panic and revolt.

We begin to feel both the horror of the plains and their attraction, a tension that, perhaps, only the map-making mind can bring under control. For, if the horizontal is the realm of Flinders's childhood, unenclosed by hills, open in all directions, the place where all futures are possible, then it is also the focus of annihilation, the inescapable point of return, where all variety is reduced to a level. In this latter aspect, it signifies the waste of vital energies, the dissipation of promise, the oblivion of an imprisonment without walls. This is the double aspect of the plain: that it releases, but releases into nothingness. Directionless and equal, it inhibits motion, it resists exploration. The solution to the plain is the mountain. But this, too, has its ambiguous aspect. If, in the form of cascades, it encourages the current of associative thought, it also leads to the prospect of extinction. Obeying the vertical impulse of its nature, the cascade inexorably wears itself out, loses its nobility, in the vicissitudes of time grows perhaps serpentine. The hill Flinders once desired, perhaps, bounding the fen, a point of departure, grows, in adulthood, into a coronet of mountains, symbolizing not release but enclosure. The variety of the world, fanned out by his arduous career, is closed up again in an island as round as the first horizon.

It is interesting, too, that, in transforming this destructive tension between vertical and horizontal into a constructive force, it is the sea that mediates. It is the sea that is supremely fluid, a devourer of horizons, charged with muscular currents, site of drowning. The sea is the ambiguous element in which Flinders turns the tension in his intimate spaces to healthy account. For the sea, like a river, is a mountain that moves: it carries towards and beyond horizons. But the sea is also a plain, a furrowed and central level where there is no threat of falling or of ever being worn out. The sea is a prison that releases.

In this profounder context, we may speculate that the attention Flinders paid to the unemphatic outlines and hazes of Spencer Gulf expressed more than a sentimental journey, more than a laboured contrivance to advance himself professionally. In naming those low islands and coasts, in miniaturizing them and standing over them, it may be that Flinders was able to transform deep feelings of imprisonment felt in the Fens to a kind of command and control; that, in this way, he could reconcile himself to his home horizons without the nightmare of being drowned there.

There is a suggestive passage in Ernest Scott's biography where he draws attention to Flinders's reaction to the mountainous west coast of Tasmania. Scott quotes Flinders:

> The mountains which presented themselves to our view . . . were amongst the most stupendous works of nature I ever beheld, and it seemed to me are the most dismal and barren that can be imagined. The eye ranges over these peaks, and curiously formed lumps of adamantine rock, with astonishment and horror.[39]

And Scott comments,

> Flinders was a fenland-bred man, and, passing from the low levels of eastern England to a life at sea in early youth, had had no experience of mountainous country . . .[40]

Scott is right to recognize something unusual about Flinders's reaction, but I doubt if he is correct in regarding it as merely 'a curious psychological fact'. For, in itself, a dislike of mountains is hardly conclusive – Scott himself quotes Ruskin to indicate that the taste for mountain scenery was a relatively recent fashion. Again, as we have seen, in the context of Australian description generally, Flinders's language is quite conventional. 'Astonishment and horror' at the 'dismal and barren' are the monotonously repeated expressions of a host of Australian explorers, from Grey to Giles.

Rather, I would say, we must seek the basis of Flinders's reaction in his characteristic mode of reasoning, in his way of seeing and making sense of the world. For, unlike the cascade in Mauritius, the associative processes that characterized Flinders's thought were horizontal. They spread themselves out in space. He thought in terms of clear views, uninterrupted vistas; he grasped mental concepts most easily in terms of geometrical images natural in a landscape where canals stretched to the horizon or intersected as expected. Where others found the view monotonous, he found it gave him room to speculate. Wherever he stood, at the centre of horizons, he was not dwarfed.

Rather than decisive objects, Flinders cultivated the continuity of spaces. There is interesting evidence of this in an amendment Flinders made to his Fair Log. On 12 March 1802, Flinders despatched a body of men to climb a hill which was duly called after their leader, Mount Brown. In his Fair Log Flinders recorded Brown's opinion that,

> The view from the summit did not furnish any lakes or bays to the eastward, but a dead, uninteresting, flat country everywhere presented itself.[41]

When, much later, Flinders returned to this passage, in the course of writing his *Voyage to Terra Australis*, he altered Brown's words to read simply,

> In almost every direction the eye traversed over an uninterruptedly flat, woody country . . .[42]

Brown's country is no longer 'uninteresting': it is 'uninterrupted'. A landscape that stifled Brown's imagination Flinders found an endless source of associations. In this way the spaces of

Flinders's intimacy informed his life; in this way his biography became part of Australia's spatial history.

Writing to his wife in 1805, Flinders referred to a request for help he had directed to one of France's leading scientific patrons, the Comte de Fleurieu, and in a postscript added,

> 'I can't get out!' cried the starling. God help thee, says Yorick, but I'll let thee out. May Fleurieu feel as much humanity.[43]

The allusion to Sterne's alter ego is far from casual. Not only did Laurence Sterne, the parson of York, delight in geo-biographical puns; he was the author of a journal 'of the miserable feelings of a person separated from a Lady for whose society he languished'; he was the writer who, in *Tristram Shandy*, came nearest to transforming the narrative tradition of the novel into a map of the passions. He was the wit who, in his abundant good humour, made capes of noses, passages of breeches . . . who could convince himself 'there is a North west passage to the intellectual world'.

Less lyrically, more gravely, in his own sphere Flinders was comparably experimental. His exploration was primarily a matter of epistemological stance, a stance characterized by sympathy or the logic of association. It implied care for the small and insignificant. It equated the God-like gaze with attention to the particular. It recognized that rhetorical trans-positions were not necessarily senseless. Place names, conventional at home, abroad acquired once more their spatial charge. They reacquired, as it were, their metaphorical force – to intimate, by way of spatial association, directions, relation-ships, gradients and topographies. It could be that, in order to characterize new places, what was needed was not names that conformed to local truth but, on the contrary, names that brought the whole mechanism of association into question, revealing it as either a metaphorical mode of knowledge or else mere superstition. At any rate, Flinders's Spencer Gulf names enabled him to express (as never at home) his intimate sense of home. In this sense they were an epitome of the *Voyage* as a whole – a book that found ways to speak clearly even where nothing was clear. For whether or not Flinders found inspiration in Sterne, there is little doubt that in *Tristram Shandy* he could have found one of the best glosses on his own life, as explorer and as writer. Says Tristram Shandy,

> There is nothing more pleasing to a traveller – or more terrible to travel-writers, than a large rich plain . . .[44]

7

Elysiums for Gentlemen

It may be as well to notice here a peculiar characteristic of the free
labouring class in Australia: it is in a state of constant migration.

'The Emigrant Mechanic'

Geometry cannot take the place of myth.

Octavio Paz, *The Labyrinth of Solitude*

One result of Flinders's Spencer Gulf survey was that he became
a founding father. A little over thirty years after his passage
Edward Wakefield formed in London the South Australian
Land Company. Its object was to initiate

> a grand experiment in the art of colonization and for the
> formation of a community among which industry would be
> wholly unfettered either by restrictions on trade, by monopo-
> lies or by taxation.[1]

The experiment was clearly utilitarian in inspiration and, as the
historian Douglas Pike has shown, Jeremy Bentham was
personally involved in its planning.[2] One of its curious features
was that the colonizers set sail for the general region of Spencer
Gulf's eastern shores with no clear idea of where they would
settle. The idea was that their surveyor, William Light, who in
theory at least was to arrive in the area some time before the main
party, would examine the coast to find a suitable location for the
capital of the future province. When the colonists arrived, they
would with any luck be able to disembark almost immediately;
and almost immediately begin their utilitarian experiment.

In the event, Light had only a few weeks in which to assess
the eligibility of various sites. And, inevitably, his siting of what
was to become Adelaide on plains near the mouth of the River
Torrens on St Vincent's Gulf drew hostile comment. One critic,
for example, argued that 'until the line of sea coast has been
surveyed, the most eligible site cannot be determined on'.[3] Who

knows, he said, whether the site of Adelaide may not turn out to be like Cook's Botany Bay, which was 'an excellent place . . . as long as Port Jackson lay unknown within a couple of hours' sail of it'. As he observed, the fault lay not with Light but with the planners: 'Col Light could as easily walk from Australia to England in three weeks, as examine 1,500 miles of coast in three months.'[4] Light himself could only agree. As he complained, 'I ought to have been sent out at *least six months* before any body else, which would have given me time to settle emigrants or stores as they arrived.'[5]

Even so, in his own defence, Light could argue that his choice of St Vincent's Gulf, rather than Spencer Gulf, had not been wholly arbitrary. For, and this was where Flinders came in, a comparison between Flinders's Port Lincoln on Spencer Gulf and his own proposed site on St Vincent's Gulf proved the latter was decisively superior, both as a harbour and in its agricultural potential. Not only this: in arriving at this conclusion, Light had been immeasurably helped by Flinders's own account of St Vincent's Gulf and, in particular, of the Mount Lofty Range bordering it on the east with its promise of rain. To this extent, his decision had been a rational one.

The debate over the *site* of Adelaide was in marked contrast to the general approval of Light's *town plan*. There were many features of the town plan that were attractive. For one thing, Light made imaginative use of the River Torrens, siting the northern part of the capital across the river at an angle to the city's southern half. For another, Light punctuated his streets with open central squares. On top of this, provision was made to preserve the integrity of the plan by buffering it against future development with a 'green belt'. But the main reason why Light's Adelaide met with approval was that it employed the rational principle of the grid. Light's picturesque additions were desirable, but it was the rational and equal division of the land into purchasable blocks that was the essential precondition of capitalist settlement – of the self-regulating 'democracy', based on free trade, which Wakefield was promoting.

The colonists' acceptence of Light's plan is easy to understand. After all, their initial willingness to invest in Wakefield's experiment had depended on their acceptance of the proposition that land *there* could be regarded very much like land *here*. Empty spaces on the map, accountably and equally subdivided, should yield returns that could, more or less, be computed in advance. This attitude was not only capitalist: it was also akin, of course, to the character of a nineteenth-century map. Such a map, with its ability to fix even blankness beneath the inflexible (and now reliably located) grid of longitude and latitude, was essentially an instrument for performing geometrical divisions. Located against the imaginary grid, the blankness of unexplored country was translatable into a blueprint for colonization: it could be divided up into blocks, the blocks numbered and the land auctioned, without the purchasers ever leaving their London offices. Light's grid plan met with approval because it was the physical embodiment of this map-like mentality. Oriented towards the cardinal points of the compass, its grid was a container for real estate; its streets were conduits for auctioneers.

All of this might suggest that the grid plan is immune, as it were, to spatial history. Exemplifying the principles of Euclidean geometry, the grid would seem to negate such spatial properties as direction, nearness, even 'here' and 'there'. For, by definition, the grid plan equalizes parts, rendering everywhere the same. In this sense, the grid plan is characterized, like the map grid, by its 'placelessness', by its elimination of viewpoints, of comings and goings, and indeed of history. If the grid, with its rectilinear arrangement of roads and buildings, has any historical significance at all, it is as the container of historical events: nothing more. In this sense, it exhibits the same historical neutrality or invisibility as the imaginary theatre in which the imperial historian sets his narrative. For it is one of the features of that theatre that it reconciles all viewpoints into one unifying cause-and-effect perspective. And this logic, equally applicable everywhere and at all times, is in reality no different from the spatial logic of the map. For the map connects up everything in advance. In advance, it presumes the unity of the space it covers.

The assumption that the grid plan is historically neutral, somehow a 'natural' or *a priori* solution to spatial organization, has been fairly widespread among urban historians. They have, on the whole, shared Christopher Tunnard's view that 'the orthogonal plan', so resistant to change, so indifferent to locality or the impress of personality, 'is a generic urban solution, of no critical significance'.[6] Towns laid out on grid principles resemble each other, at least on paper. And, since the grid is geographically characterless, the assumption has been that *therefore* it is also historically neutral. Indeed, its persistent uniformity throughout recorded time and space seems almost an affront to the notion of history. John Passmore, for instance, writes,

> Nothing could better display the despotic concept of perfection than the American-style grid town, with its echoes of Rome and, more remotely, of Pythagoras.[7]

And one of the notions such displays of arithmetic harmony appear to rule out is history itself.

But is this assumption justified? For one thing, as Light's experience demonstrates, the conception of perfection has frequently come into conflict with geographical reality. Light's critic might want complete geographical knowledge before reaching a decision but, in practice, any spatial decision on the ground was bound to be strategic: if only in this conflict between theory and practice, it might be said, the rationalism of the grid mentality leaves its mark on history. But the chasm that opens up between the rational principles of the grid and the strategic principles implicit in travelling reveals itself in other ways. It may, for example, not have been mere oversight that Light was given the impossible task of surveying 1,500 miles of coastline in only a few weeks, for one of the persistent effects of the map is to persuade the map-reader the country displayed is much smaller than it is. Evidence of this illusion is the strange story of a group of colonists who, emigrating in the early days of South Australian colonization, insisted on being landed on Kangaroo Island at the south end of St Vincent's Gulf, saying

> they would walk through the bush and should most likely reach Nepean Bay (on the island's north side) as soon or sooner than the ship.[8]

The same writer reports,

> Three of them, after wandering in the woods nearly a week
> were discovered and brought in exhausted through fatigue and
> want of nourishment . . . whilst the other two have never
> since been heard of.[9]

Here would seem to be tragic evidence of the danger in taking
that microcosm of the world, the map, literally.

Where the grid plan *has* been allowed a historical significance,
it has still been regarded as an essentially ahistorical catalyst of
events. This is particularly clear where it is cited as an urban solution associated with acts of colonization. In a fascinating study
of the segregation of Spanish and Indians in colonial Central
America, the American historian S. D. Markman points out
that, although both the *pueblos de indios* and the *pueblos de
españoles* were planned as gridirons with a central plaza,

> the symbolic values associated with the plaza in *pueblos de
> españoles* were totally foreign to those of the *pueblo de indios*.
> The plaza mayor of Spanish towns was the location and seat of
> political authority, of the market and of commerce, and was
> the main religious center. To live in its proximity implied that
> one was either a member of the power structure or of the elite
> of local Spanish society. In the *pueblo de indios*, the plaza was
> just a vaguely defined vacant space dominated by a church, its
> sole architectural distinction.[10]

In other words, the symbolic properties associated with the
urban layout of the grid were imported. They were a function
of the political, social and economic organization of the
transplanted culture in question. And, while the grid plan might
have been made to symbolize different cultural configurations,
it in no sense influenced them. It was not itself a symbolic
figure, simply a malleable container: indeed, it was this, if
anything, that made it such an efficient agent of colonization –
that it lent itself impartially to any organization of power.

Much the same conclusion can be drawn from most
discussion of the use of the grid plan in Australia. Commentators on Australian towns have expressed opposite views about
its symbolic significance. Take its political meaning, for

instance. The historian Ernest Favenc describes as an 'amusing eccentricity' Governor Gipp's insistence that

> all the towns laid out during his term of office should have no public squares included within their boundaries, being convinced that public squares encouraged the spread of democracy.[11]

But an opposite view of the square's political meaning was held by the anonymous author of *Melbourne As It Is, and As It Should Be*. Melbourne, founded one year before Adelaide, was a grid plan with none of Adelaide's redeeming features: in particular, as this writer argued, one of Melbourne's chief shortcomings was that it 'boasts no large central square' (see plate 17). This, he thought, was particularly regrettable, for the central square is

> the focus of commerce and civic authority, the residence of Municipal Authority.[12]

Had Robert Hoddle's original plan included a central square,

> Melbourne would now have had a commanding feature, and would have been more worthy of its position as the capital of a colony that seems rapidly taking the lead among the Australian group.[13]

If the anonymous critic thought that the grid signified a lack of authority, two modern writers, Cox and Stacey, regard the rectilinear layout of Australian towns as signifying the very opposite quality:

> Standardization and regularity of arrangement were the hallmarks of Authority: each town was related in a hierarchical manner to Westminster . . . generally towns were laid out as geometrical abstractions . . .[14]

and they add:

> in a similar manner to the Greek and Roman colonial towns that had been laid out some 2000 years previously.[15]

But what exactly do they mean by 'Authority'? Cox and Stacey base their view on Governor Darling's 1829 Regulations. Apart from stipulating that 'Townships of the Interior' should have a rectilinear form, the same Regulations spelt out the widths of streets, footpaths, front gardens and even the height of the 'Door-Sell' above the level of the crown of the street. Certainly, such instructions were designed to ensure uniformity. But were they authoritarian or democratic? After all, the same Regulations also announced that

> The extent of Ground, given to any one Individual, will be any number not exceeding four of the above mentioned (half-acre) Allotments.[16]

If, on the one hand, such strict egalitarianism was a means of preventing the concentration of private power, it was, on the other, a way of protecting the democratic interests of the people. The city square was an incitement to civil disobedience or it was an incitement to civic cohesion and unity of purpose.

Equally contradictory have been the claims made for the grid plan's social significance. The same anonymous critic regretted that Melbourne

> possesses no main arterial roads, conducting to the heart of the town . . . has no broad suburban roads, giving access to the country.[17]

As it is, he complains,

> The only skill exhibited in the plan of Melbourne is that involved in the use of square and compasses. Pope's couplet, slightly modified, exactly describes Melbourne . . .
>
> > Street answers street, each alley has its brother,
> > And half the city just reflects the other.[18]

In the verse epistle parodied here, Pope was lamenting a country estate whose chequered formality ruled out any picturesque inducement to explore. The English novelist Anthony Trollope expressed exactly the same feelings about Melbourne. In Sydney, he wrote, 'no arithmetic will set the wanderer right'. And, in his view, this made it a place of greater interest to the visitor: Sydney

> is not parallelogrammic and rectangular. One may walk about it and lose the direction in which one is going.[19]

In Melbourne, though, Trollope found

> I forget the numbers which I should remember and have no aid
> to memory in the peculiarity either of the position or of the
> name.[20]

The anonymous critic and Trollope shared a feeling that the
grid-plan town was paradoxically placeless and directionless.
Everywhere was alike. But, as both were candid enough to
admit, this spatial tedium did not seem to hold back social or
economic activity. On the contrary, Trollope thought, in their
preoccupation with numbers, Melbourne folk exhibited the
same commercial spirit he had encountered in Philadelphia:

> every house in it has its proper place, which can be found out
> at once, so long as the mind of the seeker be given to ordinary
> arithmetic.[21]

The journalist Richard Twopeny went even further, making an
explicit connection between Melbourne's commercial vitality
and its grid-plan layout. The newly disembarked visitor, he
reported,

> can hardly fail to be impressed by the size of the buildings
> around him, and by the width of the streets, which are laid out
> in rectangular blocks.[22]

The benefits of this spatial arrangement were, according to
Twopeny, social as well as economic: in comparison with
Sydney folk, Melbourne people

> dress better, talk better, think better, are better, if we accept
> Herbert Spencer's definition of Progress.[23]

Rectilinear town plans were chaotic or coherent; directionless
or full of direction; they were stimulating or monotonous. It is
even difficult to ascribe to the grid plan a decisive economic
advantage. The urban historian Tunnard notes that, historically,
it has been the plan of business cities. But it would be hard to
say the grid plan had been of critical importance in promoting
economic activity.[24] Certainly, even with a central square, the
grid plan was no guarantee of mercantile enterprise. The
rectilinear towns of the New World, for instance, which the

Spanish founded in the interior, did not of themselves promote trade. In such towns 'urban industries were almost always on a small scale, generally composed of workshops of the family type'.[25] By the same token, successful trading centres that conspicuously lack grid plans have been, as Tunnard himself admits, just as common.

The grid plan has no direct economic significance, no direct impact on social development. It cannot even be said to have a clear political meaning. In this context, any historical importance the grid might have would seem to be so circumstantial as to be negligible. But, even as we say this, it is hard not to see in this a paradox. For, if the grid has no historical significance, how does it enter history? How is it recognized as an urban solution? It is clearly absurd to suggest that each time the grid is used its spatial significance is invented *ab ovo*.

The fact is that, even if the nature of its historical significance is hard to define, the grid plan has undeniably been a *traditional* urban solution. The historian Dan Stanislawski, who many years ago traced the beginnings of the grid plan back to the Middle Eastern fortified cities of the second millennium BC, has observed that one constant feature of the grid plan is its association with the notion of authority or the idea of control: 'A straight street lends itself to control from without.'[26] But surely something else has to be said, which is that *the grid plan has not only been imposed from without: it has also been accepted from within*. It has not only been the tool of authority: it has itself been accepted as authoritative. And it has been regarded as authoritative, not because it is supremely rational, but because it is a traditional solution. When the colonists take up residence in Hoddle's Melbourne or Light's Adelaide, they do so not because they spontaneously react to the government's authority but because they recognize the space. It is familiar. It speaks to them.

It is precisely this familiarity which makes the grid plan a historical solution and not simply a Platonic form without spatial or temporal charge. Indeed, far from standing outside history, it could be argued that the grid, as the traditional matrix of new urban beginnings, is the supremely historical figure: it belongs to the progress of the West as quintessentially as the discourse of history itself. Why, then, is this overlooked? For much the same reason, I think, as imperial history tends to overlook the spatial dimension of history. For imperial history springs, as I have already suggested, from the epistemological assumptions of Enlightenment and positivist science. According to Adorno and Max Horkheimer, the chief defender of this kind of knowledge,

> Bourgeois society is ruled by equivalence. It makes the dissimilar comparable by reducing it to abstract quantities. To the Enlightenment, that which does not reduce to numbers, and ultimately to the one, becomes illusion; modern positivism writes it off as literature.[27]

The implications of this for spatial history are obvious. Those documents which specifically deal with unique beginnings and unrepeatable differences – the journals, diaries and unfinished maps that evoke the spatiality of historical experience – are relegated to the realm of literature – biography, fiction and epic poems. And, by a neat irony, the process of colonization becomes, as it was for Wakefield and his followers, a foregone conclusion. But, although the authority of the grid plan was not political, economic or social, it was historical. And one thing this means is that grid-plan towns did not signify the same thing in Australia as they did, say, in Mexico, in Greek Sicily or in Mohenjo-Daro. Their significance was a product of historical consciousness and one feature of a historical consciousness, as I pointed out in the previous chapter, is that it recognizes the unrepeatability of events, the sense in which any repetition is an interpretation. Even if it seeks to cancel out the difference, it has to take account of it. While Melbourne might remind Trollope of Philadelphia, it would be a mistake to suppose that the grid in both places authorized the same kind of social, political and economic conditions. Even the more idealistic Light did not proceed as William Penn had done – at any rate, he would certainly have shied away from pronouncing his grid plan a means of making 'our Wilderness' flourish 'as a Garden'.[28] It would equally be a mistake to suppose that Hoddle's repetition of a traditional solution was merely a repetition.

If we want to understand the historical success of Hoddle's Melbourne, there is no doubt that we need to seek it in the city's extraordinary economic growth. Melbourne, like Adelaide, represented a dream of utilitarian settlement. In the event, it became, as a result of the gold rushes, not so much the generator of wealth as its recipient. Although the rapidity with which bullion was translated into capital investments, for example, was a tribute to local confidence in the economic viability of the place. Even so, the economic success of the place was not fortuitous: it was implicit in Hoddle's original plan, where the arithmetical cast of mind that characterized Melbourne's capitalists was already a spatial matter of fact. At that time and in that place, the grid acquired certain economic impulses. But these were not imposed on the grid: rather, they were recognized there. They were possibilities generated by the grid's historical character. To be sure, what the grid generated was wealth: but wealth itself was spatially conditioned. Buildings were imagined before they were built. Trade was envisaged before there was anything to trade. And it was the form of the place and how it was perceived that generated this speculative confidence.

The ground of Melbourne's commercial success was spatial, not economic, and the considerable documentation to do with the early Melbourne land sales, which occurred in June and November 1837, enables us to understand how this worked. Hoddle's original grid plan (see plate 17) comprised twenty-four 10-acre blocks, arranged in three rows of eight, and each divided up into twenty allotments. These blocks were bounded on their long sides by Flinders Street and Lonsdale Street, on their short sides by Spencer Street and Spring Street. However, this apparent symmetry and simplicity on paper belied the fact that, in reality, only the south-western part of the site (towards King Street and William Street) was cleared. As Fenton recalled,

Russell Street was not even visible, for it was enclosed in a grass paddock by a rough post and rail fence. To the east there was nothing but a grass-covered slope, with gum trees, thinly scattered.[29]

At the first two sales only ten of the twenty-four blocks were put up for auction, the central group of nine blocks bounded by Flinders, William, Lonsdale and Swanston Streets and a tenth adjacent block to the south-west, between Flinders Street and King Street. But the significant feature of the two 1837 sales is that they were an overwhelming success. All blocks offered were purchased. In part, no doubt, this reflected the limited number of allotments offered. But, in part, too, it reflected the success of the grid plan in inducing buyers to invest anywhere and everywhere, regardless of the actual state of the ground. Of course, the local topography could not be wholly ignored. Given that the crossroads of William Street and Collins Street where they crossed were among the few cleared and partially settled areas, that Elizabeth Street was a creek and Russell Street was not even visible, it was hardly surprising that, at the June sale, the highest bid was made for a single lot on the north-east corner of Collins Street and William Street; that the lowest prices were paid for the lots on the north side of Collins Street, between Elizabeth Street and Swanston Street.

But more remarkable is the fact that purchasers showed a willingness to invest in every part, and the significance of this emerges when we bear in mind that among the purchasers were the founding members of the Port Phillip Association, whose land speculations the government survey and sales were intended to outlaw and supersede. Batman, Wedge and Fawkner all bought in to the new town and, as the historian Henry Turner noted, in his *A History of the Colony of Victoria*, their choice of lots was determined by a desire to reassert their position in the new scheme of things:

> Mr John Pascoe Fawkner strengthened his claim to pose as the father of the settlement by buying the first lot offered for £32. It was the eastern corner of King and Flinders Streets, about the nearest lot to the landing-place in the Yarra basin. His rival, John Batman, secured the corners of William and Flinders Streets and William and Collins Streets, at the enhanced price of £75 and £60 respectively. Another of the discoverers, Mr John Helder Wedge, the Surveyor, secured

three valuable corner lots in the centre of the town at about the same figure.[30]

Turner is surely right to recognize the personal motives behind these purchases. But the pioneers did not simply hope by their purchases to maintain things as they had been prior to the survey. It is true that Batman bought land as close as possible to what he had made the original centre of the place, Batman's Hill. But Hoddle's survey had displaced the centre; or, rather, it had made every crossroads a potential centre – a fact reflected in the consistently higher prices paid for corner blocks. The Port Phillip pioneers recognized this. Fawkner not only bought land near the site of his old home. He also invested in land on Bourke Street, between William Street and Queen Street and between Elizabeth Street and Swanston Street. The Batmans were equally far-ranging. At the November sale, John acquired corner blocks at the Swanston Street intersections with Flinders Street and Collins Street.

The behaviour of these pioneers illustrates the point made earlier: the success of Hoddle's grid plan did not depend on imposing a new authority. It depended on being accepted as authoritative. The new space did not necessarily exclude Batman or Fawkner. If they accepted its novel equality of parts, its conspicuous lack of a centre, *if they bought in*, they could continue to play an important political role in the colony, even influence perhaps where the new centres of authority might concentrate. This was a possibility clearly recognized by Batman when he requested the colonial government to remove some buildings belonging to his rival, Fawkner. Personal animosity aside, he explained that he intended to use his lot on Flinders Street as an 'Inn'. Fawkner's buildings opposite would, he said, 'become a nuisance to the house if not removed'.[31] But clearly, whatever their private territorial disputes, progress no longer depended on the pioneers. It depended now on investing in a new spatial arrangement, relocating themselves as part of a wider project where society would multiply with or without them. In this sense, Hoddle's geometry replaced the mythic claims of Batman and Fawkner.

But, in the nineteenth century at least, a myth *was* associated with the rational grid plan: the myth of Progress. And it is the idea of progress that helps explain what in Melbourne's urban plan symbolized advancement to the real estaters. There is little doubt that, in its first fifty years, Melbourne was the very embodiment of 'Progress'. Economically, Melbourne was forward. 'Magic offspring of the almighty dollar', Fenton called it,[32] but well before gold bullion started to pour in from the Victorian goldfields, Melbourne attracted investors. As early as 1840, only three years after the first allotments were sold, the squatter Philip Russell could declare, 'We were much surprised with the appearance of Melbourne: it has certainly advanced rapidly.'[33] (And Russell's brother, George, had described Melbourne four years earlier as 'three or four wattle-and-daub huts, a few turf huts, and about twelve or fifteen tents . . .').[34] Hoddle's simple grid plan seemed to encourage growth. The streets might be rivers, the first buildings 'wretched in the extreme, being little better than barns',[35] as another squatter, John Cotton, thought, but all Melbourne's critics agreed that, if not well located, it was at least well laid out, that, as a design to encourage and promote settlement, it was admirable. As 'Garryowen' remarked,

> Melbourne in 1840 was certainly not a city, and could hardly be called a town; nor did it even partake of the characteristics of a village or a hamlet. It was a kind of big 'settlement' . . .[36]

A quarter of a century later, the progress was evidently social, as well as economic. Trollope commented,

> One cannot walk about Melbourne without being struck by all that has been done for the welfare of the people generally. There is no squalor to be seen . . .[37]

As we saw, Richard Twopeny concluded from his observations that, in comparison with Sydney, Melbourne people 'are better, if we accept Herbert Spencer's definition of Progress'.

In fact, Spencer's idea of progress, set out in his 1852 essay 'Progress: Its Law and Cause', and elaborated in 'Transcendental Physiology' (1857) and 'The Social Organism' (1860), offers a useful insight not only into the mechanisms of self-interest at work in early Melbourne but also – and perhaps more surprisingly – into their distinctive spatial expressions. Of course, it is not that Melbourne in any conscious sense embodied Spencer's ideas. But what he made explicit was undoubtedly already at work there. In his essay, Spencer put forward an evolutionary theory of social development. He characterized primitive societies as 'homogeneous' and he contrasted them with the complex 'heterogeneous' society of industrial England, in which he lived. Progress, he argued, was 'those changes in the social organism' which have led from the former to the latter. He thought of the changes in the social organism as resembling the changes a living organism undergoes as it grows and develops. Progress from a state of homogeneity to one of heterogeneity depended, he argued, on two conditions: firstly, that 'the condition of homogeneity is a condition of unstable equilibrium'; and, secondly, that 'every cause produces more than one effect', that is, two or three others.[38]

Pursuing the organic analogy, Spencer explained,

> As fast as each organ of a living animal becomes confined to a special action, it must become dependent on the rest for those materials which its position and duty do not permit it to obtain for itself.[39]

The condition of the individual in modern society was analogous. His survival was intimately dependent on the activities of his neighbour, his fellow countrymen and even people in other countries. In a heterogeneous society, the individual's survival depended on good communications. So, Spencer argued, with progress

> comes the formation of more definite and complete channels of communication. Blood vessels acquire distinct walls; roads are fenced and gravelled.[40]

With further progress, those 'main channels of communication' become still more distinguished by their perfect structures, their comparative straightness and the absence of those small branches, which the minor channels perpetually give off.[41]

Spencer's characterization of branching channels as primitive recalls the explorers' frustration with Australia's indistinct river systems. It is also clear, even from this brief description, that, as a spatial version of Spencer's theory of progress, Hoddle's Melbourne could hardly be bettered. On the morning of the first land sale, the homogeneity of its parts represented a condition of 'unstable equilibrium'. By the end of that day's bidding, the differentiation of prices and positions was well begun. The results fully vindicated Spencer's prediction:

> Endow the members of a community with equal properties, positions, powers, and they will forthwith begin to slide into inequalities.[42]

Hoddle's town plan provided the momentary equality that precipitated the maximum rate of change, differentiation and progress. He had supplied not only the straight channels of communication, so necessary a part of progress, but even, in the form of crossroads, those causes leading to more than one effect, those choices leading to more than one choice.

Spencer's essay is interesting from our point of view because, almost incidentally, it shows the way in which progress, both economic and social, was, at least in Spencer's mind, associated with a particular *spatial* configuration, namely the grid. Why should straight lines and right-angles facilitate 'Progress'? For Spencer perhaps, they were little more than illustrative metaphors. But is it possible that it was Spencer's notion of progress that was the metaphorical term, and not his geometry? Could it be that it was the grid itself that was the mechanism of social change? Judging from Spencer's own ideas about space, the answer to both questions must be yes. At any rate, Spencer subscribed to a psychology of spatial perception that would seem to have been ideally suited to life in a grid.

Spencer owed his conception of space to Hume, and it was appropriate therefore that he expressed his notions in the course of reviewing the philosophy of Hume's great critic, Kant.

In that review, Spencer took exception to the German philosopher's doctrine of 'absolute' space. According to Spencer, a
space without objects was not only imperceptible, it was
inconceivable:

> the consciousness of Space is . . . wholly composed of
> infinitely numerous relations of position, such as those which
> every portion of it presents . . . every portion of Space,
> immense or minute, cannot be either known or conceived save
> in some relative position to the conscious subject, and . . .
> besides involving the relations of distance and direction, it
> invariably contains within itself relations of right and left, top
> and bottom, nearer and farther.[43]

Not the least interesting aspect of this criticism, which in large
part paraphrases Hume, is its rejection of Euclidean geometry –
at least as something perceptible. For properties of relation,
distance and direction, right and left, are precisely what
Euclidean geometry neutralizes. But, perhaps even more
significantly, this same passage enables us to see how, despite
their resemblance on paper, the grid plan was not a Euclidean
figure, but one with a distinct set of topological properties. For
it was of the essence of the grid that it expressed in the clearest
terms the relations of distance and direction – these were the
distinctive properties of the straight street regularly crossed by
other straight streets; again, it was precisely right and left that
the grid plan's crossroads articulated as distinct choices.

Indeed, Hume himself had clearly described the perceptual
appeal of the grid. Hume's sceptical contention that 'there is
nothing in any object, which can afford us a reason for drawing
a conclusion beyond it'[44] had as its corollary the proposition
that we have no reason to imagine the space elsewhere unlike
the space we now occupy. Our powers of reflection depending
on association, and not on reason, it follows that 'instances of
which we have no experience must necessarily resemble those of
which we have'.[45] The relevance of this argument to the grid is
evident. Hoddle's centreless plan of settlement is a spatial
epitome of the associationist psychology: alike in every part, it
confirmed the associationist assumption that 'there' resembled
'here'. It rendered the distant immediately conceivable, it made

the invisible visible. It meant that, wherever the observer stood, he stood at the centre. Wherever he turned, wherever he walked, his relationship with neighbouring allotments and adjacent streets was unaltered. It meant that, whatever he did, his surroundings implied the possibility of progress and change.

And it is precisely as a spatial structure transcending individual psychology, as a layout expressing the spatial ground of speculation, that the grid plan is so closely akin to Spencer's own doctrine of progress. For what distinguished Spencer's notion of progress motivated by the prospect of 'greater happiness' from the Utilitarian formula, 'the greatest happiness of the greatest number', was that Spencer's happiness might be deferred, perhaps for generations. What permitted this deferral of gratification or delayed association were what Spencer thought of as evolutionary laws operating on man's moral nature. Man's advance did not depend on individual acts of will but on the constitution or 'structure' of the mind, which was determined by an 'infinitude of previous experiences'.[46] In a comparable way, the grid plan not only confirmed an infinitude of previous experiences, being a traditional form, extending back in time far beyond the individual horizon, but it also laid out clearly the structure of the future. It established the cardinal points, giving form and direction to spatial expansion and hence social development. It established in lines the laws of improvement.

In the context of spatial history, we begin to see that, however much the grid might in theory preserve the uniformity of space, in practice it was perceived as a network instinct with qualities of convergence, divergence, centre, edge, direction and promise. In reality, as the matrix of physical progress, it shared the qualities of the explorer's track and the appeal of the picturesque view. However much its geometrical principles represented the Enlightenment project to neutralize locality, to universalize the principles of experience, in practice the grid merely channelled the intentional gaze, giving it the confidence it could be 'wherever there is something to be done'. It externalized what the philosopher Maurice Merleau-Ponty describes as the pre-temporal (because pre-reflective) perception of simultaneity. 'When one says simultaneity, is it time he means or space?',[47] Merleau-Ponty asks, and the same might be asked of the grid:

does it belong to geography or history? The grid precedes both. It is the matrix where time and space begin to differentiate themselves and *hence* acquire significance *as* history and geography. But to begin with, 'That line from me to the horizon is a rail my gaze may move upon.'

Whether in the form of a surveyor's line, creating an imaginary boundary, whether as a street, a meeting place and means of passage, the straight lines of the grid facilitated communication, they promoted the difference on which communication depended – after all, but for the authority of the survey, how could Batman have formulated his complaint about Fawkner? How could there have been disagreement or agreement? The grid could not decide the issue, but it could display it. In this context, we might also note that the anonymous critic's regret that Melbourne contained 'no broad suburban roads, giving access to the country' was, in a certain sense, to get things back to front. For it was precisely the artificial space of the grid which brought the 'country' into being as country, which created the dialectical boundary between town and non-town. It was through the frame of the town that the bush acquired direction, became a focus of strangeness and an object of desire. Striking testimony of this occurs in Alfred Joyce's *A Homestead History*, where the author recalls the early 1840s and his first impressions of Melbourne and the country beyond:

> A strange feeling impressed me as I moved about the town and contrasted the rude and crude settlement with the illimitable space of the primeval bush . . . There seemed to be such an incongruity in the raw newness of everything pertaining to the settlement and the unsubdued nature all around . . .[48]

It is the limits of the town that make manifest the 'illimitable' nature of the country. It is the finite space of the settlement that enables Joyce to name that immensity, to characterize it, to bring it into focus. And, 'naming' the country in this way was, incidentally, to proceed by way of association. For, as Hume argued, even the recognition of contrariety was a form of association, arising as it did from a deeper perception of resemblance.

Rectilinearity, whether in the form of a town plan or in the form of the survey, was a spatial stratagem for bringing space within the realm of communication. It was, despite its appearance of expository straightforwardness, a spatial metaphor: it was a means of speeding up the appearance of things, for hastening the nearness of distant objects. It was the most efficient medium of exchange, whether understood spatially or socially. As Major Mitchell discovered, when he set out to survey new roads to and from Sydney, the squatters were as keen as he was to see the introduction of straight roads. Referring to one squatter's complaints, Mitchell wrote in a notebook,

> The present road subjects him to constant depredations owing to its winding nature and running through the cultivated part of his farm . . . proposed line perfectly level and better in every respect.[49]

The 'depredations' referred to here were not thefts of property but losses of useful land, caused by successive travellers attempting to avoid the ruts or mud of earlier passers-by. But in any case the effect of a decisive track would be to eliminate these trespasses. A straight road would clearly differentiate what was public and what was private. It would speed up communication: and, according to Mitchell, this was even more true of intersections, if they were arranged according to rectilinear principles:

> All crossings, intersections, and abuttings of roads should be made at right-angles for the obvious reason of facilitating the turning from one road to the other or the more speedily crossing.[50]

Far, then, from being a static, even transcendental design, the elements of the grid were means of translating the country into a place for reliable travelling. Rendering the topographical peculiarities of the country 'level', at least in theory, they rendered travelling itself an activity independent of place. Ultimately, the effect of this geometrical tendency was to iron out spatial differences, to nullify the strangeness of here and there: a person who travels by timetables is always able, in a sense, to be at his destination without ever leaving home. But the road makers were still a long way from this completely 'smooth' travelling, and in the nineteenth century, along Australian seaboards and in the Australian bush, straightness was still emotionally charged. It was still a figure of speech. Thus, a 'respectable settler', referring to the plains he inhabited, informed the sceptical Breton that 'he once rode, *in a straight line*, during nearly a *month*, and then returned hopeless of reaching their utmost verge'.[51] To say he rode 'in a straight line' is to suggest the empirical rigour of the settler's geographical evidence. But it is also a figure of speech designed to suggest immensity: for what could be further away than something that eludes direct approach?

This is the paradox of the straight line: that, on the one hand, with a distant object in mind, it is a symbol of hope and expectations speedily realized; but, on the other, as a mere continuity of placelessness, it turns into its opposite, becoming the very expression of imprisonment. Straight lines that form crossroads are emblems of hope, but lines that exclude all hope of ending rapidly turn into signs of despair. Lhotsky, for example, complained,

> I found the road enclosed for miles with a heavy substantial fence, which I could not pass . . . these fences, quite useless at present, have been erected by the gratuitous labour of prisoners, to enrich further people who are already in comfortable circumstances.[52]

But the fences complained of here are not useless: they are potent spatial figures of speech. They communicate authority; they express, in this case, social difference. Bounding the traveller, they colonize even him.

Whatever social or economic or even political ambition was associated with it, the straight line was the offspring of the intentional gaze. It was not, for example, equal in both directions, but distinctly one-directional. Straight lines were addressed to the 'country'; they engaged the 'other' like arrows. The first land grants on the Swan and Canning rivers in Western Australia were made before any survey of the country had been carried out. And, geographer J. M. R. Cameron comments,

As no accurate map of either river existed, Stirling personally marked the frontage to each grant . . . This gave rise to grossly elongated allotments at right-angles to major rivers.[53]

David Collins reports a comparable situation which arose at Sydney Cove when settlers from the *Sirius* were granted river frontages along Cascade Stream.

They had originally been laid down without the assistance of proper instruments, and being situated on the side of Cascade Stream, which takes several windings in its course, the different allotments, being close together, naturally interfered with each other when they came to be carried back.[54]

In both cases, the strip-like allotments were the result of the settler's personal orientation, his sense of 'facing' the river and having an illimitable extent of bush stretching behind him. His backward extension might have obeyed Euclidean laws, but, in intent at least, it was decidedly projective. And it should be stressed that this elongation was not necessarily evidence of greed. Lying behind and beyond, it represented the unenclosed future, a track of possible actions proportioned to the life of a man. It was like a shadow.

To attempt to limit those unlimited perspectives, to reduce the corridors of settlement and passage to the sides or axes of the survey grid, to subordinate individual routes and holdings to the rectilinear uniformity of the chequerboard was, undoubtedly, to silence the expression of individual intentions; but it was not necessarily to eliminate from the landscape all sense of spatial direction and progress. On the contrary, the uniformity of the grid could, under certain conditions, be turned into a powerful inducement to settle in distant places.

One of the chief incentives behind the grotesque backward extension of the Cascade and Swan allotments was undoubtedly expressed by Peter Cunningham, when he advised prospective emigrants,

In searching for a suitable grant, it is a great point to fix upon a place where the land *round* it is all so indifferent that no new settler is likely to place himself near you, for a considerable period at least, enabling you thus to have a free run for your stock for miles without being encroached on.[55]

Hemmed in to left and right and in front by water, it was understandable that allotment holders might seek to resist encroachment in the one direction still open to them. But, left to their own devices, the Swan and Canning river settlers, at least, would, it seems, have stretched out their isolation to infinity. It was in limiting the settler's isolation, while at the same time guaranteeing a degree of security from encroachment, that the principles of the grid survey could, in theory, prove so useful.

For, if the grid system reduced the surveyed space to uniformity, its divisions also guaranteed equality in difference. The prospective settler who chose his rectilinear block on paper could calculate to a nicety his proximity to neighbours and, even more importantly, his distance. He could balance up the need to 'have a free run' with his need to trade. This was a formula for encouraging settlement recognized from the beginning. When, for instance, Arthur Phillip decided to settle fifteen convicts whose terms of transportation had expired, he did so 'on allotments in a district named the Ponds':

> Between every allotment, a space had been reserved equal to the largest grant on either side, pursuant to the instructions which the governor had received.[56]

In this instance, the threat of aboriginal attack meant that,

> It was soon found that this distribution might be attended with much disadvantage to the settler; a thick wood of at least thirty acres must lie between every allotment . . .[57]

But this did not undermine the general principle. The grid survey not only assured the uniformity of blocks, it also guaranteed a uniform interval between them. In this way, the individual settler's bush background, stretching away indefinitely, was both guaranteed and limited. The thick wood became a common background.

Phillip applied a version of the same principle to the arrangement of huts at Parramatta. 'The huts', Phillip wrote, are building at the distance of one hundred feet from each other, and each hut is to contain ten convicts . . . and having good gardens which they cultivate, and frequently having it in their power to exchange vegetables for little necessaries which the stores do not furnish makes them begin to feel the benefits they may draw from their industry.[58]

Again, by this arrangement, Phillip sought to preserve difference by equalizing it. The method of preservation was to supply equal intervals – in this case of gardens – between individual settlers.

The survey grid's satisfaction of a psychological desire for what we might call a sociable isolation, based on an assurance of equality in difference, was a chief source of its practical value as an instrument of settling new country. A century after Phillip, a Gippsland settler, Caleb Burchett, was using exactly the same principles to choose his own selection. A secluded, but not completely secluded, situation was what Caleb Burchett looked for, when he took up a selection, which, 'looking at the survey map . . . struck me as being favourably situated and lay about 4 miles to the east of Mr L's land . . .'.[59] But the success of the survey depended wholly on its uniformity: a survey which was limited to one region, which had edges, which therefore could not guarantee intervals beyond its limits, could only lead to the concentration of property in a few hands.

It was, for instance, the absence of a complete survey that was in large part responsible for the breakdown of Wakefield's plans for colonizing South Australia. When Light's replacement, G. S. Kingston, reached Adelaide in June 1838, he found that, while two-thirds of the settlers had taken up lots within the 150-mile radius of Adelaide surveyed by Light, a significant third of settlers

took a different view of 'the most complete liberty of appropriation'. Explorations to the south had convinced some of them of the superiority of the southern areas and they refused to take their selections in the 'salt bogs and arid plains' around Adelaide.[60]

This rejection of Wakefield's plan for settler concentration deteriorated into mere self-aggrandizement for the simple reason that no survey of the southern areas existed. Instead the government was forced to institute local surveys wherever land had been taken up. Sturt described the result:

> The Special Surveys have secured all that is valuable in the shape of water to a few individuals and rendered invaluable more than one-third of the provincial lands . . . The idea of chequering . . . [the country] as it suits the fancy of the applicants is preposterous and the consequences will be severely felt as the population increases.[61]

In short, discontinuity in the survey rendered it null and void as an instrument of organized colonization. This was a point not lost on the South Australian surveyor, George Goyder. Much as he was opposed to the northern expansion of the 1870s beyond his 'Line', he was a firm advocate of surveying before settling. Only by dividing the land into equal parts could the government prevent the firstcomers from picking out the 'eyes of the country', to the disadvantage of later settlers. The survey equalized the country. It made each hundred, each farm block, each township, in theory at least, equally central; potentially at least, equally prosperous. It gave everyone an equal chance. Donald Meinig quotes the Clare editor of the *Northern Argus*, who, referring to the surveyors' rigid adherence to straight roads, commented,

> We have only to look around us to see evidence of the folly of such a course. The most formidable barriers exist in very many places, the roads leading over hills and rocks most unsuited for public thoroughfares.[62]

And Meinig shows how, in practice, deviations from the ideal were common. But, whatever its practical shortcomings, as an ideal formula for controlling the dispersion of settlers, the grid was no folly: it was, rather, a foil to isolationism.

In all these cases, whether in Parramatta, in one of the nineteen counties or in Gippsland, this sociable isolation was a function of the survey. The regularity of its squares and rectangles enabled the settler to measure his nearness and distance, to conceptualize the possibilities for commerce and privacy. The survey enabled him to 'leapfrog' settled land and put a definite interval between himself and others because the interval was as precisely limited as the land he occupied. It was a symbolic rather than actual barrier. It communicated a limited independence. The settler's isolation avoided the complete desolation of placelessness experienced by many travellers: it was rather *isolation by association*.

The grid survey, like Hoddle's town plan, embodied the Humean principle that nothing in any object suggested any reason for drawing a conclusion beyond it. The grid survey guaranteed, in fact, that what lay beyond resembled precisely what was already familiar. In this way, the effect of seclusion could be balanced exactly. There was no question of total isolation, no threat of overcrowding. In this sense, far from being a direct instrument of economic, social or even political ambition, the value of the grid in promoting settlement was, rather, spatial and imaginative. If it could be translated into something useful, it was probably in the realm of morality. This is certainly the implication of Cunningham's view of convict reform, that,

> It is, in sober sadness, time fruitlessly expended to attempt the reformation of these people when crowded thus 'knave upon knave'.[63]

In Cunningham's view, only separated from each other and working as labourers on widely dispersed farms was there any chance of improvement:

> By seclusion in the country, and keeping their bodies and minds in healthy state through wholesome food and wholesome labour, their old thievish habits gradually wear off.[64]

Much the same opinion was expressed by the landholders J. T. Bigge circulated a quarter of a century later. As John Macarthur explained,

> When Men are engaged in rural occupations their days are chiefly spent in solitude – they have much time for reflection and self-examination, and they are less tempted to the perpetration of crimes than [they] would [be] herded together, in Towns, amidst a mass of disorders and vices.[65]

The convict's moral reform did not depend on swapping concentration for isolation, but on finding his place in a limited society, whose seclusion and respectability the survey made possible. As Archibald Bell wrote in his reply to Bigge,

> Instances have been very frequent of men assigned to farmers having formed attachments for the female Servants and after marriage becoming useful, & in many cases valuable members of the community – whilst gangs of men, in large numbers, segregated & foreclosed from such communication & its influence, seem to become indifferent to themselves & their future fate & are exposed to intercourse, vicious & depraved as we find in the extreme.[66]

'Such considerations', Bell concluded,

> tend to the adoption of the opinion that agricultural occupations are most conducive to religious & moral habits & most likely to promote a legitimate & well disposed population.[67]

The grid alone ensured that difference did not become opposition, that seclusion did not mean segregation. To be sure, complete surveys did not always precede rural settlement. But the grid, with its promise of communication beyond the horizon, with its guarantee of a uniform distribution of centres, was the geometrical ideal to which the settlers, balancing nearness with distance, aspired. The grid was, in this sense, an expression of optimism. Its authority was, in one aspect, the authority of benevolence. It produced, not only the prospect of elysiums for gentlemen, as Light wrote somewhat ironically of Adelaide, but also, if the 'Emigrant Mechanic' was not wholly deluded, something like 'Eden' for the labourers.[68]

Certainly, there were circumstances when the *absence* of a grid-like structure seemed to lead not to a heady sense of freedom but to a wandering state of mind bordering on insanity. More than once during his travels William Howitt was struck by the 'strange effect' that 'bush life' had on shepherds, their solitary existence

> at once destroying their minds, and yet inspiring them with
> such a fascination for what is so dreary in itself, and which
> ends in such misery and desolation.[69]

Near Bendigo, Howitt met a shepherd who exhibited all the
usual symptoms of madness, tales of wandering, delusions,
interminable talking, imaginary conversations.

> I asked him what books he had read. He said he had read
> Burns's Poems and the Bible. And he had read some of
> Shakespeare. Two of Shakespeare's dramas that he had read
> were *Hamilton* and *Macbeth*. These were all he could remem-
> ber. But he sometimes got a map to read, which was very
> amusing. To trace out the roads, and the places of market-
> towns, was very interesting. He complained much of the want
> of fruit in this country, and seemed to remember with a
> wonderful relish russet apples. 'Oh! those russets! They are
> beautiful fruit. I remember eating them somewhere in
> England; I don't remember where, but they were beautiful.'[70]

It is tempting to see in this poor man's obsession with maps a
desire to find himself, to trace his own place in the world. As for
the 'russets', so much bigger than the circles distinguishing
'market-towns' on the map, perhaps they represented the relish
of roads, which, for all their strict linearity, implied the location
of places, the roundedness of return. In the imaginary spaces of
the map, he glimpsed perhaps a lost home; in the familiar
names, a lost society. At any rate, the Euclidean certainty of the
map did not deter him: the very authority of its grid seemed to
bring remote things near and balance his mind.

A More Pleasing Prospect

Nothing is to be found in any country at all resembling an English park.

J. H. Pott, 1783

So much has been said of the scenery of N.S.W. resembling noble
English domains that the comparison is rather trite.

J. Cross, *Journal of Several Expeditions Made Into Western Australia*, 1833

About the time Cook returned from his *Endeavour* voyage, a poet or poetaster from my home town wrote a poem called 'Faringdon Hill'. From its modest heights, Henry James Pye, local squire and, later, Poet Laureate, surveyed the 'various objects scatter'd round' which 'charm on every side the curious eye':

> Here lofty mountains lift their azure heads;
> There it's green lap the grassy meadow spreads;
> Enclosures here the sylvan scene divide;
> There plains extended spread their harvests wide;
> Here oaks, their mossy limbs wide stretching meet
> And form impervious thickets at our feet;
> Through aromatic heaps of ripening hay,
> There silver ISIS wins her winding way;
> And many a tower, and many a spire between,
> Shoots from the groves, and cheers the rural scene.[1]

This passage is a useful gloss on the eighteenth-century associations of a number of words discussed in this book: it reveals that the plain was associated with fertility and plenty, that even uncultivated meadows were signs of richness. Since Pye's 'lofty mountains' are the Berkshire Downs, which rise little more than 300 feet above the Vale of the White Horse, the passage further reminds us of the change of meaning the word 'mountain' has undergone during the last two hundred years.

Pye's lines are also a pleasantly little-frequented way into the vast literature of the picturesque. Pye, like many of the 'landskip poets', considered himself something of an expert on beauty; so his eclectic mingling here of almost every kind of pleasant prospect is not accidental. It underlines the point that, until aesthetic theorists like Archibald Alison, Richard Payne Knight and William Gilpin began to systematize the study of landscape appeal, the picturesque – that which pleased the curious eye – could include lofty mountains as easily as enclosures, spreading meadows as easily as 'impervious thickets'. Late eighteenth-century students of landscape were not primarily interested in aesthetic orderliness. Rather, they saw themselves as experimental psychologists.[2] In describing the kinds of country that pleased, they were exploring the nature of visual perception. How did the mind organize the data of sensation? Why did some views attract, others repel? They were providing empirical data as a preliminary to solving these questions. Pye, for example, no sooner describes the scene before him than he asks why this particular view appears more charming to him than others comparably lovely. And he concludes,

> when in MEMORY's fond mirror shewn,
> The country smiles with beauties not it's own . . .[3]

It is Pye's pleasant childhood associations that invest the country with a special beauty. And Pye's association of beauty with memory was not unusual: it is little more than a variation on Edmund Burke's influential thesis, set out in 1757, that, in contrast with our idea of the Sublime, which is associated with feelings of pain and danger, our notion of Beauty is founded on pleasure.[4]

In saying, then, that different prospects corresponded to different states of mind, one is not indulging in a naive emotionalism. True, different kinds of country might acquire special, personal associations. But the pleasure of certain landscapes went deeper than this, and was based, in fact, on the presumption of a structural analogy between the perceiving mind and what was perceived. Picturesque prospects were ones that allowed the eye to wander from object to object: they had their mental counterparts in complex ideas that sparked off trains of thought. Picturesque views might give rise to all kinds of pleasant ideas, but the primary pleasure they gave resided in their picturesqueness itself – in the fact that their structure of casually interlinked and contrasting forms enticed the eye (and the mind) to wander. They were places where the lie of the imagination was made visible.

Picturesque views allowed the mind's eye to 'rove', to 'explore'. In the context of eighteenth-century landscape painting and poetry, the spatial imagery used to evoke the picturesque's appeal was metaphorical, even conventionally so: the eye that 'wanders', that is 'attracted' or 'enticed forward' by the prospect advances in fancy only. (Although, even here, I doubt whether the spatial appeal of the picturesque was wholly internalized: when, for instance, William Gilpin published his series of *Tours*, his object was as much to encourage picturesque travel as picturesque art.) But in other situations, particularly where the writer *was* travelling, whether exploring or merely roving, this was not the case. There, to call a view picturesque was not to lapse passively into the conventional vocabulary of approbation, but to indicate a particular spatial appeal – an appeal based not on any kind of personal association but on the recognition of the view's epistemological value, as a *place for travelling*.

It was not that the traveller, and the Australian traveller in particular, ascribed to the word a different, or even a more precise, meaning, simply that he used it with a different intention. And, if we find the term 'picturesque' invoked in a bewildering variety of contexts, we should not necessarily assume it had very little empirical value. On the contrary, it may be that this simply reflected the double aspect of travelling – an experience that, as pointed out earlier, required places to rest as much as roads. Indeed, in this context it is striking how, in the Australian travel literature, picturesqueness was a quality ascribed to two very different kinds of countryside. On the one hand, it was applied to 'grassy meadow' and extensive 'plains'; on the other, it was thought appropriate to regions of 'lofty mountains', 'impervious thickets' and winding streams.

Sturt in his last expedition, writes,

On ascending the bank myself, I looked to the west and saw a beautiful park-like plain covered with grass, having groups of ornamental trees scattered over it . . .[5]

This is similar to the country Mitchell describes near the Bogan on his Second Expedition:

> We crossed some good, undulating ground, open and grassy, the scenery being finer, from the picturesque grouping and character of the trees, than any we had hitherto seen.[6]

An overlander like Thomas Walker could be equally lavish in his praise. A cottage on the Murrumbidgee near Yass inspires him to write,

> The view and country around are very picturesque and pretty . . . They consist of the banks of the Murrumbidgee River . . . flowing circuitously through a very broken country. There are a few flats, but the country is chiefly very hilly on each side, and bounded by rather high ranges; the hills are, however, very thinly timbered, and covered with grass, so that the whole view . . . is very beautiful indeed.[7]

Or take the first reactions of William Waterfield, on sailing into Port Phillip Bay:

> The Bay was very splendid and picturesque as it opened on every hand. The green pasture-like appearance of the land was gratifying to the eye, and in the distance it seemed as if we were approaching a nobleman's park.[8]

The selector, too, had a well-developed taste for 'picturesque seclusion', as the Gippsland poetess Miss M. C. Johnson called it. She extolled the 'sunlit glade', the 'peaceful aisles of shade', not to mention

> the gullies where the rippling creek,
> Midst fern and bracken plays at hide and seek
> With merry sunbeams . . .[9]

Another Gippsland pioneer, Caleb Burchett, recalls how, after the burning had cleared a space,

> we came upon a site for the future home. This was a beautiful valley with tall tree ferns shooting fresh and green again after the burn. In this valley there was a pretty little hill or mound, rising gently above a fresh water creek, where small fish could

be seen disporting in the shallow clear waters, in the sunlight.[10]

At first sight, the sheer variety of the country these writers find in one form or another pretty or picturesque strongly suggests that Breton was right when he wrote,

> ask any person for a true and impartial account of the colony, or of one of its districts, and the probability is, the account will be unsatisfactory in all its bearings; for what one traveller considers a beautiful country, is by another deemed quite the contrary, and *vice versa* . . .[11]

What resemblance exists between Sturt's open plains and Walker's view 'bounded by high ranges'? What could be less alike than Waterfield's distant prospect of a nobleman's park and the intimate space of Burchett's 'pretty little hill or mound'? To find them all picturesque is surely to undermine any empirical value the word might have. Even so, however diverse the views described, the viewers themselves at least share a common attitude. For they are all, in one sense or another, travellers looking for – and looking forward to – places.

Sturt's pleasure cannot be dissociated from the character of his narrative, his biography of the journey. At least as Sturt conceptualized it, the explorer's track was given to sudden transformations and reversals. But, since it was only by a very sudden change that the desert could be transformed into an Eden, suddenness was integral to Sturt's pleasure. So it comes as no surprise perhaps to find that Sturt's enthusiasm for his 'park-like plain' depends on the contrast it makes with the preceding country, rather than on its own intrinsic qualities:

> Whether it was the suddenness of the change, from barrenness and sterility to verdure and richness, I know not; but I thought, when I first gazed on it, that I never saw a more beautiful spot.[12]

But Sturt's beautiful spot had in common with Mitchell's 'good, undulating ground' another property: it signalled a place of passage, a convergence ahead where one could get on. It is not only that the picturesque grouping of the bush does not impede one's progress: the ever-changing parallax of trees dotted across the plain is visible proof of one's own advance. Such park-like zones give the illusion of changing one's situation. There is a sense in which they travel with you. This is their human aspect, their companionship, and what is intimated by likening them to man-made parks in England. So artful is Nature's artifice, it persuades you the journey is for pleasure only; and before long a stable boy will be leading away your horse and you will be relaxing with old friends, looking back through the window (possibly with the help of a telescope) at the deer grazing where you recently passed.

The prospect of the journey ending is quite as important an ingredient of the picturesque as the promise of passage. The relish with which Burchett and Johnson welcome intimate enclosure embodies their own intention to settle, to gather the country round them in picturesque profusion. And, in this context, Walker's reaction to the Murrumbidgee is particularly interesting: for if, as a traveller going on, he recognizes the homely appeal of the place, then, as a potential settler, he finds the country insufficiently homely, intimate, enclosed. So, having acknowledged the beauty of the place, Walker goes on to reflect,

> notwithstanding all that, it was not such a place as I should like to live at, there is a wildness about it, or something else, which prevented me from feeling that it was a place I should choose for my residence; it is rather too extensive to be considered a snug sheltered valley, and yet it is nothing more than a valley of broken though beautiful ranges.[13]

Despite its apparent variety of meaning, the traveller's picturesque resolves itself into one or other of two kinds of country; and the picturesqueness imputed to these differing landscapes reflects as much the traveller's circumstances as any objective feature of the country. It is clear that the country he finds desirable depends very much on what he is looking for, whether he is after an attractive backdrop to his house or seeking an easy way over the horizon. The nature of these two kinds of picturesque is well brought out by the explorer P. E. de Strzelecki in his *Description of New South Wales and Van Diemen's*

Land; and the style of his description admirably imitates its subject matter:

> Amid the apparent sameness of the forest, may be often found spots teeming with a gigantic and luxuriant vegetation, sometimes laid out in stately groves, free from thicket or undergrowth, sometimes opening on glades and slopes, intersected with rivulets, carpeted with the softest turf, and which lack only the thatched and gabled cottage, with its blue smoke curling amid the trees, to realize a purely European picture. Sometimes, again, the forest skirts an open country of hill and plain, gracefully sprinkled with isolated clumps of trees, covered with the richest tufted herbage, and enamelled with flowers of varied form and colour; or it is lost in immense thickets, where innumerable flowering shrubs, and elegant interwoven creepers form bowers as impenetrable and as picturesque as those seen in the forests of Brazil.[14]

Although they are picturesquely interwoven, Strzelecki, it appears, recognizes two kinds of picturesque scene: one characterized by enclosure and impenetrability ('spots teeming with a gigantic and luxuriant vegetation' and 'immense thickets . . .'), the other distinguished by openness and freedom of movement ('stately groves . . . opening on glades and slopes' and 'an open country of hill and plain'). These two kinds of picturesque scene are different in another way. If the open scene, with its 'softest turf', implies inhabitation, then the appeal of the forest as picturesque as those of Brazil lies in its strangeness. If one view seems to lead to a house, in the other one is more likely to find oneself lost.

The suggestion that, as they emerge in spatial history, these two kinds of country represent attitudes as much as objects is borne out by the fact that individual travellers were quite capable of appreciating both. Walker might recognize the charms of wild enclosure, but this did not make him blind to the advantages of the other kind of country when it came to travelling on. South-west of the Goulburn, for example, he came upon what he thought

> the prettiest piece of country I have seen since leaving the Murrumbidgee, very thinly timbered, indeed in many parts

clear, with here and there interspersed a few trees or a clump or a belt, the soil sound and good; this part of the bank of the river is indeed, in my opinion, more beautiful than any country I have seen; there is little or no fallen timber about, the sward close, the ground undulating, gently swelling, plenty of back water too, the whole being intersected by lagoons: it is quite like a gentleman's park in England.[15]

Equally, Mitchell, who appreciated park-like country, also had an artist's eye for more rugged tracts. Naming Mount Salvator in south-west Queensland, he described a riverscape worthy of the Neapolitan painter:

The hills overhanging it surpassed any I had ever seen in picturesque outline. Some resembled gothic cathedrals in ruins; others forts; other masses were perforated, and being mixed and contrasted with the flowing outlines of evergreen woods, and having a fine stream in the foreground, gave a charming appearance to the whole country.[16]

And to underline his sensitivity to the different kinds of the picturesque, Mitchell gave to a neighbouring river, which flowed through a 'rich plain', the name of Claude. For if the landscapes of Salvator Rosa were romantic, sublime, heroic, then the calm vistas of Claude suggested the beauty of fertile regions long settled and civilized, whence the forces of Nature might be contemplated serenely. But, whatever their physical differences, both kinds of landscape gave the impression of visual cultivation, of an aesthetic history with a civilized future. It was in this sense that Stokes's park-like Plains of Promise (plate 8) and Mitchell's Salvator River (plate 11), though physically unalike, were equally picturesque.

Of course, as an aesthetic distinction, this contrast was hardly original. There was even a picturesque antecedent for it in the protracted debate in Regency England between the landscape gardener Humphrey Repton and his academic gentleman critics, Uvedale Price and Payne Knight. Although a follower of 'Capability' Brown, Repton thought his own approach to the laying out of grounds decidedly more picturesque. His critics disagreed. Take, for example, Repton's habit of introducing isolated clumps of trees. This 'clumping' Repton borrowed from Brown. The result of 'th'improver's desolating hand', as Payne Knight had explained in his poem 'The Landscape' (1793), was to leave the gentleman's 'mansion' standing alone,

> 'Midst shaven lawns, that far around it creep
> In one eternal undulating sweep;
> And scatter'd clumps, that nod at one another,
> Each stiffly waving to its formal brother.[17]

Against this 'scene, so dull and bare', Payne Knight proposed to reinstate 'moss-grown terraces', to 'spread the labyrinth's perplexing maze'. At least, by this means, he said

> we should obtain,
> Some features, then, at least,
> To mark this flat, insipid, waving plain;
> Some vary'd tints and forms would intervene,
> To break this uniform, eternal green.[18]

And, in support of his view that dead trees were quite as picturesque as living ones, Payne Knight even invoked the example of Salvator Rosa:

> If years unnumber'd, or the lightning's stroke,
> Have bar'd the summit of the lofty oak,
> (Such as, to decorate some savage waste,
> Salvator's flying pencil often trac'd);
> Entire and sacred let the ruin stand,
> Nor fear the pruner's sacrilegious hand.[19]

If Repton favoured Claude's pastoral, Payne Knight advocated the wilder picturesque of his Neapolitan rival.

Mitchell was familiar with Gilpin's writings and no doubt he was also conversant with this debate. But more significant than the derivation of his views is the use to which Mitchell put them: for, unlike the critics, he felt no need to choose between one kind of landscape and another; and this for the good reason that he employed both kinds of picturesque strategically, as means of travelling. If there is a feature of the landscape gardening debate that illuminates Mitchell's position, it is to be found in Repton's reply to his critics and, in particular, the distinction he made between what was picturesque in nature and what was picturesque in art.

For instance, Repton argued, in real landscapes foregrounds were always less impressive than they appeared in paintings. The painter, who only expected the viewer's gaze to wander, could afford to cultivate wildness, 'nettles and rugged thorns'. However, the visitor who contemplated wandering in a real park was likely to prefer 'a neat gravel walk'.[20] Again, theorists of art, like Uvedale Price, might define picturesque views in terms of 'novelty' or even 'surprise', but were these desirable, even attainable, qualities in a real landscape? (This, of course, is the point 'Mr Milestone', alias Humphrey Repton, makes in Thomas Love Peacock's satire, *Headlong Hall*: ' "Pray Sir," said Mr Milestone, "by what name do you distinguish this character [Unexpectedness], when a person walks round the grounds for the second time?" ')[21] Instead of novelty, Repton preferred to speak of 'Contrast'. 'Contrast', in his definition, 'supplies the place of novelty, by a sudden and unexpected change of scenery, provided the transitions are neither too frequent nor too violent'.[22] Contrast is what novelty becomes on second viewing.

In Repton's view, picturesqueness in landscape was an illusion. It was not a property of the landscape itself, but a product of looking. In fact, the task of both the painter and the landscape gardener was to create picturesque points of view. Seen in this way, the difference between the two professions was obvious. Where the painter catered for a static observer, the landscape gardener dealt with one who was mobile. The painter portrayed an ideal combination of elements, but the gardener's project unfolded in an empirical time and space. The romantic view in the style of Rosa might be picturesque to the static observer, but to the mobile observer an open, lightly timbered gentleman's park was infinitely more appealing. Thus, the 'strong chiaroscuro' which the painter used to 'preserve composition' was out of place in the arrangement of real trees, which must remain attractive under all lights. Equally, the narrow, unifocal viewpoint of a picturesque painting was ineffectual in a landscape, where every view must seem attractive. In reality, as Repton pointed out, our 'field of vision is much greater'. To portray the gardener's achievement accurately, it would require 'even a different drawing at the most trifling change of situation'.[23]

Repton clearly understands that the different kinds of picturesque do not reflect objective differences: they are the offspring of viewing the landscape either statically or in motion. But Repton also brings out another point – that, underlying these differences, both kinds of picturesque illusion have a fundamental feature in common: they both aim to heighten the impression of visibility. What constitutes 'visibility' depends on whether the picturesque view is a park or a painting. For the park-viewer, whose view of space is externally determined by the limitations of his viewpoint, the *desideratum* is an illusion of increased visual command: he wants to be able to see his way to the horizon. By contrast, the picturesque critic of painting already enjoys such a privileged command of space: it is vouchsafed him by the picture frame. He already sees all there is to see. For him, therefore, the appeal of the picturesque lies in its active *disclosure* of space. The picturesque screens of oaks, the impenetrable thickets – anathema to the traveller in the field – are, for the critic indoors, the means of bringing the country before the mind's eye, as a place of active exploration, a pleasure park.

Enhanced visibility characterizes the picturesque, but it is a visibility that implicates the viewer. There is no question here of viewing a stage; no question of a disinterested viewpoint or a unified perspective. Picturesqueness is the offspring of the viewer's orientation, his cast of mind, his exploratory urge, his pleasure in imagination. It is this argument, incidentally, that resolves the empirical paradox that, in early nineteenth-century Australia, a love of the picturesque went hand in hand with the unimaginative replication of the grid. An empirical account of the organization of space finds the co-existence of two frames of spatial reference such as these unwieldy and messy. Its classic strategy – exemplified in Jean Piaget's book *The Child's Conception of Space* – is to rank the different modes of conceptualizing space hierarchically, to argue that the Euclidean conception of space evolves out of, and transcends, the topological conception (to which the picturesque belongs).[24] The net result of this for the history of Australian space is that historical geographers pay attention to the survey, but not to travellers' accounts. The latter are relegated to the category of 'first impressions' with the implication that they are ill-informed and represent naive attempts to impose European aesthetic categories where they do not belong. The topographical, in short, is treated as mere literature. But by stressing the intentional nature of the gaze we overcome this artificial paradox. As we saw, the grid's historical significance was strategic. So, too, the forms of the picturesque emerge in answer to the directed gaze. They are offspring of our perception – a perception of the world which is not god-like but rooted in our physical make-up. This is the point the philosopher Merleau-Ponty makes so eloquently when he writes:

> Our perception would not comprise either outlines, figures, backgrounds or objects, and would consequently not be the perception of anything, or indeed exist at all, if the subject of perception were not this gaze which takes a grip upon things only in so far as they have a general direction; and this general direction in space is not a contingent characteristic of the object, it is the means whereby I recognize it and am conscious of it as an object.[25]

It is their quality of lending space direction that the grid and the picturesque share and that enables them to interpenetrate the same historical world.

The significance of this intentional visibility emerges in endless Australian contexts. The surgeon-superintendent of convict transports Peter Cunningham wrote of trees in the New South Wales county of Eden that they 'are so sparingly scattered as to resemble more a nobleman's park than a natural forest'. And he continued,

> It is really delightful to ride through these open spots, where there is scarcely a tree you would wish to see cut down, so much do they beautify the prospect; while, if a kangaroo or an emu should start up in your path, you enjoy a clear and animated view of the chase, until the dogs finally surround and seize upon their victim.[26]

Here the subject is not the hunt, but hunting as a metaphor expressive of the pleasure of seeing. In the field, as John Fenton in Tasmania observed, a taste for the 'romantic' had its limitations:

> The prostrate gum tree, shivered to atoms in its fall, with its decayed heart scattered over a large extent of ground, is beautifully screened from observation by an overgrowth of delicate fern-leaves, shrubs, and mosses, while the tree ferns, sassafras, musk-trees and myrtles, with lichens, parasites, and creeping vines adorning their trunks, make a Devon scrub look like an earthly Paradise. Go into it, however, and spend a day toiling and fighting to make headway through its impenetrable mazes, and you will come to the conclusion that 'a thing of beauty is *not* a joy for ever'.[27]

Different as they appear, the habitats Cunningham and Fenton describe have one thing in common. Like figures of speech, they both render the invisible visible. For the mobile Cunningham, the open spots give him a view of the hunt normally denied him. It is as if they magnify his control of the world. His clear and animated view takes him where the action is instantaneously. It increases his speed. It realizes the object of his desire. It brings distant things close, like a metaphor. Fenton's impenetrable 'earthly Paradise' achieves the same effect by other means. For Fenton finds that the static picturesque reveals what is hidden only so long as the observer is content to contemplate the teeming plants which 'beautifully' screen the fallen tree from a fixed spectator's point of view. He penetrates only by not penetrating. The magnificence of the fallen tree is in proportion to the observer's immobility. Once Fenton attempts to advance, the illusion of picturesqueness disappears.

The picturesque in Australia made the space of travelling visible to the traveller. It realized for him his own historical destination – to travel or to settle down. And, just as travelling and settling were dialectically related, so, also, the two kinds of picturesque, like landscape gardening and painting, were related to each other, revealing spatiality in its double aspect of motion and rest, journey and journal-writing. Implicit in both spatial modalities was always the sense of symbolic boundaries defined and rendered eloquent. The screen of vegetation, the trees one would not wish to see cut down, might, in other contexts, be a bar to physical and imaginative progress. To call them picturesque was to attribute to them the observer's own heightened sense of possession, his sensation of suddenly being at home in the world. The connection between the visible picturesque and the invisible prospect of home, the tension between motion and rest always implicit in travelling, is apparent in Robert Dawson's remark that,

> Where the soil is pretty good it is lightly timbered, occasionally resembling a gentleman's park; but the traveller soon loses this idea from finding no mansion at the end of the scene. He plods on from park to park, as it were, and rests at night, with his horse tethered beside him, near some pool of water.[28]

Captain Fyans recorded his comparable experience in the Western District of Victoria:

> The country between Timboon and the Hopkins River would remind any person lately from home of a nobleman's park, with the expectation of coming soon to a magnificent house. Many a dreary ride I have had over this magnificent, splendid country, lying waste and idle . . .[29]

In a sense, these Australian scenes retained their picturesqueness only so long as the spectator remained in one place. To explore them was to transform expectation into disappointment, splendour into dreariness. Thus Howitt, travelling through a country of 'fine slopes, and grassy swells and uplands, formed by the feet of the hills', is inevitably reminded of 'an immense and splendid park'. The resemblance is so strong

> one cannot, every now and then, help fancying that, on some height or slope amongst the trees, we shall catch sight of some gentleman's seat, or perceive a carriage, with all its finished appointments, rolling downward to the road.[30]

But it is, of course, only fancy:

> A moment's reflection reminds you that all is solitary wilderness; that there is no road in reality; and that such houses

and carriages lie, perhaps, hundreds of years in the back-ground.[31]

Among its other properties, then, the picturesque appears to telescope time.

Unpicturesque views by contrast are views that exhibit no heightened sense of time or space; they are horizontal vistas where the eye can gain no purchase. Walker, looking across level forest, found it 'a dreary sight' because it held out no promise of inhabitation, no hope of

> the cultivated fields, the numerous farm-houses, the innumer-able cottages, the peasantry, the smiling villages, the busy towns, that ought to have filled up the landscape.[32]

As Walker remarked,

> The hope of them would even have gratified and satisfied the mind, and imagination in that case would readily have filled up the picture, so that cheerful and pleasing ideas would have arisen, but no such thing could be permitted.[33]

The picturesque, then, permitted the illusion of hope. It allowed not only the contraction of future time but also, to judge from Walker's list of objects, the bringing near of distant objects, the magnification of the minute, the God-like survey of the great. The picturesque assembled time and space, presenting society as a community of objects.

This picturesque interplay between space and time, between present loneliness and future sociability, between visible Nature and invisible Culture, was equally the appeal of picturesque views after Salvator Rosa. It was the promise of the invisible, as much as what was visible, the promise of the horizon being brought into view and grasped that mattered. When Mitchell wrote ecstatically of a 'distant valley', it was with the temporal and spatial beyond primarily in mind:

> In such a clime, with these romantic hills, that valley must be a paradise if watered well, as I hope it is. So flowed the 'spring' of hope at least, as it was fed by the scene then before me.[34]

In this passage, the Claudean valley suggests stasis, the romantic hills onward motion. Later, in the fourth expedition, Mitchell again took advantage of the complementary nature of the mobile and static picturesques. On 14 September 1846, Mitchell recalled, he was making his way towards a 'rocky gap [in a ridge]' – a gap sufficiently significant in his epic tale to find a place for itself on his map (see plate 12) – and he commented,

> The sun nearly set and not a blade of grass visible amongst the brigalow bushes. But what was all this to the romantic uncertainty as to what lay beyond![35]

The following day, Mitchell's expectations are more than fulfilled. That other picturesque comes into view:

> I hastened towards the gap, and ascended a naked rock on the west side of it. I there beheld downs and plains extending westward beyond the reach of vision, bounded on the S.W. by woods and low ranges, and on the N.E. by higher ranges . . .[36]

And Mitchell commented:

> To an European, the prospect of an open country has a double charm in regions for the most part covered with primeval forests, calling up pleasing reminiscences of the past, brighter prospects for the future – inspiring a sense of freedom, especially when viewed from the back of a good horse.[37]

In effect, Mitchell recognized, the two picturesques provided the viewpoints to appreciate each other: a romantic backdrop of forested mountains was necessary to complete the appeal of the plain. The plain was most visible from a prominent ridge. The pleasant prospect of home was best seen at a distance. And, in interweaving these two countries, Mitchell was also taking into account the picturesque demands of his own narrative. As *Tristram Shandy* pointed out, however it might appeal to the traveller, a spacious plain made dreary reading. Whether or not the more romantic prospects of Rosa contributed to Mitchell's progress, they were a great help in urging the reader forward. Mitchell's landscape was one where traveller and poet, colonist and critic, might feel equally at home. It looked forward to a cultivated society.

In this context, also, we can make fuller sense of the photograph of the first settler at Hall's Gap (plate 13), which I discussed in chapter 5. For, not only is his hut sited on the edge of a plain, it is also located against a backdrop of mountains – the very Grampians, in fact, which Mitchell discovered and named. It lies, in short, at the intersection of the two kinds of picturesque. But these are not so much ecological or even topographical divisions as products of the double point of view which characterizes the history of settlement. It is only the settler, looking reflectively back towards his cottage, and beyond it to the nestling horizon, who finds the backdrop of hills attractive: to the traveller they are merely an obstacle. To the traveller, it is the plains in the foreground and the shaded veranda which occupy his mind. For him, the house is a place for looking back where he has been and forgetting the hills temporarily behind him.

This is the double-vision of the photograph taken in all likelihood by an itinerant photographer. But the tendency has been to ignore the photograph's point of view, the sense in which it reveals the settler's place as something picturesquely constructed and not merely reported. In a manner analogous to imperial history's invention of the heroic pioneer, making a place out of nothing, pictures like this have been treated as if the settler took them, as if he made the picturesque, and not vice versa. A true history of photography in Australia would have to do primarily, not with the visible content, but with the invisible point of view, the 'here' on which 'there' was dialectically predicated.

Picturesqueness was a form of eloquence, it was a spatial figure of speech. With its implication of natural places, nameable things and parts composed to form a harmonious whole, it belonged to the order of language. It lent itself to description. It exhibited a spatial grammar. Picturesque country was country that spoke for itself. There is a striking passage in one of Hannah More's letters that illustrates this point. Not without irony, she reports on a 'very agreeable two hours' spent with 'Capability' Brown, the landscape gardener:

He illustrates everything he says about gardening with some

literary or grammatical allusion. He told me he compared his art to literary composition. 'Now *there*,' said he, pointing his finger, 'I make a comma, and there,' pointing to another spot, 'where a more decided turn is proper, I make a colon; at another point where an interruption is desirable to break the view, a parenthesis; now a full stop, and then I begin another subject.'[38]

Such landscapes could be read. And we begin to realize that when writers like Howitt and Walker spoke about the homeliness of the scene it was not necessarily the old country for which they felt nostalgic. 'Home' was a metaphor for the place of speech, the place where language made sense. To be at home in Australia was to be at home in speech. It was the ability to manipulate space, to concentrate it here, to spread it out there. This was the focal power of Strzelecki's cottage with its plume of smoke, its ability to translate views into surroundings, and surroundings into significant histories, to render foreground details promising, chance events poetic. Bright birds flew through the trees and on out of sight and an overlap of trunks at last began to promise a street of opening doors.

The intentional nature of the picturesque throws light on the familiar colonial charge that the Australian bush was 'monotonous'. There was no habitat immune to this accusation: open sclerophyll forest or the undulating sea of stunted mallee gums; riverine plains and waterless salt flats. Even the coastline was often felt to be devoid of objects of note.[39] But monotony was not an objective fact: it was a function of the intention to travel and settle down. If a natural 'nobleman's park' ceased to please, after traversing it for days, it was because it failed to show asymmetry in depth. It became monotonous because it did not share the traveller's sense of direction. And, indeed, even the traveller's rate of progress could contribute materially to his sense of repetition.

In other contexts, monotony was the quality of what was unnamed. But, whatever the case, implicit in it was the charge of being uninhabitable. R. L. Heathcote, for example, in his excellent study of marginal settlement, *Back of Bourke*, cites 'the monotonous repetition of natural phenomena', in the literature of the 1840s and 1850s, as if it were a natural fact. And he ascribes to a shift in sensibility the sudden 'awareness of contrasts' that occurred in the 1880s and 1890s.[40] But, rather than reflect a change in aesthetic fashion, this changed perception of surroundings was undoubtedly bound up with the fact that the resident selector was replacing the peripatetic squatter; smallholdings were replacing vast ranches. Thus there was nothing mystical about the dispersion of monotony: among other things, it was the selector himself who made the country picturesque – or, at least, began to imagine it that way.

The settlers themselves intruded symbolic boundaries and directions. Writing of the regionalization of Western Australia, Gentilli has pointed out that a sense of differentiation and contrast does not precede residence, but is the product of it:

> Such regions are usually distinguished after man has been associated with them for some length of time. It is no accident that at the beginning of the century no such type of region was recognized in Western Australia (with the obvious exception of the gold-fields): but now, 70 years later, Wheat Belt, Great Southern and Esperance Plains have acquired individuality through their agricultural settlement.[41]

What Gentilli identifies at a regional level was true more intimately, too: picturesqueness, the condition of differentiation that rendered identity of place and its communication possible, did not precede exploration and settlement. It followed the travellers wherever they went and decided to set up camp permanently. By the 1890s there was a market for books like J. E. Brown's *A Practical Treatise on Tree Culture in South Australia*, in which the South Australian government botanist declared,

> How different . . . the contrast of appearance between a country well stocked with trees and one bare of these. The one looks clothed and picturesque, while the other has that barren unproductive look which wearies the eye.[42]

Recommending that fence lines and poor spots about the farm should be planted up, Brown reminded his reader that the resulting trees give such a clothed look to his farm as to enhance its value very much in the estimation of persons of refined taste; and this often goes far in securing a high price for land.[43]

In view of these utilitarian arguments, it might well be asked why squatters and the selectors who followed them after the Selection Acts frequently added, if anything, to the monotony of the place. As early as 1836, for instance, Thomas Shepherd was pleading with fellow Tasmanians for picturesque restraint in clearing land:

> In place of cutting down our splendid forests right forward without distinction, we have only to thin out, and tastefully arrange and dispose them, to produce the most pleasing effects. The country could by this means, at a very small cost, and with less labour than is required by the indiscriminate destruction of our native trees, present an exterior to the eye of a stranger and the resident of the Colony, such as no other country in the world I believe could furnish. Besides the pastoral nature of this country would favour such embellishments, as not an acre of ground would be lost – sheep might feed on our lawns and parks, adding the pleasure of seeing living objects enjoy the benefits of improved scenery.[44]

But despite Shepherd's commercial common sense, one has the impression that pastoralists of all descriptions continued to remove timber indiscriminately, as if their mission was, in James Bennett's words, 'to destroy everything that grows above 2 feet'.[45]

Part of this apparent indifference has to do with the nature of the survey itself, as I suggested in chapter 5. But it may also be that, despite appearances, the settlers remained in mind at least on the move, that they thought of themselves not so much as settled but as permanently camped. For it was the transient who were most destructive. The traveller and journalist Howitt, for instance, who had a highly developed taste for the picturesque, noticed that no sooner had he begun to pan for gold than all his aesthetic principles abandoned him. 'We diggers', he wrote, 'are horribly destructive of the picturesque.'[46] And Howitt attributed the destructiveness of the squatter to the same cause:

A squatter is a nomade [*sic*] by his very name. He is not a proprietor; he is not a cultivator, but a king of the desert, and can reign there alone. When it ceases to be a desert, he ceases to reign, and either assumes the shape of a denizen of cultivated earth, a lord of ploughs and enclosures, or moves on.[47]

Just as fence lines could transform the terrifying wilderness into an object of pleasure, so, too, the picturesque that foretokened possession could, in retrospect, come to signify wildness and the romance of beginnings. This, perhaps, is the gesture implicit in the earnest adoption of aboriginal names. Names that were once effaced are now used to disguise a too suburban familiarity. Names that once marked the intent to settle now allude to the luxury of imaginary flight. There is a nice nineteenth-century instance of this process. Near Swan Hill, on his third expedition, Mitchell gave the name 'Moonlight Creek' to one of his camping places.[48] The name itself was conspicuously picturesque, but A. M. Campbell, one of the first settlers in the area, evidently decided to go one better than Mitchell:

Without A. M. Campbell's early knowledge of the Aboriginal language the word 'Kerang' may never have been. The Aboriginal word for 'moon' in certain tribes was Kewang, therefore the creek named Moonlight by Mitchell would be Kewang in the Aboriginal tongue. One is left to wonder did Mr A. M. Campbell misinterpret the word Kewang as Kerang?[49]

But the question of Campbell's linguistic qualifications is beside the point. Quite aside from the possibility that 'Kerang' may have nothing to do with moonlight – it may even have something to do with 'Kerangyala', meaning 'plenty of game and fish'[50] – Campbell clearly had no intention of restoring to the place its original name. Campbell did not approach the renaming of Moonlight Creek in a spirit of antiquarian zeal. What he wanted to stress was not wilderness, but the picturesque illusion of it. He wanted to incorporate nature within the framework of settlement, to authorize his own place there and by his art to give back to nature its artlessness.

There was no question of effacing his presence – which no doubt explains why Kerang is not even situated on Moonlight (now Barr) Creek, but merely nearby. Nor was his object to honour the region's displaced inhabitants. Campbell's aim was picturesque – to cultivate the illusion of a natural place. In his history of Deniliquin, John Bushby describes the controversy that arose over the naming of the town's first public gardens. Some, he says, thought 'it should be a native name linking "the present state of ornamentation and that of the past wilderness" '.[51] Campbell's purpose was comparable: by commemorating the picturesqueness of the aboriginal language, the white namers rendered the Aborigines tacit conspirators in their own destruction. In retrospect, the country had formerly been populated not with people but with vaguely beneficent spirits, who smiled on the invaders' artistry and on their own posthumous fame.

In this context of attributing to nature an artfulness that allied it strategically to white plans for settlement, we can also make sense of another kind of 'native spirit' frequently associated with picturesque Australia: the fairy. John Fenton, for example, writes of 'a remarkably grand fall':

> When I first saw this cascade it was a charming sight in the bosom of the primitive unbroken foliage. The tree-ferns were growing within touch of the water; the sombre colour of the myrtles, with the pale green tints of the young leaves just bursting into life, and the countless shades of other beautiful shrubs, forming, as it were, a leafy arc round the terraces of dancing waters, made the place look like a fairy scene.[52]

There is an animation here that suggests the presence of mindful creators. They are geniuses of the place of the kind Wordsworth recommended to Sir George Beaumont in laying out his picturesque garden at Coleorton.

> In this little glade should be a basin of water inhabited by two gold or silver fish . . . these little creatures to be the 'genii' of the pool and of the place.[53]

Wordsworth's fancy also illuminates, incidentally, Caleb Burchett's reference to 'small fish . . . disporting in the shallow clear waters, in the sunlight . . .' which I quoted earlier in this chapter. The presence of such fish does not attest to Burchett's interest in natural history: it is their animation, the light on water and scales, that renders them numinous. And this quality of glitter, of things moving between visibility and invisibility, is eminently picturesque.

As the Gippsland poet Marie Pitt wrote in her poem 'Doherty's Corner',

> There's no bush to-day at Doherty's Corner,
>   Only strange green hills and the glint of a far bay;
> . . .
> There are no fairies now at Doherty's Corner,
>   Where dusky spider-flowers and wild white daisies grew;
> . . .
> Perhaps they died when the old black log and the bracken
>   And the box bushes were gone. [54]

In Pitt's poem, it is the cleared land that appears strange, not the original bush. The new visibility has rendered the fairies invisible. It has destroyed that picturesque animation, that fairy realm where 'every sense was a-leap'. Against the loss of that chiaroscuro of 'dusky spider-flowers and wild white daisies', the poignancy of the line 'Only strange green hills and the glint of a far bay' is overwhelming. For, it seems, the fairies have not been wholly lost: they have been metamorphosed and revived in the suddenly strange 'green' hills and in the 'glint' of the far bay. That green, that remote twinkle of the sea were previously the qualities of pellucid forest water, of fishes disporting in the sunlight, of luminous canopy.

More generally, Australian travellers and settlers detected in the picturesque a vision of future civilization that both rebuked their initially destructive intrusions and, ultimately, legitimized them. Writing of the Tasmanian forest, Fenton expressed the view that,

> The natural foliage, undisturbed by the woodman's axe, grows so luxuriantly, adapting itself to the situation, as though vegetation were not altogether devoid of mind. [55]

The picturesque seemed to anticipate the traveller's intentions. As Mitchell wrote,

> We crossed a beautiful plain; covered with shining verdure, and ornamented with trees, which, although 'dropt in nature's careless haste', gave the country the appearance of an extensive park. [56]

Such country was naturally civilized. Walker said of the squatter Ebden's run near Mount Macedon:

> We were indeed enchanted with this country, and well we might, for *no art could improve it*, either for use or ornament. [57]

Such places did not merely resemble parks: they were more park-like than parks themselves. Like the orator's picturesque figures of speech, they revealed, as no bare statement could, the nature of the place. Such places held up a mirror to art. Referring to a wooded and hilly scene on the Claude River, Mitchell was reminded of the landscapes of John Martin, and he commented,

> I never saw anything in nature come so near these creations of genius and imagination. [58]

Not surprisingly, then, the picturesque, and trees in particular, were endowed with the newcomers' own highest social aspirations. Echoing sentiments expressed by G. P. Marsh, in his book *Land and Nature*, and, nearer home, by Sir Ferdinand Müller, Brown argued

> In an ornamental point of view, then, trees are a necessity of our life; they instruct the mind in the work of the Creator, and they elevate the soul to things noble and cultivated . . . trees have a wonderfully refining influence upon human nature, to such an extent that by our cultivation of trees, so I think, may our social standard be estimated. [59]

So, picturesque meanings multiplied around settlement and the promise of settlement. So, manipulated in various ways, the picturesque taught the country to smile, in Pye's phrase, 'with beauties not it's own'. But it would misrepresent the historical nature of its appeal to close an account of the picturesque on a static note. For the essence of the picturesque was that it drew the traveller on: it *led him* to settle. J. M. Powell, in his exhaustive studies of George Russell and the wool-manufacturing Clyde Company, suggests that the company's head-station came to be sited on the Leigh near Geelong through a process of 'trial-and-error'.[60] But Russell's own testimony reveals that the site of the future headquarters was decided in advance of any empirical inquiry. It was the result of a picturesque impression gained in the course of a tour *prior* to establishing a run:

> We reached the hill where Golfhill now stands about midday. Here we camped, and had our midday meal. We both admired the view down the valley of the Leigh: covered as it was with such an abundant crop of grass, it had a very rich and fertile appearance. I remarked to Mr Clarke that if I settled in the country I should choose the Leigh valley to settle down in; and that, if so, I should build my house upon the hill. Which afterwards turned out to be the case.[61]

First of all, the picturesque was a traveller's viewpoint, a possible stopping place, a punctuation mark, an opportunity to reflect on the future. And, since it was a mode of journeying, it seems appropriate to conclude here with a picturesque journey.

Nowhere, perhaps, is the impact of the picturesque on Australian settlement better documented than in the history of the Major's Line. Although Mitchell may have intended his fourth expedition to mark the culmination of his ambition to locate a picturesque paradise, it was his earlier third expedition of 1836 that came closest to realizing his hopes in the field. Mitchell's elaborate descriptions of the country he dubbed Australia Felix had a considerable influence on the pattern of overlanding from Sydney and the distribution of squatters' runs north of the Victorian Divide. Australia Felix – roughly Victoria's Western District, but extending as far east as the Pyrenees and Mount Macedon – was, in Mitchell's well-known formulation,

> a country ready for the immediate reception of civilized man; and destined perhaps to become eventually a portion of a great empire. Unencumbered by too much wood, it yet possessed

enough for all purposes; its soil was exuberant, and its climate temperate; it was bounded on three sides by the ocean; and it was traversed by mighty rivers, and watered by streams innumerable. Of this Eden I was the first European to explore its mountains and streams – to behold its scenery – to investigate its geological character – and, by my survey, to develope those natural advantages, certain to become, at no distant date, of vast importance to a new people.[62]

In short, Australia Felix was a picturesque country. Its rhetorical nature is underlined when we remember that, in Mitchell's published narrative, the description just quoted occurs in the entry for 13 July, *before*, that is, Mitchell had entered Australia Felix.

But, as valuable as Mitchell's account of a region that displayed both the Claudean picturesque of the plains and the romantic mountains of Salvator Rosa, was the Major's Line – Mitchell's well-marked return route from Portland to Sydney: it was by way of the Major's road that Sydney-siders hoped to gain access to the promised country. The mere existence of the Major's wheelmarks, dividing the country in two, to left and right, seems to have had a remarkable impact on how the overlanders 'saw' the country they passed through. Mindful of Mitchell's picturesque formulations, they seem to have regarded his track as dividing the good country decisively from the bad. This is brought out in an early sketch map of the Port Phillip district (plate 19), which shows quite dramatically how Mitchell's return route acted as a boundary to settlement – all the squatters, whether originating in Tasmania or Sydney, seeking runs south of his Line. At the same time, of course, Mitchell's route was a boundary that communicated difference: it was a limit inviting transgression, a fact the map-maker graphically symbolized by writing 'Advance Australia' across the as yet unoccupied interior north of the Line.

Curr, for example, describing his northward journey from a run near Carlsruhe to his new station on the Murray, recalls crossing the line near Seymour on the Goulburn:

The next day I crossed the Sydney-road, which ran between the ranges and the flat country. On the east side of the road I found the mountainous district abounding in green grass and running streams – what a new chum would think the beau idéal of a sheep country; and in effect this neighbourhood was in high repute at the time, whilst the flat country to the west, which was noticeable for its dry, burnt-up appearance, and the prevalence of salsolaceous vegetation, was considered to be very inferior. On this head the mountaineers at that time plumed themselves not a little, rather looking down on the dwellers in the plains.[63]

As Curr goes on to emphasize, these first impressions based on aesthetic associationism were not borne out by experience:

Of course we all know now that the estimate formed on this subject was quite an erroneous one, and, as a fact, that those overlanders who took up country to the eastward of the Sydney-road, amidst abundance of water and green grass, met with but scant success as sheep-farmers; those whose fortune led them westward, or down the rivers, as a rule doing exceedingly well. Indeed, now-a-days, green grass country and bad country are pretty generally synonymous terms.[64]

William Brodribb, who recalled overlanding to Port Phillip in 1839, put it more bluntly:

At that time, on the right of our route, *not one acre was occupied in the salt bush country. In those days, the whole country to the right of the track was considered a desert.*[65]

But, empirically valuable or not, as a picturesque incentive to overland the Major's Line was clearly invaluable. If only as a rhetorical place, it provided the traveller with a decisive direction and the pleasant prospect of home beyond the horizon. It enabled the overlander to speak of his prospects. Thus, having followed the Major's Line some miles west of the Campaspe, specifically 'in the hope of seeing something of that highly extolled country', Walker ascends a range of hills and reports, 'It looked beautiful, and we all exclaimed – "There is Australia Felix!"' [66] But Walker's narrative has a more than anecdotal interest. Earlier, travelling along the Major's Line, Walker had caught up with the overlander Charles Ebden, who was on his way to establish a new station in the Port Phillip direction. Walker's account of Ebden's progress and eventual selection of a run, making him the first squatter north of the Divide, enables us to trace in remarkable detail the impact picturesque criteria had in determining the pattern and distribution of Victorian squatting.

Walker overtook Ebden on the Goulburn River and travelled with him and his flock of 9000 sheep, following the Major's Line as far as the Campaspe. At the Campaspe crossing, Walker and Ebden parted company, Walker to view Australia Felix, Ebden to head southwards up the Campaspe towards Mount Macedon. Ebden's decision to look up the Campaspe for a suitable run was itself a tribute to the power of the picturesque. In October 1836 Ebden had written from the Murray to his partner, explaining his intention to move their flocks, the runs there not having equalled 'our first expectations'. A preliminary expedition to Port Phillip had persuaded Ebden that a run much closer to that port, 'say to a distance of 80 miles', made good business sense. But the move itself seems to have depended on Ebden receiving, early in 1837, a version of Mitchell's expedition report. This emerges from the fact that, when Walker overtook Ebden on the Goulburn, on 21 May 1837, Ebden informed him that he was 'going to the westward of Mount Macedon, about 60 miles from Port Phillip'. And, until Mitchell rechristened it the previous year, Mount Macedon had been known by the name Hume and Hovell had previously given it: Mount Wentworth.[67]

The economic reasons for choosing the Mount Macedon region were obvious. The previous year, Mitchell had made a south-easterly detour from his homeward Line, crossing and briefly following the Campaspe, in order to climb Mount Macedon. The view from its summit towards Port Phillip Bay led him to name the gap to its west Expedition Pass. He was

> confident that such a line of communication between the southern coast and Sydney must, in the course of time, become a very considerable thoroughfare.[68]

Clearly, this region would suit Ebden's purposes very well. However, although Mitchell's picturesque narrative gave Ebden a *general* idea of where to look, it did not help him to locate *precisely* the place to settle. It had brought him by way of the Major's Line to the verge of Australia Felix; it had even indicated a promising valley between his Line and Mount Macedon – with his customary vague optimism, Mitchell had said of it he had never seen 'a more pleasing or promising portion of territory'.[69] But, within that portion of territory, Ebden still had to select where precisely to settle. And here, also, it was picturesque considerations which proved decisive.

This, again, emerges from Walker's narrative. At the point where the Major's Line crossed the Campaspe, Ebden had found the country unattractive: 'He thinks these plains too bleak and cold for winter,' Walker reported.[70] But, as Walker discovered, when he returned from his Australia Felix detour and followed Ebden southwards, a few miles up the Campaspe the country was quite different. Travelling south from Mitchell's crossing place, the bleak plains were left behind. After a mile or two of forest, he descended to an alluvial flat formed by the Campaspe. Beyond this (the future site of Kyneton), the valley of the Campaspe suddenly grew picturesque:

> We entered upon a magnificent piece of country, and continued on it, for at least a dozen miles, towards Mount Macedon: through it the Campaspe (or water we take to be the Campaspe) flows.[71]

This was the country that, just two days earlier, Ebden had selected for his head-station, Carlsruhe:

> The country itself *is superb*, the soil very rich, and well clothed with grass, with very few trees, certainly with no more than required for ornament, and they are not the gums, but wattles (mimosa) of different kinds, forest oaks, honey-sucles (banksia) &c., and a great portion is totally devoid of trees. The surface of the ground is also beautifully diversified by all manner of slopes and plains, and vales, also a few hills, beautifully wooded.[72]

The site Ebden chose for his head-station reinforced this park-like appearance. Located at the south-west extremity of his run, on the eastern bank of the Campaspe, backed to the south and

11 "River Salvator," engraving
from Mitchell's *Journal of an Expedition into the Interior of Tropical
Australia*, 1848

The Country and the Routes
between the
Maranóa and Mount Mudge
Chapters V. and VIII.

RIVER VICTORIA
Chapter VII.

English Miles.

12 River Victoria, map
from Mitchell's *Journal of an Expedition into the Interior of Tropical
Australia*, 1848

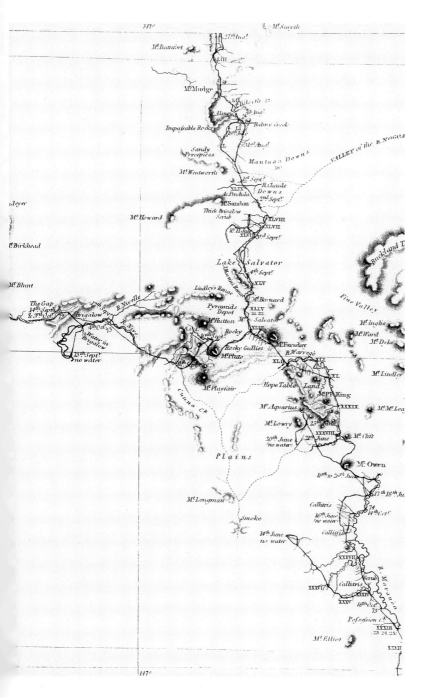

13 (Photographer unknown) Robert Graham, first settler at Hall's Gap,
Grampians, Victoria; photograph, 1880s

14 Fred Kruger, *View on the Bass River, near Queen's Ferry, Western Port,*
Victoria, photograph, *c.* 1878

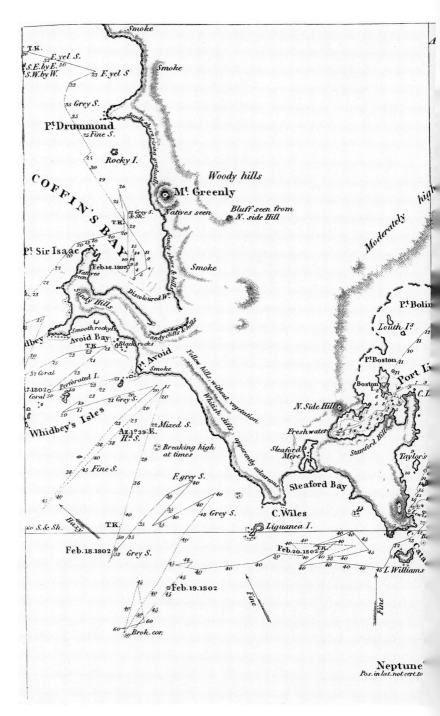

15 Spencer's Gulf, detail of map
from Flinders's *A Voyage to Terra Australis*, 1814

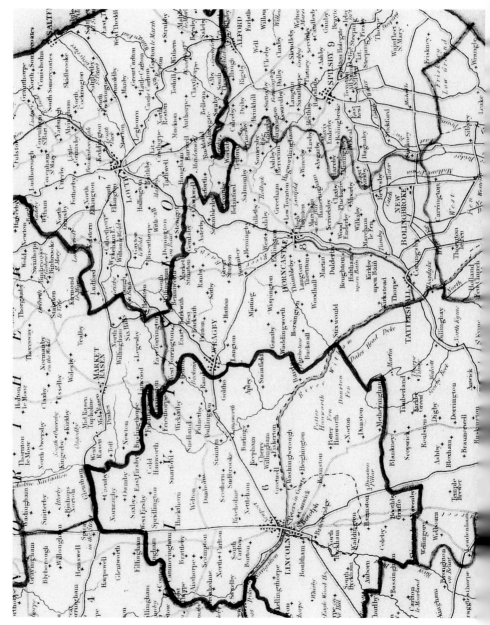

16 Lincolnshire, England, detail of map
   from S. Lewis's *A Topographical Dictionary,* 1842

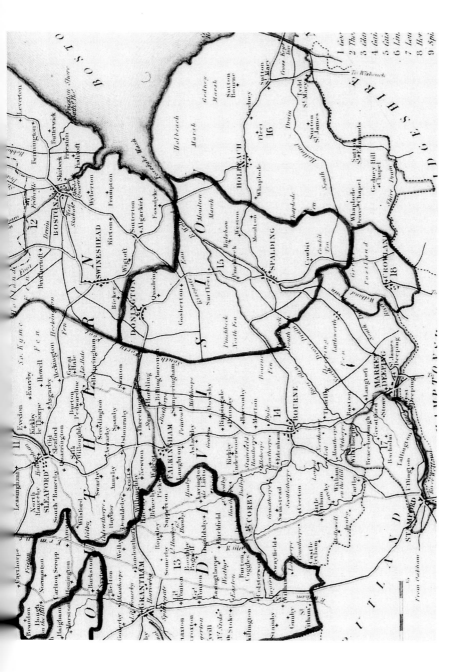

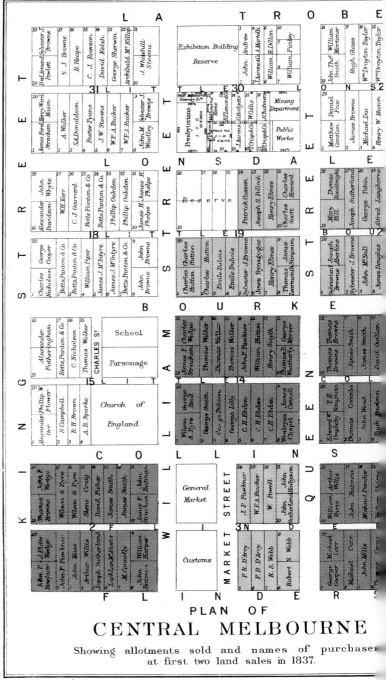

PLAN OF

CENTRAL MELBOURNE

Showing allotments sold and names of purchasers
at first two land sales in 1837.

George Philip & Son Ltd

17 Melbourne's First Land Sales, map
from H. G. Turner's *History of the Colony of Victoria*, 1904

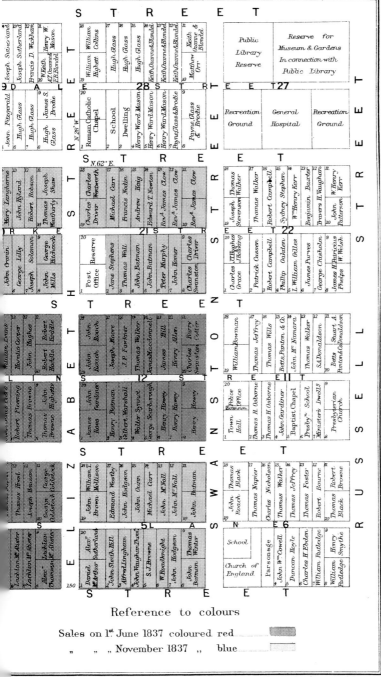

Reference to colours

Sales on 1st June 1837 coloured red

" " " November 1837 " blue

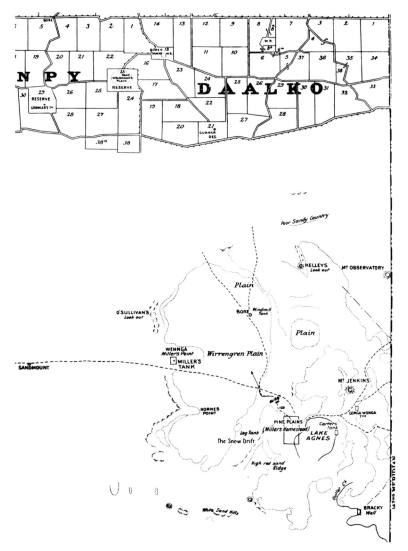

18 Squatters and Selectors in the Mallee, detail of map of Weeah,
Division A, County of Millewa, Victorian Crown Lands
and Survey Department, Melbourne, *c.* 1890

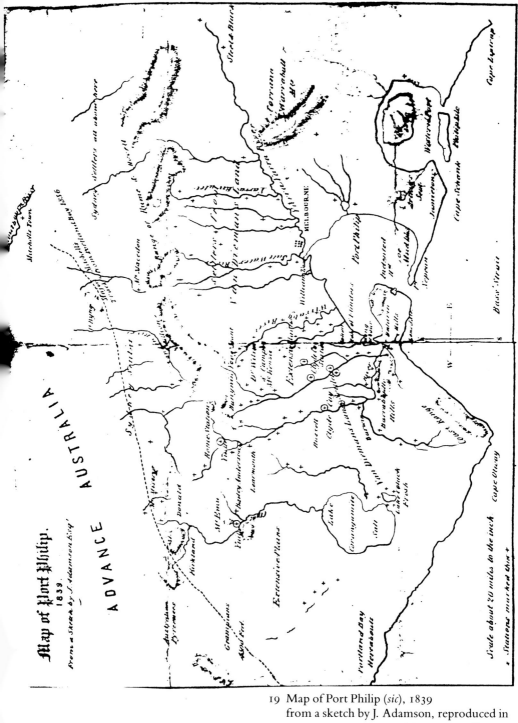

19 Map of Port Philip (*sic*), 1839
from a sketch by J. Adamson, reproduced in
Narrative of George Russell, 1935

20 Tree-house, made by J. D. Wells, Childers, Gippsland, photograph, 1892

21 Frederick McCubbin, *The Pioneer*
oil on canvas, 1904

NATIVE OF WESTERN AUSTRALIA

Capt.ⁿ Grey del.^t_G Foggo lith.   M.& N.Hanhart, lith Printers

Published by T.& W.Boone, London.

22 "Native of Western Australia," engraving
from Grey's *Expeditions in Western Australia*, 1841

west by the densely forested slopes of the Macedon Range, Carlsruhe faced north or north-west. Occupying a picturesque point of view, it imposed on the immediate country the asymmetry essential to its continuing appeal. It looked 'down' the valley, northwards. The picturesque horizon of hills lay 'at its back', a romantic backdrop. Even today, it makes an enormous difference whether you approach the site of Carlsruhe from the north or the south. Only from the north does it reveal itself as *the* picturesque place. From the south it remains invisible.

But the significance of Ebden's picturesque motives does not end here. For Ebden's choice of location helped determine the entire pattern of squatting throughout the Campaspe and Coliban valleys. As J. O. Randell's squatting histories reveal, the runs of later squatters in the area were all located and oriented in relation to Carlsruhe. John Coppock and W. H. Yaldwyn, who were second in the area, took up a run between Ebden's northern boundary and the Major's Line. Alexander Mollison, who arrived on the Campaspe only a few months after Ebden, scoured the region south and north of the Divide before settling adjacent to Ebden across the Coliban to the west. This jigsawing not only determined the route that major roads took. It even had a decisive influence on the later location of towns: Mollison's head-station was close to the present town of Malmsbury. In this sense, Ebden's picturesque journey and choice of site effectively decided the country we now see when we pass through that region. He selected the points of view we now identify as typical. The roads we follow are travellers' constructions, ways to find home.

Ebden's journey evidently made good picturesque sense. And instances of picturesque criteria determining site choice and settlement could no doubt be multiplied. It is strange to realize that throughout much of settled Australia what we take to be 'Australia' is the product of picturesque strategies. This has nothing to do with whether or not the revealed views conform to canons of taste formulated in Regency England. It is bound up with the profounder intention that roads and windows have of making the world visible, of rendering it an object capable of translation. In this sense, when we travel over many Australian roads or tracks, we do not travel 'Australia'. Rather, we relive those first journeys and campsites. But, going over the ground with the advantage of history, we do not come to these places as the first squatters and selectors did. In order to share their experience, we must interpret what was obvious to them – the attraction of the picturesque. To understand their routes and resting places, we have to travel reflectively, even picturesquely. But, then, without reflective travel, their history would remain invisible.

9

Intimate Charm

La flamme est une verticalité habitée.

Gaston Bachelard

The candle flame, the light at the window, the glow of an inviting interior: these are not only the memorable images of home in European fiction. They were, in nineteenth-century Australia, visions representing familiar spatial experiences. Both the traveller and the settler recognized in them the essence of what they meant by homecoming. When the Reverend J. R. Wollaston returned to Albany after one of his long pastoral circuits in the 1840s, he recorded his arrival in these terms:

> Saw light at parlour window – sung out – 'Halloa! How are ye! All right?' Immediately saw two female figures flitting and jostling one another behind the curtain. Door opened – candle blown out – entered home, thank God, safe and well etc., etc., etc., etc. [1]

The most significant part of this extract is the repeated 'etc's with which it concludes. The image of the light and the candle are so widely understood as images of homecoming that they render further description unnecessary. Wollaston's account draws attention to another characteristic property of the flame – its feminine aspect. The light is tended by women, the same women whom it shelters and protects and whose outlines it throws invitingly against the curtains. The flame manifests the double aspect of the house: as seducer and seduced, as mistress and servant. The house makes of the returning traveller both master and child.

The light at the window not only signifies 'home' to the traveller. In the night it also reveals to him his road. In

Gippsland, we learn, in the old days,

> The traveller was guided into Rosedale after dark by the candle
> which always glimmered in the window of Tom Timbs's house
> which is, alas, no more. Old Mr Timbs used to keep the light
> twinkling in the window frame for the benefit of the benighted
> wayfarer, until a reasonably late hour of the evening.[2]

The light at the window keeps the road open. It seems to await
the traveller, musing on his arrival. It implies a vigilant inmate,
but it also implies the reverie of the road. In the last chapter I
suggested that our own progress over roads was a form of
travelling reflection. This property of roads was well known to
early travellers. The road was a place where one's mind could
wander, where one could dream, as if at home reading by
lamplight or with one's eyes closed.

Forty years before the considerate Mr Timbs hung a light in
his window, the site of the future Rosedale was occupied by a
shepherd known as 'Blind Joe'. Blind Joe's hut

> was on the first primitive track from Melbourne to Sale, with a
> junction road leading away from that point to Port Albert, a
> very important place in those days, and the main gateway into
> Gippsland.[3]

'Of course,' the same writer remarks, Blind Joe 'was blind only
in one eye', but the anecdotal association of an unseeing man
with the meeting place of roads – that fundamental site of
nocturnal vigil – may be far from trivial. Albeit by way of a
characteristically Australian rhetorical device, which deflates the
strange and threatening by giving it a nickname, the memory of
Blind Joe at the crossroads may preserve the recognition of a
paradox: that a place associated with far-seeing was once
inhabited by one who saw poorly. Yet, in view of his disability,
Blind Joe could not have chosen a better place to live. For to
some degree, roads removed the need for seeing.

The road at night, revealed in the distant window, was like
the *terra incognita* Stokes described, where there was nothing to
divert the current of one's thoughts. In R. S. Medew's
admittedly fictionalized account of early days in Gippsland, we
meet lay preacher Henry Sutherland:

It is doubtful if Henry is taking much notice of his surroundings because his Bible is open on the pommel of the saddle and
from this altar he is noting the passages to be read and going
over in his mind all he shall say when he comes to preach to his
fellow settlers.[4]

Roads allow one to be where one's thoughts are at once. In this
sense, houses are arrested roads. By the same token, roads were
also houses on the move – as an overlander like Walker knew
only too well: in his tent, laboriously writing up his journal by
candlelight while the others yarned or fell asleep, Walker
experienced the pleasure of the hermit and the pilgrim. His
journal was a road punctuated by lamps glowing in the dark.

This sense of the road as an extended home promising arrival
could be expressed in other ways. In his book *The Unfolding
Hills*, Warwick Eunson describes an early Mirboo settler:

> as he was unused to such densely timbered country and to
> make sure that he could return to his selected land, he tore a
> red handkerchief into strips, and attached the strips to trees
> here and there, to mark the track he had taken.[5]

In effect, the selector was making a road and what he meant by a
road was a place where one could not get lost, where one was
always at home, a place that, one day, might be arrested and the
red rags transformed into geraniums blossoming in the crown
of a tree stump. The strips of handkerchief emblemized his
intent to make the way visible, to see through and over the
picturesque foreground. In this context, as places of reverie,
where the intentional gaze looked beyond to find the object of
its desire, cleared tracks were raised *above* the adjoining
countryside. They transcended their surroundings. Their horizontality lent the traveller the dignity associated with seeing
over things. Travellers on them assumed the tallness of ships at
sea. 'The bullocky', E. S. Sorenson writes, 'takes as much pride
in his wagon as a captain does in his ship, and, like the ship, the
wagon is always "she".'[6] In fact, implicit in the horizontal
swathe of the road was always the uprightness it permitted the
traveller – just as the beams he laid overhead and underfoot lent
the settler's posture the rectitude of a tree. And the consequence

was the traveller's enhanced verticality, his conviction that the road was indeed a 'high' road.

The horizontal and the vertical, the light and the dark: these are the twinned dialectical properties that characterize the burning light. They are also the fundamental modalities characterizing the intimate space of the first white Australian travellers and settlers. And it is the historical significance of these most essential and intimate of spatial experiences that I want to trace in this chapter. For much as the public man might dwell in the realm of the map and the picturesque view, the dreamer, the reflective reader and writer (so conspicuously absent from the pioneer myth) travelled and dwelt in the spaces of his intimacy. The spaces he inhabited at night or on the road were neither the conceptual intervals of the grid nor the visible harmonies of the picturesque: they were imaginative spaces, where he realized (as he never could in deed) the fullness of his own spatiality, the spatial command he knew in dreams, where he was no stranger to flight.

It would be revealing, in the context of exploring the history of travelling and settling, to have a history of travellers' and settlers' dreams. Without seeking to psychoanalyse them, we might find writ large there the newcomers' spatial fantasies as they lay asleep beneath the stars or else meditated from a veranda on the mid-afternoon haze. But, in the absence of such a history, we can at least approach such intimate knowledge by way of the image that, throughout the early travel literature, serves to symbolize most profoundly for the newcomers the idea of place. And this is not the candle flame but the tree – and, more specifically, the gum tree, with its dappled, cloud-shadow trunk and limbs. Such trees with their twinned qualities of light and shade, height and length, emerge in the literature of travelling and settling as fundamental expressions of the newcomers' desire to inhabit.

The identification between the gum tree and the bright, welcoming hut is made very clear in an early South Australian poem. A woman is lost in the bush:

> . . . in the distance [she] saw a small white speck –
> A cottage it might be! She then pursued

With eager step her way; but near approach
Her last hope crushed – it was the gum tree's stem,
Its snow-white bark whose beauty had deceived.[7]

The ease with which a shining gum bole might be mistaken for
a sunlit veranda is also excellently illustrated in the photograph
of the Hall's Gap pioneer (plate 13). But perhaps the focal point
in this view is the pioneer himself, with his white shirt and cap,
in whom all the lightness of the scene is concentrated. In
Kruger's photograph of the Bass River farm (plate 14), it is a
woman's blouse twinkling on the heavily shadowed veranda
which serves the same function. As an image of homecoming,
her bright figure is like a glowing window, and no less enticing.

Another metonymy of home that, like the gum tree, could be
deceptive was the moonlight. An early naturalist in the
Victorian Mallee, A. H. E. Mattingley, recalls making for Pine
Plains station after nightfall:

> The sky was presently lit up by the pale moonbeams, and as
> we made no noise in tramping along the soft sand, the stillness
> had a lonely, dispiriting effect, accentuated further by an
> occasional wailing cry from a Curlew. Frequently my com-
> panion would ejaculate – 'Here is Pine Plains!' as he saw a
> white sand dune show up in the distance through the tall
> timber. The white sand appearing like open country ahead
> gave him the impression of an open plain.[8]

The fact that *sounds*, as well as sights, could also spell loneliness
or arrival is a point we shall come back to. Here what is
interesting is that, although Mattingley explains the reasoning
that makes his companion connect lightness with openness, he
feels no need to elaborate the further connection between these
properties and the prospect of home – so generally is the glow
of light understood to intimate the end of the journey. Indeed,
to the homemaker, whiteness was the predominant quality of
such places – a point poetically underlined by the name 'The
Snow Drift' given to dunes near Pine Plains (see plate 18).

Not surprisingly, moonlight and the snow-white gum tree
were, when taken together, powerful inducements to fall into
reverie and indulge the far-fetched fantasies normally entertained only gazing into the fire in the hearth. Howitt, for

example, riding through the Black Forest near Mount Macedon writes,

> If you traverse these woods in the dusk or in the moonlight, your imagination has abundant scope for exercise. All the blackened stumps, or fallen trees bleached to whiteness, assume characters many of which never really existed in these lands . . . Some appear like dark images of the natives, who have been pushed from their hereditary seats by the white man . . . But far oftener these dark masses appear in the shapes of your own native regions, and your own history. Kings of lofty stature, and in flowing robes, sit on ebony thrones; bishops and abbots stand arrayed in stole and mitre; silent women, seated with their heads stooped on their knees, seem lost in profound grief . . .[9]

These are home thoughts from abroad of a most extravagant kind. They could hardly be entertained by day. Moonlight and forest make visible to the traveller his own mythical origins, the jumble of gothic images that constitute his history. With the phantasmagoric clarity of a dream, they conjure up before him his own gods and keepers on the way.

By daylight, too, the gum trees, like beams of light filtered through clouds, inspired the thought of other places. But such fantasies were characteristically dialectical: they were flights of fancy that brought the dreamer back home. Thus Nellie Clerk's poem 'Imprisoned' begins with the poet's longing to escape from the Gippsland forest:

> There's a gap in the forest fortress
> That circles this clear-topped mound,
> A blue, broken-lined suggestion
> Of unknown beauties beyond;[10]

But, were the poet able to 'fly from the forest' that way, could she 'soar with the birds in the morning,/Peer down at its mysteries', it would not be in order to escape the bush, but rather in order to share her experience of it,

> Thrilling the world with its praise,
> And telling . . .
> How fair gleam at eve the white branches,

Smooth as round limbs of a maid:
Cloud-rolled are their garments of foliage,
  In sun-gilded plumes they're arrayed;
Great gum-boles, like pillars of silver,
  Shine out from deep aisles of shade
And softly the rosy sky kisses
  Tall crests that have heavenward strayed.[11]

Clerk's poem ends conventionally with the resolution of her conflict. Resigning herself to her isolation, she entreats the trees to teach her obedience:

Oh! giants which bound me
Bid my restless longings to cease!
Centuries of steady obedience,
  Of silent, upward increase,
With but one aim – to grow nearer heaven,
  Prove you wiser than man, oh! ye trees![12]

But, although the prayer-like attitude of these lines may be commonplace enough – and might lead one to mistake the whole poem for a pastiche hymn – Clerk's imagery is anything but derivative. The metaphor that expresses Clerk's resignation to her situation is phenomenologically precise. For she settles herself where she is by stabilizing her horizontal impulse to flight through the contemplation of the trees' vertical estate. And, we may note, the same contemplation of the trees, shining 'like pillars of silver', also quells her own longing to fly like a bird and *see* the whole world. In short, the subject of Clerk's poem is home, its symbolic emergence through the metaphor of trees. The trees, which are a physical barrier, become, in her poem, an imaginative window, a site of reverie – which is one definition of home.

As lighthouses, then, trees exhibited a double aspect: they were markers along the way; they were also tall and wall-like. They suggested the brightness of the road and the lofty port of arrival. The association of roads (and trees) with light is clear in the phrase 'blazing a trail'. To mark the route, trees were 'blazed', their bark cut away. The white blaze marks were like lanterns along a street. Implicit in roads was the experience that King described at sea when he wrote of the dangers of 'the glare of the sun, shining in the direction of our course'.[13] 'Dark with excessive light', as King put it, there was a danger of not taking the right route – a danger roads also made possible. At the same time, though, roads made the horizontal, sea-like interior (whether of forest or desert) bearable. Roads were metaphors of the horizon, bringing it close, rendering it tangible.

But, while many eucalypt species offered powerful emblems of light in both its horizontal and vertical aspects, they were less conspicuous for their powers of casting shadows. In an obvious enough sense, trees *were* a source of shelter. But it is significant that Hamilton, in his picturesque memoir, *Experiences of a Colonist Forty Years Ago*, thought it necessary to affirm this. 'Speaking of shade,' Hamilton wrote,

> an erroneous statement has gone forth that the Eucalyptus affords no shade; that in consequence of its leaves being pendent they do not offer shelter from the sun; this is one of the many wicked scandals against the noble tree – it does not give so deep a shadow as the oak or elm, but it is not shelterless.[14]

In reacting to an opinion expressed by writers as various as Barron Field, Peter Cunningham and Darwin, Hamilton may seem to us to be only stating the obvious. But the terms in which Hamilton expresses his denial also suggest why it was necessary. To be sure, no one could deny that the fragile foliage of the eucalyptus cast shade of a sort. Yet it was not the decisive shadow that, in European eyes, emblemized the prospect of almost house-like shelter. There was no sense of a natural roof beneath a gum tree. The pool of shadow cast by the low, densely foliaged branches of the oak or elm was an invitation to sit down. It invited reflection on the world outside. One sat, as it were, at the mouth of a cave. But such room-like properties were wholly absent in the lofty, cloud-like neighbourhood of the gum. While it offered the vision of light-filled courts and temples, it gave no inkling of shady interiors, no sense of looking out. And, in this connection, we may also note that the kind of ascent into invisibility, which the low, horizontally limbed European trees vouchsafed, was also denied to the denizen of gum groves.

To transform the forest into an inhabitable interior, light had to be made dark and the dark light. The tall had to be laid low, revealing widening horizons; and the horizons had, once again, to be bandaged up between vertical door-jambs. Roads had to lead to smoking chimneys and disappear. And the medium of this was what one writer in *The Land of the Lyrebird* calls 'the intelligent axeman', the selector who, unlike the squatter, aimed to reside, not to travel on. His object was not to exclude nature – a gratuitous act – but to incorporate it, to make it a living place. The axeman's weapon partook of his ambition. In her poem 'The Song of the Axe', Marie Pitt celebrates the blade that 'leaped with a flash and a quivering crash'.[15] The axe, swinging left and right or up and down, its lightning glint followed by a growing thunder, emblemized the transformational character of home-building. If, in Mary Fullerton's words, the pioneer struggled to 'subdue the scrub', he also had 'to woo the virgin soil of his selection'.[16] He felled in order to raise up again.

But this was as much an architectural as an agricultural function. To build a house out of the split remains of a forest giant was not so much to destroy the tree as to climb inside it and raise oneself up. Home did not exclude the forest: rather, it invested the inhabitant with a tree-like permanence and resistance to change. In her book *Bark House Days*, Fullerton describes the riverflats her father was attempting to clear:

> So thickly they grew, and so befoliaged were the tall trees, so dense was the scrub between them, with the sun-swallowing ranges close behind them, that truly the place was always dank and dewy.[17]

And something of that coolness, that shade, also characterized her own birthplace:

> The house of my memory was all of stringybark, on a framework of bush timber. If not beautiful to the eye . . . it was cosy in winter, and cool in summer. The heavy, thick sheets of bark kept the fierce sun at bay, as we realized later when the era of the iron roof set in.[18]

But the coolness of the tall trees has been made useful by laying them low: it is pinioned over a vertical framework, in the horizontal dimension of the roof, that they preserve their weighty darkness, their coolness. It is as tables, chairs, window-sills and lintels that they become conformable to human needs. Similarly, they supply slab floors: their single-minded tallness, implying lofty views, now becomes a means of physical passage. Fallen trees are literally bridges:

> At the crossing there is the usual friendly log with axe-notches in it to prevent one slipping into the water.[19]

Even in their vertical aspect, the trees are now proportioned to their inhabitants. Clerk, describing her Gippsland home, says

> Keeping well to the centre, 'twas easy to enter,
> Unmolested by ridge-pole or rafter . . .[20]

Fallen trees provided refuges in other ways. Fullerton recalls her young cousin Dick 'once hid himself in an old hollow fallen trunk by the first barley paddock, and was lost for several hours'.[21] The fantasy of living inside trees was sometimes realized literally. There is, for example, the case of the Budgeree pioneer caught in a huge bushfire who,

> At the height of the fire . . . with the two boys and a pet dog took refuge in a huge hollow log clear of the scrub, placing wet blankets over the entrance hole.[22]

They could be permanent homes, too. Around 1892, the pioneer J. D. Wells built himself a dwelling in South Gippsland inside the stump of a giant gum (see plate 20). With its tall, hexagonal wizard-hat slab roof, and its curiously blind, slatted door, set between the tree's enormous buttresses, it gives the eerie impression that its inhabitant has been transformed rather than the tree. One is reminded of Marie Pitt's description of a house whose inhabitants have left: 'Draw down the blinds, like lids o'er weary eyes . . .'[23] Another Gippsland tree was about the same time being used as a church. A photograph, inscribed a 'huge tree stump near Foster . . . used for church services', shows twenty or thirty worshippers congregated between the spread wings of the giant.[24]

To hew down trees was not merely to put out their light and make them harbours of shade: it could also be to display the light locked inside them. As one pioneer writer put it,

Remote, hidden recesses of the hill land gullies yielded their wealth to him and the rough logs were brought out of the hills to be sawn and dressed, so that the inner beauty of their wood was revealed.[25]

In this sense, the sawyer was a sculptor. He realized the wood's character and history, made it his own. And its liveliness also informed his dwellings. In a poem addressed to 'The Rusted Wedge' ('a wedge is a piece of metal sloping to a thin edge used for splitting logs'), a Mrs Ruth Young of Yarragon conjures up its original pioneer owner, his wife and

> their little home of split palings,
> The bark roof cool and sappy . . .[26]

The skin of this house still breathes. It is airy, light and temperate.

It was not the trees themselves that excited the settler's interest, but the spatial fantasies they harboured, their possibilities of darkness and light, height and depth. In Straw's family memoir, *The Hazeldeane Selection*, an account of the Poowong settler Caleb Burchett and his wife, Amy, the writer describes how, after clearing the original forest, the settlers established a vegetable plot and orchard:

At the entrance to the home enclosure . . . two pines stood on guard.[27]

These trees were no more of value in *themselves* than the trees they replaced. As Straw writes, their value was symbolic:

They had been planted by Caleb when he first cleared the block, and although singed by the bush fire had now grown to giant proportions and were a landmark in the locality. These grand old trees were identified with the pioneers, having witnessed throughout the years events incidental to the family life within. It was ordained that they should also be partakers in the tragedy and sorrow which inevitably descends on all human activity.[28]

The pine trees marked a place of habitation. They stood at the focus of the road. They also stood for the inmates' verticality. They were like flames, green, aspiring, vital. They stood for stability, endurance. They externalized a growing depth of attachment – and perhaps their dark, bosky plumage assisted in suggesting their rootedness and antiquity. But, as trees, they were only ciphers. For the pioneer who found the pines ennobled and assured his existence was the same who recalled the *original* forest trees in these terms:

> On the house site chosen by me there were 40 of them in that acre and it took the cutting down of over 60 to make the home secure.[29]

Like fire, it seems, the trees make good servants but bad masters.

In this context, we can make better sense of the at first sight curious fetish of the tree stump. In early photographs of bush dwellings, a tree stump almost invariably appears at the left- or right-hand corner of the house front: two tree stumps are visible, for instance, in the garden of the Bass River farm (plate 14). Sometimes headless wooden columns figure prominently by the front gate. Their function is made poignantly clear in *Bark House Days* where, while father felled the tree that leaned ominously towards their house, mother and children retired to the tree stump:

> There we were, Jack and mother and I, away to the stump by the front gate for safety.[30]

The tree stump stands for the family. It is a wall and a viewpoint; it gathers light and shade. It is an image of solidity. It supports a column of air. The light in the sky above it is a phantom foliage. Incorporated within the garden enclosure, obstinate to one side of the entrance, it has the amiability of a priest interrupting conversations with the recollection of another world. It grazes paddocks like the farmer's cattle or sheep. In time, the axeman sights his land by way of such mighty stepping-stones.

If 'with his implements of destruction' he 'lays the beautiful plantation low to be consumed in the devouring flames', still, as Fenton puts it,

> The ornamental products of the vegetable kingdom are replaced by the useful; happy homesteads and verdant meadows rise from the wreck of the 'burning off', and the desert places bloom as the rose.[31]

The stump, wreathed with flowers, a resting place, a talking point, house-like in its form and spirit, not only bears witness to this resurrection but guards over it. So, in her remarkable poem 'My First Garden Flower', Nellie Clerk finds the stump is the ideal planting place for her geranium:

> Ah! that headless trunk will hold
> You safely, sweet Geranium,
> On his broad breast some pliant mould
> Shall, 'mid the cairn, your roots enfold,
> No more I'll mourn his grandeur bold,
> His scars hid by your beauty.[32]

The geranium is a candle lit and tended at the tomb of a lost one. It keeps alive the vertical instinct.

The intimate charm of trees is perceived not only with the eyes. It has its counterpart in the world of sound. Tree noises were equally sources of imaginative reverie, making apparent to the settler the essence of what was meant by home. Take this passage, again from Fullerton's *Bark House Days*:

> We have sometimes deliberately on gloomy evenings worked ourselves into eerie moods, to hearing strange cries of tortured ghosts from those mystic flats; sounds that made us run homeward, stumbling and tumbling in our haste. It was this flapping of the loosened bark that in other moods became the bridle-reins of the wind driving the trees. There was nothing our fancy was not equal to in those days, ere the 'prison house' shut us in.[33]

This passage should not be put down to some naive fear of the bush. On the contrary, as Fullerton makes clear, it is the communicable qualities of the bush that enable her and her brothers to work themselves into eerie moods. It is the familiarity of its strangeness that makes the mystic flats a site of fancy. And the fancy located there is the nightmare of homelessness. But, if the flapping of the loosened bark conjures up darkness and inarticulateness, it does so most eloquently. And, in this sense, it is an antidote to the prison-house of daytime and adult rationality.

The eerie sounds of the forest, then, *communicate* the loneliness of the place: they speak to the newcomer of *their* own desolation or destruction. In this sense they ally themselves to his fate. They take on human feelings, resentments and concerns. Even their hostility is strangely comforting, for it makes the bush a theatre, with the animation of human drama. Take this familiar enough story:

> Another memory is of an old prospector being lost out from Combienbar. The men of the district congregated at our place and went out to search; but, although his pipe and clothing was found, he was never found. One of the searchers described the eerie sound of the long strips of bark scraping against the tree trunks as they searched.[34]

In this passage the subvocal scraping of the bark communicates the opposition between home and non-home. For, if the men 'congregate', then the remains of the lost prospector disperse. If the trees maintain a mocking chatter or hoarse rasping, then the man coming home speaks out loud and clear. In a comparable way, Mary Fullerton concludes her account of the eerie bush by recalling that,

> There was, though, a very practical use to which the dry and curling bark, at last come to the ground, was sometimes put. My mother liked it better than anything else when she wanted a quick fire for baking small cakes. Many a large bundle of the light stuff used we to bring her for that purpose; our sweet and crisp reward not far away.[35]

Sounds find themselves transformed into tastes and scents. One is tempted to meditate on the profound connections between wood smoke and pipe smoke.

These eerie sounds of the forest are the sounds of a deserted house. They recall the 'house that was "home" but yesterday' in Marie Pitt's poem, where

> The naked floors ring hollow to my tread
> Like cries of inarticulate regret.[36]

By the same token, though, if absence of community is suggested by sounds that are hollow, dull, and full of 'mute reproach', then the sounds that characterize presence, animation, life have all the qualities of the flame: they are bright, they shine, they laugh, quiver and resound. They are 'silver' sounds. Silver, both aurally and visually, is a fundamental quality of home – a fact that emerges, for instance, from descriptions of the bell-bird's song. George Hamilton refers to its notes as 'silver-toned', while Jennings Carmichael, in a poem that contains the line, 'Look! there is the homestead – here the gate . . .', writes,

> Here is where the bell-birds tinkled
> Fairy chimes for me all day.[37]

Walker amplified the associations of the bell-bird's song when he noted that it was 'indicative of a warm sheltered country, with water in it'.[38] And if Breton found its note like 'the single tinkle of a sheep bell' and 'melancholy as well as monotonous', it was not least because here as elsewhere he was bent on attacking the 'common opinion', that held that 'the bell-bird denotes the proximity of water'.[39]

Chiming sounds, sounds that ring out, are the bright sounds that symbolize society. A correspondent of the *Morwell Advertiser* in Gippsland recalls how, in the early days of the town,

> As the train drew up at the Morwell Station, the first sound usually heard was the ring of the hammer on the anvil and the cheery voice of the blacksmith.[40]

I doubt if this was literally true. But the ringing hammer was the first *human* sound. It was a signal for the cheery voice of the blacksmith. Sound ringing out also brings us back to the axe. A traveller north of Melbourne, wanting to evoke a picture of settlement literally in full swing, could think of no better way than to describe the sounds:

> The air, melodious with the song of the whistling crow, or Australian magpie, was laden with the aroma of wild flowers, and one heard at intervals the distant sound of the fall of the axe, the laughter of the sawyers' children, and the barking of dogs, blended with the rush and swirl of the fresh breeze in the tree-tops as the branches creaked and groaned overhead.[41]

The fall of the axe in this context is a sound full of animation. Like the sound of the hammer, it is a 'ringing' sound, a sound redolent of habitation, a sound musically amplified by the magpie's song. The wind itself seems like a glittering waterfall of bright glinting sounds. The trees themselves assume the burden of human activity, creaking and groaning with lively effort.

Central to this scene of human activity is the axe. As Mary Fullerton writes,

> There is to this day no more delightful sound to my ears . . . than the ringing sound of axe and maul and wedge . . .[42]

It is a sound that, as emerges in Marie Pitt's poem 'The Song of the Axe', is also light. The axe in her poem not only produced, in 'The echoes of axe-strokes ringing', 'a music more meet for singing'; it also 'leaped with a flash and a quivering crash'. In these terms, Pitt addresses the axe as

> O music and mirth of the cities of earth
> O levin of light and laughter![43]

By the penultimate verse of her poem, the axe has become a talisman, not only of the bushman's life, but of a just society as a whole. It has been transformed into

> a steadfast star,
> Set high o'er the ways of error.[44]

By an extraordinarily rich transformation of sensuous experience, based on the profound phenomenological reverberations of certain sounds and qualities of light, Pitt evokes a progress of settlement characteristic not just of a minority of settlers in

Gippsland but of mankind as a whole. So that, addressing 'the cities of the earth', she finally asserts:

> From the forests ye sprang where the axes sang
> Their lyrics of ridge and rafter.[45]

The link between the lonely hermit's hut and the sprawling suburbs of industrial towns is the desire to inhabit, to cultivate those intimate spatial qualities bound up with the sense of home.

Marie Pitt's vision of cities springing up in the wake of the pioneer recalls *The Pioneer*, the triptych by a painter of the Heidelberg school, Frederick McCubbin (see plate 21), a painting whose three panels, to borrow the words of a contemporary reviewer, 'give pictorial insight to three episodes in the life history of those strong spirits who opened up this Continent'.[46] Of course the mood and even the historical vision informing McCubbin's painting are not Marie Pitt's, a consequence in part, no doubt, of his very different personal background. McCubbin, born, bred and trained in Melbourne, might enjoy camping in the bush. But he visited it from suburbia: and the pioneering images he brought home adorned suburban walls. For one who, like Marie Pitt, had actually been brought up in the bush, it was the city, not the wild, that beckoned. Camping out was romantic self-indulgence. As she wrote, 'A tent 'neath the gum tree? No! Not I!/I'll march with the rabble, clean and unclean.'[47]

Even so, despite these biographical and philosophical differences, poem and painting evoke the idea of settling in strikingly similar terms. It is not simply that the axe is central, symbolically and literally, to both McCubbin's composition and Pitt's poem. More profoundly, McCubbin's painting realizes the light of the axe. Stars leading ever onward may be poetic images but they do not translate easily into paint. Another light source has to be found. This, I would suggest, is the meaning of the plumes of smoke rising in the left-hand and central panels. Associated iconographically with the act of homemaking, smoke is also, pictorially speaking, bright. It illuminates the ghost of the absent tree – a theme taken up in the central panel where the bright pinpoint of the selector's cottage stands in a vertical shaft of light. It is associated with reflection, with thoughts of elsewhere, with lighting a pipe. In the right-hand panel, a generation later, the memory of these things is no longer smoky: it has become a permanent patch of sky fixed brightly above the city. (In urging this interpretation, it may be relevant that between first exhibiting *The Pioneer* at a one-man show in Melbourne in 1904 and exhibiting it again the following year more publicly with the Victorian Artists' Society, McCubbin retouched the city in the manner of that artist who, better than any, understood light as history: J. M. W. Turner.)[48]

More recently, the pioneer myth has been enshrined in the historian Russel Ward's thesis, that the Australian character owes most to the 'frontier spirit' of the nomadic bushman. But, at least in the Gippsland context, this has been decisively refuted by the critic and local historian Patrick Morgan. The 'pioneers' of Gippsland from the 1870s onwards were, he points out,

> in general . . . a respectable lot, many being Melbourne people with a business background, and often of the artisan –craftsman type.[49]

They were literate; they were often family men – or hoped to be: they were conscious of putting down roots. They were self-consciously pioneers. Unlike the itinerant bush worker, that 'nomad tribe' who, according to Russel Ward, 'moved in a peculiarly male world',[50] the Gippsland selector lived with his wife – and it was the women who were, in the main, the bush historians. In this sense, despite the physical appearance of the place, the selector in Gippsland – and elsewhere in Victoria – was reproducing conditions he was familiar with in the city.

Rather than thinking of a nation growing tree-like from humble roots in the bush, one has to recognize that there was a constant, two-way intercourse between bush and city. As Morgan points out, many selectors found the land they had taken up too hard to work profitably. It has often been forgotten that they drifted back to the city. And, arguing against the Ward thesis, Morgan thinks it likely that the middle-class values the failed selectors brought with them, their ambition to be respectable, to achieve security and a stake in property, have been at least as important in the formation of contemporary Australia. Unless we posit the influence of the smallholder ethos, how can we explain 'the seemingly unbridgeable gap between outback behaviour and the quiescence of suburbia'? The smallholder's impact on urban development is apparent, Morgan points out, 'even in a physical sense':

> The detached, self-owned house on its quarter-acre block, surrounded by its high paling fence, is an urban memory of the country farm. The emphasis on being independent and self-contained is common to both. [51]

Whatever the sources of the Australian character, a study of its perceptions of intimate space reveals the profound metaphorical relationship between bush and city environments. For, however different its physical aspect, the spatial imagery of that distinctively Australian urban form, suburbia, exactly resembles the signs of dwelling in the bush. Cities did not leave the bush behind any more than artists forgot where they came from when they 'went bush'. The two were symbolically equivalent. This emerges most obviously in what might be described as the vertical deprivation that characterizes the suburbs. The French philosopher Gaston Bachelard has forcibly made the point that a characteristic of modern cities is their lack of verticality – he argues that the height of modern buildings is purely exterior, not being matched by a comparable sense of interior tallness. At times, Bachelard says, he can comfort himself with the image of the city as 'a clamorous sea'; at other times, it imprisons him. He cites Courbet's desire in prison to paint a view of Paris, 'all its houses and domes imitating the tumultuous waves of the sea'. [52]

This sense of chaotic horizontality is perhaps the primary spatial experience of the suburbs. In their intimate interiors the high ceilings of suburban dwellings may preserve a private verticality, but the public space is flat, uranian. It resembles the sea-like interior described by Sturt. To a newcomer seeking to differentiate it, suburban space can elicit exactly the same baffled response expressed by a Gippsland pioneer who, on first seeing her 'home',

> could not speak, and my eyes filled with tears. That one spot of iron, in the midst of a sea of logs and stumps, looked so desolate . . . [53]

But the single-storeyed horizontality of suburbia, its minimaliza-
tion of public spaces, its repetition of sentinel trees, its paradisal
gardens, its verandas and plaster fairies: these are equally the
qualities of the bush dwelling. Before long, we learn from Straw,
the Poowong pioneer Burchett had cleared his land:

> English trees and shrubs planted seven or eight years ago
> formed a background for a wild country garden which had a
> charm of its own. [54]

It was not only in the city that the house-owner liked to
reproduce the wildness of nature.

The sense in which the proliferating suburbs of late nineteenth-century Melbourne and Sydney seem like the ruins of a
pastoral arcadia – a dream of self-sufficient independence which
has turned into a prison-house – cannot be traced back simply to
the local fact of a drift back from the land. It is bound up with
the much wider phenomenon of migration itself. The fact is that
selectors might differ from squatters and bushworkers in terms
of wealth and social ambition. They might seek respectability
and security. But, like it or not, they, too, led at least partially
nomadic lives. As Ward points out,

> A great many selectors were, at the same time, itinerant
> bushmen who went shearing, horsebreaking, and so on for
> months at a time to help make ends meet on the farm, and
> when the farm failed many of these remained permanently as
> casual hands in the pastoral industry. [55]

The dwellings of the bush were, in this sense, migrant
dwellings. As Mary Fullerton remarks of her childhood Bark
House,

> The old house is no longer there. The structures of pioneer
> days are not for permanency. [56]

But bush dwellings were migrant dwellings in a profounder
sense – in that their builders belonged to a society that was itself
migrant: and it is this that explains the remarkable continuity of
form between private dwellings in city and country. The key to
what might be called the architecture of migration is the
phenomenon of privatization. The people who flocked to the

suburbs, whether they came from other suburbs, alighted from ships or drifted back from the bush, came from outside. They colonized privately, not communally. In theory at least, they occupied land without ever speaking to a neighbour. Roads were channels of private communication. Each property was an end in itself. As we saw in relation to Hoddle's grid plan of Melbourne, an important incentive to settle was the literal placelessness of the place, the fact that, spatially, the burgeoning suburbs had much in common with the wilderness.

How, then, did the palaces of suburbia resemble bush dwellings? They resembled each other in their intimacy and closure, in their burning of symbolic trees and their erection of others. Think of the candle flame, casting its bowl of light on the velvet tablecloth. It is an image of balance, of active calm or reflection. It is vigilant, it leans attentive to every sound. It listens, tall and erect. But it also watches over: its light suggests rest and dreams. Over recumbent bodies it makes the shadows leap tall. Think of the light at the window, which also suggests the hearth, and the glow of firelight reflected along gun barrels, copper pans and rows of crockery. Shining out from the darkness of the wall, the pale square of the window signals, too, the house's intimate connection with darkness and night. Cool and shadowy in the heat of the day, the house comes alive at night, making shadows dance, like puppets in a theatre. At night, it opens its eye. This is how suburban dwellings celebrated their origins in what Bachelard has referred to as 'the spaces of our intimacy'. And, in this context, we can only speculate about the deprivation caused by the electric light bulb. Could it be there is a connection between the installation of light and the investment in Heidelberg landscapes, where the hues of sunset were preserved?

Writing about London and Paris, the American historian Richard Sennett has put this intimate history on a sound sociological footing. In the nineteenth century, the impact of migration on urban life – for the new urban population was not merely larger but also shifting – was, he argues, of decisive importance in determining the contraction of public spaces and the expansion of privacy. The accelerated rate of economic and technological change such a growing pool of labour precipitated led, in Sennett's view, to the rapid decline of the public space as a zone of significant social intercourse. With it disappeared the figure of the 'public man', the Enlightenment man at home in a society outside the family. There emerged, instead, what Sennett calls the 'tyranny of intimacy', which he defines as 'the aspiration to develop one's personality through experiences of closeness with others'.[57] And the spatial corollary of this psychic retreat from the civil domain was the cult of suburbia with its anti-urban, pseudo-sense of community.

In nineteenth-century Australia this process of privatization was even more marked – as was the phenomenon of migration. Newcomers to grid-plan suburbs, like selectors on their blocks of land, had long retreated from (if indeed they had ever known) the impersonality of the public domain. They may have written much but, with notable exceptions, in public they were habitually taciturn, even tongue-tied. In these circumstances, the cultivation of intimate space assumed an extraordinary importance. Each house became its own theatre, a world in miniature, complete with its own sky and earth, its own hearth, its own breathing walls and its complement of birds whistling on the chimney-top. Here the world could be dreamed of.

One consequence of recognizing how, in terms of focusing interest on the spaces of our intimacy, suburbia and the bush expressed a common historical shift towards privatization – a process itself expressing a strategic function of travelling – is that it casts doubt on the often repeated assertion that the nationalist myth of the bush represented a kind of anti-urban nostalgia. The argument is summarized by Richard White, when he writes of the 'new intelligentsia' – by whom he means primarily the artists of the Heidelberg school and the writers of the *Bulletin* – that they

carried into their image of the bush their own urban bohemian values – their radicalism, their male comradeship, their belief in their own freedom from conventional restraints – and presented it as the 'real' Australia. They also projected on to their image of the bush their alienation from their urban environment.[58]

From this point of view, a critic like Ian Burn can argue very convincingly that, in the paintings of the Heidelberg school, the people are

> city folk and the incidents narrated are part of the social relationship to the bush of an urban class. The perception of the bush which the artists have portrayed conforms to their social relationship.[59]

But are these paintings or the literature of the *Bulletin* writers about the bush at all? They represent rural life and do so in a romanticized way betraying an urban viewpoint and an urban audience. But the world they conjure up is not a world of alienation: as they hang on their suburban walls, their brightness glowing in the gloom, do they not rather suggest the fantasy life of suburbia itself? They may make metaphorical use of certain rural activities and myths, but the images refer rather to certain qualities of light and dark, window view and green, pink and orange prospect, expressive of life in the suburbs. Is it in the bush that one thinks of elsewhere, as McCubbin suggests in *The Pioneer*, or in suburbia? The conspicuous 'warmth' of, say, Tom Roberts's paintings may have nothing to do with the climate of the interior and everything to do with the warmth that Sennett describes as an essential ingredient of the tyranny of intimacy.

Sennett may ascribe the cultivation of this feeling to social and psychological causes. But warmth is also a sensation, which, in the context of home-making, has the profoundest phenomeno- logical reverberations. It may well be that we should ascribe to these pale, almost blank landscapes the quality of the candle flame. To contemplate this art was not to indulge in a train of association, taking one back to when one last went sketching, photographing, botanizing or fishing. It was to feel more than ever at home. It was to realize the imaginary dimension of dwelling, the sense in which the house and its garden were a device for imaginative travelling, for making the walls speak. Such paintings were signs of habitation – and, much as the imagery of the bush may have *represented* certain urban preoccupations, this may not have been what such paintings *symbolized*. Their symbolism may have had little to do with the choice of subject, much more to do with their particular worship of earth and sky, their assertion of a private traveller's window on Arcady in suburbia. Like windows and doorways, they were the horizontal made vertical.

In one obvious sense, at least, suburban living certainly resembled bush living, and this was in its pursuit of linear repitition. Just as huts were strung out along pack-tracks, so, albeit with greater geometrical regularity, quarter-acre blocks were threaded along suburban orthogonals. It was a spatial procedure that recalls Lhotsky's description of the Australian creek, which I discussed in chapter 2. The creek, according to Lhotsky, resembled an organism too primitive to have developed a 'vascular system'. And I suggested there a parallel between its physical form and its resistance to naming and description: it was a geographical form that defied the organizing principles of syntax and grammar. Similarly, the prevalence of the horizontal and a rectilinear refusal of convergence in public spaces were the signs of a form of settlement that lacked an articulate public discourse.

Recognition of a distinguishing quality of Australian settlement – its horizontality – not only serves to identify the common strand connecting settlement in the cities and in the forests. It also identifies the sense in which, despite their apparent differences, another pair of environmental opposites – the forest and the desert – were also spatially similar. The idea that the bush can be divided into two zones, a fertile coastal crescent (inhabited by the selector) and the outback of the great inland plains (mythologized as the realm of the bush nomad) makes good sense as historical geography. But, at a more intimate level, the distinction melts away and we find that, in the context of home-making, the 'closed' world of the forest and the 'open' environment of the plains presented similar challenges, challenges defined by the newcomer's irremediable lack of commanding height.

The sense of claustrophobia that could overcome a newcomer to the forest is well evoked by R. S. Medew, in his fictionalized account of pioneering days at Jeeralang in South Gippsland:

The steep declivities, falling away to apparently bottomless depths terrified Robert. The thick mountain mists seemed to suffocate him. He began to cry, 'I can hardly breathe, I want to go back.'[60]

But it was not only in the forest that the would-be settler felt, like Nellie Clerk, 'imprisoned'. It was equally a sensation felt in the grasslands, too. Randell, in his book *The Pastoral Pattersons*, relates 'an old story, apparently unconfirmed', to the effect that,

> one very good year at Binya the grass grew so tall John Patterson could tie it over the bow of his saddle. This is said to have frightened him as such grass was little use to sheep and he is then supposed to have made up his mind to sell the station.[61]

Again, the scrub of the Mallee, in places so low 'that a man on horseback could look over it for miles',[62] could be quite as enclosing as the Mountain Ash of Gippsland. Consider the remarkable experience of a Mallee pioneer, a Hopevale woman, reported by T. G. Allen in her book *Shears in Hand*:

> Three year old Les must have been quite a problem for his mother as the area around the Hopevale house was thickly clad in scrub and the child was a wanderer. Mother overcame this by clothing him in a red dress and tying a bell to dangle from the back of the collar. Thus Les could be both seen and heard from a distance. Often he was allowed to venture forth to where a man was stump-picking half a mile away. When the child arrived the man would lift him up so that mother, atop a shed roof, could see the red frock had reached there safely.[63]

In the context of our analysis of the spaces of the settler's intimacy, this passage reveals itself as a rich site of spatial history reflection. The colour red – like white, the colour of flame – is a colour associated with the illumination of place. Similarly, the bell is a pre-eminently cheery sound, bright with nearness. At the same time, though, the recollection of the Hopevale woman is saturated with a deep pathos, which I think derives from the image of the mother 'atop a shed roof'. For this is the pathos of vertical deprivation. How different this episode would appear, if the mother awaited the arrival of her offspring from an upstairs window. Then, if the child was like a ship at sea, the house would have been a resounding lighthouse. There would have been pleasure in the view; fear would have been replaced by nostalgia.

It may be noted in passing that placelessness in the Mallee provoked much the same kind of reaction it elicited in the rain forest. It was not only Mary Fullerton who found the bush eerie. An early traveller in the Mallee recalled,

> There is a dry sort of rustle, like the inarticulate murmur of many parched tongues, from the leaves, and the innumerable strips and shreds of dead bark beat against the stems like the wasting garments against the bones of a gibbet.[64]

This kind of description offers, it seems to me, an auditory image not remote from the visual image that McCubbin creates in paintings like *Down On His Luck*, *The Lost Child* and even *The Pioneer*, where the very indifference of the trees seems to collude in the newcomer's loneliness. Friendly or not, the Mallee is certainly articulate. It seems to anticipate the traveller's end – much as the sympathetic foliage and the viewpoint of McCubbin's paintings seem to frame and lament in advance its solitary figure's fate. Just as light signalled home, so to perceive the dullness of the bush was to experience the feeling of being lost. And, being lost, sandhills could appear quite as dark as rain forest. The explorer Stuart, finding himself among apparently interminable sandhills near Mount Finke, writes, 'I could see a long distance but nothing met the eye save *a dense scrub as black and dismal as midnight.*'[65]

Hand in hand with vertical deprivation in these migratory environments went its dialectical counterpart: vertical longing. As the explorers' hilltop soliloquies and the picturesque sites chosen by settlers for their cottages both indicate, an enhanced height usually meant a greatly extended visibility. Height above and beyond the human was a means of commanding the space, of giving it focus and edge. In this regard, both in the desert and in the forest, where cleared elevations were lacking, the presence of climbable trees was essential in this respect. In the absence of two-storey buildings or the privileged viewpoint of attic windows, trees were rooftops in advance. R. S. Medew describes Henry and David at work tree-felling:

they worked twenty or more feet from the ground, balancing themselves on the springboards . . . In this laborious work they often paused for rest, looking about them or engaging in conversation. The mountains of the Great Divide loomed blue in the distance. The plains of the valley lay straw coloured in their grazing lands. Near at hand, the green wall of the virgin forest rose from the gorge of the creek and timbered the eastern range about Jung Knob.[66]

It is significant that this extended grasp of the world is the occasion of an ecstatic meditation on the biblical story of Abraham: 'Lift up now thine eyes, and look from the place where thou art . . .' For the significance of being raised up did not lie merely in the extended physical grasp of the world. It consisted also in the prevision of community that it suggested.

This profound connection between enhanced verticality and a sense of community is illustrated very clearly in the journal of the marine surveyor Stokes. In an earlier chapter, I quoted his peroration on the charms of novelty as he stepped out across the Plains of Promise near the Albert River on the Gulf of Carpentaria. Stokes had earlier noted how

A vast boundless plain lay before us, here and there dotted over with woodland isles. Whilst taking the bearings of one of these to guide us in the direction we were to steer, I sent a man up a tree to have a further view; but nothing beyond an extension of the plain was to be seen . . . We were now once more stepping out over a terra incognita; and though no alpine features greeted our eyes as they wandered eagerly over the vast level, all was clothed with the charm of novelty.[67]

In a physical sense sending a man up a tree had no great significance: in the open plain, Stokes and his men could get on with or without a horizon object. But the spatial impulse represented by the tree-climbing was not insignificant. It was a bid for exactly the same verticality enjoyed by the pious timber-fellers in Gippsland. For the consequence of that increased height was not simply to enhance the viewer's grasp of this world: in looking down, he felt a magnified sense of the cultural significance of his journey. He enjoyed a degree of other-worldliness, the freedom of flight. He could dream of the sky. But he could also envisage a marriage of sky and earth, in short, the prospect of a Christian community:

> [I] could not refrain from breathing a prayer that ere long the now level horizon would be broken by a succession of tapering spires rising from the many christian hamlets that must ultimately stud this country, and pointing through the calm depths of the intensely blue and gloriously bright skies of Tropical Australia to a still calmer and brighter and more glorious region beyond.[68]

In a similar sense, Nellie Clerk had embraced the upward growth of the forest trees as an emblem of her own eventual elevation and transfiguration. In a similar vein, we may add, fifty years later the painter Arthur Streeton was recording 'the great hidden poetry that I know is here but have not seen or felt . . .' and depicting it predominantly in the key of blue.[69]

The longing for enhanced height had, then, a double aspect. It reflected the awareness of place as a correspondence between view and viewpoint. But it reflected something more: the fact that a sense of place depended not only on its visual and conceptual distinctness, but also on its suggestiveness as a site of reverie, as a zone where one was borne aloft to dream. It is perhaps this sensation of place as a bridgehead between earth and sky that is preserved in our colloquial usage of the adverbs 'up' and 'down'. In saying we walk 'up' to a house or go 'up' to town, even though, physically, no ascent is involved, we recognize such places as centres where space congregates, loci of heightened psychic activity, regions of lightness in a double sense.

In the desert and in the forest, it was not only the traveller's height that was diminished, but the tallness of the world; yet this diminution of worldly tallness gave the traveller a delicious illusion of upward power. It was precisely the fact that the giant gum trees bounded her view of the far higher sky that gave Nellie Clerk the feeling the trees might draw her up towards the 'Tall crests that have heavenward strayed'. Similarly, as J. W. Gregory noted in his book *The Dead Heart of Australia*,

> One of the main charms of the desert is the sky. Never does it look so solid, nor feel so close.[70]

In the desert, he writes,

> The sky seems to creep down closer, until it appears almost within touching distance.[71]

Despite their obvious physical differences, the opposite environments of the plain and the forest resembled each other spatially. They revealed to the traveller the fundamental dimensions of his desire to inhabit. For, manifesting extreme horizontal and vertical fantasies, and extremes of light and dark, they suggested the tenuousness of his balance and stability in the world. In this sense, they were alike 'wilderness', the antithesis of home, revealing to the traveller what he meant by 'home'. He was, in both environments, at risk of drowning or drifting. He was at sea, like Sturt, without anything to steer for. Indeed marine imagery often characterizes wilderness descriptions. Seeing Aborigines shinning up trees after koala bears, the Gippsland traveller G. H. Haydon remarks, they 'ascend nearly as easily as a sailor would up a rigging.'[72] Nellie Clerk writes of the wind-swept, ring-barked gums, which rose 'Thick as masts on the Thames',

> Like ships on rough seas, they rocked in the breeze . . .[73]

In the plains, of course, the only trees *were* masts. Off the north-west Australian coast, Stokes reports,

> From the maintop gallant yard I was enabled to take an almost bird's eye view of the level country stretched apparently at my feet . . .[74]

But, in either environment, the grasp on space attained in this way was temporary and even sickening. As Nehemiah Bartley wrote of the Mallee,

> Woe to the traveller who gets lost in this terrible desolation; he can see no distance; he can climb no hill; and if the Mallee sticks would bear him on the top, he would only see Mallee, Mallee, Mallee all around him.[75]

What was spatially implicit in the forest was made spatially explicit in open country; and vice versa. Thus, as Bartley's remark makes clear, to see in the Mallee was to see nothing.

And this feeling of being nowhere, perhaps surprising when one could in theory see to the horizon, was, of course, precisely what the forest made quite explicit. As Christy Palmerston said of the Atherton Tableland rain forest: it was 'a jungle in which one's eyes could not pierce much further than one's own length'.[76] In this context, it is not surprising that, while early settlers often referred to the forest as 'gloomy', 'gloomy scrub' was also the phrase Sturt used to describe the vegetation of the Mallee.

Both environments were wildernesses, places where space failed to congregate into picturesque forms, where nature failed to speak. In both environments, to anticipate freedom was also to court self-immolation; to magnify one's reach and breathe deeply was to risk being swallowed up or drowning. In the desert as in the forest, identity, like direction, was dispersed; the subject himself immersed in a greater medium, hidden, invisible. Yet this delicious sensation of being curled up in the pocket of the night could not be separated from terror of the immensity. In this world of streaming winds, to travel was never to walk or ride: it was to fly or to drown. These spatial sensations, entertained alike in the open and closed worlds of the desert and the forest, had their origins not in the personal psychology of the traveller but in the fact that to be conscious was to be conscious of being in the world. The ambiguity of these realms grew out of the settler's existential necessity to inhabit, to come into being through differentiating himself and his surroundings.

This sense of spatial ambiguity brings us back once more to the image of the suburbs. For, it might be argued, the extreme atomization of space that occurs in suburbia, the proliferation of individual dwellings that do not add up to a communal space, can be seen as so many travelling strategies for rendering the wilderness habitable. By way of floor, window, doorway and ceiling, by way of fence and garden, the suburban dwelling successfully incorporates and represents the world in such a way that it speaks. But the mere repetition of individual solutions, the proliferation of intimate space, cannot add up to a communal image of sky and earth, such as, say, the church and the marketplace symbolize. Sennett criticizes the kind of town planning that does not allow for 'multiplicity of function', that segregates different social activities.[77] But, in the suburban environment most Australians inhabit, the public space of streets and pavements, parks and car parks, has not even one clear function. Spaces serving different functions are not noticeably different. In this sense the public space is more accurately described as ambiguous. The visual chaos that characterizes many suburban streets is, spatially speaking, no different from the wilderness. It is a space where travellers cannot settle, like the sea.

In this context, we begin to understand more clearly the peculiar interest the semi-nomadic settlers had in trees. It was not trees in general that attracted them or that they sought to reproduce in their gardens and paintings; it was not the space of the forest or the bush that they wished to inhabit imaginatively at home. Nostalgia for the wide open spaces of the outback had nothing to do with it. It was the tree as icon of place that they worshipped. It was the tree as a figure of their own verticality they clung to. And they clung to it in order to articulate the spaces of their intimacy, in order, that is, to inhabit. To this extent, they succeeded in settling. But the space of the forest and the desert, the 'public' space, as it were, this remained flat, featureless and uninhabited, a reminder of the traveller's vertical deprivation. Its urban counterpart was the suburb. In this regard, the forest of chimneys and television aerials that dominates urban skylines is a faithful reflection of the migrant's silence in the lonely spaces of the bush.

One of the more memorable passages in George Johnston's novel *My Brother Jack* – reputed to be one of the most popular of all twentieth-century Australian novels – relates the narrator's rooftop meditation on the complete absence of trees in his suburb.[78] Davy resolves to plant a sugar gum in his front garden, an act that symbolizes his contempt for the world of *Phlox drummondii* and *Tropaeolum*, a world of utter emotional and social sterility. The gesture works, Davy's marriage breaks up and he escapes. Is this, as is often assumed, a rejection of false urban values in favour of something more authentically natural? Not at all: the sugar gum is itself a thoroughly suburban gesture. Planted in the front garden, it is a statement about and in terms of the intimate spaces of suburbia. It treats the 'bush' as an intimate icon, a mark of identity. It may signify Davy's break with convention, but its most profound transgression consists in the simple fact of its flame-like verticality. It is a plea for what Bachelard calls 'cosmicity', but it is made in the sign language of suburbia. As for any longing to rove the great Australian plains and forests, Davy's later adventures show there was none of that.

10

The Road to Botany Bay

. . . some villains broke into the dispensary at the hospital, and stole two cakes of portable soup . . .

David Collins, *The English Colony in New South Wales*

The place in which a pioneer like Caleb Burchett lived was not *there* in advance of him. His living space was the offspring of his intent to settle. His ability to interpret symbolically the language of longitude and latitude enabled him by 'looking at the survey map' to select a piece of land. But this limited blankness was still a potential place. It was not possessed at once simply by thinking of it. The subject of hearsay, rumour and doubt, it harboured a multitude of possibilities. To begin with, it was dark with horizons. It was uncleared, unnamed: as a place, invisible and silent. Reaching his selection, Burchett had to see it first, to make a picturesque selection. He chose a valley where 'there was a pretty little hill or mound'.[1] Even then there was nothing to mark the spot, except his intention, a finger pointing. To climb the hill, to look down from it, required that ways be cleared and lined. Light lines and barriers proliferated. Axes were honed, candles lit. Eventually, the clouds parted and the sun shone down.

Nothing could be less appropriate to the evocation of historical space than the one-way logic of positivist chronology. Pioneers did not yield to citizens. Men went bush and they came back. They passed on to other countries and began new lives. They changed their names. In different parts of Australia, quite different traditions of building, travelling, even weather-watching evolved; and, after years of drought, were given up and begun again elsewhere. Imagination was constantly on the move. Solutions were nomadic, variable, easily forgotten. The famous Australian taciturnity would seem to embody a profound scepticism about generalized explanations of any kind. 'Bullshit,' they say in response to any kind of intellectualizing – as if ideas were not everywhere: and indeed, in Australia, you cannot get away from theories, from lives relived as endless stories. Bullshit is the result of chewing the cud, the repetitive detritus of trying too hard to conjure oneself from the ground. The close scrutiny of hides, tracks, horizons, even impassive extracts of city pavements, seems like a form of magic designed to ward off the broader absence of a historical destiny. Bullshit is full stop to this, an act of defiance, a reminder to look at what's in front of you.

So a spatial history does not go confidently forward. It does not organize its subject matter into a nationalist enterprise. It advances exploratively, even metaphorically, recognizing that the future is invented. Going back, it questions the assumption that the past has been settled once and for all. It undermines the empirical stability of roads and buildings. It runs the risk of becoming as intangible as distant views. Its objects are intentions and, suggesting the plurality of historical directions, it constantly risks escaping into poetry, biography or a form of immaterialism positivists might think nihilistic. After all, what can you do with a horizon?

For all this, though, spatial history does not simply restore men and women to themselves; it does not merely haul them from the stream of time and ask them to reflect on their own destinies, as if they were something apart from history. It suggests even our inviolable 'personal space' expresses a community of historical interests. The viewpoints we take for granted as factual began in someone else's fantasy: it is not so much that the travellers and settlers belong to our past, but that we belong to their future. But their fantasies, too, were historical. Just as the travelling writers did not invent the language they used, so they did not make the world in their own image. They entered historical space as they entered life, finding a use for themselves where they lived. It was their intention to make a place for themselves which links us to them as much as any marks they succeeded in making. And it is by reflecting on their intentions, by understanding what lies behind the finished map, the elegant journal, the picturesque view, that we recover the possibility of another history, our future.

Consider, in this context, the observation of the First Fleet scholar and editor G. C. Ingleton:

> Perhaps the most serious omission in our records is the lack of narratives or letters written by the convicts themselves, or by the lower-deck seamen or the rank-and-file marines sent out as guards. Enlightening details of epic stories, such as those of the Bryants and the Kables and other convicts, appear to have been lost forever.[2]

What details we have come to us, as Ingleton recognizes, through the more or less distorting mirror of the First Fleet chroniclers – Phillip, Tench, Collins, Hunter and White. But for the most part these writers tend to treat the convicts as irrational beings little superior in either intellect or morals to the Aborigines. Is it likely then we can recover their history? The 'convict' who comes down to us in the pages of his oppressors is a social and political construction: he exists as a reflection of a body of rules, as a personification of transgression, a figure of speech necessary to the ruling class's self-justification and the perpetuation of its power. To let the convicts speak for themselves would have been to entertain the unthinkable: mutiny, another history.

But there is another possibility – that, by returning to Botany Bay reflectively, and by interpreting the accounts of the First Fleet journalists spatially, we can recover from the Enlightenment logic of cause and effect something of what that logic suppressed. In particular, we may be able to recover that dimension of the convict's existence which imprisonment and transportation were specifically designed to exclude: his occupation of a historical space. Recovering this lost space may not change the official history but, proposing another place, another Botany Bay, it does represent a timely mutiny against imperial history's methodological assumptions.

The feasibility of pursuing this inquiry arises from the fact that all the First Fleet historians were amused by what Tench refers to as the convicts' 'fertility of invention'. The convicts, it seems, were great story-tellers, myth-makers and dreamers. Appearing, as this habit did, to confirm the received truth of their warders – that the convicts were incapable of reason – the official historians felt no inhibition about reporting convict tales. They were a welcome diversion from the boredom of daily routine and, presenting a contrast to the officers' adherence to reason, they confirmed the colonial administration in its position of power. Yet these 'fabrications' of the convicts were not evidence of mental or moral aberration. On the contrary, they represented strategies for constructing a believable place – a place in which to speak and, no less important, a place from which to escape.

The striking fact is that the majority of the convict inventions which the First Fleeters so amiably record are *spatial* fantasies. Relegated to the realm of fairy-tales and, ironically, recorded for the very reason that they are thought harmless, the tales of hidden countries and routes which characterized convict gossip were not simply evidence of geographical ignorance or psychological stress. They were in fact fragments of a communal fantasy, a fantasy to do with the invention of another historical space. Yarns of El Dorado were not spun as a pastime: they were cryptic bids for power. And, in this sense, they held up a mirror to the pretensions of those in command, revealing to them the rhetorical nature of their exclusive claim to possess the one and only historical truth.

Consider the case of the convict James Daley. In August 1788, Collins writes,

> The settlement at Sydney Cove was for some time amused with an account of the existence and discovery of a gold mine; and the imposter had ingenuity enough to impose a fabricated tale on several of the officers for truth. He pretended to have found it at some distance down the harbour . . .[3]

Daley's mine turns out to be an invention but Collins concludes, somewhat sententiously,

> Among the people of his own description, there were many who believed, notwithstanding his confession and punishment, that he had actually made the discovery he pretended, and was induced to say it was a fabrication merely to secure it

to himself, to make use of at a future opportunity. So easy is it to impose on the minds of the lower class of people![4]

And not only on the minds of the lower class. At first all were willing to be taken in. Tench, in his reference to the incident, points out that it was not the first time that the authorities had been duped in this way.

> We found the convicts particularly happy in fertility of invention, and exaggerated descriptions. Hence large fresh water rivers, valuable ores, and quarries of limestone, chalk and marble, were daily proclaimed soon after we had landed. At first we hearkened with avidity to such accounts; but perpetual disappointments taught us to listen with caution, and to believe from demonstration only.[5]

Daley was punished for his 'imposition' but, as Collins writes, he 'was observed from that time to neglect his labour, and to loiter about from hut to hut, while others were at work'.[6] In December 1788 Daley was arrested on a charge of housebreaking; he confessed to 'several thefts, to which he had been induced by bad connections'.[7] For these Daley was hanged in the same month.

White was inclined to think 'Daily's' (*sic*) behaviour proved the man was 'insane', a 'lunatic'. But White also adds the information that, when the gold-mine report was found to be false, not only Daley but two other men were arrested. White acknowledges that some were of the opinion 'that time will disclose a deep-laid scheme, which he had planned for some purpose hitherto undiscovered'.[8]

We gather some inkling of the nature of this scheme from Collins. According to Collins, when he was arrested, Daley confessed that his gold-mine was an invention designed to induce the people belonging to the supply ships, *Fishburn* and *Golden Grove*, to trade with him: 'he expected to procure cloathing and other articles in return for his promised gold-dust'.[9] This seems inherently implausible: how would Daley have explained his new acquisitions to the authorities or his fellow convicts? How would he have hung on to them? At any rate, Tench, like White, assumes Daley's behaviour was irrational, only introducing the gold-mine story as a pretext for 'the following observation':

> the utmost circumspection is necessary to prevent imposition, in those who give accounts of what they see in unknown countries.[10]

For Tench, Daley's career is little more than an Aesopian fable illustrating what happens when Reason nods.

If we had no other account to go on, we might well conclude that Daley's case was exceptional. Hunter, however – and Hunter alone of the First Fleet chroniclers – gives Daley's fabrication a rational motive. If Daley's report proved true, Hunter recalls, the lieutenant-governor had promised Daley a reward:

> this reward was, (as there were ships upon the point of sailing) his own and a particular woman convict's enlargement, and a passage in one of the ships to England, together with a specified sum of money.[11]

Daley's 'deep-laid scheme' was, in short, nothing more or less than escape. In the light of Hunter's explanation, it seems unlikely that the convict's subsequent loitering about from hut to hut described by Collins was motiveless. May it not have been connected with Daley's continuing ambition to abscond?

Circumstantial support for this interpretation comes from the case of the convicts who apparently sought to escape by walking to China. This 'very extraordinary instance of folly stimulated to desperation', as Tench calls it, occurred in November 1791. A group of twenty-one convicts absconded from Rose Hill with all their belongings and were seen by settlers making their way northward. Asked where they were going, the settlers 'had received for answer, "to China" '. This ambitious 'elopement' rapidly petered out and, in dribs and drabs, the convicts gradually returned to Sydney Cove.[12] The chroniclers' reactions to this escape attempt were various – although, again with one exception, they agreed in treating the convicts' reasoning with derision. Phillip, for example, attributed it simply to 'ignorance' and, according to Hunter, Phillip was

> less inclined to inflict any punishment on these people, than to

punish those who had deceived them by the information of 'not being far from some Chinese settlements, and near people who would receive them, and where they would have everything they wanted, and live very happy . . .'[13]

It would seem from this that the convicts gave at least two reasons for escaping: to reach China and (perhaps or) to discover a Land of Cockaigne. This double motive was certainly confirmed by Tench, who pointed out that some at least of the escapees 'had general idea enough of the point of the compass, in which China lies from Port Jackson, to keep in a northerly direction'.[14] But the majority lured by the promise of China had been the victims of deception and their own ignorance:

> Upon being questioned about the cause of their elopement, those whom hunger had forced back, did not hesitate to confess, that they had been so grossly deceived, as to believe that China might easily be reached, being not more than a hundred miles distant and separated only by a river.[15]

In addition to these, however, Tench reports others among the convicts who

> ashamed of the merriment excited at their expence, said that their reason for running away, was on account of being overworked, and harshly treated; and that they preferred a solitary and precarious existence in the woods, to a return to the misery they were compelled to undergo.[16]

Whatever their motives, the escapeees were largely pardoned, although this did not prevent some from remaining rebellious: according to Hunter, 'they even talked of seizing on the soldiers' arms'.[17]

The impression one has from Hunter, Tench and Phillip is that the convicts involved in the China bid were a group of people who, like the convict Daley, were incapable of sustained reasoning even where their own interests were concerned; a people given to sudden excitement, inexplicable changes of mood; as ignorant as gullible. But once again one of the First Fleet's writers – in this case, Collins – puts forward a rational explanation for their apparent folly. According to the Judge-

Advocate 'the chimerical idea of walking to China' was only a ploy:

> It was generally supposed . . . that this improbable tale was only a cover to the real design, which might be to procure boats, and get on board the transports after they had left the cove.[18]

This suggests they may have anticipated the strategy of the group of convicts who attempted to escape in September 1793. According to Collins, that group took to the woods where, by raiding settlers' properties, they were able to stockpile equipment, and particularly a boat, preparatory to sailing away.[19] If Collins's supposition is right, the convicts' rhetorical China assumes a quite different meaning. Far from being the product of ignorance and deception, it may have reflected a strategic coolheadedness quite comparable with, say, that exhibited by the soldiers who, in August 1793, deserted with the intention, Collins says, of escaping in a long-boat. No less capable than the convicts of playing on the El Dorados of the colonists' imagination, when these soldiers were intercepted 'in the path to Parramatta', they 'told an absurd story of their being sent to the Blue Mountains'.[20]

This was not mere rhetoric: on occasion the spatial figures of the convicts' imaginations did translate themselves into history. In March 1791, eleven convicts led by William Bryant seized a government cutter and made their escape by sea. In September the previous year, five rather less well-prepared convicts had seized a small boat and, although it was 'very small and weak', they purposed, according to their friends, 'steering for Otaheite'. This latter party 'had each taken provisions for one week; their cloaths and bedding; three iron pots, and some other utensils of that nature'.[21] And, ambitious as this voyage may have seemed, it embodied an optimism about distance shared by professional navigators. It was Bass, after all, who in February 1798, rescued five escapees from an island in Bass Strait and, depositing them on the Gippsland coast, left them 'to begin their march to the northward, at the distance of upwards of 400 miles from Port Jackson'.[22]

The behaviour of Daley, the convict, was not then necessarily irrational and inexplicable. His gold-mine may have been a ploy to give him access to the supply ships – perhaps to trade his passage (as became common) or to reconnoitre and lay plans for stowing away. When such plans were thwarted, it is at least likely that Daley devised an alternative scheme and that his loitering and housebreaking were part of a plan to secrete supplies of clothing and the like preparatory to another escape attempt. It is clear, at any rate, that Daley was not alone in prosecuting both these plans and that his behaviour was not necessarily a sign of lunacy.

The significance of the convicts' rhetorical gold-mines and Chinas is not that it clarifies the hardly surprising fact that prisoners were interested in freedom. It lies less in their desire to escape than in the strategies they used to that end. For, whatever else they were, Daley's gold-mine and the convicts' China were rhetorical places outside the bounds of the penal colony. They were figures of speech which made the possibility of escape conceivable: they gave escape direction. They gave it a metaphorical name. More than this, although the First Fleet chroniclers treated the convicts' spatial inventions condescendingly, they accurately mirrored and articulated the spatial history of the white settlement as a whole. In this sense, recovering them we gain access to a dimension of Australia's founding which the foundational histories leave out.

Daley's gold-mine was not, as Tench called it, an instance of 'fertility of invention'. On the contrary, it conformed remarkably to official expectations. As Tench himself recalled:

> Previous to leaving England I remember to have frequently heard it asserted, that the discovery of mines was one of the secondary objects of the expedition.[23]

In 'discovering' a gold-mine Daley was only articulating a mineralogical fantasy on everybody's mind. The same was true of those tales of 'large fresh water rivers, valuable ores, and quarries of limestone, chalk and marble' with which the convicts regaled Phillip and his men. Such familiar geographical phenomena had an obvious utilitarian value. But they had another value as well: the empirical confirmation of their

presence in the new country was an important strategic tool in
getting a grasp on the country. The discovery of mines and
quarries was bound up with the validation of Enlightenment
epistemology. The convicts who announced their discovery
flattered the discourse of power. Such valuable objects not only
lent those in authority increased material power: more profoundly, they substantiated the proposition that 'here' was a
repetition of 'there'; that there was, in fact, no escape from a
cultural regime that could command space quite as effectively as
it regulated time. But who could tell what the net effect of this
reassurance might be? Perhaps the officers and soldiers would
feel they could relax. Perhaps these imaginary rivers and mines
would make it easier to slip away unnoticed.

It was not surprising that governor and officers paid attention
to convict tales: they were what they wanted to hear. They were
tales that appealed to geographical Reason. And it was on behalf
of the same Reason – the reason that Voltaire had celebrated,
'the same for all thinking subjects, all nations, all epochs and
cultures' – that the chroniclers relegated the convicts' tales, once
disproved, to the realm of ignorance and myth. In the interests
of founding a new society, it was essential to establish a clear,
hard and fast, publicly coherent place. And such a place
depended on establishing factual foundations. It could not
accommodate rival hypotheses, alternative histories, unofficial
stories. It could certainly not countenance fugitive countries
beyond the palisades. In this situation, it is small wonder that
the chroniclers fail to give a coherent account of the convicts'
actions. When, for example, Tench remarks that, under
questioning, certain convicts 'did not hesitate to confess, that
they had been so grossly deceived, as to believe that China
might be easily reached',[24] one is bound to wonder at the
miraculous power of 'experience' that instilled in these ignorant
folk so considerable a grasp of world geography in so short a
time in the bush. In other words, it looks very much as if the
convicts have had words put into their mouths. They have not
contested their interrogator's leading questions. The convicts'
prompted confessions, leaving unspoken their real motives,
permit Tench to exclude their actions from History. And,
colluding in a map-like vision of the historical world, the

convicts are deceived again: for their confirmation of government reasoning obtains them no official recognition. It merely excludes them further from a history of their own.

But this relegation of convict tales to the realm of myth was itself based on a mythic notion of history, a notion of history where space was passive, where events unfolded according to the logic of cause and effect. The official attitude of more or less benign amusement towards convict inventions was, amongst other things, a rhetorical stratagem designed to discredit the possibility that space might have a historical role and be actively implicated in the emergence of a settlement. The passivity or emptiness was a sign of reason, a device for concealing those spatial uncertainties which no rational plan of action could wholly foresee or neutralize. When, in January 1792, some villains, in Collins's account,

> broke into the dispensary at the hospital, and stole two cases of portable soup, one case of camomile flowers, and one case containing sudorific powder . . . which perhaps they had taken for sugar or flour . . .[25]

their action was not one of mere villainous theft: it, and break-ins like it, were the clearest statement that the penal colony was a prison; they asserted the possibility of a beyond where the traveller was not subject to Enlightenment hierarchies. In this sense the theft of portable soup was emblematic of a history whose content was light and dynamic, was not for permanent stockpiling but for strategic use. It symbolized nomadic transgression as against imperial appropriation. Such behaviour suggested that even 1788, the date, was negotiable: when William Bryant made his successful escape attempt in 1791, his term as a convict had all but expired. In escaping as a free man he was, in a sense, denying that Botany Bay had ever existed for him.

Whether in the form of burglaries or stories, the spatial fantasies of the convicts revealed the true nature of the new settlement, the fact that its law and order were not self-fulfilling, but the offspring of the convicts' collusion in the dream. The convicts' 'depredations', like their 'elopements', represented a hypothesis about the plural nature of historical space. They revealed the colony, not as a necessary and irreplaceable institution, but as a possible history, a possible place among others. They asserted the possibility that travellers, as well as city-founders, might have histories. Perhaps the most significant feature of Daley's gold-mine was that 'He pretended to have found it at some distance down the harbour.'[26] It lay, if anywhere, beyond the clearing, out of sight – a place where, as happened on the first excursion to verify his discovery, Daley could elude his officers by slipping into the bushes. A place 'at some distance', the gold-mine was also sufficiently close to function as a symbolic 'other' place. Implicit in it was the possibility of repeated journeys, a new orientation for the colony, a new view of Sydney Cove.

But the convicts' spatial history did not only reveal the real motives of the government's appeal to axiomatic and incontrovertible Reason. It also revealed that, even as they appealed to it, the policy-makers at Sydney Cove did not rely on Reason. The space, as they well knew, had to be possessed and named: it was not like a stage. It only 'presented' itself to the intentional gaze, the roving eye. Had this not been so, the convicts' tales could have held no conceivable interest. Imperial space which, as we saw in the Introduction, has been taken over uncritically by a tradition of Australian historians, with its ideal neutral observer and its unified, placeless Euclidean passivity, was a means of foundation, a metaphorical way of transforming the present extent into a future enclosure, a visible stage, an orderly cause-and-effect pageant. It was no less of a myth than the convicts' China. Thus in one of the founding passages of Australian history Phillip writes of the preparations for settlement:

> There are few things more pleasing than the contemplation of order and useful arrangement, arising gradually out of tumult and confusion; and perhaps this satisfaction cannot any where be more fully enjoyed than where a settlement of civilized people is fixing itself upon a newly discovered or savage coast. The wild appearance of the land entirely untouched by cultivation, the close and perplexed growing of trees, interrupted now and then by barren spots, bare rocks, or spaces overgrown with weeds, flowers, flowering shrubs, or under-

wood, scattered and intermingled in the most promiscuous manner, are the first objects that present themselves; afterwards, the irregular placing of the first tents which are pitched, or huts which are erected for immediate accommodation, wherever chance presents a spot tolerably free from obstacles, or more easily cleared than the rest, with the bustle of various hands busily employed in a number of the most incongruous works, increases rather than diminishes the disorder, and produces a confusion of effect, which for a time appears inextricable, and seems to threaten an endless continuance of perplexity. But by degrees large spaces are opened, plans are formed, lines marked, and a prospect at least of future regularity is clearly discerned, and is made the more striking by the recollection of the former confusion.[27]

It was precisely this model of order emerging inexorably out of chaos, according to an inner historical logic, which the testimony of the convicts revealed as mythic, as a rhetorical rationalization designed to neutralize the reality of a space that was turbulent, unpredictable, rebellious. The dispassionate, contemplative viewpoint embodied in Phillip's theatrical account is a narrative fiction. In truth, the 'objects' of nature did not 'present themselves': rather, they remained invisible and had to be distinguished by the intentional gaze. It was not 'chance' that presented 'a spot tolerably free from obstacles', but the travelling eye. And the travelling eye scanned the ground ahead tactically, 'sizing it up', rehearsing spatial hypotheses, adapting itself to conditions. Phillip's notion of settlement as an evolutionary civilization of 'promiscuous' nature, by way of the picturesque rearrangement of 'obstacles' and, eventually, their reduction to the logic of the grid, 'the prospect of future regularity': this has the strategic advantage of simplicity. As a spatial strategy, it corresponds admirably to Locke's injunction to avoid the sinuous paths of metaphor when writing the expository prose of reason.

But, as the convict antics revealed, from the first day and night of their own 'promiscuity', the world Phillip imagined constructing was only a stage: its reality depended on the engagement with the active regime of space so fully attested to by the convict narratives. The passivity of objects in Phillip's narrative belongs to the world of Bentham's device for keeping all prisoners constantly in view – in this connection, it may be that Phillip had a polemical, rather than poetic, reason for penning his elaborate description. After all, it was at about the time Phillip was writing that Bentham published his description of the 'Panopticon, or the Inspection House' based on

> a new principle of construction applicable to any sort of establishment in which persons of any description are to be kept under inspection.[28]

And Bentham suggested that, among other advantages, the arrangement of inmates around a central, all-seeing eye offered a mode of imprisonment considerably more rational than that of sending convicts to Botany Bay.[29] In a sense, Phillip was showing that Botany Bay, too, was a place where nothing was invisible, where no one could escape.

More picturesquely, Phillip's mechanisms for a change which, by merely clearing away the chaos, reveals space as it is, empty – and therefore changes nothing – this manipulation of the world, as if it had no motives of its own, recalls the renowned eidophusikon of De Loutherbourg, a six- or eight-foot stage in which painted scenes of nature were 'so manipulated it was a perfect picture of reality'.[30] But, as the metaphorical world of the convicts exemplified, the process of settlement was not one of gradual exclusion and reduction: it proceeded by way of an increasingly intricate and elaborate history of metaphors. It created zones of symbolic difference rather than exclusive opposition. What constituted Sydney Cove as a place and compacted its roads and walls was the crowding pressure of other places, imaginary rivers, delicious interiors, nearby Chinas.

In this context of rival spaces we can give proper weight to what must count as the first convict escape attempt. One would hardly guess from Phillip's description of regularity replacing wildness that the beginnings of the colony had been surrounded by uncertainty, that, contrary to expectations, the Botany Bay which Tench had greeted as a second Ithaca was found unsuitable for permanent settlement. Nothing in Phillip's stage directions reveals the fact that the site of the future colony had to be moved only a few weeks after arrival from Botany Bay and improvised at a hitherto unknown reach of water, Sydney Cove. Phillip's triumph of progress might have been written before the event it describes. Still the fact is that, late on 23 January 1788 (only five days after his arrival), Phillip returned from a reconnaissance of Port Jackson and ordered the evacuation of Botany Bay:

> In consequence . . . every preparation [was] made to bid adieu to a port which had so long been the subject of our conversation; which but three days before we had entered with so many sentiments of satisfaction; and in which, as we had believed, so many of our future hours were to be passed.[31]

The unexpected appearance of the French explorer La Pérouse, when the First Fleet was on the point of setting sail, delayed departure a further couple of days. Even so, by the 27th the new camp was established at Sydney Cove, while the French ships remained in Botany Bay until mid-March.

Beyond recording this removal from one place to another, the First Fleet historians attribute no particular significance to it. Indeed, they go on to narrate the proceedings of the colony much as if the move had never occurred. But the decision to leave behind Botany Bay had a significance for the exploration and settlement of the neighbourhood which extended far beyond considerations of security and safe anchorage. This emerges from a passage in Tench, where he describes the reaction of the convicts to the transfer of headquarters – and to the appearance of the French ships. Although no longer the main port, Botany Bay was by no means forgotten. Before January was out, when 'confusion' had hardly given way to 'system' in the Sydney Cove camp, Tench was obliged to record that,

> As the straggling of the convicts was not only a desertion from the public labour, but might be attended with ill consequences to the settlement, in case of their meeting with the natives, every care was taken to prevent it . . . In spite, however, of all our precautions, they soon found the road to Botany Bay, in

visits to the French, who would gladly have dispensed with their company.[32]

What was 'the road to Botany Bay'? Tench clearly refers to the overland route which the convicts took in an attempt to escape to the French ships. But what was the nature of this 'road'? It was not a road in the modern sense of a more or less metalled highway; nor, apparently, was it a road in the eighteenth-century sense of an established pathway or track. The exploration of Port Jackson, where Sydney Cove was selected as the site of the settlement, was conducted wholly by water. The transportation of convicts and soldiers from Botany Bay to Sydney Cove also occurred by water. And, prior to the establishment of Sydney Cove, there could have been no reason for anyone, soldier or convict, to attempt an overland journey in that direction. The probability is that the 'road' in question was any one of the numerous aboriginal tracks that criss-crossed the country between the two harbours. Whatever the case, it is clear that the route in question was not at this stage, from the white point of view, in any sense a constituted two-way passage, an official channel of communication. It was at best a gap suggesting escape, a promise of direction. Were it anything more, it would be hard to explain how the convict Ann Smith and an unnamed man, whom the French turned away, 'missed their way as they returned' and, according to White, probably 'perished for want'.[33]

Certainly, this view is supported by Hunter who, over the succeeding months, was primarily responsible for the thorough exploration and survey of Botany Bay and its environs. True, some eighteen months later by September 1789, when Hunter set off to survey Botany Bay, he could remark that 'The route being now well known, and the path well trodden, it was not an unpleasant walk.'[34] Even as early as March 1789, Collins reports a man murdered by the Aborigines found 'stripped, and lying in the path to Botany Bay'.[35] But, when the convicts made their way back to Botany Bay, only a week or so after first disembarking there, the country they traversed was densely wooded, and even the aboriginal tracks did not lead directly from one place to the other. Hunter, who made an overland journey from Botany Bay to Sydney Cove in March 1788, described the country in these terms:

> The distance from Botany Bay to Port Jackson, across the land, and near the sea shore, is, in a direct line, eight or nine miles; and the country about two miles to the southward of Port Jackson abounds with high trees, and little or no underwood; but between that and Botany Bay, it is all thick, low woods or shrubberies, barren heaths, and swamps; the land near the sea, although covered in many places with wood, is rocky from the water-side to the very summit of the hills.[36]

Tench's 'road' was not, then, a fixed and immobile conduit of communication: however real or otherwise the path which the convicts took, it was from their point of view one-way, open-ended. In this sense, the convicts' first escape attempt not only revealed the contingent nature of historical space, but directly contradicted (and revealed) the falsehood of Phillip's rhetorical pretence that one place was very much like another. For it was precisely by removing from Botany Bay that Phillip constituted Botany Bay as a place, the first 'other' place in the colony. It was in terms of, and in contrast with, this other place that Sydney Cove (and the authority of Phillip) was now, for the first time, defined. But, by defining the colony as a place in contrast to other places, as an enclosure of order, Phillip inevitably gave focus to what lay outside. For the first time, it became possible for the convicts to contemplate escape, to *conceive* of a road to Botany Bay. The significance of their pathetic efforts to elude further punishment is that it brings to the surface what the official accounts suppress: the spatial constitution of the nascent colony.

In this light, Tench's 'road' is a significant misrepresentation of the spatial reality. For the implication of the word is the prior existence of two opposite and equal termini – in this case, Botany Bay and Sydney Cove. It suggests the convicts followed what was already there – and in this way imprisons them, once again, within the all-seeing survey of those with power. There is already implicit in this characterization of the escape route the nullifying authority of Enlightenment reason – the conviction that all places are central, all roads the prisoners of authority;

that, ultimately, the convicts must return and neither place offers refuge, only detention. For a 'road' runs backwards and forwards, equally, unemphatically, without intention or promise.

And yet this was precisely what the escape attempt disproved: the two 'places' the convicts travelled between were by no means equal. If one was open, the other was closed: if one was ahead, the other lay behind. The ideas that, a few days earlier, had been associated with Botany Bay, ideas of confinement or, from the official point of view, security, had now been transferred to Sydney Cove. In turn, Botany Bay assumed a new significance as the first place *outside* the settlement. If Botany Bay now provided those in authority with a definite focus for their surveying and exploring activities, it now enabled the convicts to reconstitute it as a *place* of escape. The place name changed its meaning. The road itself was pushed forward without thought of going back. The road was a journey: it retained the charge of direction. It was precisely the difference between the actual beginning here and the possible destination there that brought the road into being.

The historical significance of the road to Botany Bay, then, is not confined to the particular fantasy which occasioned it. Whether or not any of the convicts succeeded in getting aboard the French ships by bribing the sailors with the promise of women, is by the way in this context. Like Daley's gold-mine or the Chinese settlement beyond the river, the road to Botany Bay was a fantasy about the other place. It was the act of imagining oneself there which brought the other place into being as the occasion of a historical event. In this sense, from the point of view of spatial history, the road is richly metaphorical. Not only does it lead back, against the imperial tide of events, towards another beginning, but also by its definition of historical space as intentional space, it articulates the historical experience which the Englightenment apologists of settlement left out. In its own way, it is a foundational event, although what it establishes is not another cause leading to other effects, but simply the presence of human beings who, though they were actors like the rest of us, did not strut the same stage as their historians and captors.

These actors did not take the world for granted: their right to live in it had been forfeited. Nor were they taxonomists or cartographers. Unlike the government, they had no interest in making the future like the present. They wanted to break out of their enclosures, whether historical or physical. Whether or not they successfully translated their wishes into historical events, they embodied a historical attitude which was not exhausted in its local causes and effects. Phenomenologically grounded, it belonged to the history of space and, wherever such people found themselves, it was likely to emerge. Thus the spatial revision of history adumbrated on the road to Botany Bay is evident again, and much more dramatically, as soon as Phillip embarks on his second spatial initiative, the settlement of Norfolk Island.

Following instructions, Phillip despatched a small contingent of officers and convicts to Norfolk Island only two months after his own arrival at Sydney Cove. The speed and confidence with which he could contemplate founding a satellite colony was, of course, another testimony to the thoroughness of Cook's voyaging and to the ease with which islands, unlike coastlines, could be possessed. And, in theory, at least, Norfolk Island was the ideal prison: unlike the mainland, it seemed inconceivable that it should harbour the stuff of revolutionary myth. No rivers could be expected; there were no promising interiors. Natural and symbolic boundary coincided. From the outset, the map-maker and musket-bearers commanded the routes of escape and arrival. Trespass was unthinkable. Unlike anyone unfortunate enough to become lost in the bush near Sydney Cove and for whom, as Collins put it,

> the westward was an immense open track before him, in which, if unfriended by either sun or moon, he might wander until life were at an end[37]

the wanderer on Norfolk Island was almost bound to find his way back. Two Norfolk Island convicts who missed their way on 16 March 1788 and 'lost sight of the sun from the thickness of the woods', wandered about

> till eleven o'clock when they heard the noise of our church

bell, which was a man beating on the head of an empty cask, and presently afterwards they returned to the settlement.[38]

But, perhaps surprisingly, the qualities which recommended Norfolk Island to Phillip also appealed to the convicts. The nine male and six female convicts who sailed with King were, according to Collins, 'mostly volunteers'. In October the *Golden Grove* brought a further, larger consignment of convicts, with the result that by January 1789 the population of Norfolk Island consisted of sixty-three persons, seventeen of whom were free (including six marines), the remainder convicts. Very shortly after this King was informed that the convicts were planning an insurrection, and the plan they had adopted makes it clear why the island appealed as much to them as to the government. The idea was that King was to be seized 'when going to or returning from' his farm; a forged message from King was to be used to lure the surgeon away so that he could be seized 'as soon as he got into the woods'. And, Collins goes on,

> the serjeant and the party (who were out bringing in cabbage palm, also 'from the woods') were to be treated in the same manner.[39]

The convicts were then to use similar ruses to gain control of the *Supply* anchored offshore:

> and then, as the last act of this absurd scheme, the ship was to be taken, with which they were to proceed to Otaheite, and there establish a settlement.[40]

There was, after all, little which was absurd in the scheme, and the spatial imagination it expressed was shared by soldiers and convicts alike. It was, for instance, the fact that the island was felt to be a natural prison which gave the convicts an unusual freedom. King himself attributed the plot in part to the informality that had grown up between the soldiers and the convicts – and it was the same indiscipline that was blamed for the attempted mutiny of soldiers on the island in 1794. Further, fixed natural boundaries limited the authority and freedom of the gaolers quite as effectively as it constrained the imprisoned. An island which offered no 'other' place except the wood placed the two sides on an equal spatial footing – and, therefore, undermined the rhetoric of command.

The security of the island, its easy supply of symbolic boundaries and a given centre, served the interests of both parties. It made the mobilization of opposition easier for the same reason it made the process of administration smoother – the progress of settlement, like the prospect of escape, could not only be conceptualized: it could also be visualized. Even the convicts' object of desire was highly conventional. Ever since Cook's glowing account of it, Tahiti had been high on the official agenda of colonization. The convicts simply put into words what was on everyone's mind at some time or another. So, when William Bryant made his successful escape, Tench attributed it to the example of that best known of Tahitian sailors, Bligh:

> After the escape of Captain Bligh, which was well known to us, no length of passage, or hazard of navigation, seemed above human accomplishment.[41]

In dealing with authority, the convicts revealed its rhetorical foundations: maps and memos were instruments of strategy, not incontestable facts. Place names were figures of speech, places where one could speak. Imagining them lent one authority. But this, after all, was how reason worked, by persuasion rather than demonstration. For, before there were facts, there had to be the fiction of facts. There had to be agreement that space was not historical, that language was not metaphorical. It is in demonstrating the falseness of these premises that the convicts not only subverted Enlightenment reason but held up an ironic mirror to it. In the process, their spatial fantasies revealed the possibility that, despite official plans, Botany Bay was not settled before it was reached and not even fixed finally once it was surveyed. The road to Botany Bay represented a history still to be written.

Significantly, while the First Fleet historians disparaged what the convicts said, explorers took their words seriously. In January 1798 it was discovered that the most recently arrived convicts were planning to escape to

a colony of white people, which had been discovered in this

country, situated to the S.W. of the settlement, from which it was distant between three and four hundred miles, and in which they were assured of finding all the comforts of life, without the necessity of labouring for them.[42]

Collins further reports that

it appeared, that the history of the supposed settlement had its rise from some strange and unintelligible account which one of these men, who had left his work, and resided for some time with the natives, had collected from the mountain savages.[43]

Collins affects to find the whole story preposterous, but it was this or a very similar tale of an inland society which Flinders adduced in support of his theory of a trans-continental channel. Again, it was another criminal report, this time of a mythical river, the Kindur, which inspired Mitchell's first expedition. Explorers, unlike legislators, welcomed these imaginary places as hypotheses necessary to rational travelling. Fiction or fact, they lent the traveller a direction. The confirmation of these tales was less important than the ideal other place they offered as a goal. The mythic and the marvellous were essential to travel, as Flinders recognized, and in this respect the convicts' stories only spelt out what was officially known but suppressed.

In effect even the colonial administration itself could not afford to ignore the convicts' tales. Whether empirically respectable or not, these other places represented knowledge and therefore power. It is significant that the strategy used to dissuade the convicts from their scheme of seeking an inland colony was to send four of them out with three people 'accustomed to the woods of this country', so that they might see for themselves their 'fancied paradise' did not exist.[44] This free lesson in empirical reasoning sounds admirably benevolent, but it is at least as likely that the governor's real motive was to pre-empt any claim the convicts might make to an important discovery. As the eagerly transcribed accounts of the convict Wilson's inland wanderings indicate, Collins and others recognized that they owed much of their intimate knowledge of what was outside to those most at home there: the convicts.

Ridicule of the convicts' ignorance went hand in hand with the appropriation of their knowledge. And, such was the nexus between knowledge and power, it was impossible for the convicts to keep anything for themselves. For whatever they brought back became grist to the mill of authority. Short of disappearing for ever, the convicts' geographical knowledge could never liberate them. Short of proposing spaces that could not be mapped, they were doomed to remain imprisoned in someone else's theory. In this light we can see that Tench's growing disillusionment with Cook's description of Botany Bay had quite as much to do with power as with knowledge. Cook's Botany Bay provided the essential conceptual scaffolding in terms of which Tench could construct his own viewpoint. But, once established, it became equally necessary to jettison the scaffolding and appear to stand free. Accordingly, he consigned Cook's description of Botany Bay to the same realm as the prisoners' stories, the prehistoric realm of childish fancy.

Nor did the imposition of power as knowledge stop here. If the removal to Sydney Cove gave Tench and the other chroniclers room to conceptualize Botany Bay as a distinct geographical object out there, it soon encouraged them to further distance themselves from their own mythic origins by restoring to the place its original 'wildness'. Indeed, by the time of Hunter's survey, there are parts of it which might more profitably be left unknown – the coastal creeks, for instance, which, Hunter remarks, 'were *with me* no object at this time to throw away time upon'.[45] The increasing remoteness of Botany Bay, which the convict escape attempt was the first to anticipate, reflected a crisis of authority. For, despite the optimistic rhetoric of Phillip, the colony did not consolidate itself easily. As crops failed and supply ships were delayed, the need to unite the settlement increased, rather than decreased. As Tench wrote referring to September 1789,

> all our attention was not directed to explore inlets, and toil for
> discovery. Our internal tranquillity was still more important.[46]

In these circumstances, it was not only the convicts who came to regard Botany Bay as their place: it was crucial for those in authority to define it similarly, as a place outside the law. After the first desertions to Botany Bay, in the course of a speech on 7 February 1788, Phillip reminded the convicts of his intention 'to let the rigour of the law take its course, against such as might dare to transgress the bounds prescribed'.[47]

There is yet another sense in which the road to Botany Bay and the fantasies it embodies illuminate the beginnings of Australia's spatial history. 'Road' was Tench's word and, in view of the failure of the escape attempt, it may be that he used the term ironically. Much as they may have wanted a road, much as they may have persuaded themselves a road existed, the fact was that it was a figment of their fevered imaginations. In effect, they fell victims to their own rhetorical artifice, to their own abuse of language: China does not lie across the river just because you say so; the bush does not cleave because you invoke the word 'road'. Only minds deaf to reason could have insisted on describing a tract of bush as a track. This, or something like it, may well be the irony implicit in Tench's phrase. But, if so, the irony risks turning on Tench himself. For it may well be that Tench was obliged to treat the convicts' behaviour ironically for the simple reason that he could not describe it in any other way.

As I have suggested, the most striking feature of the convicts' stories is the way in which they parody the language of reason. It is as if all its devices, its figures of speech, its extrapolative logic, its insistence on facts, are taken and turned on their heads. With the greatest gravity, the convicts send up the pretensions of power. They march the soldiers down the beach to look for gold and, while they are scrabbling in the sand, slip away into the bushes. And, when captured, rather than explain, they let their captors make up their stories for them. But it is precisely this submissiveness which reveals their intransigence. For underlying it is a refusal to attribute to words the unambiguous substance and historical materiality with which the governor and officers invest them. The complaint that, in King's words, some of the convicts were 'incorrigible', 'notwithstanding every encouragement was held out to them',[48] runs through First Fleeters' accounts. The convicts seemed to give no weight to promises, contracts and threats. You could not talk to them or interpret reliably what was said.

When the November 1791 escapees straggled back to camp, they were asked their destination. They replied 'to China'. And Tench remarks,

> The extravagance and infatuation of such an attempt was explained to them, by the settlers; but neither derision, nor demonstration, could avert them from pursuing their purpose.[49]

They would not, in short, listen to reason.

But this was not simply a failing. As Tench and his fellow officers recognized, it was intentional. The convicts' ironic appropriation of the tricks of the dominant discourse revealed its flimsiness. Those Chinas and inland kingdoms may well have represented imperial figures of speech especially concocted for the interrogators' consumption. They may have been metaphors which concealed, rather than revealed a plot to travel, to set out, a scheme where portable cakes of soup were more useful than maps. But who could tell? There was something ridiculous about Lockean empiricism when there were not even words to name things. The 'infatuation' with fantastic ideas, which men like Phillip and Collins found so irritating, was a rebuff to the Enlightenment boast that it could vindicate its world view empirically. It was a rebuff to the view that saw history occurring in a world already fully furnished with barracks, court-houses, prisons and roads.

This explains Tench's objection to the convicts' 'flash, or kiddy language'. It is a language of many 'dialects':

> The sly dexterity of the pickpocket; the brutal ferocity of the footpad; the more elevated career of the highwayman; and the deadly purpose of the midnight ruffian.[50]

Underworld cant, it is also the language of the roads, the language of illicit exchange, where objects change name as they pass from hand to hand. It is a language designed to baffle detection – and, significantly, Tench's first argument against it is the difficulty it creates in courts of law. Significantly, too, Tench sees the practice of this language as an integral part of the convicts' physical practice: cant and crime, word and deed, cannot be separated. Predictably, Tench is of the opinion that 'an abolition of this unnatural jargon would open the path to reformation'.[51] Here we see the Enlightenment project of reducing the world to uniformity, replacing local difference with universal intelligibility. But, underlying the superficial benevolence of this linguistic imperialism, is something approaching panic, the chaos of unintelligibility. The path to reformation, like the road to Botany Bay, leads to a prison. The difference is that it involves no transfer of power.

The convicts' ironic presence suggested the strategic, deceptive power of language – the administrative nightmare of 'roads' that might, after all, just peter out. Their cant functioned as an agent of travel, of secret commissions and metaphorical exchange. It was part of an act which revealed the world as a stage. Nor was improvisation confined to making up stories; there were, to quote Tench again, 'many persons of perverted genius, and of mechanical ingenuity'. Tench cites an ironworker called Frazer, convicted as a thief, who was not only a wizard with locks but, in his previous life, 'a travelling conjuror'.[52] White records a comparable case of 'ingenuity': a convict called Thomas Barrett who, in the confinement of the transport, had succeeded in forging passable quarter dollars.[53] As masters of deception, such men were both above and below nature: they were perverters of reason. No less significantly, they were manufacturers of the tools of passage.

This is the last revenge of Enlightenment reason, to describe the road to Botany Bay as nothing but a deception. In an effort to suppress the irony of another history, Botany Bay and the convicts who escape there must be stigmatized as unnatural and deceptive. By a final irony, the official historians *will* the convicts to take to the woods: for is it not where they belong, in the prehistoric, pre-rational realm of Australian nature? Already, early in 1788, Lieutenant Southwell, writing of the approaches to Sydney Harbour, was lamenting ''Tis greatly to be wish'd these appearances were not so delusive as in reality they are.'[54] A few years later, the artist Thomas Watling referred in similar vein to 'Mangrove avenues, and picturesque rocks, entwined with non-descript flowers', and regretted 'were the benefits in the least equal to the specious external, this country need hardly give place to any other on earth'.[55] Human nature, as it appeared in convict behaviour, and Australian nature, in its specious picturesqueness, belonged to the same order of unreason.

In this sense, the convicts' recidivist habit of, in Collins's words, 'flying from labour into the woods', like their habit of retreating into an impenetrable argot, only served to bring home the urgency of clearing a space, of marking out conceptual, as well as physical, boundaries. For to call the road to Botany Bay a 'road' may have been a rhetorical means of suggesting the deceptiveness of appearances, but it also recognized the wood as the place of masked schemes, the place of highwaymen, unseen violence and strange translations (from white to black, from confinement to freedom), an environment predicated on the formalized and continuous transgression of fixed boundaries.

So there is pathos in Tench's 'road' as well as irony: for while the convicts might prey on roads, in their own travelling they avoided them. Roads were for other people, for people who had an official destination in mind and were where they wanted to be at once. The more inconvenient they were for travellers, the better they suited the man of the road. For convicts, roads were proof that the fruits of travel were there for the taking, that roads bearing bullion distributed largesse. Roads were like laws, for crossing at night. But, confined to the high way of reason, how could Tench have acknowledged this? Only by settling it with roads of his own could Tench order Botany Bay's thieving spaces and deceptive meadows.

11

A Wandering State

From the quick and eager exercise of their eyes, in seeking for their prey,
they are exceedingly keen-sighted, and discover birds in the trees, or
venemous reptiles in the grass, where Europeans see nothing.

London Missionary Society Deputation, Hunter's River, 1824

The end of linear writing is indeed the end of the book . . .

Jacques Derrida

The road to Botany Bay leads back not only to the world of the
convicts but also to Australia's earlier inhabitants, the Aborigines. It does this quite literally in the sense that, if the escaping
convicts did take a 'road' of any description, it must have been
an aboriginal track. Botany Bay was apparently an aboriginal
meeting place – in addition to a 'village' on the north-west arm
of the bay, inhabited by perhaps sixty people,[1] Tench records a
party of 'more than three hundred persons, two hundred and
twelve of whom were men', encountered by Phillip at the head
of the bay early in 1788.[2] From early days, taking the road to
Botany Bay implied a confrontation with savage nature.
Tench's ill-fated excursion to Botany Bay in 1790 was designed
to avenge aboriginal attacks on the settlement.[3] Convicts who
took to the woods did not simply seek freedom or respite from
work: they sought the company of savages. They relied on the
good will of the Aborigines for their survival. More than this,
leaving the pale of order behind, convicts behaved like savages.
In Botany Bay, the name and the symbolic place, convict and
savage were fused into the figure of unreason.

Identified with nature, the Aborigines enter white history in
much the same role as the convicts. As credulous victims of
superstition, they are entertaining. As more or less reliable
informants about the country beyond the settlement, their
statements are eagerly transcribed. But, as vehicles of reason,
they are uniformly disappointing. Attempts at civilizing them
encounter insuperable resistance. They keep on taking off their

clothes. To reason with them is to debate with the air. They seem to take no account of Sydney Cove's logical arguments and moral distinctions. They are people of the night, adept at stealing, suddenly violent, communicating in a language as bereft of grammar as the breeze. Children of nature, they are convicts without a criminal record. In this sense, they reproach the convicts' vicious habits. Referring to the action of convicts in destroying an aboriginal canoe, Collins observes

> How much greater claim to the appellation of savages had the wretches who were the cause of this, than the native who was the sufferer?[4]

Disarmed of their savagery, the natives become figures of irony. They stand in for irredeemable nature. Forty years later, Breton could refer quite casually to a notorious bushranger as 'this gloomy savage'[5] – as if the Aborigines had never existed, except as a figure of speech.

The Aborigines' crime was to be primitive, to have no history. In this sense it was quite natural that nineteenth-century ethnologists meticulously compared the skull measurements of slaughtered Aborigines with those of executed white criminals, as if the volume of unreason might be plotted on a graph. The dead were more informative than the living. In the absence of history, science was a form of decent burial. Whatever the difference of their racial and cultural origins, convicts and Aborigines constituted the rebellious nature which the authorities had to subdue. They were the prehistory history had to fight. Their antics brought history's task into focus. Always shifting ground, they corrupted benevolence. If they could not be counted, how could blankets be ordered or bullets? How could they be given a history? People who did not understand causes and effects had, historically speaking, no employment. What, then, could be done except to hire their services to kill each other?[6]

The tendency of the First Fleet journalists to treat the Aborigines like convicts might suggest that their history can be treated like the convicts'. It is tempting to imagine that by attending to the occasion and context of aboriginal appearances in, say, the First Fleet chronicles, we can recover their history of travelling. Instead of making fleeting appearances and baffling pronouncements, the Aborigines might emerge as the proponents of a different, spatial history. This alternative history might, once again, be seen to reflect on certain profound preoccupations of the Sydney Cove settlement suppressed or 'rationalized' in official accounts.

The First Fleet accounts themselves certainly seem to lend support to this possibility. In June 1792, when the colony was anxiously looking out for ships, Collins reports:

> On the last day of the month, some natives residing at the south shore of Botany Bay, whether from a hope of reward, or from actually having seen some ships at a distance, informed the governor that a few days before they had perceived four or five sail, one of which they described to be larger than the others, standing off the land, with a westerly wind. Little credit was given to the report.[7]

Here, for instance, Botany Bay is not only the place of the Aborigines: it is associated with the future security of the colony. The people who reveal this connection are the Aborigines themselves. Their testimony reveals history's need of a place of far-seeing, where the observer merges with the seer, history into hope. A few pages later, Collins again refers to the Aborigines' report:

> The natives who lived among us assured us from time to time, that the report formerly propagated of ships having been seen on the coast had a foundation in reality; and as everyone remembered that the *Justinian*, after making the heads of Port Jackson, had been kept at sea for three weeks, a fond hope was cherished that the sun had shone upon the whitened sails of some approaching vessel, which had been discovered by the penetrating eyes of our savage neighbours at Botany Bay. In this anxiety and expectation we remained till the 26th, when the long-wished-for signal was made, and in a few hours after the *Britannia* storeship, Mr William Raven master, anchored in the cove . . .[8]

Passages like these underline the connection between the Aborigines and the convicts, and their common historical function. Like the convicts, the Aborigines make their appearance in the pages of history as tale-bearers. Like the convicts' gold-mines, the Aborigines' whitened sails are not random fabrications: they articulate what is on everyone's mind. This is why they are recorded. In this sense, the Aborigines' horizon visions articulate the emotional and physical needs of the colony even more immediately than the prisoners' tales of China.

The supply ships are overdue. Despite every precaution, predictions have not been fulfilled. Temporarily at least, the horizonless logic of Enlightenment reason is in question. In this threatening situation, it is not surprising that Collins treats the Aborigines' sightings much as he treats the convicts' claims. At first they are given little credit; afterwards, they are superfluous – for it is highly significant that Collins leaves it an open question whether or not the Aborigines' original sightings were genuine. In this sense, the Aborigines' stories are the emotional scaffolding on which Enlightenment history must build, but which it must also reject. If false, they demonstrate once again the need for scepticism. If true, they are immediately rendered superfluous to history by their transformation into facts. As a result, any evidence of unreason in the colony is attributed to the Aborigines. And, by a final ironic twist, true or false, their stories are consigned to the unverifiable realm of the hearsay prehistoric.

There is no question that stories of ships did articulate communal fantasies. On an earlier occasion in April 1790 when the colonists' stores had been almost exhausted and supply ships were long overdue a mate on the *Sirius*, Daniel Southwell, wrote,

I early and late look with anxious eyes toward the sea; and at times, when the day was fast setting and the shadows of the evening stretched out, have been deceived with some fantastic little cloud, which, as it has condensed or expanded by such a light, for a time has deceived impatient imagination into a momentary idea that it was a vessel altering her sail and position while steering in for the haven; when, in a moment, it has assumed a form so unlike what the mind was intent upon, or become so greatly extended, as fully to certify me of its flimsy texture and fleeting existence.[9]

Southwell scans the sea not because he *expects* to find a sail there, but because *he would like to*. In his anxious state of mind, he is easily deceived into imagining 'some fantastic little cloud' is 'a vessel altering her sail'. But this is not a lapse into mechanical associationism: it implies a heightened state of concentration; a poetic state of mind capable of transforming perceptions almost instantaneously into signals of desire. The play of light on cloud suggests a hypothesis that can be tested in an instant. For, so certain is the mind of what it is intent upon, that chimeras *cannot* deceive it. Thus it continues its hunt, its provisional pursuit of promising clouds.

Apart from anything else, Southwell's description of his visual perceptions evokes in the precisest terms an intentional state of mind – a state of mind that is neither a blank page passively waiting to be written on by events, nor a storehouse of associations incapable of judging novelty except by the light of custom and previous experience. Southwell's single-minded orientation towards the horizon is at once empirical and imaginative. Instead of waiting on facts, Southwell concentrates on phenomena. His narrative reveals the primary act of perception as interpretation. His poetic precision keeps the horizon open, and it also opens up the possibility of the kind of history attempted here, a history of intentions.

The important point, though, is that Southwell's fantasies, or anything like them, are largely excluded from the narratives of Tench and his fellow chroniclers, except as they appear in the stories of the Aborigines, where the context neutralizes their emotional appeal. Even there, they appear in the most harmless and conventional of linguistic guises. Collins may acknowledge the power of infatuation, albeit in an impersonal passive construction: 'a fond hope', he writes, 'was cherished that the sun had shone upon the whitened sails of some approaching vessel'. But how lifeless Collins's image is in comparison with Southwell's 'fantastic little cloud' suggesting 'a vessel altering her sail'. Collins's conventional expression, 'fond hope', implies the mood of 'anxiety and expectation' is not to be taken too seriously. Passing like the clouds, it is only of interest because of its coincidental connection with a historical fact – the arrival of the *Britannia* and its master, Mr William Raven.

The story-telling Aborigines preserve for us states of mind which, but for rare private testimonies, like Southwell's, we would have to infer from the official narratives. This much is clear, but it does not follow that we can treat the Aborigines as a kind of black convict, attempting to recover them from history dialectically. Gold-mines and cloud-like sails may be alike in holding up a critical mirror to the epistemological assumptions of the rulers. But this is no reason to suppose that they were put forward with the same intention. To treat the Aborigines as an oppressed group within white society or for that matter to write of their history beyond the frontier, as if they were spirited opponents of white colonization, is only to achieve by different means what Tench and his colleagues had already done before: their appropriation to a white discourse, history. It is to suppose that the Aborigines moved in the same historical space as the Europeans – a space constituted culturally, according to social, economic and, above all, intellectual criteria. And, while this assumption may be made for the convicts, it is not valid for the Aborigines: we have no grounds for presuming that aboriginal history can be treated as a subset of white history, as a history within history.

If Aborigines, unlike convicts, remain outside white history, even when the dominant positivist methodology is brought into question, this reflects, not on the Aborigines, but rather on the essential nature of history as imperial historians have defined and practised it. Its essential feature as a discourse has been identified by Adorno, where he writes, 'History does not merely touch on language, but takes place in it.'[10] The foundational history which Tench or, for that matter, most of our contemporary historians practise is essentially a legitimation of selected earlier documents. As my own quotations from the First Fleet writers illustrate, even the primary sources consist largely of the narration of quotations and are themselves, in this sense, secondary. Quotations are the historian's raw facts. By arranging and narrating them, he not only constitutes certain documents of the past as 'authorities', but also earns his own writing the authority and legitimacy of history.

This process occurs entirely within language, and it has important consequences. As the cultural critic Walter Benjamin has pointed out, the fact of quotation also testifies to the loss of the original source, its lapsing from historical memory and the necessity to revive it.[11] In this sense the value of writing history is that it continues to remind us of our origins. But there is also an opposite implication. The fact that history is essentially an act of interpretation, a re-reading of documents, means that it *hides* our origins from us. For, by its nature, history excludes all that is not quoted or written down. Only what has been transcribed is available for interpretation. Only documents can be compared, ordered, interpreted and judged. Ironically, the originality of historical personages, like the uniqueness of historical events, depends on their *not* being original or unique but part of a wider already constituted historical pattern. History has a historical horizon which is constituted by the activity of history itself: the horizon of writing. It offers the mechanism for generating a tradition, but not the means of reflecting on the validity of the tradition itself. In this sense, it may exclude much of the past which matters to us – our own spatiality, for instance.

Usually, the fact that history occurs within history, as it were, is not crucial. It does not, for example, affect our discussion of the convicts. For the fragmented testimonies of the convicts, which appear as quotations in the First Fleet journals, fall within a historical tradition. They belong to a historical pattern in terms of which we can judge their originality. We have numerous texts from Homer and Genesis onwards that enable us to authenticate the notion of escape. There is no reason to doubt the convicts 'read' the symbolic spaces of the Sydney Cove settlement as the soldiers did, although they may have assigned opposite values to them. There is a history of captivity in the Bible. There is even, thanks to the author of *The Anatomy of Melancholy*, a history of lunacy. Above all, there is the shared tradition of language as a social activity, whether in the form of dialogue or as writing. The First Fleet writers could question the convicts and draw conclusions from their answers: implicit in the historians' activity was a shared world of intentionality. For the same reason, we can contest their conclusions and offer plausible readings of our own. For, beyond the quotations, there is always the authority of earlier texts and our own history of reading. To draw attention to the lost history of the convicts is to engage in a genuinely dialectical activity: it not only reflects critically on the dominant historical tradition, but also gives the convicts a place within it, a place from which to speak and be heard.

None of this applies to the Aborigines, for the simple reason that, from the beginning of white occupation, the Aborigines were made to speak a language which was not theirs. From the beginning, Whites made little effort to learn aboriginal languages. It is striking how often missionaries, for instance, have to start from scratch in learning the local language: there was no tradition of bi- or multi-lingualism out of which the documents of aboriginal history might have emerged and in terms of which they might have been interpreted. Instead, Aborigines appeared only in so far as they could successfully ape European cultural paradigms and command the rudiments and rhetorical occasions of English speech. Their motives, unlike those of the convicts, remained hidden: there was no history in terms of which to interpret them. When Stokes remarks that

> None but those who have made the experiment, are aware of what has to be overcome before any sort of intercourse can be carried on by signs . . .[12]

and, elsewhere,

> many words put down by us as meaning a certain thing, signify in reality, 'What do you mean?' 'I do not understand' . . .[13]

there can be little doubt that he encapsulates the main epistemological reason for the exclusion of the Aborigines, from both white space and white history. If the Aborigines loiter on the edge of our historical clearing, throwing spears or performing corroborees with equal alacrity, it is because, except in these theatrical manifestations, which speak as it were for themselves, they cannot be appropriated and carried away as cultural treasure by the victors.

Consequently, by a deadly irony, it is the attempt of the Aborigines to speak English which consigns them to historical silence. To take again the passage where Collins quotes the Aborigines' tale of ships. What undermines its authority is not merely that it is superseded by the arrival of ships, but the fact that no motive can be assigned to it. 'Whether from a hope of reward, or from actually having seen some ships at a distance . . .', Collins writes. Were the storytellers aping white desires? Perhaps they thought ships were something else. But, in the absence of a shared history, there was no way of interpreting their intentions. There was no way of distinguishing figures of speech from facts, lies from mere politeness.

This self-effacement arose directly from the character of empirical history itself – from its project to hunt out and ascertain the facts. Contesting Ricoeur's notion of a kind of symmetry between writer and reader, the critic Edward Said has argued that

> far from being a type of conversation between equals, the discursive situation is more usually like the unequal relation between colonizer and colonized, oppressor and oppressed.[14]

It is the writer who sets out the terms of any exchange: and the same was true of the Europeans who engaged the Aborigines in dialogue with a view to legitimating a new society. When, for example, Lachlan Macquarie records in his journal,

> One of the natives . . . tells us that the real and proper name of this newly discovered river that we are now exploring is the Warragombie,[15]

the authority for this name resides with the governor, not with the informant. It resides with Macquarie who asked the question, in this way, from the outset, locating the name, not within an aboriginal context, but within the rhetorical ambit of a white geo-historical discourse. Macquarie decides whether or not this name will be preserved; and, if it is preserved, it is because it has the authority of a quotation. A white name, as Macquarie well knew, could draw criticism, particularly if it commemorated one's own importance, but a native name was beyond cavil: it expressed the *ultra qua non* of history.

Preserved out of context in a linguistic environment quite foreign to it, a stuffed bird in a museum case, it scarcely mattered whether the aboriginal name was the 'real' one or not. When Giles gave the name 'Petermann' to a mountain range, he commemorated a geographical personality. But he also commemorated a coincidence, explaining that the word was 'a transliteration of the aboriginals' insistent comment'.[16] His name was a quotation which concealed its origins, a name which cancelled out any traditions attaching to it. It had the authority of a pun and, shrugging off inherited meanings, it functioned magically to found a new place. It symbolized verbally a horizon beyond which history could not stray. In its foreignness to reason, it was a secular version of the phenomenon Strehlow noted in connection with the use of Walbiri words in certain Western Aranda charms:

> It is a curious fact that strange and foreign verses are often imagined as having greater potency than the local charms . . .[17]

In the absence of a shared intentional space in which translation could occur, possession by puns was the rule rather than the exception. Quotations were from the beginning quotations out of context: there was no way of authenticating them, no shared authorities. There is, then, nothing paradoxical about, say, Mitchell's eagerness to obtain aboriginal names and the superficiality of his inquiries. On his Third Expedition, according to Brough Smyth,

> There is tolerably plain evidence that he either misunderstood his own supposed interpreter, or was grossly deceived by him, in the fact that scarcely one of his native names of localities in this colony has been verified.[18]

But the value of Mitchell's 'aboriginal' names is not in the least diminished by showing them to be incorrect. Whether correct or not, the names, transcribed, fixed in maps and narratives, made sense. They enabled Mitchell to name the journey – which was precisely why he took an Aborigine with him, rather than rely on chance, and probably unintelligible, encounters. It may be of anthropological interest to ascertain that 'the true native name of the lake called "Boga" by Mitchell is "Goorm" . . .'[19] but, historically, the two names are equally meaningless, equally authoritative. Any syllable uttered would have answered, would have satisfied the dialectical condition of exploring. Any sound was a historical starting point.

In order to speak, place names had to be stripped of their meaning, reduced to mere sounds, like bird songs. If they could be translated, the purportedly aboriginal place names of the early maps might reveal themselves as nothing more than figures of speech for the act of naming, the names of what cannot be said. This is the irony of their euphony, that it signifies less than nothing, a clearing away of meaning preparatory to a history of jokes. Certainly this process is at work in the matter of personal names. Take the names appended to a petition prepared on behalf of the Aborigines of Flinders Island in Bass Strait in 1838. Amongst those 'desirous to accompany the Commandant, G. A. Robinson to Port Phillip' were Alexander, Achilles, Leonidas, Tippoo Saib, Napoleon and Neptune.[20] Comparable 'English Names' occur in Warner's 'Nominal Return of Natives present at the issue of Blankets at Lake Macquarie, and Names of those absent in the District' reported in 1833. In addition, this list included such notables as 'Nobody', 'Little Nobody' and 'Macquarie'.[21]

There is at work in these names a very interesting form of irony. Quite clearly, the names are ironic. But what is it that is being ironized? It is not the Aborigines, but rather the project of imperial history itself. For these names are not nicknames – they are not humorous appellations drawing attention to individual peculiarities. On the contrary, they are names supplied in the absence of particularities – a fact strikingly brought out by the name 'Nobody'. In calling an Aborigine 'Napoleon' or 'Macquarie', the namer is, in fact, testifying to the impotence of his historical paradigm to locate these people. The Aborigines who bear these names, the namer implies, bear no resemblance whatsoever to their names. No dialectical relationship binds the Aborigine to the cultural genealogy suggested by his name. Because of this the Aborigine transcends irony. For, as Adorno points out, irony's medium is 'the difference between ideology and reality'.[22] But, in this case, the reality and the ideology were identical. From the point of view of the census, there was no reality beyond the names. So long as there were names, it made no difference whether nobody was present or absent. He had been accounted for. As a result, history was free to go on without him.

At the very moment he is named, the Aborigine becomes someone else or nobody. But my point is that, if this process effaces the Aborigine, it also reflects on the limitations of history itself. By displaying the arbitrariness of historically important names, like Leonidas and Alexander, the namer reveals the conventional nature of historical knowledge, its dependence on authorities. Historical meaning is defined by tradition. Without shared tradition, naming falls on deaf ears. Names are laughter disguising an embarrassing silence. In this sense, what the namer ironizes is history's pretension to deal with the real world. This is mockery which is self-destructive and in this sense different from the irony of, say, Cook's place names. As I pointed out in chapter 1, Cook's names were ironic – there was apparent in them a conspicuous disproportion between the particularity of the epithet (Warning, Eagle, Glass House, etc.) and the generality of the descriptive term (Mountain, Island, etc.). But, whereas the aboriginal names work to efface difference – or better give it no room in which to emerge – Cook's names tend to preserve difference. Both terms of Cook's names belong to a single geo-historical discourse, the literature of travelling. We understand that, in naming a 'mountain', the traveller is writing his journey over the world; and, by the same token, the anecdotal character of the individual name reminds us this is not a Euclidean world, but the world of the journey. Implicit in Cook's names is the irony implicit in geography itself – that it is a travelling discourse, a historical discipline, which, at the same time, aspires to the transcendent placeless-ness and timelessness of a map. It is the constant negotiation between these different orders of knowledge which forms the basis of the explorer's irony.

But, in giving Aborigines 'English' names, naming worked quite differently. Names like 'Nobody' neither classified nor particularized. Their sole function was to distinguish. They did not function geometrically, to suggest a disposition of objects through space, but arithmetically. They were numbers, nothing more. They belonged to an Enlightenment project, not to engage the world dialectically, but through the procedures of classification and taxonomy to reduce its otherness to the uniformity of a universal knowledge. And, in this project, the early missionaries and aboriginal protectors responsible for the kind of names I have quoted were faithful servants. Their primary task was neither to convert nor to protect: it was to census. It was necessary, not only to number the Aborigines present, but, for future reference, to fix them with names. Names made them facts which could be written down time and again. Against names information (Native Names, Probable Age, Wives, Designation of Tribes, etc.) could be tabulated and preserved. Names, in short, made them white history.

The constitutional inability of imperial history to engage the Aborigines, to recognize the possibility of a different history, emerges in a variety of ways. But, underlying them all, is the question of language. The poverty of aboriginal and white exchanges prevented the development of a tacit dimension of shared assumptions out of which a common language might have come. In the absence of this, it was predictable that Australia's namers should have been afflicted by the kind of onomastic megalomania which seems to have afflicted Governor Macquarie. Macquarie, as contemporary critics pointed out, seemed incapable of making an excursion without commemorating himself and his family in place names. It was equally understandable that those in power should have been afflicted by moods of ironic self-doubt, where they lapsed into deflationary puns.

Predictably, these difficulties expressed themselves in discussions of the Aborigines' language. Was there one or many? Did the Aborigines' speech conform to rules and, if so, what were they? To what family of languages did the aboriginal tongues belong? But questions like these belonged to the same world as Banks's botanizing. They betrayed no sympathy with occasion and context. They were the questions of strangers more used to taking notes than talking. Implicit in them was a paradigm of language predicated on the fixed and repeatable conventions of writing. And, as a result, would-be students of aboriginal languages were continually baffled by what appeared to be their fluidity, their localness and changeability, their refusal to conform to a general grammar. For stability in space and time was the condition of being translatable, and hence of appropriation to a literate culture. The missionary Threlkeld gives an amusing instance of the difficulties he faced in 'getting' the language:

A man stood on the North Shore, while we were on a fishing
excursion, I noted down what the Black said was the North
Shore, using the phrase sometime afterwards, I found it was
not so, a native came to a fire one evening and the same word
was used and on paying particular attention found that it was
the Adverb over there.[23]

Has Threlkeld 'got' the word now? If we take as our authority
Beveridge, who writes of the Murray dialects, 'The adverb
stage is still a long distance off,'[24] the answer is: clearly not. In
any case, to understand the word's meaning he would need to
follow its progress through successive contexts. He would need
to see, not only where it was used, but in what circumstances
and by whom. It is the arbitrary cut in the flux of usage,
imposed upon Threlkeld by his own ambition to copy the word
down, which makes the semantic and grammatical properties of
the word obscure. What Threlkeld eloquently describes is the
character of the historical interview – that curious strategy of
colonization which, by mimicking the dialectic of dialogue,
attempts to translate a genuinely oral and spatial culture into the
book-like, museum-like discourse of a culture which claims
universal validity.

Generalizations about the Aborigines' language were even
more fraught with difficulty. According to Grey, for instance,
'a language radically the same, is spoken over the whole
continent'.[25] Brough Smyth, on the other hand, took the view
that 'The diversity of speech, the number of dialects, and
probably of distinct languages, are amazing.'[26] Anthropologists
and linguists may still debate whether aboriginal languages are
genetically related – and equally whether many aboriginal
'languages' are in fact 'dialects' – but the point here is not
merely that authorities disagreed, but that there was no other
authority they could appeal to in order to reconcile their
differences. The information on which Grey and Brough Smyth
based their conclusions almost certainly reflected their mode of
inquiry, rather than any facility with aboriginal languages.
They were answers to questions put during more or less
contrived interviews. But, when they were interviewed, the
Aborigines often seemed to mimic white preoccupations to the

point where their own identity was wholly concealed. The Aboriginal Protector Robinson, for example, writes of one such encounter:

> I had some difficulty in inventing names for them. They were not satisfied unless they had one; they wanted to be served all alike. I looked up and thought of the stars.[27]

The explorer Giles reports a comparable situation:

> Everything with them was 'What name?' They wanted to know the name of everything and everybody, and they were no wiser when they heard it.[28]

The stars provided as good a genealogy as any. In the absence of something more definite, late nineteenth-century cultural evolutionists like Brough Smyth were free to speculate that by a series of transformations the aboriginal 'kiradjee' was cognate with Greek 'cheirourgos' and hence 'surgeon'; that the aboriginal 'marrey' was cognate with 'mer' and 'mar' and even connected with Weston-super-mare.[29] These were sound arguments for drawing the Aborigines within the fold of the great human family, but they revealed nothing of the Aborigines' state of mind. Etymology had nothing to say about intentions. Any speculation about the mental world of the Aborigines could only be guesswork. Giles, for example, supposed

> The knowledge possessed by these children of the desert is preserved owing to the fact that their imaginations are untrammelled, the denizens of the wilderness, having their faculties put to but few uses, and all are concentrated on the object of obtaining food for themselves and their offspring.[30]

Grey, in flat contradiction, writes:

> to believe that man in a savage stage is endowed with freedom of thought or action is erroneous in the highest degree. He is in reality subjected to complex laws, which . . . deprive him of all free agency of thought.[31]

Whom are we to believe? Arising from interviews in which, from the outset, the Aborigines' words were plucked from their social context, transcribed (and probably misheard) and served up as piquant quotations, the authority of Grey and Giles depends on no other text than their own. Or, rather, their interpretations are no better or worse than those of the psychologists they have read.

Enough has been said to demonstrate the impotence of an empirically-based historical method in coming to terms with the historical experience of Aborigines. The traditional description of much of the content of aboriginal testimony as referring to 'myths', 'legends' and 'superstitions' reflects the poverty of a world view which cannot entertain the logic of other worlds. Perhaps this explains why there appears to be a direct relationship between the failure of history to embrace the Aborigines' post-settlement destiny and the gradual appropriation of aboriginal culture by anthropologists and, latterly, sociologists. In the great majority of 'Narratives' written in the first hundred years of European settlement, any more than passing mention of the Aborigines is relegated to the back of the book, usually to an appendix. The Aborigines are grouped together with the 'natural productions' of the country, with its fauna and flora. They find themselves, if at all, consigned to the category of miscellaneous information, sailing directions, prospects for trade, geological specimens and the climate. They inhabit the realm of the 'etc.'.

And yet, despite their marginal place in the hierarchy of knowledge, the Aborigines are, in another sense, an obvious presence throughout the same explorers' and settlers' narratives. The Aborigines may be historically enigmatic, but *spatially* they come into prominent view. The newcomers may not communicate with the Aborigines themselves, but they certainly communicate with their country. In some sense – which remains to be defined – the Whites did occupy the same country. And this obvious fact opens up the possibility that, where conventional history fails, a spatial history may succeed in suggesting the dimension in which the two cultures did interact, to create a joint and mutually intelligible tradition. Of course, this suggestion runs into difficulties of its own: for the same authorities which could not comprehend aboriginal behaviour also wanted to de-territorialize the Aborigines. It was the Aborigines' spatial command of the country which presented the greatest threat to white interests. As one of Governor Bourke's correspondents wrote, regarding the establishment of native villages around Port Phillip in 1835,

> I fully enter into the spirit of your design, which I perceive is first to get these wanderers to settle, then to endeavour to give them a taste for the enjoyments and security of civilized life.[32]

The refusal to live in one place, and hence to be accountable, was the major obstacle to the process of civilizing. As another writer complained,

> The various tribes hitherto discovered, all live in a wandering state, having neither village nor hut; but each tribe retains its peculiar province, under the jurisdiction of a petty chief.[33]

Here, in the succinctest terms, was expressed the true motive behind the establishment of villages. Herding the natives into centres, the government further centralized its own power. It was not that the Aborigines were unorganized, only that their power was distributed horizontally, dynamically. Their wandering did indeed constitute a 'state' – a form of social and political organization. But this was expressed, not as a power over past and future – the pet obsession of the usurping historical culture – but as a power over space. In view of this fundamental difference, it is not surprising that commentators steeped in the teleological lore of the Bible were baffled that 'They appear to have no reflection, no forethought.'[34] For theirs was a world of travelling, where succession, rather than stasis, was the natural order of things: succession as a spatial, rather than temporal, phenomenon. It was space which was problematic, the field of history and tactical address, not the metaphysical past and future. In this sense, it was an astute remark when one missionary observed, 'A sailor's life would suit these blacks more than any other except a gentleman's . . .'[35] But it overlooked one point: that the Aborigine did not travel for the sake of seeing new countries, but in order to continue to inhabit his own. If the white historian feels the need to validate his present by reliving the past, the Aborigine travelled in order to stay where he was. If one society saw self-loss and cultural amnesia as a function of mobility, the other saw it as a function of immobility.

Spatially, if not linguistically, the Aborigines informed the Whites at every turn. And it is this fact which enables us to get beyond the solipsism of a history merely reflecting on itself. A historical journey which begins at Botany Bay only to return to it at the end may have enriched our historical perceptions, but its symmetry risks reinforcing our isolation from all that went before 1788. Introducing the spatial history of the Aborigines, we discover that asymmetry in depth, not only indispensable to the process of exploration, but inseparable from our perception of the real world.

In 1788, Australia was already a highly cultivated space. Aboriginal occupation had created tracks and clearings: it had been responsible in all probability for the 'meadows' Cook remarked on. Instead of confronting chaotic nature, map-like in its uniformity, explorers and overlanders entered a country replete with directions. The very horizons had been channelled and grooved by aboriginal journeys. But for this, colonization would not merely have been a vastly more costly and protracted affair. In more remote regions it would have been difficult to the point of impossibility. But, as we review the overwhelming evidence for white dependence on the Aborigines' cooperation, it soon becomes clear that the bare fact that the two peoples frequently travelled together along the same tracks, that they admired and contested the same country, does not of itself throw light on the Aborigines' experience. To conceptualize the historical space of the Aborigines in terms of tracks, journeys and regions is already to appropriate it to the symbolic language of white history. The Aborigines' keen-sightedness, which so impressed the whites, was not a physical endowment: it reflected the fact that the Aborigines knew what they were looking for.

It is not simply that Aborigines ascribed different meanings to a country already there: the country itself was the product of their journeying, coming into being like a familiar text read aloud. It may be that the incidents and accidents of travelling that constituted the explorer's history of the country did not exist for the guides. They shared the same sensory experiences. Kangaroos were run down and the flesh shared. Hills were seen and names accurately ascertained. Everyone saw the clouds. But the meaning of these events, the historical significance of their spatial appearance was another matter. The world of the journey furnished a symbolic text where each culture read its own intentions. Physical overlap was no guarantee of mutual understanding. The recognizable kangaroos and clouds may have been nothing more than physical puns, objects able to bear equal and opposite meanings.

In his book *Aboriginal Tribes of Australia*, the anthropologist Tindale observes:

> A study of the tracks of explorers and pioneers who have opened up the country are [*sic*] of particular interest. Often it can be noted how they were led along tracks that happen to be boundaries between tribal groups. Where such men were accompanied by aborigines with local knowledge, it is probable that to avoid transgression of the territories of others, for which the aborigines could be held responsible, pioneer whites were always steered along tribal boundaries and through other neutral areas. Once these lines of European movement became established, they persisted. Anyone studying maps can find instances. For example, the boundary between Kitja and Malngin in northwestern Australia is followed almost exactly from Hall's Creek to Wyndham and even when approaching Wyndham the track divides two tribal territories.[36]

Even viewed empirically as lines on the map referring to real geographical objects, it is clear that tracks could bear different meanings, what was marginal to one culture serving subsequently as a central artery to another.

In the closed environment of the rain forest native tracks were not simply a convenience, but a necessity. Where one could see no further than a few feet, paths were sight-lines, literally rendering the space visible. A characteristic entry in Christy Palmerston's journal of a journey made through thick forest near the Atherton Tableland, Queensland, in 1882, reads:

> . . . scrub dense. In one mile struck a large nigger path, the largest I have seen as yet – could take horses along it easily; after travelling along it for one mile, we came into a large niggers camp.[37]

In no sense did the Whites 'come across' signs of aboriginal habitation and cultivation. The park-like open forests and plains, the tracks and water holes were not so many charming geographical exhibits in an otherwise neutral museum-like space. On the contrary, occupation occurred within the Aborigines' landscape, a cultural space whose views, horizons, scale and gradients already answered to a cultural history. It was these human signs which made the imposition of a new cultural landscape, with its own symbolic spaces, intimate, picturesque and linear, at all possible.

Like the explorers, the settlers made use of native tracks. The Western Australian anthropologist Sylvia Hallam brings together a host of material to support her statement that

> Not only in a general sense, by utilizing the same tracts of country, but in a very specific sense, by using the same network of nodes (at water sources) linked by tracks, the European pattern of land use was based on (and modified) the Aboriginal pattern.[38]

The same was true throughout colonized Australia. And it was significant, not only in a relatively closely settled area like King George's Sound in Western Australia, but also in 'outback' regions, like the mid-nineteenth-century Wimmera in Victoria. There,

> The first roads followed Aboriginal tracks from spring to spring . . . The squatters, the drovers with their flocks and herds, the shearers and the teamsters used these native ways and, to gain access to stations, added to them. The big junctions where tracks met or crossed, such as those at Dimboola, Nhill, Lawloit and Lillimur South, became natural campsites from which settlements grew.[39]

The Aborigines themselves actively collaborated in this process. To quote Hallam again, 'Aboriginal guides led the way for aboriginal dispossession in the Victoria Plains.'[40] The same was true in Victoria. With due respect to Tindale, there seems to have been no question of guiding the Whites *away* from tribal waters, although it may well have been that guides selected aboriginal springs and ponds which were then out of season.

Captain Hepburn, speaking of the occupation of country north of Mount Macedon, told Robinson: '. . . the natives had made the principal and best roads through the ranges for the whites.'[41] Referring to another squatting family, Robinson wrote, 'The black . . . first showed the Manifolds the way through the stony rises so Scott and Manifolds say. And yet they drive them away.'[42] This was the universal pattern: aboriginal cooperation followed by usurpation of aboriginal resources.

> They have been employed as guides to exploring parties and searches after land. And when the purpose of the whites have [sic] been learned the natives have been turned adrift, away, and frequently in a strange country, and destroyed by the other natives.[43]

And, if Robinson was even approximately right, when he said that in western Victoria 'half the runs have been shown by the natives',[44] the devastating impact of this expulsion on aboriginal culture can easily be imagined.

Where travellers might have met and passed, the nomadic overlanders squatted and stayed. At the very moment where the newcomers might have discovered an unfamiliar knowledge, they set about grazing and watering their stock. The Aborigines were trapped inside white space and pushed to its margins. Perhaps they unwittingly hastened their own historical eclipse in another way. Aborigines not only supplied guides, they also provided scouts. More often than not the European explorer did not lead, but was led. Mitchell comments, in the course of the third expedition, that his guide

> . . . usually explored the woods . . . for several miles in front of the column . . . my attention was, for the most part, confined to the preservation of certain bearings in our course, by frequent observations of the pocket compass; but in conducting carts where no roads existed, propitiating savage natives, taking bearings . . . I believe I was indebted to the sympathy even of my aboriginal friends.[45]

This is an eloquent description of the Aborigine's function in the Whites' spatial history. There is little difference between Mitchell's reliance on his guide to show him the way and Sturt's pleasure in floating down the Murray. The aboriginal guide allows Mitchell to retreat from his surroundings, to treat it as already discovered, and proceed to its picturesque and carto-graphical representation. His guide enables him to pretend the horizon is not there, the landscape already possessed.

But there was a further ironic result of this aboriginal leader-ship, which was that white travellers often gained the impres-sion the country they were passing through was relatively unpopulated. In explanation of Mitchell's under-estimation of the Victorian aboriginal population, the historian of the Gipps-land Aborigines, Peter Gardner, has offered two reasons: '. . . his lack of encounters with the blacks, and that he did not travel through areas of high aboriginal population . . .'[46] Some support for the first reason comes from Robinson, who reports asking natives if they knew who made the Major's Line: 'They said white man a long time ago and that black fellow too much frightened and plenty ran away.'[47] To judge from Stapylton's diary, the truth seems to have been more complicated. Mitch-ell's habit of setting up temporary depot camps, under his second-in-command, while he himself made two- or three-day forays in various directions, had the interesting consequence that, while Mitchell saw few Aborigines, Stapylton back at camp was frequently aware of their presence. Aborigines who might shadow a moving column often only appeared when the expedition camped – and Mitchell was away. Judging from Stapylton's diary local Aborigines were an almost constant presence, particularly at the more permanent camps. But it was Mitchell's narrative which was published. In any case, the fact was that, when travellers were being guided through and among a travelling nation, the interior could appear decep-tively uninhabited – an ironic fulfilment of Banks's earlier pre-diction.

Aboriginal culture unwittingly colluded in its own disrup-tion in yet another way. The tracts of open country – Cook's fine meadows – were created and kept open by the Aborigines, who periodically fired the undergrowth as a means of facilitat-ing hunting: and the result, a careful balance of visibility and invisibility, of open and closed spaces, greatly appealed to the European counterpart of the aboriginal hunter. As Mitchell acknowledged, such country gave the pastoralist an unusual advantage too:

> Fire is necessary to burn the grass, and form these open forests . . . But for this simple process the Australian woods had probably contained as thick a jungle as those of New Zealand or America instead of the open forests in which the white men now find grass for their cattle.[48]

Early overlanders who, like Ebden, were attracted to picturesquely natural places were, in fact, being drawn to a highly artificial aboriginal landscape. And, writing of south-western Australia, Hallam quotes numerous remarks from early visitors and settlers which indicate a recognition of the relationship between the open country they so prized and the Aborigines' policy of periodic firing.

As if this were not enough, the memory of the Aborigines' country was further weakened as those survivors of the usurpation were drafted into the workforce as shepherds and stockmen. Less than twenty years later, the Manifolds, whom Robinson criticized for expelling the Aborigines, were employing the survivors, noting that they were

> . . . far better acquainted with stock, more active in duty, more ready and willing, and not more expensive, although in addition to 10s. a week wages, rations have to be supplied to as many of the race and connexions as choose to hang about . . .[49]

In North Queensland, as D. May has shown, the aboriginal population represented for the pastoralists 'a large pool of cheap labour displaying attributes most advantageous to their industry.'[50] And May makes the point that 'this occurred at a time when squatters found it almost impossible to secure suitable white labour'.[51] But for the anonymous toil of generations of Aborigines, the process of colonization in more remote and economically marginal areas might have been impossible to sustain.

The influence of aboriginal culture in succouring and locating European society in Australia was considerable. But, as even this brief sketch indicates, it did not lead to any form of symbolic exchange. Spatial translation was almost wholly one way. This impression is reinforced by the character of the records themselves. The individual perpetrators of the rapes, massacres, poisonings and systematic starvation that the Aborigines endured have often been well aware that strength of arms and strength in law did not necessarily go together. They have often suppressed the events of invasion – with the curious result that historians have been tempted to invent a new dialectic, no longer between invader and invaded, but between pioneer and nature. The narratives of Tench and Hunter, for example, show that this self-censorship was at work from the earliest days of the colony: much as they denigrate the convicts, these writers close ranks with them when it comes to the issue of aboriginal attacks.

The Aboriginal Protector Robinson came across the same phenomenon in a dramatic form in Victoria half a century later. There, barely four years after the first squatter incursions, he found it almost impossible to obtain accurate information about the extent of the aboriginal massacre. Shepherd and squatter closed ranks. The circumstantial evidence was there – like the dairy station in the western district where 'In front of the hut . . . is a swivel gun to shoot blacks.'[52] But oral testimony was hard to come by. Judith Wright has described the same mason-like seal of silence among squatters in southern Queensland. But perhaps one of the most remarkable examples of this historical self-censorship occurs in the diary of Patrick Buckley, a squatter who entered Gippsland around 1840, ahead even of the explorer Angus McMillan. According to Gardner, 'A close examination of the diary proves almost conclusively that it was re-written in the years 1869–71, just before the author's death.'[53] The significance of this is that, in the re-written version, Buckley appears to have censored entries dealing with his part in the black hunts of the early 1840s.

By their conspicuous absence, by the silence surrounding them, the Aborigines have made the history of white settlement a peculiarly narrow and brittle narrative of the ruling class – for, in this context, the humblest ex-convict shepherd with a gun and the governor himself belonged to the same race of oppressors. Their wandering state has made the Aborigines

343

peculiarly easy to manipulate rhetorically, as well as physically. Their occasional nature has made them the servant of white occasions. They have been moved about the stage of white history with the ease of stage props – in order to create an effect, to authenticate a particular vision. Thus, on one occasion, Eyre can write, '. . . the very regions, which, in the eyes of the European, are most barren and worthless, are to the native the most valuable and productive'.[54] On another, though, Eyre blandly refers to '. . . the native grass affording subsistence to the kangaroos of the natives, as well as to the wild cattle of the Europeans'.[55] The first observation occurs in the context of Eyre's own continuing inability to penetrate the interior, the second in the context of a benevolent essay appended to his expedition journals: it is the rhetorical place which lends these contradictory remarks coherence, not any advance in knowledge. Similarly, Mitchell, the punctilious observer, could openly acknowledge that the characteristic Australian plains, so attractive to white pastoralists, were an aboriginal creation. He could even understand

> How natural must be the aversion of the natives to the intrusion of another race of men with cattle: people who recognize no right in the aborigines to either the grass they have thus *worked* from infancy, nor to the kangaroos they have hunted with their fathers.[56]

But this did not prevent him from writing, at the climax of his fourth expedition, when he was intent on realizing his epic vision of a country reserved for the white man,

> Those splendid plains where, without a horse, man seems a helpless animal, are avoided, and are said to be shunned and disliked by the aboriginal man of the woods.[57]

The Whites treated the Aborigines' spatial history like their language. Pools, pastures and tracks were taken out of context and used, like quotations, to symbolize their own historical presence. They were punning authorities which made cultivation look natural. Here was a country *waiting* to be occupied. All too quickly the brittle criss-cross of the newcomers' gaze sliced up and fenced off what had formerly been imagined. The result was the collapse of aboriginal space, its flight inwards into isolated objects, its fragmentation into farms. The tension of history which held the country open like a book closed up. What was left of the aboriginal presence was not a history in Nietzsche's sense of a 'history for life', but accumulating piles of archaeological relics, objects in the absence of a spatial tradition, boomerangs which no one could throw.

Aboriginal ways of thinking about the world they inhabit, their historical space, have been increasingly clarified by recent anthropologists. Tindale might have felt a methodological need to plot aboriginal 'boundaries' on the unhistoried space of the white map, but as he himself notes elsewhere, when he questioned Aborigines about their territories, they tended to describe them as a succession of camp-sites. As they spoke, they might draw what they were talking about in the sand; and what they drew was a line, a way, rather than a circled territory. The last and the first camp-site might be the same place, but they were represented at opposite ends of the line. Another anthropologist, R. Moyle, amplifies this point in his discussion of the Alyawarra and their 'country'. Boundary points are almost always water sources. Any water source between boundary points is itself a boundary point. On the other hand, relatively little significance attaches to the land between such boundary points. Moyle observes that, besides representing the most distant points over which informants had exclusive religious rights, these boundary sites

> . . . are also ecologically reliable outposts beyond which the location, quality and quantity of drinking water cannot be consistently guaranteed in any given direction or within any given distance.[58]

For the Alyawarra, boundary sites lie at the centre of things, not at their periphery. The idea of the boundary area as 'points capable of confirmation by means of a visual survey from a single position on the ground' is, Moyle says, 'foreign to Alyawarra thinking'.[59]

These observations reinforce the point that the anthropologist's interest in fixing boundaries and territories resembles the archaeologist's fascination with relics and sites: both activities divorce the objects of study from the context of their production, that living space in which places have histories and implements are put to use. To describe a country is not to stand back, as if one were not there, but to travel it again. For Aborigines, to travel a country is to *tell* it, to represent it to oneself. The anthropologist Helen Payne draws attention to how, in the Pukatja community in northern South Australia, '. . . whenever women visited their sites, or were questioned about them, they would enact the items naming them'.[60] Journeying with a group of central Australia women, another anthropologist notes, '. . . all the way out from Willowra, the women sang the songs of the country as they travelled through it . . . they sang, danced and felt the country'.[61] Here the idea of spatial history is a tautology. Travelling and story-telling are inseparable from each other. The country is not the setting of stories, but the stories and songs themselves. The re-enactment of the country does not occur on a stage: it is what brings the country into being and keeps it alive.

History is not a form of writing, a linear archive manufactured after the event. Instead, history and the making of history are one and the same thing. It is not simply that there is no writing: in the spatial history of the Aborigines, even the voice enjoys no special privileges. Dancing and drawing are equally important means of spatial telling. According to Nancy Munn, the Walbiri of the Northern Territory make no distinction between drawing and story-telling. In her experience, as the women related their everyday experience or dreams, as the men narrated journeys of their ancestral beings, they drew designs in the sand. Walbiri designs did not 'illustrate' the story. On the contrary, the songs and designs were '. . . treated as complementary channels of communication; each is a repository of narrative meaning, and the production of one may evoke the other'.[62] The character of this unwritten, enacted spatial history is ably generalized by the French cultural theorists Gilles Deleuze and Felix Guattari in their book *Anti-Oedipe*.

Primitive forms of expression are oral, vocal, but not because they lack a system of writing: a dance on the earth, a pattern on a wall, a design on the body are systems of writing, spatial writing [*un géo-graphisme*], a geography. These forms of expression are oral precisely because they possess a system of writing which is independent of the voice, which neither aligns itself with the voice nor is subordinated to it, but which is linked with it, coordinated within a radiating, multi-dimensional structure. (And it is necessary to say that the opposite is true of linear writing: cultures only cease to be oral when they forfeit the independence and autonomous dimensions of a system of writing; it is in aligning itself with the voice that writing both supplants the voice and introduces a fictional voice.)[63]

The fictional voice is the voice which can tell its story anywhere and over and over again. It is the voice of white history. Short of abandoning linear writing, short of writing no more books, how, then, is a history of aboriginal space to be written? What kind of representation could make present to us the historical space which has been so effectively excluded from our own historical narratives?

There can surely be no question of naive imitation. An anthropologist like Charles Mountford might travel the country of the desert nomads and produce a book in which, in fascinating detail, he narrates, draws and photographs the Aborigines' historical space.[64] But, while this respects the spatial reference of the aboriginal texts, it cannot, of course, initiate us into the history of the journeys it describes. Mountford's one-way journeys, his extraordinarily detailed, but nevertheless unique and linear narrative, can hardly evoke the wandering state in which things are fixed by virtue of motion, a state in which the Aborigines' travelling is a form of eternal return and, in this sense, highly self-referential. For the Aborigines, their journeys are a way of not forgetting, of conjuring up what might be otherwise lost. Re-enacting stories, bringing distant things near, they give back to metaphor its primary spatial meaning.

But, even taking account of this may involve one in an imitative fallacy of another kind. It is not, for example, enough – as some Australian historians and artists are now doing – simply to 'deconstruct' the devices of imperial history. To replace the uni-vocal linearity of conventional history with a 'bricolage' of 'texts' (photographs, oral testimonies, theoretical commentary, anthropological notes) is undoubtedly a spectacular way of imitating, amongst other things, the open-ended, occasional character of the journal and the journey. It demonstrates clearly the incommensurability of authorities or, better, the authority of all viewpoints. But such an approach still perpetrates an illusion of its own: that, in some way, the multidimensional spatiality of aboriginal culture is hereby being *imitated*.

The device of the historian absenting himself as author, that the Australian writer and academic Stephen Muecke adopts in his 'co-authored' book *Reading the Country*[65], where he edits visual, oral and written texts to suggest multiple routes across a particular tract of country near Broome in north-western Australia, certainly illustrates the 'textuality' of our knowledge of a place – the sense in which cultural frames of reference influence how we see. Krim Benterrak, the artist in this book, records one country, Paddy Roe, a local Aborigine (and inspiration of the enterprise) narrates another, the theoretically informed Muecke constructs yet another: but the implication that, by editing these different versions, by cutting them and overlaying them, we can attain to the multi-dimensionality of an aboriginal narrative seems to me an editorial illusion. 'This book', writes Muecke of *Reading the Country*, 'is a record of Paddy Roe's dreaming at its most important nexus: the country itself.'[66] But, rather, it is a valuable record of the dismantling of certain white historical myths: to suppose there is a natural correspondence between this and the 'nomadic discourse' of the Aborigine is to be guilty, it seems to me, of an imitative fallacy.

The limitation of this kind of deconstructive reading is that, while it reveals a sophisticated understanding of 'reading', it remains fundamentally empirical in its assumptions about spatial experience. The 'country' may be 'written over' by many discourses, but it remains, for all that, there, an *a priori* place, something to be read. Spatial, unlike discursive, horizons remain unmapped. It may be symptomatic that, while Muecke follows the thesis of Deleuze and Guattari, that nomadic knowledge represents an alternative kind of power to that implicit in the centralized, imperial discourses of the West, he appears to imagine the contest between these world-views taking place in a space already constituted imperially. Muecke concludes,

> It is the country, therefore, which slowly produced the nomadism of the Aboriginal peoples who had lived there for so long. It was not they who suddenly decided to choose among a variety of 'social systems' and found nomadism to be the most suitable.[67]

But, as we have seen, historically speaking, the country did not precede the traveller: it was the offspring of his intention. His distinctive way of viewing the world did not develop under the impress of external circumstances alone. The country did not teach him how to read. Rather, he found there what he was looking for. And what he, the nomad, black or white, symbolized, when he wrote or danced or simply made tracks, was not the physical country, but the enactment of a historical space. In his writings, whether in the form of fences or journals, what he sought to re-enact symbolically was the figure of intention that brought the country into focus in the first place.

It is here, in recognizing the intentional nature of historical activity, that the possibility of *writing* an aboriginal spatial history emerges. A cross-cultural history, as Muecke shows us, has to be, in some sense, dialectical: it has to see what aboriginal perceptions have to tell us about the limitations of white history. But, after the critical dismantling, there has to be something more: a restoration of meaning, a process which cannot avoid being interpretative and imaginative. This is what the philosopher of intentionality, Edmund Husserl, understood when he complained that 'Greater and greater segments of this life lapse into a kind of talking and reading that is dominated purely by association.'[68] Husserl imagined '. . . the possible activity of a recollection in which the past experiencing is lived through in a quasi-new and quasi-active way'.[69]

Recollection is not passive imitation inspired by antiquarian zeal. It is active re-creation. Belonging to the 'activity of concurrent actual production', its relation with the past is at best metaphorical. In this way, by shifting the emphasis from the *object* of recollection to the reflective *attitude* in which recollection occurs, Husserl argues, '. . . what has now been realized in original fashion is the same as what was previously self-evident'.[70]

An aboriginal history of space would, then, be a symbolic history. It would not be an anthropologist's account of the Aborigines' beliefs. Nor would it be a history of frontiers and massacres. Rather than seek by a newly ingenious means to translate the otherness of their experience into empirical terms, it might take the form of a meditation on the absent other of our own history. It might begin in the recognition of the suppressed spatiality of our own historical consciousness. It would not be a question of comparing and contrasting the *content* of our spatial experience, but of recognizing its form and its historically constitutive role. A history of space which revealed the everyday world in which we live as the continuous intentional re-enactment of our spatial history might say not a word about 'The Aborigines'. But, by recovering the intentional nature of our grasp on the world, it might evoke their historical experience without appropriating it to white ends.

A spatial history of this kind would stand in a metaphorical relationship to the history the Aborigines tell themselves. It would be a comparable reflection on different historical content. And, naturally, since the medium of white history is writing, it would not simply be a book about the language of recollection. If it were to avoid the kind of passive associationism Husserl refers to, it would have to enact the language of recollection. Such a history, giving back to metaphor its ontological role and recovering its historical space, would inevitably and properly be a poetic history.

There is a passage in the journal of the explorer Grey where he describes an Aborigine setting out to hunt:

The moment an Australian savage commences his day's hunting, his whole manner and appearance undergo a won-drous change: his eyes, before heavy and listless, brighten up, and are never for a moment fixed on one object; his gait and movements, which were indolent and slow, become quick and restless, yet noiseless; he moves along with a rapid, stealthy pace, his glance roving from side to side in a vigilant uneasy manner, arising from his eagerness to detect signs of game, and his fears of hidden foes. The earth, the water, the trees, the skies, each are in turn subjected to a rigid scrutiny, and from the most insignificant circumstances he deduces omens – his head is held erect, and his progress is uncertain, in a moment his pace is checked, he stands in precisely the position of motion as if suddenly transfixed, nothing about him stirs, but his eyes, they glance uneasily from side to side, whilst the head and every muscle seem immoveable; but the white eye-balls, may be seen in rapid motion, whilst all his faculties are concentrated, and his whole soul absorbed in the senses of sight and hearing.[71]

Here, in a metaphorical way, is set out the scope of a spatial history, one which takes us back, not to chronological origins, but to the study of intentions. For here is described a figure ready for any eventuality; a figure at once spontaneous and wholly dominated by the space of his desire. Here, in this attitude, at once active and recollective, is history in motion. But here, too, is the historian, consciously re-creating what is self-evident, striving for a comparable immediacy, achieving it by careful revision. And not only by stylistic means, but also by adopting a point of view, isolating his hunter in the ring of a telescope, his silence the product of distance. Here, then, is the writer as hunter, tracking down *his* prey. Here, in the intentional space of their activity, two cultures meet without bloodshed – a fact which Grey perhaps wished to signify when he portrayed a native hunting as the frontispiece of his book (plate 22). At any rate, the Aborigine, whose stance so closely, and ironically, prefigures that of the flag-waving sailor of Captain Cook's Landing (plate 1) is a salutary reminder of those invisible differences which imperial history's attachment to visible, repeatable facts effectively leaves out.

Recovering the intentional common place of history, we could begin to understand how it was possible for the natives to remain 'intirely unmov'd' by the *Endeavour*, why they continued 'attentive to their business', why the 'Idea of traffick' did not cross their minds. We would come to understand an intensity of intention which the proliferation of the unreflective media does all in its power to suppress. We might come to see the way in which historical activity, day-to-day experience, is never merely routine, but always, possibly, an original recovery of what was previously self-evident. There would be no question of imputing this quality of introspection to the Aborigine 'in his natural state': it would be the outcome of what Husserl calls the 'activity of concurrent actual production'. This history might be a beginning.

Notes

Introduction

1. Banks, Sir J., *The Endeavour Journal, 1768–1771*, ed. J. C. Beaglehole, Sydney, 1962, vol. 2, p. 63.
2. Clark, C. M. H., *A History of Australia*, vol. 1, *From the Earliest Times to the Age of Macquarie*, Melbourne, 1962, p. 87.
3. Tench, W., *A Narrative of the Expedition to Botany Bay*, Sydney, 1961, p. 38.
4. McIntyre, K. G., *The Secret Discovery of Australia*, Sydney, 1982, p. 214.
5. Blainey, G., *Our Side of the Country*, Sydney, 1984, p. 17.
6. Boswell, J., *Journal of a Tour to the Hebrides*, ed. F. A. Pottle, Yale, 1963, p. 165.

Chapter 1

1. Robertson, J., *The Captain Cook Myth*, Sydney, 1981, pp. 140ff.
2. Cook, James, *The Journals of Captain James Cook on his Voyages of Discovery*, Cambridge, 1955, ed. J. C. Beaglehole and others, vol. 1, *The Voyage of the Endeavour, 1768–1771*, p. cciv.
3. De Quincey, T., 'On Style' in *Works*, Edinburgh, 1854, vol. VI, pp. 169–70.
4. Beaglehole, J. C., *The Life of Captain James Cook*, London, 1974. See chapters 2, 3 and 4 for these details.
5. Cook, James, *op. cit.*, p. 299.
6. *Ibid*, pp. 315 and 374.
7. *Ibid*, p. 342.
8. *Ibid*, p. 48.
9. Anon. (James Magra?), *A Journal of a Voyage round the World . . . Undertaken in Pursuit of Natural Knowledge, at the Desire of the Royal Society*, London, 1771, p. 116.
10. Bonwick, J., *Captain Cook in New South Wales*, London, 1901, pp. 28–9.

11. Watson, F., 'Lieutenant James Cook and his Voyages in H.M. Bark Endeavour', Sydney, 1933, p. 37.
12. Cook, James, *op. cit.*, p. ccix.
13. Bonwick, J., *An Octogenarian's Reminiscences*, London, 1902, p. 205.
14. Watson, F., *The Beginnings of Government in Australia*, Sydney, 1913, Preface.
15. Mitchell, Dr. A. M., 'Frederick Watson and Historical Records of Australia', *Historical Studies*, vol. 20, October 1982, p. 185.
16. Beaglehole, *op. cit.*, p. 698.
17. Cook, James, *op. cit.*, p. 501.
18. Cook, James, *op. cit.*, p. 172.
19. *Ibid.*, p. 172.
20. Beaglehole, *op. cit.*, p. 198.
21. Stearn, W. T., *Three Prefaces on Linnaeus and Robert Brown*, Weinheim, 1962, p. xi.
22. *Ibid.*, p. xii.
23. Goldsmith, O., *History of the Earth and Animated Nature*, London, 1876, vol. 1, p. 230.
24. Quoted by Stearn, *op. cit.*, p. xiv.
25. Sachs, J. von, *History of Botany (1530–1860)*, trans. H. E. Garnsey, Oxford, 1890, p. 108.
26. *Ibid.*, p. 109.
27. Banks, Sir J., *op. cit.*, vol. 2, p. 59.
28. *Ibid.*, p. 100.
29. *Ibid.*, p. 112.
30. *Ibid.*, p. 116.
31. *Ibid.*, p. 122.
32. Cook, James, *op. cit.*, p. 52.
33. *Ibid.*, p. 399.
34. Beaglehole, *op. cit.*, p. 252n.
35. *Ibid.*, p. 246.
36. Cook, James, *op. cit.*, p. 501.
37. *Ibid.*, p. 505.
38. *Ibid.*, p. 500.
39. *Ibid.*, pp. 387–8.
40. *Ibid.*, p. 222.
41. Banks, Sir J., *op. cit.*, vol. 2, p. 52.
42. Locke, J., *An Essay Concerning Human Understanding*, ed. P. H. Nidditch, Oxford, 1975, p. 508.
43. Ricoeur, P., *The Rule of Metaphor*, trans. R. Czerny, Toronto, 1977, p. 143.
44. *Ibid.*, p. 17.
45. Adorno, T., *Minima Moralia*, London, 1978, p. 218.

Chapter 2

1. Fletcher, B. H., *Ralph Darling, A Governor Maligned*, Oxford, 1985, p. 73.
2. De Quincey, T., 'Wordsworth and Southey', *op. cit.*, vol. II, p. 330.
3. *Ibid.*, vol. II, p. 330.
4. Tench, W., *Sydney's First Four Years*, ed. L. F. Fitzhardinge, Sydney, 1961, p. 31.
5. *Ibid.*, pp. 31–2.
6. *Ibid.*, p. 65.
7. *Ibid.*, p. 155.
8. *Ibid.*, p. 215n.
9. *Ibid.*, p. 116, n. 22.
10. Hunter, J., *A Historical Journal of the Transactions at Port Jackson and Norfolk Island*, London, 1793 (reprint 1968), p. 162.
11. Tench, W., *op. cit.*, p. 319.
12. Hawkesworth, J., *An Account of the Voyages undertaken by the Order of His Present Majesty for making Discoveries in the Southern Hemisphere*, London, 1773, 3 vols., vol. 3, p. 97.
13. Cook, James, *op. cit.*, p. 309.
14. Field, Barron (ed.), *Geographical Memoirs on New South Wales: By Various Hands*, London, 1825, pp. 423–4.
15. Smith, B., *European Vision and the South Pacific, 1768–1850*, Oxford, 1960, pp. 182–3.
16. Hume, D., *A Treatise of Human Nature*, ed. A. D. Lindsay, 1934, London, vol. 1, p. 22.
17. *Ibid.*, vol. 1, p. 77.
18. Field, Barron, *op. cit.*, p. 430.
19. Hovell, W. H., and Hume, H., *Journal of Discovery to Port Phillip, New South Wales*, ed. W. Bland, Sydney, 1831, p. 51.
20. Eyre, E. J., *Journals of Expeditions of Discovery into Central Australia and overland from Adelaide to King George's Sound, 1840–1*, London, 1845, 2 vols., vol. 1, p. 94.
21. Breton, W. H., *Excursions in New South Wales, Western Australia and Van Diemen's Land*, London, 1833, p. 373.
22. Sturt, C., *Narrative of an Expedition into Central Australia*, London, 1849, 2 vols., vol. 1, p. 168.
23. Sturt, C., *Two Expeditions into the Interior of Southern Australia*, London, 1833, 2 vols., vol. 1, p. xliv.
24. Eyre, E. J., *op. cit.*, vol. 1, p. 65.
25. *Ibid.*, vol. 1, p. 41.
26. Stokes, J. L., *Discoveries in Australia*, London, 1846, 2 vols., vol. 2, p. 268.
27. *Ibid.*, vol. 2, p. 484.

28. Mitchell, T. L., *Three Expeditions into the Interior of Eastern Australia*, London, 1838, 2nd edition, 1839, 2 vols., vol. 2, pp. 252–3.
29. Eyre, E. J., *op. cit.*, vol. 2, p. 113.
30. Sturt, C., *Narrative*, vol. 1, p. 88.
31. Richards, J. A. (ed.), *Fourteen Journeys Across the Blue Mountains*, Hobart, 1979, p. 82.
32. Mitchell, T. L., *Three Expeditions*, vol. 1, p. 158.
33. *Ibid.*, vol. 2, p. 179.
34. Grant, A. J., 'Cartography and Australian Place Names' in *Cartography*, vol. 5, 1964, p. 103.
35. May, J., *Kant's Concept of Geography*, Toronto, 1970, p. 72.
36. McKinlay, J., *Journal of Exploration in the Interior of Australia*, Melbourne, 1861, p. 2.
37. Warburton, P. G., *Journey across the Western Interior of Australia*, London, 1878, p. 194.
38. Stuart, J. M., *Exploration across the Continent of Australia*, Melbourne, 1865, p. 179.
39. Gregory, A. C., and F. T. Gregory, *Journals of Australian Explorations*, Adelaide, 1884, p. 128.
40. Eyre, E. J., *op. cit.*, vol. 1, p. 26.
41. Hume, D., *op. cit.*, p. 21.
42. Warburton, P. G., *op. cit.*, p. 285.
43. Sturt, C., *Two Expeditions*, vol. 2, p. 86.
44. *Ibid.*, vol. 1, p. xiii.
45. *Ibid.*, vol. 1, p. 76.
46. Burnet, T., *The Theory of the Earth*, London, 1684, pp. 230–1.
47. Cotton, J., *The Correspondence of John Cotton*, ed. G. Mackaness, Sydney, 1953, part 2, p. 36.
48. Mitchell, T. L., *Three Expeditions*, vol. 2, p. 34.
49. Mitchell, T. L., *Journal of an Expedition into the Interior of Tropical Australia*, London, 1848, p. 76.
50. Lhotsky, J., *A Journey from Sydney to the Australian Alps*, Sydney, 1835, p. 26.
51. *Ibid.*, p. 223n.
52. *Ibid.*, p. 100.
53. Curr, E. M., *The Australian Race*, Melbourne, 1886, 4 vols., vol. 1, p. xvii.
54. Smyth, R. Brough, *Aborigines of Victoria*, Melbourne, 1878, 2 vols., vol. 2, p. 3.
55. Parker, E. S., 'The Aborigines of Australia, A Lecture' in E. Morrison, *Frontier Life in the Loddon Protectorate*, Daylesford, Victoria, 1967, pp. 20–1.
56. Beveridge, P., *The Aborigines of Victoria and Riverina*, Melbourne, 1889, p. 174.

57. *Ibid.*, p. 125.
58. *Ibid.*, p. 173.
59. Cunningham, P., *Two Years in New South Wales*, ed. D. S. Macmillan, Sydney, 1966, p. 21.
60. Stokes, J. L., *op. cit.*, vol. 2, pp. 241–2.
61. Corris, P., *Aborigines and Europeans in Western Victoria*, A.I.A.S., Canberra, 1968, p. 53.
62. Mitchell, T. L., *Three Expeditions*, vol. 2, p. 174.
63. *Ibid.*, vol. 1, pp. 174–5.
64. *Ibid.*, vol. 2, p. 285n.
65. Curr, E. M., *op. cit.*, p. xvii.
66. Mitchell, T. L., *Journal*, p. 124.
67. *Ibid.*, p. 81.
68. Johnson, S., *The Idler*, No. 97, 23 February 1760.
69. Jameson, F., 'Postmodernism and Consumer Society' in *Postmodern Culture*, ed. H. Foster, London, 1983, p. 114.
70. Darwin, C., *Journal of Researches into the Natural History and Geology of the countries visited during the voyage of H.M.S. Beagle etc.*, New York, 1896, p. 417.

Chapter 3

1. Bunce, D., *Australasiatic Reminiscences*, Melbourne, 1857, p. 1.
2. *Ibid.*, p. 1.
3. *Ibid.*, pp. 1–2.
4. Hamilton, G., *Experiences of a Colonist Forty Years Ago*, Adelaide, 1880, reprint 1974, p. 38.
5. Hamilton, G., *A Journey from Port Phillip to South Australia in 1839*, p. 43.
6. Greig, A. W., 'The Official Foundation of Melbourne' in *Victorian Historical Magazine*, vol. 7, no. 1, p. 39.
7. Advertisement in Sturt, C., *Narrative*, vol. 1, p. 418.
8. *Ibid.*, vol. 1, p. 417.
9. Sturt, C., *ibid.*, vol. 1, pp. 405–6.
10. Robinson, G. A., *Journals*, ed. G. Presland, Records of the Victorian Archaeological Survey (RVAS), no. 5, p. 23.
11. Stuart, J. M., *op. cit.*, p. 333.
12. Leichhardt, F. W. L., *Journal of an Overland Expedition in Australia from Moreton Bay to Port Essington . . . 1844–1845*, London, 1847, p. 267.
13. Forrest, Sir J., *Explorations in Australia*, London, 1875, p. 192.
14. Giles, E., *Australia Twice Traversed*, London, 1889, 2 vols., vol. 1, p. 157.
15. Gregory, A.C. and F. T., *op. cit.*, p. 137.

16. *Ibid.*, p. 137.
17. Stuart, J. M., *op. cit.*, p. 345.
18. Giles, E., *op. cit.*, vol. 1, p. 23.
19. *Ibid.*, p. 23.
20. Warburton, P. G., *op. cit.*, p. 221.
21. Sturt, C., *Narrative*, vol. 1, p. 63.
22. Mitchell, T. L., *Journal*, p. 332.
23. Bowles, J., *Poetical Works*, Edinburgh, 1855, vol. 1, p. 288. See also Cowper, W., *Poetical Works*, Edinburgh, 1854, vol. 1, p. 110.
24. Coleridge, S. T., *Notebooks*, ed. K. Coburn, Princeton, 1973, vol. 3, no. 3921.
25. Southey, R., *The Poetical Works*, London, 1850, p. 106.
26. Stokes, J. L., *op. cit.*, vol. 1, p. 347.
27. Sturt, C., *Two Expeditions*, vol. 1, p. 137.
28. Warburton, P. G., *op. cit.*, p. 250.
29. Stokes, J. L., *op. cit.*, vol. 2, p. 317.
30. *Ibid.*, pp. 285–6.
31. Giles, E., *op. cit.*, vol. 2, p. 153.
32. Leichhardt, F. W. L., *op. cit.*, pp. 265–6.
33. Webster, E. M., *Whirlwinds in the Plain*, Melbourne, 1980, pp. 47–8.
34. Eyre, E. J., *op. cit.*, vol. 1, p. 327.
35. Sturt, C., *Narrative*, vol. 1, p. 222.
36. Dutton, G., *The Hero as Murderer*, London, 1967, p. 114.
37. Beale, E., *Sturt: The Chipped Idol*, Sydney, 1979, p. 227.
38. Sturt, C., *Narrative*, vol. 1, p. 400.
39. Beale, E., *op. cit.*, quoted from Browne's *Journal*, p. 228.
40. Sturt, C., *Narrative*, vol. 1, p. 405.
41. *Ibid.*, vol. 1, p. 403.
42. Eyre, E. J., *op. cit.*, vol. 2, pp. 1–2.
43. *Ibid.*, vol. 2, p. 113.
44. Ricoeur, P., *op. cit.*, pp. 81–2.
45. Stokes, J. L., *op. cit.*, vol. 1, p. 105.
46. Banks, Sir, J., *op. cit.*, p. 104.
47. Eyre, E. J., *op. cit.*, vol. 1, pp. 348ff.
48. *Ibid.*, vol. 2, p. 68.
49. Sturt, C., *Narrative*, vol. 1, p. 176.
50. *Ibid.*, p. 179.
51. *Ibid.*, p. 319.
52. *Ibid.*, p. 397.
53. *Ibid.*, p. 252.
54. *Ibid.*, vol. 2, p. 43.
55. *Ibid.*, vol. 1, p. 370.
56. *Ibid.*, vol. 2, p. 38.
57. *Ibid.*, vol. 1, p. 398.

58. Hutton, J., 'Theory of the Earth', 1788 in *Contributions to the History of Geology*, ed. G. W. White, vol. 5, New York, 1973, p. 46.
59. Sturt, C., *Narrative*, vol. 1, p. 33.
60. *Ibid.*, vol. 1, p. 34.
61. *Ibid.*, vol. 1, p. 382.
62. *Ibid.*, vol. 2, pp. 29–30.

Chapter 4

1. Grey, Sir G., *Expeditions in Western Australia, 1837–1839*, London, 1841, vol. 1, p. 224.
2. Foster, W. C., *Sir Thomas Livingston Mitchell and his World, 1792–1855*, Sydney, 1985.
3. Mitchell, T. L., *Field Books*, Mitchell Library, Sydney, C52.
4. Mitchell, T. L., *Outlines of a System of Surveying for Geographical and Military Purposes*, London, 1827, p. 26.
5. Mitchell, *Field Books*, C52.
6. Mitchell, T. L., *Journal*, p. 309.
7. Mitchell, T. L., *Three Expeditions*, pp. 174–5.
8. Stapylton, G. C., *With Major Mitchell's Australia Felix Expedition, 1836*, ed. E. J. Andrews, Hobart, 1986, p. 128.
9. *Ibid.*, p. 138.
10. *Ibid.*, p. 49.
11. Mitchell, T. L., *Journal*, p. 332.
12. *Ibid.*, p. 332.
13. *Ibid.*, p. 332.
14. *Ibid.*, p. 309.
15. Foster, *op. cit.*, p. 402.
16. Sturt, C., *Narrative*, vol. 2, p. 86.
17. Finlayson, B., 'Sir Thomas Mitchell and Lake Salvator: An Essay in Ecological History' in *Historical Studies*, vol. 21. October 1984, p. 212.
18. Gardiner, L. B., *Thomas Mitchell*, Melbourne, 1962, p. 30.
19. Stapylton, G. C., *op. cit.*, p. 49.
20. Mitchell, T. L., *Outlines*, p. 52.
21. Randell, J. O., *Pastoral Settlement in Northern Victoria*, Melbourne, 1982, vol. 1, p. 154.
22. *Ibid.*, p. 154.
23. *Ibid.*, p. 155.
24. Robinson, G. A., *Journals*, ed. G. Presland, RVAS, p. 80.
25. *Ibid.*, p. 74.
26. Robinson, G. A., *Journals*, ed. G. Presland, RVAS, no. 11, October 1980, p. 80.
27. Robinson, G. A., *Journals*, RVAS, no. 5, p. 60.
28. Mitchell, T. L., *Three Expeditions*, vol. 2, p. 171.

29. Mitchell, T. L., *Journal*, p. v.
30. See Jeans, D. N., *An Historical Geography of New South Wales to 1901*, Sydney, 1972, pp. 108–9, for the advantages and disadvantages of the rectangular grid survey.
31. Flanagan, R., *The History of New South Wales*, London, 1862, p. 142.
32. Maslen, T. J., *Friend of Australia*, p. 21.
33. *Ibid.*, p. 62.
34. *Ibid.*, p. 96.
35. Mitchell, T. L., *Field Books*, C21, p. 15.
36. *Ibid.*, C34, 19 January 1826.
37. *Ibid.*, C21, p. 183.
38. *Ibid.*, C28, n.p.
39. *Ibid.*, C39, February 1827 *passim*.
40. *Ibid.*, C19, frequent references and *Three Expeditions,* vol. 2, p. 190.
41. Mitchell, T. L., *Journal*, p. 245.
42. Mitchell, T. L., *Three Expeditions*, vol. 1, p. 5.
43. *Ibid.*, vol. 1, p. 5.
44. Mitchell, T. L., *Field Books*, C42, 15 June, 1830.
45. Mitchell, T. L., *Journal*, p. v.
46. Stapylton, G. C., *op. cit.*, p. 124. Andrews (*ibid.*, p. 117) assumes the name Ilyssus alludes to Dido's Tyrian name, Elissa. However, in classical times a stream called the Ilissus actually existed near Athens (see *The Oxford Classical Dictionary*, ed. N. G. L. Hammond and H. H. Scullard, Oxford, 1978, p. 142). Whatever Stapylton and Mitchell thought the name alluded to, the epic association with the foundation of a civilization was clearly uppermost in both their minds.
47. *Ibid.*, p. 148.
48. *Ibid.*, p. 179.
49. Mitchell, T. L., *Three Expeditions*, vol. 2, p. 179.
50. Mitchell, T. L., *The Lusiads of Camões*, London, 1853, p. vii.
51. *Ibid.*, p. vii.
52. *Ibid.*, p. vi.
53. *Ibid.*, p. vii.
54. *Ibid.*, p. vii.
55. Mitchell, T. L., *Three Expeditions*, vol. 1, p. 165.
56. *Ibid.*, vol. 2, p. 171.
57. Mitchell, T. L., *Journal*, p. 292.
58. *Ibid.*, p. 332. It may be worth stressing here that, although his translation of the *Lusiads* was published in 1853 – some five years after the Journal of his Fourth Expedition – Mitchell's interest in the poem *was* 'life-long'. Apologizing in the Preface for the 'rough chiseling' of his translation, Mitchell claims that 'most of it came into shape . . . under water, in a small clipper, during a voyage round Cape Horn' (i.e. in 1851–2). Is this evidence of a prodigious literary feat or a pardonable

exaggeration? The higher poetic quality of Mitchell's rendering of the earlier stanzas suggests the latter and that Mitchell was already immersing himself in Camões's world years before rounding Cape Horn.

59. Mitchell, T. L., *Field Books*, C28, n.p.
60. Mitchell, T. L., *Three Expeditions*, vol. 1, pp. 231–96.
61. *Ibid.*, vol. 1, p. 221.
62. *Ibid.*, vol. 1, p. 241.
63. *Ibid.*, vol. 1, p. 244.
64. *Ibid.*, vol. 1, p. 266.
65. *Ibid.*, vol. 1, p. 235.
66. *Ibid.*, vol. 1, p. 304.
67. *Ibid.*, vol. 1, p. 241.
68. *Ibid.*, vol. 1, p. 249.
69. *Ibid.*, vol. 1, pp. 246–8.
70. *Ibid.*, vol. 1, p. 269.
71. *Ibid.*, vol. 1, p. 270.
72. *Ibid.*, vol. 1, p. 271.
73. Tindale, N. B., *Aboriginal tribes of Australia*, Los Angeles, 1974, p. 198 (for Ngemba) and p. 195 (for Kula).
74. *Ibid.*, p. 197.
75. *Ibid.*, p. 192.
76. Mitchell, T. L., *Field Books*, C52, 9 August 1835.
77. *Ibid.*, 9 August 1835.
78. Mitchell, T. L., *Lusiads*, p. 171.
79. Mitchell, T. L., *Journal*, p. 224.
80. *Ibid.*, facing p. 225. I say 'presumably' because, quite as remarkable as Mitchell's disappearing lake is the lacuna in Mitchell's text at this point: although Martin's Range is included in the List of Illustrations, the engraving itself is mysteriously absent from most copies of Mitchell's *Journal* I have consulted. Finlayson himself reproduces a sketch for the engraving, not the engraving itself.
81. *Ibid.*, pp. 202–3.
82. *Ibid.*, p. 295.
83. *Ibid.*, p. 297.
84. *Ibid.*, p. 309.
85. *Ibid.*, p. 310.
86. *Ibid.*, p. 310.
87. *Ibid.*, pp. 311–12.
88. *Ibid.*, p. 226.
89. *Ibid.*, p. 296.
90. Finlayson, B., *art. cit.*, p. 217.
91. *Ibid.*, p. 217.
92. Eyre, E. J., *op. cit.*, vol. I, p. 59.
93. Stapylton, G. C., *op. cit.*, p. 124. See also note 46 above.

94. *Ibid.*, p. 129.
95. *Ibid.*, p. 142.
96. Finlayson, B., *art. cit.*, p. 212.

Chapter 5

1. See *The Victorian Historical Magazine*, vol. 1, No. 3, 1911, p. 99.
2. Bride, T. F., *Letters of Victorian Pioneers*, ed. C. E. Sayers, Melbourne, 1969, p. 97.
3. *Ibid.*, p. 97.
4. *Ibid.*, p. 97.
5. Curr, E. M., *Recollections of Squatting in Victoria*, Melbourne, 1965, p. 161.
6. Walker, T., *A Month in the Bush of Australia*, London, 1838, p. 19.
7. Bacon, F., *Essays*, London, 1892, p. 71.
8. Smith, B., *European Vision and the South Pacific*, 1960, p. 8.
9. Wollaston, J. R., 'Original Diaries', 26 November 1840–19 April 1841, typescript, Battye Library, Perth, p. 34.
10. See chapter 3, note 10.
11. Clerk, Nellie, 'Imprisoned' in *Songs from the Gippsland Forest*, ed. C. P. Nind, Mirboo, North Gippsland, Victoria, 1887, n.p.
12. Mill, James, *Analysis of the Phenomena of the Human Mind*, London, 1869, vol. 1, p. 186.
13. *Ibid.*, p. 186.
14. *Ibid.*, p. 185.
15. Williams, M., *The Making of the South Australian Landscape*, London, 1974, p. 171.
16. Bushby, J. E., *Saltbush Country*, published privately, 1980, p. 122.
17. Breton, W. H., *op. cit.*, p. 103.
18. Fenton, J., *Bush Life in Tasmania Fifty Years Ago*, London, 1891, pp. 117–8.
19. *Ibid.*, p. 118.
20. Breton, W. H., *op. cit.*, p. 75.
21. *Ibid.*, p. 92.
22. *Ibid.*, p. 92.
23. Curr, E. M., *op. cit.*, p. 42.
24. *Ibid.*, p. 42.
25. *Ibid.*, p. 45.
26. *Ibid.*, p. 45.
27. *Ibid.*, p. 48.
28. Midgley, S. and R. Skilbeck, *Diaries*, ed. H. A. McCorkell, Melbourne, 1967, p. 4.
29. *Ibid.*, p. 79.
30. *The Land of the Lyrebird*, originally published 1920, republished by The Shire of Korumburra for the South Gippsland Development League, 1966, p. 213.

31. *Ibid.*, p. 349.
32. *Ibid.*, p. 349.
33. *Ibid.*, p. 349.
34. *Ibid.*, p. 350.
35. *Ibid.*, p. 351.
36. Cerutty, A. M., *Tyntyndyer*, Kilmore, 1977, p. 84.
37. Derrida, J., *Of Grammatology*, trans. G. C. Spivak, Baltimore, 1976, p. 86.
38. *Records of Castlemaine Pioneers*, Adelaide, 1972, p. 21.
39. Perry, T. M., *Australia's First Frontier*, Melbourne, 1963, p. 123.
40. *Ibid.*, p. 123.
41. Reynolds, H., *The Other Side of the Frontier*, Melbourne, 1982, p. 1.
42. *Ibid.*, p. 163.
43. Eliade, M., *Australian Religions, Part V: Death, Eschatology, and some Conclusions*, History of Religions, Chicago, 1968, p. 261.
44. Reynolds, H., *op. cit.*, p. 163.
45. *Ibid.*, p. 163.
46. Cited by Reynolds, *ibid.*, p. 51.
47. Biernoff, D., 'Safe and Dangerous Places' in L. Hiatt (ed.), *Australian Aboriginal Concepts*, Canberra, 1978, p. 98.
48. Turner, D. H., 'Levels of Organisation and Communication in Aboriginal Australia' in Peterson, N., *Tribes and Boundaries in Australia*, Canberra, 1976, p. 185.
49. Peterson, N., *ibid.*, p. 6.
50. Berndt, R. M., 'Territoriality and the Problem of Demarcating Socio-cultural Space', in Peterson, N., *ibid.*, p. 134.
51. Gardner, W., 'Boundaries of the Blacks' in *Records of Times Past*, ed. I. McBryde, A.I.A.S., Canberra, 1978, p. 243.
52. *Historical Records of Victoria*, vol. 2A, Melbourne, 1982, p. 128.
53. *Ibid.*, p. 131.
54. Tindale, N. B., *Aboriginal tribes of Australia*, Canberra, 1974, p. 57.
55. Berndt, *art. cit.*, p. 142.
56. Tindale, N. B., *op. cit.*, p. 66.
57. Reynolds, *op. cit.*, p. 52.
58. Bride, T. F., *Letters from Victorian Pioneers*, p. 62.
59. *Ibid.*, p. 64.
60. Billis, R. V., and A. S. Kenyon, *Pastoral Pioneers of Port Phillip*, Melbourne, 1932, endpapers.
61. Randell, J. O., *op. cit.*, e.g., p. 136, pp. 298–9.
62. Priestley, S., *Warracknabeal: A Wimmera Centenary*, Brisbane, 1967, p. 7.
63. Hartnell, R., *Pack Tracks to Pastures*, Poowong, 1974, p. 28.
64. *Ibid.*, p. 29.
65. *The Land of the Lyrebird*, p. 351.

66. Birtles, T., G., 'Changing Perception and Response to the Atherton –
    Evelyn Rainforest Environment, 1880–1920', paper given at The Insti-
    tute of Australian Geographers, 15th Annual Conference, Townsville,
    August 1978, pp. 14–28.
67. *Ibid.*, p. 30.
68. *Ibid.*, p. 28.
69. *The Land of the Lyrebird*, p. 213.

Chapter 6

 1. See J. J. Shillinglaw *Papers*, La Trobe Library, Melbourne. Manuscript
    Collection, Box 81.
 2. *Ibid.*
 3. *Ibid.*
 4. *Ibid.*
 5. *Ibid.*, also in Flinders, M., *A Voyage to Terra Australis,* London, 1814,
    vol. 2, p. 455.
 6. Flinders, M., *ibid.*, vol. 2, p. 469.
 7. *Ibid.*, vol. 2, p. 458.
 8. *Ibid.*, vol. 1, pp. 132–3.
 9. Shillinglaw *Papers*.
10. *Ibid.*
11. Flinders, M., *op. cit.*, vol. 1, p. 157.
12. Cooper, H. M., *The Unknown Coast*, Adelaide, 1953, p. 134.
13. Shillinglaw *Papers*.
14. Flinders, M., *op. cit.*, vol. 1, p. 120.
15. Shillinglaw *Papers*.
16. Flinders, M., *op. cit.*, vol. 2, p. 470.
17. Cooper, H. M., *op. cit.*, pp. 137–9.
18. *Ibid.*, p. 140.
19. Flinders, M., *op. cit.*, vol. 1, p. 147.
20. *Ibid.*, vol. 1, p. 134.
21. Shillinglaw *Papers*.
22. Rogers, S., *Poems*, London, 1849, p. 29.
23. *Ibid.*, p. 5.
24. *Ibid.*, p. 25.
25. Flinders, M., *op. cit.*, vol. 2, p. 512.
26. *Ibid.*, vol. 2, p. 522.
27. *Ibid.*, vol. 1, p. 112.
28. *Ibid.*, vol. 1, pp. 68–9.
29. Wordsworth, W., *Poetical Works*, ed. T. Hutchinson, Oxford, 1969,
    p. 736.
30. *Ibid.*, p. 738.
31. *Ibid.*, p. 739.

32. Scott, Sir E., *The Life of Captain Matthew Flinders R.N.*, Sydney, 1914, p. 12.
33. Coleridge, S. T., *Omniana*, ed. R. Gittings, London, 1969, p. 353.
34. *Ibid.*, p. 353.
35. Flinders, M., *op. cit.*, vol. 2, p. 438.
36. Rogers, S., *op. cit.*, p. 26.
37. Shillinglaw *Papers*.
38. Bachelard, G., *La Poétique de l'espace*, Paris, 1957, p. 28.
39. Scott, E., *op. cit.*, p. 139.
40. *Ibid.*, p. 139.
41. Cooper, H. M., *op. cit.*, p. c.77.
42. Flinders, M., *op. cit.*, vol. 1, p. 159.
43. Shillinglaw *Papers*.
44. Sterne, L., *The Life and Opinions of Tristram Shandy*, New York, 1935, vol. 2, p. 650.

Chapter 7

1. Pike, D., 'The Utopian Dreams of Adelaide's Founders', *Proceedings of Royal Geographic Society of Australasia*, vol. 53, 1951–2, p. 72.
2. *Ibid.*, p. 71.
3. Light, W. E., *A Brief Journal*, Adelaide, 1839, p. 45.
4. *Ibid.*, p. 45.
5. *Ibid.*, p. 20.
6. Tunnard, C., *The City of Man*, New York, 1953, p. 57.
7. Passmore, J., *Man's Responsibility for Nature*, London, 1974, p. 37.
8. Horton, James T., *Six Months in South Australia*, London, 1838, p. 22.
9. *Ibid.*, p. 22.
10. Markman, S. D., 'The Gridiron Town Plan and the Caste System in Colonial Central America', in *Urbanization in the Americas from Its Beginnings to the Present*, ed. R. P. Schaedel, J. E. Hardoy and N. S. Kinzer, The Hague, 1978, pp. 480–1.
11. Favenc, E., *The Explorers of Australia and their Lifework*, Christchurch, 1908, p. 94.
12. Grant, J., and G. Serle, *The Melbourne Scene, 1803–1956*, Melbourne, 1957, p. 66.
13. *Ibid.*, p. 66.
14. Cox, P., and W. Stacey, *Historic Towns of Australia*, Melbourne, 1973, p. 14.
15. *Ibid.*, p. 14.
16. *Sydney Gazette*, vol. XXVII, 28 May 1829.
17. Grant, J., and G. Serle, *op. cit.*, p. 65.
18. *Ibid.*, p. 65.
19. Trollope, A., *Australia*, London, 1873, p. 213.

20. *Ibid.*, p. 213.
21. *Ibid.*, p. 213.
22. Twopeny, R., *Town Life in Australia*, London, 1973 (originally published 1883), p. 4.
23. *Ibid.*, p. 3.
24. Tunnard, C., *op. cit.*, pp. 61–2.
25. Hardoy, J. E., and C. Aranovich, 'The Scale and Functions of Spanish American Cities around 1600', in Schaedel, Hardoy and Kinzer, *op. cit.*, p. 92.
26. Stanislawski, D., 'The Origin and Spread of the Grid-Pattern Town', *Geographical Review*, vol. 36, 1946, p. 107.
27. Adorno, T., and M. Horkheimer, *the Dialectic of Enlightenment*, trans. J. Cumming, London, 1973, p. 7.
28. Illick, J.E., *Colonial Pennsylvania: A History*, New York, 1976, p. 37.
29. Fenton, J., *op. cit.*, p. 56.
30. Turner, H. G., *A History of the Colony of Victoria*, London, 1904, vol. 1, p. 210.
31. *Historical Records of Victoria*, vol. 3, 1984, p. 23.
32. Fenton, J., *op. cit.*, p. 56.
33. Russell, P., *Clyde Company Papers II 1836–40*, ed. P. L. Brown, Oxford, 1952, p. 343.
34. *The Narrative of George Russell*, ed. P. L. Brown, Oxford, 1935, p. 80.
35. Cotton, J., *Correspondence*, p. 22.
36. Finn, E. ('Garryowen'), *The Chronicles of Early Melbourne*, Melbourne, 1888, p. 108.
37. Trollope, *op. cit.*, p. 385.
38. See Spencer, H., 'Progress: Its Law and Cause', 1852, p. 35, and 'Transcendental Physiology', 1857, p. 81, both in vol. 1 of *Essays, Scientific, Political and Speculative*, 3 vols., London, 1891.
39. Spencer, H., 'The Social Organism', *ibid.*, vol. 1, p. 292.
40. *Ibid.*, vol. 1, p. 295.
41. *Ibid.*, vol. 1, p. 295.
42. *Ibid.*, 'Transcendental Physiology', vol. 1, p. 83.
43. *Ibid.*, 'The Ethics of Kant', vol. 3, p. 198.
44. Hume, D., *op. cit.*, vol. 1, p. 139.
45. *Ibid.*, vol. 1, p. 106.
46. Kennedy, J. G., *Herbert Spencer*, Boston, 1978, p. 67.
47. Merleau-Ponty, M., *Signs*, trans. M. C. McCleary, Northwestern University Press, 1964, p. 15.
48. Joyce, A., *A Homestead History*, ed. J. F. James, Melbourne, 1942, p. 37.
49. Mitchell, T. L., *Field Books*, C42.
50. *Ibid.*, C42.
51. Breton, W. H., *op. cit.*, p. 91.
52. Lhotsky, J., *op. cit.*, p. 16.

53. Cameron, J. M. R., 'Patterns on the Land' in Gentilli, J. G. (ed), *Western Landscapes*, Nedlands, W. A., 1979, p. 205.
54. Collins, D., *An Account of the English Colony in New South Wales*, vol. 1, London, 1798, p. 197.
55. Cunningham, P., *op. cit.*, p. 259.
56. Collins, D., *op. cit.*, vol. 1, p. 144.
57. *Ibid.*, vol. 1, p. 144.
58. *Historical Records of New South Wales*, 1, Part 2, Sydney, 1892, p. 362.
59. Straw, E. E., 'The Hazeldeane Selection', December 1956, La Trobe Library, Melbourne, MS 8814.
60. Pike, D., *Paradise of Dissent*, London, 1955, p. 175.
61. *Ibid.*, p. 178.
62. Meinig, D. W., *On the Margins of Good Earth*, 1963, p. 97.
63. Cunningham, P., *op. cit.*, p. 308.
64. *Ibid.*, p. 280.
65. Ritchie, J., *The Evidence of the Bigge Report*, Melbourne, 1971, vol. 2, pp. 73–4.
66. *Ibid.*, p. 62.
67. *Ibid.*, p. 62.
68. 'Emigrant Mechanic', *Settlers and Convicts*, Melbourne, 1969, pp. 129–30, although the reality was very different – see *ibid.*, pp. 182–90.
69. Howitt, W. E., *op. cit.*, Letter XX, p. 360.
70. *Ibid.*, p. 361.

Chapter 8

1. Pye, Henry James, *Poems on Various Subjects*, London, 1787, vol. 2, p. 5.
2. See, for example, Hipple, W. J., *The Beautiful, the Sublime and the Picturesque in 18th Century British Aesthetic Theory*, Carbondale, Ill., 1957, pp. 306ff.
3. Pye, H. J., *op. cit.*, p. 6.
4. Burke, E., *A Philosophical Enquiry into the Origin of our Ideas of the Sublime and Beautiful*, London, 1757, p. 142.
5. Sturt, C., *Two Expeditions*, vol. 1, p. 286.
6. Mitchell, T. L., *Three Expeditions*, vol. 1, p. 192.
7. Walker, T., *op. cit.*, p. 11.
8. Extracts from the Diary of Rev. William Waterfield in *Victorian Historical Magazine*, vol. 3, no. 3, p. 106.
9. *The Land of the Lyrebird*, p. 412.
10. Burchett, C., 'Memories of Pioneer Days, by an Old Pioneer', 1916, La Trobe Library, Melbourne, MS 8814.
11. Breton, W. H., *op. cit.*, pp. 106–7.
12. Sturt, C., *Two Expeditions*, vol. 1, p. 286.
13. Walker, T., *op. cit.*, p. 12.

14. Strzelecki, Count P. E. de, *A Physical Description of New South Wales and Van Diemen's Land*, London, 1945, p. 242.
15. Walker, T., *op. cit.*, p. 34.
16. Mitchell, T. L., *Journal*, p. 222.
17. Knight, P. R., *The Landscape*, London, 1793, Book II, ll. 190–4.
18. *Ibid.*, Book II, ll. 200–4.
19. *Ibid.*, Book III, ll. 29–35.
20. Loudon, J. C., *The Landscape Gardening and Landscape Architecture of the late Humphrey Repton Esq.*, Edinburgh, 1840, pp. 96ff.
21. Peacock, T. L., *Three Novels*, ed. J. Mair, Edinburgh, 1940, p. 33.
22. Loudon, J. C., *op. cit.*, p. 113.
23. *Ibid.*, p. 96.
24. Piaget, J., and B. Inhelder, *La Représentation de l'espace chez l'enfant*, Paris, 1948.
25. Merleau-Ponty, M., *The Phenomenology of Perception*, London, 1962, p. 253.
26. Cunningham, P., *op. cit.*, p. 67.
27. Fenton, J., *op. cit.*, p. 35.
28. Dawson, R., quoted by Jeans, *op. cit.*, p. 61.
29. *Letters of Victorian Pioneers*, pp. 184–5.
30. Howitt, W., *op. cit.*, Letter V, p. 43.
31. *Ibid.*, Letter V, p. 43.
32. Walker, J., *op. cit.*, p. 29.
33. *Ibid.*, p. 30.
34. Mitchell, T. L., *Journal*, p. 215.
35. *Ibid.*, p. 308.
36. *Ibid.*, p. 308.
37. *Ibid.*, p. 309.
38. Cited by Stroud, D., in *Capability Brown*, London, 1975, p. 201.
39. Hunter, J., *An Historical Journal*, London, 1793, republished 1968. Hunter writes of the coast south of Botany Bay, p. 27: 'a small clump of trees, something like that on Post down hill, near Portsmouth: these, I think, are the only remarkable objects here.' The modern editor comments that the area is 'indeed featureless'.
40. Heathcote, R. L., *Back of Bourke*, 1965, p. 17.
41. Gentilli, J. G. (ed.), *Western Landscapes*, Nedlands, W. A., 1979, p. 11.
42. Brown, J. E., *A Practical Treatise on Tree Culture in South Australia*, Adelaide, 1881, p. 8.
43. *Ibid.*, p. 36.
44. Shepherd, T., quoted by J. M. Powell in *Environmental Management in Australia: 1788–1914*, Melbourne, 1976, p. 29.
45. Quoted in M. Williams, *op. cit.*, p. 15.
46. Howitt, W., *op. cit.*, Letter XIII, p. 205.
47. *Ibid.*, Letter XXXI, p. 323.

48. Mitchell, T. L., *Three Expeditions*, vol. 2, p. 150.
49. Morrison, E., *Frontier Life in the Loddon Protectorate, Daylesford, Victoria*, 1967, p. 9.
50. See Letter from A. Garden in *Swan Hill Guardian*, 4 October 1944.
51. Bushby, J., *op. cit.*, p. 118.
52. Fenton, J., *op. cit.*, p. 173.
53. Greaves, M., *Sir George Beaumont, Regency Patron*, London, 1966, p. 137.
54. Burke, C., *Doherty's Corner*, Sydney, 1985, p. 77.
55. Fenton, J., *op. cit.*, p. 173.
56. Mitchell, T. L., *Three Expeditions*, vol. 1, p. 90.
57. Walker, T., *op. cit.*, p. 44.
58. Mitchell, T. L., *Journal*, p. 222.
59. Brown, J. E., *op. cit.*, p. 14.
60. Powell, J. M., *The Public Lands of Australia Felix*, Melbourne, 1970, pp. 17–22. See also *Clyde Company Papers, II, 1836–1840*, ed. P. L. Brown, London, 1952, p. 414.
61. *The Narrative of George Russell*, p. 84.
62. Mitchell, T. L., *Three Expeditions*, vol. 2, p. 171.
63. Curr, E. M., *op. cit.*, p. 64.
64. *Ibid.*, p. 64.
65. Brodribb, W. G., *Recollections of an Australian Squatter*, Sydney, 1883, p. 18.
66. Walker, T., *op. cit.*, p. 41.
67. Bremner, G. A., *History of the First Explorer and Squatter in the Kyneton District, Mitchell and Ebden*, Kyneton, 1969, n.p.
68. Mitchell, T. L., *Three Expeditions*, vol. 2, p. 281.
69. *Ibid.*, vol. 2, p. 282.
70. Walker, T., *op. cit.*, p. 38.
71. *Ibid.*, p. 44.
72. *Ibid.*, p. 44.

Chapter 6

1. Wollaston, J. R., *Albany Journals, 1848–1856*, ed. Canon Burton, Perth, 1946, p. 136.
2. *The Morwell Historical Society News*, vol. 4 (1965), p. 15.
3. *Ibid.*, vol. 8, No. 1, p. 4.
4. Medew, R. S., *The Days of Thy Youth: A Story of early Gippsland Pioneers,* 19—, privately published, p. 8.
5. Eunson, W., *The Unfolding Hills*, Mirboo North, Victoria, 1978, p. 52.
6. Sorenson, E. S., *Life in the Australian Backblocks*, London, 1911, p. 64.
7. 'A Tale of South Australia' by A.B.F., in *South Australian Magazine*, vol. 11, 1842, p. 85.

8. Allen, T. G., *Wyperfeld*, Rainbow Historical Society, 1977, p. 29.
9. Howitt, W., *op. cit.*, Letter V, p. 39.
10. Clerk, N., *op. cit.*, 'Imprisoned'.
11. *Ibid.*
12. *Ibid.*
13. King, P. P., *Narrative of a Survey of the Intertropical and Western Coasts of Australia*, London, 1827, vol. 1, p. 196.
14. Hamilton, G., *Experiences of a Colonist Forty Years Ago*, p. 2.
15. Pitt, Marie E. J., *The Poems of Marie E. J. Pitt*, ed. E. A. Vidler, Melbourne, 1925, p. 158.
16. Fullerton, M., *Bark House Days*, Melbourne, 1921, p. 12.
17. *Ibid.*, pp. 43–4.
18. *Ibid.*, p. 13.
19. Quoted by Eunson, p. 22.
20. Clerk, N., *op. cit.*, 'My Gippsland Home'.
21. Fullerton, M., *op. cit.*, p. 37.
22. *The Morwell Historical Society News*, vol. 5, p. 8.
23. Burke, C., *op. cit.*, 'A House', p. 104.
24. Eunson, W., *op. cit.*, p. 179.
25. Medew, R. S., *op. cit.*, p. 30.
26. R. Young, 'The Rusted Wedge', in *From the Dawning, A History of Yarragon and District*, ed. S. Dalziel et al., Back-to Committee, Yarragon, 1978, p. 14.
27. Straw, E. E., *op. cit.*, p. 13.
28. *Ibid.*, p. 24.
29. *Ibid.*, p. 23.
30. Fullerton, M., *op. cit.*, p. 13.
31. Fenton, J., *op. cit.*, p. 175.
32. Sladen, D. B. W. (ed.), *Australian Ballads and Rhymes*, London, 1888, p. xxx.
33. Fullerton, M., *op. cit.*, p. 35.
34. Gilbert, M. I., *Personalities and Stories of Early Orbost*, Orbost, Victoria, 1972, p. 97.
35. Fullerton, M., *op. cit.*, p. 36.
36. Burke, C., *op. cit.*, p. 104.
37. Quoted in M. I. Gilbert, *op. cit.*, p. 21.
38. Walker, T., *op. cit.*, p. 23.
39. Breton, W. H., *op. cit.*, p. 66.
40. Maddern, I. T., 'Early Morwell' in *Morwell Historical Society News*, vol. 1 (1962), p. 17.
41. McCrae, G. G., 'Some Recollections of Melbourne in the "Forties"' in *The Victorian Historical Magazine*, vol. 2, no. 3, 1912, p. 130.
42. Fullerton, M., *op. cit.*, p. 76.
43. Pitt, Marie E. J., *op. cit.*, p. 159.

44. *Ibid.*, p. 159.
45. *Ibid.*, p. 159.
46. Quoted in Clark, J., and B. Whitelaw, *Golden Summers*, Melbourne, 1985, p. 149.
47. Burke, C., *op. cit.*, 'City Hunger', p. 108.
48. Clark, J., and B. Whitelaw, *op. cit.*, p. 149.
49. Morgan, P., 'Forgotten in the Fertile Crescent', *Quadrant*, November 1983, p. 55.
50. Ward, R., *The Australian Legend*, Melbourne, 1965, pp. 182–3.
51. Morgan, P., Unpublished manuscript.
52. Bachelard, G., *op. cit.*, p. 42.
53. *The Land of the Lyrebird*, p. 349.
54. Straw, E. E., *op. cit.*, p. 13.
55. Ward, R., *op. cit.*, pp. 182–3.
56. Fullerton, M., *op. cit.*, p. 11.
57. Sennett, R., *The Fall of Public Man*, Cambridge, 1974, pp. 337–40.
58. White, R., *Inventing Australia*, Sydney, 1981, pp. 101–2.
59. Burn, I., 'Beating About the Bush: The Landscapes of the Heidelberg School', in *Australian Art and Architecture*, ed. A. Bradley and T. Smith, Melbourne, 1980, p. 85. In this sense, the advocate of an authentically Australian literature, Rex Ingamells, may have had it exactly the wrong way round when he criticized Roderick Quinn's line 'And dead leaves carpet the bush,' because it 'makes the bush seem like a drawing room': in truth the line's banality lies in the *failure* to imagine the bush as a living room. (See R. Ingamells, *Concerning Environmental Values*, 1937.)
60. Medew, R. S., *op. cit.*, p. 58.
61. Randell, J. O., *The Pastoral Pattersons*, Melbourne, 1976, p. 156.
62. Mitchell, T. L., *Three Expeditions*, vol. 2, p. 97, cited by A. S. Kenyon in 'The Story of the Mallee', *The Victorian Historical Magazine*, IV(1) p. 27.
63. Allen, T. G., *Shears in Hand*, Hopetown, 1976, p. 1.
64. F. Myers, quoted in A. J. Williams, 'Jeparit's Early History', *Jeparit Leader*, 1955, Part 2.
65. Stuart, J. M., *op. cit.*, p. 35.
66. Medew, R. S., *op. cit.*, pp. 79–80.
67. Stokes, J. L., *op. cit.*, vol. 2, pp. 316–7.
68. *Ibid.*, vol. 2, p. 319.
69. Croll, R. H., *Smike to Bulldog*, Sydney, 1938, undated letter to Tom Roberts, p. 40.
70. Gregory, J. W., *The Dead Heart of Australia*, London, 1906, p. 161.
71. *Ibid.*, p. 162.
72. Haydon, G. H., *Five Years Experience in Australia Felix*, London, 1846, p. 125.
73. Clerk, N., *op. cit.*, 'My Gippsland Home'.

74. Stokes, J. L., *op. cit.*, vol. 1, p. 84.
75. Kenyon, A. S., *art. cit.*, p. 26.
76. Christy Palmerston, *Explorer of the Rainforest*, an Eacham Historical Society Publication, n.d., p. 32.
77. Sennett, R., *op. cit.*, p. 297.
78. Johnston, G., *My Brother Jack*, London, 1973, pp. 257ff.

Chapter 10

1. See chapter 8, note 10.
2. Ingleton, G., in J. White, *Journal of a Voyage to New South Wales*, Sydney, 1962, pp. 2–3.
3. Collins, D., *op. cit.*, vol. 1, p. 39.
4. *Ibid.*, vol. 1, p. 47.
5. Tench, W., *Sydney's First Four Years*, p. 137.
6. Collins, D., *op. cit.*, vol. 1, p. 47.
7. *Ibid.*, vol. 1, p. 47.
8. White, J., *op. cit.*, p. 163.
9. Collins, D., *op. cit.*, vol. 1, p. 47.
10. Tench, W., *Sydney's First Four Years*, p. 137.
11. Hunter, J., *An Historical Journal of the Transactions at Port Jackson and Norfolk Island*, London, 1793, p. 84.
12. Tench, W., *Sydney's First Four Years*, p. 243.
13. Hunter, J., *op. cit.*, p. 563.
14. Tench, W., *Sydney's First Four Years*, p. 243.
15. *Ibid.*, p. 243.
16. *Ibid.*, p. 244.
17. Hunter, J., *op. cit.*, p. 564.
18. Collins, D., *op. cit.*, vol. 1, p. 185.
19. *Ibid.*, vol. 1, p. 310.
20. *Ibid.*, vol. 1, pp. 302–3.
21. *Ibid.*, vol. 1, p. 136.
22. *Ibid.*, vol. 2, p. 94.
23. Tench, W., *op. cit.*, p. 66.
24. *Ibid.*, p. 243.
25. Collins, D., *op. cit.*, vol. 1, p. 197.
26. *Ibid.*, vol. 1, p. 39.
27. Phillip, A., *op. cit.*, p. 122.
28. Barton, G. B., *History of New South Wales from the Records*, Sydney 1889–94, vol. 1, p. 583.
29. *Ibid.*, vol. 1, p. 583.
30. Pyne, W. H., *Wine and Walnuts*, London, 1823, vol. 1, chapter XXI, *passim*.

31. Tench, W., *op. cit.*, p. 33.
32. *Ibid.*, p. 39.
33. White, J., *op. cit.*, p. 115.
34. Hunter, J., *op. cit.*, p. 161.
35. Collins, D., *op. cit.*, vol. 1, p. 43.
36. Hunter, J., *op. cit.*, p. 76.
37. Collins, D., *op. cit.*, vol. 1, p. 69.
38. Hunter, J., *op. cit.*, p. 303.
39. Collins, D., *op. cit.*, vol. 1, p. 61.
40. *Ibid.*, vol. 1, p. 61.
41. Tench, W., *op. cit.*, p. 220.
42. Collins, D., *op. cit.*, vol. 2, pp. 75–6.
43. *Ibid.*, vol. 2, p. 76.
44. *Ibid.*, vol. 2, pp. 75–6.
45. Hunter, J., *op. cit.*, p. 162.
46. Tench, W., *op. cit.*, p. 156.
47. *Ibid.*, p. 41.
48. Hunter, J., *op. cit.*, p. 399.
49. Tench, W., *op. cit.*, p. 243.
50. *Ibid.*, p. 297.
51. *Ibid.*, p. 297.
52. *Ibid.*, p. 296.
53. White, J., *op. cit.*, p. 70.
54. Southwell, D., *Historical Records of New South Wales*, vol. 2, Sydney, 1893, p. 666.
55. Quoted by Smith, B., *op. cit.*, p. 135.

Chapter 11

1. Tench, W., *op. cit.*, p. 52.
2. *Ibid.*, p. 52.
3. *Ibid.*, p. 207.
4. Collins, D., *op. cit.*, vol. 1, p. 166.
5. Breton, W. H., *op. cit.*, p. 334.
6. See, for exapmle, John Batman's 'Importation of Sydney Aborigines into Tasmania for the Purpose of Hunting the Local Natives', cited by T. Bonyhady, *Images in Opposition*, Melbourne, 1985, p. 32.
7. Collins, D., *op. cit.*, vol. 1, p. 221.
8. *Ibid.*, vol. 1, p. 223.
9. Southwell, D., *Historical Records of New South Wales*.
10. See chapter 1, note 45.
11. Benjamin, W., *Illuminations*, trans. H. Zohn, London, 1970, p. 257.
12. Stokes, J. L., *op. cit.*, vol. 1, p. 181.
13. *Ibid.*, vol. 2, p. 23.

14. Said, E., *The World, The Text and the Critic*, London, 1984, p. 48.
15. Macquarie, Lachlan, *Journals of his Tours*, ed. P. Mander-Jones, Sydney, 1956, p. 21.
16. Giles, E., *op. cit.*, vol. 2, p. 2. Also vol. 2, p. 54.
17. Strehlow, T. G. H., *Songs of Central Australia*, Sydney, 1971, p. 258.
18. Smyth, B., *op. cit.*, vol. 1, p. 12.
19. *Ibid.*, p. 13n.
20. See Turnbull, C., *Black War: The Extermination of the Tasmanian Aborigines*, Melbourne, 1965, p. 202.
21. Threlkeld, L. E., *Australian Reminiscences and Papers*, ed. W. E. Gunson, Canberra, 1974, pp. 360ff.
22. Adorno, T., *op. cit.*, p. 211.
23. Threlkeld, L. E., *op. cit.*, p. 209.
24. Beveridge, P., *op. cit.*, p. 174.
25. Grey, Sir G., *op. cit.*, vol. 2, p. 210.
26. Smyth, B., *op. cit.*, vol. 1, p. 18.
27. Robinson, G. A., *Journals*, March–May 1841, p. 56.
28. Giles, E., *op. cit.*, vol. 2, p. 279.
29. Smyth, B., *op. cit.*, vol. 2, pp. 3ff.
30. Giles, E., *op. cit.*, vol. 2, p. 100.
31. Grey, Sir G., *op. cit.*, vol. 2, p. 217.
32. *Historical Records of Victoria*, vol. 2a, Melbourne, 1982, p. 154.
33. Dr Roger Oldfield in Threlkeld, *op. cit.*, p. 351.
34. Samuel Marsden, *ibid.*, p. 347.
35. Dr Roger Oldfield, *ibid.*, p. 353.
36. Tindale, N. B., *op. cit.*, p. 57.
37. Christy Palmerston, *op. cit.*, p. 34.
38. Hallam, S. J., *Fire and Hearth*, A.I.A.S., Canberra, 1979, p. 67.
39. Blake, L., *The Land of the Lowan*, Nhill and District Historical Society, 1976, pp. 34–5.
40. Hallam, S., *op. cit.*, p. 74.
41. Robinson, G. A., *op. cit.*, no. 5, p. 55.
42. Robinson, G. A., *op. cit.*, no. 6, p. 79.
43. Robinson, G. A., *op. cit.*, no. 5, p. 4.
44. *Ibid.*, p. 4.
45. Mitchell, T. L., *Three Expeditions*, vol. 2, p. 135.
46. Gardner, P., 'The Pre-White Population of the Gippsland Aborigines' *Journal of the Royal Australian Historical Society*, vol. 64, part 1, June 1978, p. 58.
47. Robinson, G. A., *op. cit.*, no. 11, 1980, p. 118.
48. Mitchell, T. L., *Journal*, pp. 412–13.
49. Bonwick, James, *Western Victoria: Its Geography, Geology and Social Condition*, Melbourne, 1970, p. 31.
50. May, D., 'The Articulation of the Aboriginal and Capitalist Modes on

the North Queensland Pastoral Frontier', *Journal of Australian Studies*, no. 12, June 1983, p. 43.

51. *Ibid.*, p. 43.
52. Robinson, G. A., *op. cit.*, no. 6, p. 95.
53. Gardner, P., 'The Diary of P. C. Buckley and the Aboriginals of Gippsland', *Agora*, vol. XIII, no. 3, June 1979, p. 26.
54. Eyre, E. J., vol. 1, p. 351.
55. *Ibid.*, vol. 2, p. 299.
56. Mitchell, T. L., *Journal*, p. 306.
57. *Ibid.*, pp. 315–16.
58. Moyle, R., 'Songs, Ceremonies and Sites: The Agharringa Case' in *Aborigines, Land and Land Rights*, ed. N. Peterson and M. Langton, Canberra, 1983, p. 71.
59. *Ibid.*, p. 71.
60. Payne, H., 'Residency and Ritual Rights' in *Problems and Solutions*, ed. J. C. Kassler and J. Stubington, Sydney, 1984, pp. 271–2.
61. *Ibid.*, p. 272.
62. Munn, N., *Walbiri Iconography*, New York, 1973, p. 148.
63. Deleuze, G., and F. Guattari, *Anti-Oedipe*, 1972, p. 222 (my translation).
64. Mountford, Charles, *Nomads of the Australian Desert*, Adelaide, 1976, *passim*.
65. Muecke, S., *Reading the Country*, Fremantle, 1984. Muecke (p. 230) describes his book as, amongst other things, an experiment to see if it was possible 'for the country to "write itself"'.
66. *Ibid.*, p. 14.
67. *Ibid.*, p. 227.
68. Derrida, J., *Edmund Husserl's Origin of Geometry, an Introduction*, trans. J. P. Leavey, New York, 1978, p. 165.
69. *Ibid.*, p. 163.
70. *Ibid.*, p. 163.
71. Grey, Sir G., *op. cit.*, vol. 2, p. 267.